DATE DUE

Planning

ENVIRONMENT SERIES

The Modern Metropolis: Its Origins and Growth,
selected essays by Hans Blumenfeld, edited by
Paul D. Spreiregen.

The Pollution Reader by Anthony de Vos,
Norman Pearson, P.L. Silveston and
W.R. Drynan.

Planning the Canadian Environment,
L.O. Gertler, Editor.

PLANNING THE CANADIAN ENVIRONMENT

For information address Harvest House Ltd.
1364 Greene Avenue, Montreal 6, Quebec, Canada.
First Harvest House Edition — September 1968.

Printed and bound in Canada by
Librairie Beauchemin Ltd., Montreal.

Planning the Canadian Environment

L. O. Gertler, Editor

 HARVEST HOUSE, MONTREAL

CONTENTS

DEVELOPING AND PLANNING THE REGIONS OF CANADA

PERSPECTIVES FOR REGIONAL PLANNING

INTRODUCTION

The papers presented in this volume are selections from the first five years of *PLAN, Canada,* the journal of the Town Planning Institute of Canada. Spanning a period from the end of 1959 to the first quarter of 1965, they have been chosen for the way they illuminate the evolution of planning in Canada.

The publication of a book on this theme has its justification for purely historical reasons as an exposure of the thought of Canadian planners during a period of intense activity in urban and regional development. And it fills a need to make accessible to the teacher, the student and the man of affairs, a treatment of planning issues in terms of Canadian experience —not to assuage parochial feelings, but for the greater relevance of the material to the man or woman struggling for a better environment, or studying about it, in Halifax, Montreal or Vancouver.

Important as these things are, there is still another and more fundamental reason for this book. And that is to highlight by selection and juxtaposition of these works the particularly Canadian contribution to urban and regional planning in the Western World. Those of us, like myself, who have a partisan view on this issue, must confess to a concern about the gap between achievement and assertion. We have generally not matched in the realm of scholarship what we have done in the realm of action. This book is, in a sense, the beginning of an exegesis. It will to a degree serve the purpose of showing what Canadian planning has accomplished, of explaining its particular character and flavour, and suggesting something of its potential.

The significance of this exposition will, of course, depend on the reader's view of the plusses in Canadian planning experience. These may be counted as the establishment of a legal framework for planning in the provinces (Armstrong); making metropolitan planning operational in a large urbanized complex (Jones); establishing within one provincial jurisdiction a system of regional planning on a multi-municipal base, with executive and not just advisory powers (Gertler); building citizen participation into the planning process of a metropolis (Lawson); designing in a comprehensive and integrated fashion an entire new section of a city, with innovations in the forms of multiple housing and in the ways of coping with the automobile (Hancock); applying and elaborating the technique of new town building both for a resource-based town on the frontier (Richardson), and for an industrial satellite in a dynamic western park belt region (Smith); and undertaking a national evaluation of the use and abuse of renewable resources, opening the way to an inter-disciplinary and regional approach to the study and solution of resource problems (Dakin).

Some of the clues to the Canadian planning riddle are found in this book. I will refer, by way of illustration, to only a few of these. In the beginning there was Thomas Adams, who knew and was inspired by Patrick Geddes and Ebenezer Howard—whose career included participation in the British Garden City movement at the turn of the century, the direction of the Regional Plan for New York and its Environs, from 1923 to 1930, and the teaching of planning at Harvard until 1934. Not untypically his Canadian period came as a transition between those two epochal phases of his planning work. His seven years sojourn here as Adviser on Town Planning to the Commission of Conservation was marked by a number of tangible results which reverberate to the present day. These include the founding of the Town Planning Institute of Canada, and the actual adoption of his draft statutes in seven of the nine provinces. Paradoxically, as Alan Armstrong points out, Adams became the vehicle for embedding into our law and our planning process the American prototype, slightly modified, of the separate honorary and advisory planning board. With hindsight we know this to be a mixed blessing—at least that may be said of its perpetuation half a century later in vastly altered circumstances.

On other scores, Adams' grasp of Canadian problems and needs in the 20th century was near-prophetic. He asserted the necessity of applying to the richly variegated Canadian landscape the sensitive design approach he had developed under the influence of Raymond Unwin. The technique of new towns building, which he helped to evolve as the Secretary of the First Garden City Company at Letchworth, has great relevance for a country which has been continuously engaged in opening up new resource frontiers. In his book on *Rural Planning and Development* (1917) and in his other Canadian papers, he set out a concept of planning which goes far beyond the tight little world of planning for self-contained cities which predominated until recently. He had a broad view which encompassed town and country, human and natural resources. He had a highly developed sense of the national role of community planning.

The world of Thomas Adams, that is, his adopted Canadian "world" had been formed by French and British colonial settlement, under the stimulus of military and mercantilist policies; the paper by Michael Hugo-Brunt elucidates this heritage in the Maritimes, and that by Peter Oberlander, in British Columbia. It was also the product of the occupation of the moving settlement frontier on the basis of free or cheap land, as related in the paper on the economic and social background of planning in Alberta. By the time Adams arrived on the scene, land development was greatly affected by violent speculative swings. In his final year in Canada he was impelled to observe, perhaps with some bitterness, "that the system of development . . . of land should be designed more for the purpose of promoting the prosperity of industry and less for the purpose of protecting the profits of those engaged in land speculation".

Adams would be interested in finding an echo of these ideas in Bryant's paper which catalogues the development distortions in Canada and other western countries, associated with the unbridled land market. And he would be intrigued by the suggestion of a "thinkers' group" of that arch radical political party, the Progressive Conservative, that public ownership of land is necessary to keep housing costs in check.

Forty years after the demise of the Commission of Conservation this country embarked on a second major research-conference enterprise concerned with renewable resources—the "Resources for Tomorrow" Confer-

ence (1961). It was a revealing demonstration of the Canadian preoccupation with the resource base, notwithstanding galloping urbanization.
But as John Dakin makes abundantly clear this was more than an inventory
of resource capacities and a prognostication of demands. The theme that
Adams introduced with great foresight, as a strident piccolo, had now
become an entire wind section. There emerged a strong emphasis on
resources as environment, and on regional planning as a vehicle for achieving
an integration of economic, social, environmental and resource objectives.
But there are some hazards. Dakin notes that "the idea of resource development and planning is well built into our society's system of values ... and
it may lead to a special way of approaching regional planning in Canada"
[but] ... "the erroneous impression exists that regional planning is simply
one among many activities to do with resources, when in fact it is the one
operation which embraces all others". Dakin would have the piccolo become
the maestro.

The spirit of Canadian planning is reflected as well in the development
of frontier regions. Richardson's paper through case studies of Prince Rupert
and Kitimat, British Columbia, illuminates both the special problems and
opportunities of the resources frontier. He demonstrates forcibly how broad
and deep the planning effort must be when a new community is carved
out of the primeval forest; and by the same token, the inescapable penalties
of failure. The point of interest for Canadian planning is that the discipline
of meeting this challenge—of building from resource surveys and strategies
of regional economic development to the planning and design of towns
sensitive to new societies and unique landscapes—because it is a continuous
process, can have a powerful influence on the mainstream of Canadian
planning.

The papers in this book which are philosophical or theoretical in their
bent are of more than casual interest as an indication of the ideas that
shape planning in this country today. In Canada the key planners in government, universities and consulting number not more than some three score.
Unlike meetings of the American Institute of Planners which inescapably
are mass affairs, the annual meeting of the Town Planning Institute of
Canada rarely involves more than two hundred and fifty people. Within a
"universe" of this cosy dimension, communication can be effective even if
it is sometimes across several thousand miles. Mobility of people and ideas
is high. And those who by precept and practice take the lead can make
an impact that reverberates across the land. This difference is not simply
a function of population. It is in large part a reflection of our system of
provinces. Unlike the U.S.A., Canada is not carved up into a multitude of
suzerainties, each with its own planning establishment. With territorial
jurisdiction in the hands of ten provinces and of the federal government
that directly administers the vast northland, control of land use and of
development is much more centralized. And accordingly there are fewer
chiefs.

These observations are not presented as virtue, but simply as fact.
When you add to this the devastating effect of the depression on community

planning and planners in Canada—there was a break in continuity of about fifteen years—the staggering backlog of work to be done and the slow evolution of planning education, it is perhaps not surprising that the task of bringing Canada into the second half of the 20th century in this context fell to the lot of a relatively few qualified people who exerted a substantial influence.

Some of these speak out from these pages. And we find an augury in their words—in Humphrey Carver's emphasis on suburban town centres as major elements in city-regions and on the large-scale reorganization of "the distribution of population and community services" in the broad economic regions, heretofore characterized by primary production and small scattered centres; in André Saumier's diagnosis of urban trends, leading to the presumption that "a national and systematic effort towards urban renewal of the centres of our cities might have good chances of succeeding"; in Gordon Stephenson's warm humanistic vision, of which Australia is now the beneficiary, of a city-region consisting of "a whole series of related self-sufficient communities separated by generous open spaces"; and in Hans Blumenfeld's concept of regional planning through the marriage of local physical planning and functional economic planning. One could do much worse than to present the foregoing as an account of the directions of city and regional planning in Canada today.

It is noteworthy that all of the above-mentioned individuals in addition to contributing in the realm of basic ideas, are or have been men of action, deeply involved in the struggle for a better environment. Here we may come closest to answering the riddle of Canadian planning. The outpouring of ideas, compared to the American avalanche, is small, but its relevance to the problems of our time, and its operational effectiveness is extra-ordinary. It is for the reader to determine whether this makes sense or is just plain chauvinistic conceit.

Having said all this, the editor hastens to note that in this fast-moving Canadian society, the views expressed here are already obsolete, and that we are entering a new phase of planning education and action, much more broadly based, much more promising of sound scholarship, and characterized by feedback from the field to the classroom and the book.

LEONARD O. GERTLER

UNIVERSITY OF WATERLOO
WATERLOO, ONTARIO

1. *The Evolution of Planning in Canada*

THOMAS ADAMS AND THE COMMISSION OF CONSERVATION

Alan H. Armstrong

> *Architect and city planner, Mr. Armstrong
> has contributed substantially to both fields.
> He has been the Executive Director of the
> Community Planning Association of Canada,
> Adviser on Community Planning for the
> Central Mortgage and Housing Corporation,
> and Secretary to the Royal Architectural
> Institute of Canada, Committee of Inquiry
> into the Residential Environment. He is at
> present, Executive Officer, Canada Council
> on Urban and Regional Research. While
> accepting full responsibility for the text of
> this paper, the author wishes to acknowledge
> the help of Professor Frederick J. Adams of
> Cambridge, Massachusetts.*

Fortunately for me, what I have to report took place at a time when a
remarkably complete record of events was deposited for us. In the years
before the First War, photo-engraving was far enough advanced to leave
us clear pictures of our towns and unmistakable likenesses of our heroes.
In Edwardian Ottawa (when Parliament met for only a few months in the
year) there were expert stenographers available from Parliament Hill, with
their foolscap pads, quill pens and ink bottles to take down every syllable
that was said. These records had the advantage over the magnetic tape,
in that devoted editors corrected the grammar and turned them out in
thousands of beautiful volumes with gold lettering on the back. Every
ponderous turn of phrase is reproduced exactly, through days and days of
meetings. I have just been through a few of these records, mostly Annual
Reports of the Commission of Conservation, and the flavour of the time is
in many ways delightful.

FORMATION OF THE COMMISSION

Fifty years ago, the United States had conquered its last domestic
frontier and could just see the end of its self-sufficiency in natural resources.
In 1909 we in Canada, too, were closing a remarkable quarter-century of
industrialization and were in the midst of a period of enormous immigration
(accompanied by acute epidemics). Calgary and Edmonton, each multiplying
forty times in population in the first ten years of this century, were
symptomatic of the sudden change: from the quiet, village-like and un-
cluttered cities of the beginning of that period to the chaotic bustle and
litter—with all the noise of mechanical transportation— that was found

here by the outbreak of the First World War. In that period the Prairies had been settled and fortunes had been made for the mail order houses and farm implement manufacturers of the East. The pre-Cambrian Shield had been opened up (a good deal of it by the Tyrrells) with the completion of the Temiskaming and Northern Ontario Railway in 1902; most of what we now understand by the term Bay Street had set up shop in little more than a decade.

The Chicago Exposition of 1893 had been the spring-board for the "city beautiful" movement; but its relevance to these booming towns of the frontier seemed less and less clear. On the other hand, mere size and rate of growth were no longer the only municipal virtues worth talking about. People by 1908 were beginning to have a look at the quality and cost of urban life—and to discover that the price of a serviced lot thirty-five feet wide outside Toronto had suddenly risen to $2,000 (that means $8,000 in 1958 terms). The essentials of the North American urban housing dilemma were sinking in on some men's minds for the first time.

In October of 1907, there was appointed in the United States an Inland Waterways Commission, which recommended to President Roosevelt that he should summon a conference of the State Governors to deal with natural resources conservation in general. The Governors accordingly met at the White House in May of 1908 and proceeded to the establishment of a National Commission, charged with the preparation of resource inventories and other matters. Roosevelt was aware that to safeguard some American resources would require co-operative efforts with neighbouring nations. He proposed that we should take up these questions in Canada, and his proposal was accepted by the Laurier Government. Times were prosperous, yet land and timber reserves no longer seemed "inexhaustible".

In the spring of 1909, Sir Wilfred Laurier introduced an Act to Establish a Commission for the Conservation of Natural Resources. [1] The Act had been drafted by the Hon. Clifford Sifton, a Winnipeg lawyer and Liberal Member of Parliament, who had been in Laurier's Cabinet until the two disagreed in 1905.

The Commission of Conservation Act provided for the creation of a body on which would sit *ex officio* the Federal Ministers answerable for the Agriculture, Interior and Mines Departments and also the members of each Provincial Government directly responsible for natural resources. There would also be a third class of members, appointed by the Governor-in-Council, to include at least one professor from each province in which there was a university. This body would meet at least once each year and would report to the Governor-General-in-Council, the report to be laid before both Houses of Parliament. The Commission could deal with any questions within its terms of reference that were referred to it by resolution of either House. Broadly, its scope embraced all questions related to the better utilization of the natural resources of Canada.

---

[1] 8-9 Edw. VII, Ch. 27 (1909).

The Commission was authorized to appoint a Secretary and Clerks under the Civil Service Act, and to retain expert assistants for special projects. Any person serving the Commission would be debarred from acquiring a proprietory interest in any Canadian resources. The Commission members were allowed their out-of-pocket expenses in doing the Commission's business. In September of 1909 the Honourable Clifford Sifton was named the Chairman of the Commission by an Order-in-Council which also listed the other members.

In spite of his differences with Laurier, Sifton was credited with the energetic policy of attracting immigrants which resulted in the enormous inflow of Europeans to Canada after 1899. While it now appears that other factors contributed at least as much as his ingenuity to the sudden spurt of settlement in the Western Provinces, his personal reputation remains untarnished.

Clifford Sifton has been described as "the greatest constructive statesman that Canada has yet produced". [2] A prominent member of the C.C.F., half a dozen years after Sifton's death, singled him out as "... one of our few intelligent millionaires"—high praise indeed from that quarter. [3]

A civil servant named James White was appointed Secretary of the Commission. He later reported that Sifton at the outset had laid down these rules for the Commission's operations: first, the printing and other purchases of the Commission shall be at the best prices, irrespective of political or other considerations; second, the staff is to be limited to a few expert advisers on the main resource fields, "assisted by clever members of the weaker sex"; third, special investigations will where possible be done by persons retained for specific tasks and for specified times; fourth, the Commission will strike a committee on each of the main resource areas and one on publications; fifth, the Commission will concentrate its efforts in one or a few directions at a time and will transfer continuing investigations where possible to operating departments of governments. [4]

To a considerable degree the Commission succeeded in these aims; systems of demonstration farms, water power inventories, a more consolidated Federal health service, housing and town planning were by its later years all accepted departmental responsibilities in Canadian Governments. The Commission never succeeded in its great aim of establishing a continuing inventory of all our major resources nor of developing a national policy on sources of energy; the latter remains to a Royal Commission in our day.

There was much discussion in its first days of what should be the functions of the Commission. Its Chairman said, "It is not the duty of this Commission to act in an executive capacity . . . . Our duty is to investigate, enquire, advise and inform. While . . . it will occasionally become

[2] By Augustus Bridle in *Sons of Canada*, quoted by A.R.M. Lower in *Colony to Nation*.

[3] In *Social Planning for Canada* (Nelson, 1935) by the League for Social Reconstruction.

[4] Annual Report of the Commission dated in 1919 and covering the calendar year 1918 (hereafter cited as *A.R.C.C. 1919*): pp. 12ff.

necessary for us to do things ... possibly falling within the function of a governmental department, ... never to a greater length than is necessary to arouse interest ... to point a way to improvement ... to collect information to an intelligent judgment." [5]

Looking back on the first five years of the Commission's work, the Chairman was able to report a wide range of accomplishments. He said there was no danger, as had been thought by some, that the early zest and idealism would flag. He instanced the fostering of national parks and game preserves; (Pelee Island and Percé were both national parks suggested by this Commission). He observed the encouragement given to agricultural and technical education, to the studies of mineral and energy resources, the development of safer practices in mining and in the utilization of western coal. The Commission had brought to public notice the danger to forests from the use by railways of certain types of coal; the railway board had ordered that these coals be no longer used. The impact of the war on the fur and fish industries had been studied with profit to the nation. Special studies had been made of conservation of the headwaters of the Trent (a provincial matter) to ensure the adequate flow of the canal (a federal investment). Canada's dormant concern for our share of international hydro-electric power sites had been awakened. Patronage in the giving of forest licences was reduced, the teaching of expert foresters and the establishment of a merit system among forest rangers were begun. Improvements in pulp and paper had been achieved by means of a special study conducted for the Commission by young Doctor C. D. Howe. [6]

In so wide a range of activities, relationship of the Commission to the ordinary functions and bodies in government gave rise to questions. The funds of the Commission were voted by Parliament on recommendation of the Minister of Agriculture, but he later insisted that the Commission was "neither a department nor a branch of government" and that "I had no responsibility at all ... in dealing with its various policies and so on". [7]

The Commission did have a few questions referred to it by Parliament: for instance, the Standing Committee of the Senate on Public Health, in February 1910, had noted the peril of stream pollution and asked the Commission (as a ready-made Dominion-Provincial body) to convene the Provincial Deputy Ministers of Health to consider the problem. [8] The Commission did so in October 1910, by which time its staff had collected alarming evidence. There were fifty-seven systems of inland waters receiving raw sewage from 159 municipalities, while 111 water supply systems were obtaining their water from streams or bodies of water into which raw sewage had been discharged above the intake point; there were only sixty-one sewage treatment plants in operation in Canada. [9]

---

[5] A.R.C.C. 1914: p. 17.

[6] A.R.C.C. 1915: pp. 3-33.

[7] A.R.C.C. 1919: p. 3.

[8] A.R.C.C. 1911: pp. 118ff.

[9] A.R.C.C. 1915: pp. 9-11.

The Commission recommended to the Government stream control methods observed by its staff in use in the United Kingdom and Germany.

However, the Federal Government rejected the advice, saying that most of the things the Commission wanted lay purely within provincial jurisdiction. [10] It was several years before a Federal health department was established, as another child of the Commission of Conservation.

The Commission quickly tangled too with provincial sovereignty. In 1911 the Guild of Civic Art of Toronto (which had already submitted designs for a civic square on almost the site now adopted) had prepared a Housing Bill for presentation in the Ontario Legislature. The Torontonians asked the support of the Commission of Conservation. Sifton was cautious: while much legislation of this type is "not wisely thought out ... I think we might go so far as to say that the Commission will approve of our Public Health Committee (Sir Edmund Osler, Chairman) supporting a demand for legislation after satisfying itself as to the wisdom of the provisions ... ". Nevertheless it was decided that the Health Committee should "represent" the Commission before the Ontario legislature, thus placing a Federally appointed body as advocates before a Provincial legislature. [11]

INTEREST OF THE COMMISSION IN TOWN PLANNING

One of the first permanent specialists appointed by the Commission was its Adviser on Public Health, Dr. Charles Hodgetts, who joined the staff on May 23, 1919; he had previously been a Medical Health Officer in Ontario. He was from the first convinced of the close relationship between public health and housing conditions. In his initial report he cited a great many authorities and statistics on the evils of overcrowding, including local reports from half a dozen Canadian cities. He called the tenement "a damnable architectural invention" and the apartment building "an architectural monstrosity". He said that the slum was "the great culture medium of civilization wherein great cultures of disease are growing, ready when ripe to rise and sweep the city streets". From Winnipeg, he quoted appalling conditions out of a book called *Strangers Within Our Gates* by a young clergyman of the Methodist persuasion, the Reverend J. S. Woodsworth. [12]

It was characteristic of the Commission that the experts-with-a-mission on its staff were much more extravagant in their language than the politicians who were the Commissioners. We find Dr. Hodgetts saying "There are two important factors in the question of national conservation, the physical and the vital. The former relates to the protecting of our land, our forests, our minerals, our waters, our sunlight, our fresh air; the latter, to the prevention of diseases, to health and to the prolongation of life.

---

[10] Order-in-Council P.C. 601 (March 27, 1911).

[11] *A.R.C.C.* 1912: pp. 81-83.

[12] *A.R.C.C.* 1911: pp. 50ff.

In housing and town planning we are dealing with most of the former and all of the latter." [13]

It is difficult to remember that during those days, every third death in the Dominion of Canada was caused by tuberculosis [14] and that typhoid and influenza epidemics produced death rates far in excess of those suffered later by active units in the war, and more like the casualties suffered nowadays on the roads. The battle cry again and again in the proceedings is that "population is our most valuable national asset". [15]

There are in the Commission's reports many notes of optimism, once everybody could get clearly in their minds that public health can be improved and that housing and town planning are means to that end. Hodgetts said it is "not so much the city beautiful as the city healthy that we want for Canada". He believed that legislatures were now ready to give ear to urban matters previously somewhat neglected and that if Ontario would now take the right advice "then we would not see the city of Toronto repeating the mistakes which make its outlines a hideous blunder on our map". [16]

Hodgetts said that building had tended to go forward rapidly on lines set out wholly between the owner and his surveyor and that this had left bad street layouts, lack of public open space, excessive height, coverage and bulk of buildings at the centres of cities and "shack-towns in the environs". He said we could learn from Port Sunlight, Bournville, Hampstead Garden Suburb and Letchworth. Hodgetts was especially down on great heights: he said skyscrapers were "nothing more nor less than nuisances, a menace alike to the health of those who are compelled to work in them, as well as to those who, unfortunately, fall within their overpowering and sepulchral shadow". The city of tall buildings, he said, was "the emanation of a freakish mind"; he was sure that public health would be the ground on which town planning would make headway. [17]

Others were likewise optimistic for the future while critical of present conditions. Mayor Geary of Toronto in his inaugural address of 1912 said, "there are few conditions found in the slums of European cities that have not been revealed in Toronto — the difference being one of degree only". However, the imminent extension of the civic car lines system should remove any excuse for central congestion. [18] In Winnipeg, the Medical Officer of Health was going to win the day with statistics. The aim was that every dwelling "no matter how humble" should be "a fit and proper place to bring up Winnipeg's most valuable asset—her children". He added: "Once the existing conditions are tabulated and are available in black and white

---

[13] *A.R.C.C.* 1912: p. 148.

[14] *A.R.C.C.* 1915: p. 178.

[15] *A.R.C.C.* 1910: pp. 114ff.

[16] *A.R.C.C.* 1915: pp. 270ff.

[17] *A.R.C.C.* 1912: pp. 132ff.

[18] Quoted in *A.R.C.C.* 1912: p. 144.

for the perusal of our citizens, we expect that public opinion will be ripe for a step forward in the housing problem". [19]

Even Sifton shared this optimism. While admitting that housing conditions in Montreal, Toronto and Winnipeg "demand a very radical remedy" he went on: "But our cities are not so large that they are out of control, and it is still possible within the next ten or twelve years to relieve any evil conditions which exist at the present time, and to lay foundations which will effectually prevent any serious growth of undesirable conditions in the future". While he admitted that the growth of very large cities posed many problems, he still looked for "public-spirited and philanthropic citizens to overtake the work which the housing problem presents". Speaking to a Toronto conference in 1914, he was confident "that there will probably be a pretty general agreement on policies and methods after the subject has been clarified by discussion".

Sifton's optimism of 1914 found the solution to housing problems in rapid transit. He recognized slums as "the most important social question of the modern world . . . more important than flying machines or wireless telegraphy, or battleships or armies"; but he believed that it was the difficulty of urban transit that had enforced congestion and added: "If any modern city fails to provide a proper method of transportation, in order to enable its population to extend its residential areas, then it is the fault of the people themselves, because the remedy lies close at hand". [20]

The interest of Sifton and Hodgetts in these problems led them to investigate and report fully on the planning progress being made here and abroad. They noted the establishment of the School of Civic Design at Liverpool in 1910, the appointment of one of Daniel Burnham's chief assistants, Edward H. Bennett, in 1913 to prepare a plan for Ottawa, and the work of Thomas H. Mawson and Sons in Calgary and Prince Rupert.

Dr. Hodgett's definition of town planning was very straightforward and confident: "The primary objects of town planning may be considered under three heads:

1. To encourage and facilitate thorough co-operation in the providing of housing accommodation for town dwellers whereby they will have sufficient light, air and space.

2. To ensure the exercise of foresight in reserving plenty of space for the development of main thoroughfares when required.

3. To take into account everything that helps to make town life worth living.

He elaborated the task saying: "The various constituent parts have to be arranged to form an harmonious whole, no matter how great that whole may ultimately become" and that the plan should provide for "every urban,

---

[19] *Ibid.*

[20] The preceding quotations are all from the address with which Sifton launched the business of the National Planning Conference in Toronto in May 1914, as reproduced in *A.R.C.C.* 1915: pp. 238ff.

suburban and rural area that may be built upon within from thirty to fifty years". He regarded wide streets with planting as "long ventilators . . . absorbing noxious gasses". He noted that in Europe, the work of correction had been begun "mainly on the initiative of medical health officers" but in the United States under the impulse of "the city beautiful". He was broad-minded enough to add: "public offices should be located in commanding positions, not only for the sake of the time and money saved to the public by the convenience of their positions, but because they should be dignified reminders of the Corporation's existence, and act as inspirations to the patriotism of the people". [21]

FIRST INVITATION TO THOMAS ADAMS

The Adviser on Public Health reported in 1913 that his Standing Committee had adopted a proposal to "call a National Housing and Town Planning Congress at Ottawa and secure, if possible, the attendance of one of the officers of the Local Government Board of Great Britain charged with the administration of this particular branch of that Board's work". [22] Supporting this proposal, the Chairman of the Health Committee, Sir Edmund Osler, said: "Organizations have been formed in almost all the leading cities . . . (for) the proper laying out of new towns and . . . to provide sanitary houses for workingmen, a need which is probably . . . greatest. A petition asking us to secure Mr. Adams to give advice in these matters has been very largely signed by public bodies interested and has been forwarded to the Commission." [22a]

Thus, Sir Edmund (brother of the famous physician) was the first to mention in the proceedings of the Commission the name of Thomas Adams. It was appreciated that the consent of the British Government would be required, and it was suggested that he should come for two months, the Canadian Government meeting his expenses and offering him some fee; the Prime Minister, Sir Robert Borden, was said to be willing to ask. Those in favour of Adams' visit included the Canadian Manufacturers' Association, the Imperial Order Daughters of the Empire, the National Council of Women, the Montreal Parks and Playgrounds Association, the Union of Canadian Municipalities, the Hamilton Board of Trade and "a very large number of the most prominent citizens of Canada". Osler added that perhaps they "expected a little too much of the visiting Englishman" but that "Adams was the one man (at the Philadelphia National City Planning Conference of 1911) who apparently had very sound and business-like ideas on the subjects of housing and town planning". The proposal was supported in the Commission by Sir John Gibson (Lieutenant-Governor of Ontario), by the Manager of the Toronto Globe, the President of the Toronto Housing

---

21 *A.R.C.C.* 1912: pp. 135-37.

22 *A.R.C.C.* 1913: p. 5.

22a *A.R.C.C.* 1913: p. 8.

Company, and by Dr. James Robertson, who was cautious enough to add the proviso that Mr. Adams should be accompanied about the country by a Canadian.

The National Conference on City Planning was the link between the Commission and Adams. These conventions began in 1909 in Washington (in the same atmosphere that produced the Commission of Conservation) at the instigation of the Committee on Housing Congestion of New York City. They have been held annually since, under various names, and are currently organized by the American Society of Planning Officials.

Sir Robert Borden did ask in 1913 for Adams to be loaned to Canada, but the British authorities said they could not spare him, and the matter was dropped for the time being. [23] Meanwhile the Commission pressed on with the promotion of town planning. It sent representatives to the National Planning Conferences at Boston in 1912 and Chicago in 1913; they brought back many specimens of the "districting ordinances"; tenement by-laws and subdivision control measures that were discussed at the later Conference. These were used by the Health Committee in drafting a comprehensive model provincial Town Planning Act for Canada. A separate draft Act was prepared for the condemnation of unfit housing. [24]

The Commission's ideas for procedures in planning and housing were thus grounded in American prototypes and attitudes. The Health Adviser said he was "not impressed with the achievements or the capabilities of the town councils". The model clauses drawn up by the Commission in 1914 were built around the idea of a separate honorary planning board on the American model.

These first model clauses were ascribed to Lieutenant-Colonel Jeffrey Burland, a man of considerable wealth from Montreal who left the Commission before Adams was appointed its Town Planning Adviser. Burland's draft was presented to the Sixth National Planning Conference, held in Toronto in May of 1914, for which the Commission of Conservation acted as host. This conference was opened by His Royal Highness the Duke of Devonshire, then Governor-General, and one of the invited speakers was Thomas Adams, still a British Civil Servant.

The first model Bill called for a Department of Municipal Affairs in each province, with under it a Central Town Planning Board consisting wholly of professionals with a qualified town planner as comptroller, surrounded by the regular provincial officers of finance, public health, engineering and law. This Board would see to the establishment of local planning boards, each to consist of the Mayor, the municipal engineer, medical officer of health and two ratepayers, "preferably an architect and a financier".

The local board was to be set up upon resolution of the Council, or on the petition of ten ratepayers, or by direction of the Central Board. Each local board was to have (as servant, not as voting member) a qualified

23 A.R.C.C. 1914: p. 21.
24 A.R.C.C. 1915: pp. 270ff.

Town Planning Commissioner, whose pay and tenure of office would be protected by the province, which would also supervise the local board's budget. For planning in smaller places one-fiftieth of one per cent of the total assessment was thought to be enough; and for the larger places one one-hundredth of one per cent of the total assessment; in the City of Toronto this would now produce a planning budget of about $150,000 a year.

The plans of local boards were to be called "town planning schemes", prepared in accordance with the regulations of the Central Provincial Board, which could advise on, approve conditionally or otherwise, alter, confirm or revoke local plans.

The local board subject to the province was to have considerable powers to buy property in the carrying out of plans and to pay compensation to land-owners affected by the plan. The local board could also collect betterment charges on property enhanced by its plans. The local board was to have excess condemnation powers and the approval of its scheme by the Central Board could supersede municipal by-laws. The local board could execute works and alter or remove buildings in default of action by their owners, if such action was essential to the completion of a scheme. All these powers were suggested for a board of one elected official, two municipal staff officers, and two appointed citizens. [25]

The essential unrealism of this model Act was seized on as soon as it was presented to the 1914 conference. Dr. Charles H. Mitchell (later Dean of the Faculty of Applied Science at the University of Toronto) observed that in co-ordinating the work of the local board with other municipal work "there is a chance for friction to creep in". Almost every other speaker concurred in this observation, some of them putting it in much stronger terms. A westerner observed that the Bill offered no control over railway development which was under federal jurisdiction; that federal suggestions to improve town planning might better begin at home. A man from Calgary observed that the Committee that drafted the Bill had no-one on it from west of Ottawa, that there were not enough skilled men to carry out the idea and that "the City Engineer and Medical Health Officer of a small town in the West are the last two persons that one would want to have anything to do with town planning".

The Minister of Municipal Affairs of Saskatchewan said "the Bill is a reversal entirely of our democratic order of things" and there was no hope of getting any provincial government in Canada to adopt it. He felt that "in our Province the Bill could not be entertained for a single moment" and that the town planning legislation ought to be achieved by amending the Cities and Towns Acts. The Provincial Treasurer of Quebec said of the Bill "in its present form I do not think it should be adopted". The public health people rallied to its defence and said that it was no more autocratic than the existing legislation on public health and sanatoria. [26]

---

[25] The Model Act is set out in full in *A.R.C.C.* 1915: pp. 245ff.

[26] The 1914 discussion is reported, apparently verbatim, in *A.R.C.C.* 1915: pp. 272ff.

Thomas Adams avoided direct criticism of the Bill on the Conference floor as a visitor to this country. But he dwelt on British experience at length; he said that civic planning in some continental countries had to do with servitudes in the monumental parts of the city, but he believed "town planning includes the consideration of every aspect of civic life and civic growth" and that the essence was "the provision of proper homes for the people. On that basis we have to build up the whole of our theory and practice on the subject... You can afford monumental structures as matters of luxury, after you have considered the real essentials of the home life of the people—the human units of the community." He emphasized that the British Legislation of 1909 dealt with future suburban development, saying that "the evils that have been created—while these are important—might wait a little". He also stressed the importance of the interim control provisions in the British Act. He said that it was the coming of the railways that had knocked the growth of towns out of kilter. [27]

At the close of the 1914 Conference, there was further emphasis by Chairman Sifton on the function of his Commission in town planning. He said " ... One of the main objects to be attained ... with a Conference of this kind is to secure a due measure of publicity.... The Conference has been competing for newspaper space ... at a time when ... the doings of H.R.H., a very popular prince, take up a good deal of space.... You have been holding your Conference while the spring races have been going on at the Woodbine, which is the most important sporting and social event which the good city of Toronto sees during the twelve months of the year. Then there is that incipient rebellion in Ulster, Home Rule, watchful intervention in Mexico and all that sort of thing.... So I think our friends of the Press have treated us very liberally.... "

On the same occasion, Clifton explained: " ... The germ ideal of [our] Commission is to ... save money's worth ... to preserve things that have value from being destroyed.... If [town planning] is another way of wasting public money (God knows there are enough of them now!) ... then it does not appeal to me. But if it can be shown ... that returns will be made for the money that is invested ... then we will have no trouble in getting the money.... I think this meeting will go a long way toward getting our people to understand that idea.... I.... hope this will not be the last Town Planning Conference that will take place within the limits of the Dominion of Canada." [28]

THE COMING OF ADAMS TO OTTAWA

During the summer of 1914, arrangements were completed for Thomas Adams to join the Commission of Conservation as Adviser on Town Planning. He appeared in Ottawa after war had broken out, in October 1914.

---

[27] *A.R.C.C.* 1915: pp. 258ff.

[28] *A.R.C.C.* 1915: pp. 242ff.

In introducing him to the next meeting of the Commission, the Chairman (now Sir Clifford Sifton) spoke of Adams' contribution to the Conference in Toronto and said that it "undoubtedly helped to create in the public mind a better understanding of the questions involved in what may be described as the science of town planning . . . ." The time had come to take a step which might be expected to produce something in the nature of definite results so the Commission obtained the services of Thomas Adams "one of the foremost and ablest authorities upon the subject . . . . I am determined that during the time Mr. Adams will be with us, we shall make use of his services in such a way as to secure definite and tangible results . . . ." [29] It will be noted that Adams' appointment was regarded from the outset as temporary.

Thomas Adams was born in 1871 in Edinburgh. He studied law, but early became acquainted with Patrick Geddes and the fascinating circle around Ebenezer Howard and the Garden City movement. He became Secretary of the First Garden City Company at Letchworth in 1900 and six years later entered private practice as a town planning consultant. On the passage of the British Town Planning and Housing Act in 1909 he was made an Inspector in the Local Government Board which administered that Act. He was one of the Founders and the first President of the British Town Planning Institute, being elected in the very year in which he came to Canada. Of his subsequent activities we shall hear more later. But on his arrival here he was already known as an eloquent author and speaker on the Garden City movement, on agricultural land use and on town planning and housing as aspects of local government.

On his first appearance before the Commission he commended the progress made by the Commission in these fields in its first five years. He also reviewed the steps taken locally across the country including the Winnipeg Tenement House By-law of 1909, the town planning begun in that city at the same time and culminating in the Greater Winnipeg Planning Commission of 1914, the Civic Guild of Toronto begun in 1897, the Toronto Housing Company's project of 1913, the Metropolitan Parks and Planning Commission established in Montreal as a child of the (still extant) Montreal Civic Improvement League, and on local plans prepared for Prince Rupert, Port Mann, Edmonton, Brantford, Calgary, Ottawa, Halifax and many others. He noted that Nova Scotia, New Brunswick and Alberta had Town Planning Acts, the earliest of them dating from 1912, based on the British Act of 1909 in part. He noted the movement for a National Housing and Town Planning Association or a Civic Improvement League of some sort. (He was to become the ringleader and first President of such a group the following year.) He did not hesitate to criticise what he regarded as inadequate provincial legislation. He paid full tribute to the impact of the 1914 Conference that was brought to Canada by the Commission. [30]

Adams went on in his first report to speak of the model town planning bill which the Commission had prepared. He said he had revised it, especially

[29] A.R.C.C. 1915: p. 2.
[30] A.R.C.C. 1915: pp. 158ff.

in the light of western comment. Pending the adoption of legislation, the great thing to do was to get adequate city maps at a scale useful for town planning purposes. He felt the lull brought about by the war was the golden opportunity to do preparatory work against the days of reconstruction ahead. He said past mistakes looked their most miserable in a period of interrupted development like the present. He again referred to the futility of drawing detailed plans until there were adequate local powers and fiscal means, and especially some machinery for interim control. He looked forward to extensive local consultations and to the collection of a library of literature, photos, slides and exhibits for demonstration purposes. [31]

In his second report to the Commission, at the beginning of 1916, Thomas Adams was able to report a tremendous and energetic year of work. He said the war "has cast new lights and new shadows on the old problems" and has thrown up adjustments whose necessity could now be more clearly seen. His report on 1915 contains many slogan phrases like "prepare for peace". He was already aware of the need for better systems of rural land parcelling and control, and was preparing a pioneer document on the subject Rural Planning and Development (published in 1917). He was fully aware of the Procrustean effect of Crown survey and grant systems upon later agricultural and settlement patterns. He urged the decentralization of manufacturing industries after the war and again mentioned the lack of sewerage and sanitation facilities in Canada.

Adams had by now made his own revision of the Commission of Conservation's model town planning bill and had secured wide acceptance of the draft. Adams said that the Nova Scotia Planning Act of 1915 and the regulations drafted under it had been as advocated by him in Halifax. In New Brunswick, a new set of regulations and an explanatory memorandum upon their 1912 Act had been adopted as drafted by him. In Quebec, his draft Town Planning Bill had been circulated to all members of both Houses and the Premier had personally promised him early action. In Ontario, Adams had addressed Ministers of the Legislature and submitted a draft Bill to the Premier and Provincial Secretary. In Manitoba, Adams had been asked to comment on a Town Planning Bill prepared by the Provincial Government and his suggestions were largely taken. In Saskatchewan, a Bill drafted by Adams had been given first reading. In Alberta, new regulations drafted by Adams pursuant to the old 1912 Act of the Province had been adopted. This left only two of the nine Provinces in which, after 15 months on the job, Thomas Adams did not have a statutory instrument of his own making in force. Those two Provinces were British Columbia and Prince Edward Island and to each he had sent a draft Town Planning Bill and received acknowledgment. This extraordinary effort was commended by formal Resolution of the Commission of Conservation in January 1916. [32]

We may note that Adams' revised model clauses for the Commission of Conservation as printed in 1916 contain many of the features to which

---

[31] A.R.C.C. 1915: pp. 160-179.
[32] A.R.C.C. 1916: pp. 118ff.

objection was taken by Canadian politicians in responsible positions in 1914. The local executive body is still an appointed group, on which the Mayor is the only person with a political mandate and two other members are his own employees. The arbitrary powers of the local board have been pared down somewhat but the general principles of Burland's 1914 draft are still preserved. Only in the last ten years have we moved away from the American prototype of the separate honorary planning board in some of our provinces; in some of the others we are considerably further, in a purely advisory direction from the elected city council and its full-time officials, than was Adams with his mixed local town planning board. I am reliably informed by people who knew Adams well that his British background rebelled against the North American separate commission for planning, but that he was obliged to promote that form of planning machinery (in his own somewhat blended version) by the widespread mistrust of elected local government then shared by all North American advocates of town planning.

In the fifteen months in which he had been writing town planning law across Canada he had also consulted with some forty local councils, working up a zoning by-law and a draft Official Plan for Halifax, a large town extension scheme for Saint John, New Brunswick, and two new towns— Ojibway for U.S. Steel near Windsor, and one for a pulp company on Lake Temiskaming. He had advised on the development of Stanley Park and judged the Civic Centre Competition in Vancouver. He had spoken and written extensively on the need for provincial departments of municipal affairs. He had instituted a housing survey of the City of Ottawa as a sample for methods to be used in a drafting of a Housing Act and regulations. He had written most of the material for a quarterly bulletin called *Conservation of Life* put out by the Commission of Conservation and had collected a good deal of the propaganda material in maps and photos that he wanted. He had taken steps to organize a national Civic Improvement League which held its first meeting in November 1915 and held a National Conference in January 1916. He had been consulted on a route of new highway from Toronto to Hamilton. He had been a very busy man.

APOGEE OF COMMISSION'S PLANNING WORK

For the fiscal year 1916-1917, the budget of the Commission of Conservation was cut 25 per cent out of respect for the very heavy war expenditures then faced. The budget in the first full year had been of the order of $50,000 and was now close to $100,000. Before the Commission came to an end its annual budget had reached $280,000, although in the final years it was back to about $150,000. In 1917 Adams returned to England and missed the Commission's Annual Meeting. He came back to Canada just at the time of the Halifax Explosion at the end of that year. He was immediately directed by the Cabinet to serve in the rebuilding of Halifax. He prepared a detailed scheme for the devastated area and a general scheme for the metropolitan area as a whole. He was asked by the Government to become a member of the federally created Halifax Relief Commission, and the Commission of Conservation endorsed this idea but Adams "for personal reasons" declined, while agreeing that the Halifax group needed expert staff. [33]

The burden of his work made it necessary for the Government to provide assistance to him for his consultations in western cities; Mr. Arthur G. Dalzell, an engineer, was made available to help him. [34] For his work in the eastern part of the country, Mr. Horace L. Seymour was loaned to him by the Surveyor-General of Canada. Later in 1918, Mr. W. D. Cromarty was added to his staff for the preparation of model house designs. All these men were original members of the Town Planning Institute of Canada, of which Thomas Adams was the first President, elected in 1919.

By February of that year, at the Annual Meeting of the Commission, Adams had, for the first time, to report some discouragement. Manitoba had not yet appointed the qualified comptroller provided under their act. His report on "urban planning and development" had had to be put aside for the urgent matters in Halifax and elsewhere. Ontario had amended its Planning and Development Act, but not (apart from the title, which was of Adams' choosing) along the lines which the Commission of Conservation had recommended. He was receiving an enormous stream of plans for comment and was soon to be involved as a special adviser to the Cabinet Committee on the Housing Act—passed at the end of the war as a measure to offer employment and meet the needs of veterans. [35]

One aspect of his work in 1918 is of particular interest to us, in that Alberta cities were then coming to realize that the large tracts zoned for urban development within their boundaries, but still in use as agricultural lands, were posing a serious taxing problem. Adams' advice was that these lands should be taxed as agricultural, notwithstanding their position within the city limits. It was reasonable to designate as building land only what was likely to be built upon within a reasonable time. When any land was transferred from agricultural use to building land, its great increase in value should be reflected in greatly increased municipal taxes; and until so designated no land should have urban works installed in it at the city's expense, although private persons might install such works at their own expense and with the city's approval. In agricultural lands within city limits there should be no consent to subdivision, unless the need for it was shown and at least two-thirds of the adjacent subdivisions were already built upon. Any land subdivided should immediately be put on the higher tax rate. He said that many of the existing vacant subdivisions, dating from the pre-war land boom, should be cancelled. Further, that the effect of these steps would be to "increase the value of central areas" and hence to increase municipal revenues while cutting municipal expenditures that

[33] *A.R.C.C.* 1919: pp. 102-105.

[34] Mr. Dalzell, a founder and long an officer of the Town Planning Institute of Canada, is living in Toronto and is now an Honorary Member.

[35] *A.R.C.C.* 1919: pp. 17ff.

had been based on "the extraordinary pictures conceived by real estate owners with vivid imaginations". [36]

Adams in 1919 seemed to sense that the steam was going out of federal leadership in the town planning field. He noted that the work of the Commission had not been widely enough understood. He regretted that Canada had failed to employ suitably qualified veterans to make city maps, as was done in Britain. He believed that steps must now be taken to make permanent the Civic Improvement League, which had been begun four years earlier. He also said that "a Town Planning Institute is being formed for the purpose of promoting educational courses on town planning in the Universities". [37]

END OF THE COMMISSION

At this same meeting of the Commission in February 1919 was announced the resignation of Sir Clifford Sifton, after nearly ten years in the Chair; this was met with profound regret both by the members of the Commission and members of its staff. Sifton, too, must have felt that the days of his usefulness to the Commission were drawing to a close. There were now many bureaus and departments of Federal Government carrying on as normal responsibilities in the fields which had been opened up by the Commission in its ten years of existence. A number of post-war decisions of the Judicial Committee of the Privy Council in London had underscored the general feeling that it was time to cut the Federal Government down to size and to restore to the provinces their full range of constitutional functions. The period of heroic developmental works requiring Federal Government financing or guarantees was also past for the time being, and the leaders of the business world were thus less interested in the Federal Government's help and ideas as to the best way to make a dollar.

In Sifton's absence, the annual statement of the work of the Commission was made by the Honourable Martin Burrell, the Minister of Mines; although there was no more reason why he should make it than that it should be made by the Minister of the Interior, Mr. Arthur Meighen, who was also a member of the Commission and was in the room. [38]

Meighen did not fail to notice that the Commission had presumed to present a brief in the previous September to the International Joint Commission, although the Government of Canada had its own formal brief and counsel in the same hearing before that Commission. The hearing happened to concern an application of a subsidiary of the Aluminum Corporation of America for certain water power rights in the St. Lawrence. It was an area in which the Commission of Conservation thought there should

---

[36] *A.R.C.C.* 1919: pp. 113ff.

[37] *A.R.C.C.* 1919: p. 102. See also Adams' *Outlines of Town and City Planning* (New York, Russell Sage, 1935) p. 285.

[38] *A.R.C.C.* 1919: p. 3.

be a comprehensive plan for power development and a deepened seaway. The objection of the Government of Canada, on the other hand, was lodged on legal grounds: that the application was not properly before the International Joint Commission. The conflict between these legalistic and developmental objections of the two emanations of the Government of Canada must have been puzzling to the I.J.C.

The end of the Commission of Conservation came in the Spring session of the Parliament in May of 1921, when Bill 187 was introduced into the Senate to repeal the Commission of Conservation Act. In the Senate debate there were allegations that the Commission was torpedoed because of the ambitions of one or two senior members of the regular departments. In bringing the Bill into the Commons, Mr. Meighen (now Prime Minister as successor to Sir Robert Borden for eighteen months) denied that this was the cause.

Many of those associated with the Commission have said that the full story should be told some time, but so far as I can discover the full story has not been told. [39]

The reasons given by Mr. Meighen in the House of Commons for the repeal of the Act included the following: that the Commission was "merely advisory" and had "no relationship to any Minister". He said it was in the logic of the thing that "it could only be of a temporary character" and had not "the seeds of permanency in it". He said that such a body was "not consistent with our system of government". He accused the Commission with characteristic candour of having "laid its hand on anything that looked alluring" and of having invaded one department after another with resultant overlap. He said it had taken credit for the work of others embodying their findings in its elegant and expensive annual reports as its own work. He referred specifically to the confusing appearance of representatives of the Commission of Conservation before the International Joint Commission alongside counsel for the Government. He also said that the creation of a department of pensions and national health (occasioned by the heavy budget of allowances for veterans among other things), the great development of the forest service, of the mines department and other branches, had made most aspects of the work of the Commission of Conservation redundant.

Only three speakers opposed the motion to abolish the Commission in the House of Commons: they were the Honourable Dr. Belland who was a member of the Commission; Mr. Fielding, who as a member of the Government that had formed the Commission took exception to some of the Prime Minister's remarks; and Mr. Bureau. [40]

Sir Clifford Sifton lived to add to his distinctions until 1929. Thomas Adams became more and more heavily involved with private consulting work and in 1923 was appointed Director of the Regional Plan of New York and Environs, a position he held until 1930. Adams then became

---

[39] Typical of these observations is one in a personal letter to the author to the effect that "a political feud broke up the Commission".

[40] Canada, House of Commons *Debates* 1921: pp. 3858, 3970-71.

Associate Professor of City Planning at Harvard University. He had been lecturing in Civic Design at the Massachusetts Institute of Technology since 1921. He resumed his British connections more actively after 1934, when he became Vice-President of the Institute of Landscape Architects. He conducted a substantial private practice as consultant to local authorities in the United Kingdom until his death in March, 1940 in Sussex. Mrs. Adams is still living in England.

Most of us know Adams' books on planning that date from his years in the United States. What happened to the material he prepared while in Ottawa on "Urban Planning and Development" we can only guess; it is to be hoped that most of it found its way into these later writings.

ISSUES RAISED BY COMMISSION'S EXPERIENCE

I would be rash indeed at this stage to pronounce judgment upon Sir Clifford Sifton's Commission as a Federal instrument, or about Thomas Adams' sojourn in Canada. I have tried from bits of quotation to sketch in the beginnings, accomplishments and downfall of the Commission and the background of Adams' service to it. This is not idle antiquarianism. The 1909 to 1921 experience contains lessons and issues for us to ponder today.

Uppermost in my mind are questions of this order:

1. Was the Canadian Commission of Conservation, in relation to resources management and planning, symptomatic of that phase in every new activity dominated by the enthusiastic amateur, the confident dilettante, the zealous oversimplifying missionary? Was the Commission therefore doomed by the accession of technical specialists in regular government departments (a development accelerated by the first World War)? Or was a useful adjunct of government torpedoed in 1921 by petty views and expedient ambitions?

2. With much hesitation, I ask the associated question: was Thomas Adams also representative of a talented *prima donna* phase in planning? Was he more an inspired advocate, an able solo tactician, a gifted persuader than he was a disciplined professional member of the public service? Is there some reason why we now have fewer "stars" in planning, and of those we have many seem disillusioned and underemployed? Does this arise directly from the encouraging progress that physical planning activity has made, both toward a fuller understanding of the complexity of our raw material and of our limitations as individuals in handling it, and also the attainment by planning of a normal place as a part of any well-constituted local government?

3. Can government usefully employ a detached body, dominated by elected persons, with very broadly defined and everlasting investigating duties, but the obligation to report specific accomplishments annually? Is the committee appointed by and from the legislature, active only as it receives particular questions for enquiry, a more suitable instrument for the

purpose? Does recent American experience illuminate this? Do the more or less futile Dominion-Provincial conferences of Premiers illustrate the pitfalls, and the far more effective and regular Federal-Provincial consultations of officials with funcionally limited responsibilities (health, labour, or agriculture) answer better than the Commission did? (These specialized appointed bodies tend to avoid formal recommendations: each member advises his own government in the light of shared information.) Was the Commission bound to overstep safe limits in the excitement of advocacy, in the effort to justify itself or to scrutinize the practices of operational units of government?

4. Is the management of resources, including urban wealth, a matter (as suggested by the Sirois Commission staff) so influenced by regional and partisan interests, attitudes and philosophies, that recommendations from appointed joint bodies will rarely be acceptable to enough of the sovereign bodies they represent? Is there a parallel here with joint planning boards, who must make common recommendations to competing (though adjoining) municipal councils?

5. With the increased roles since 1921 of Provincial and Federal governments in physical development (which means more and more in metropolitan regional development) should we be thinking about quite specific new machinery to reveal the inter-governmental implications of each agency's program? Are the emanations of senior governments otherwise likely to fashion the main outlines of our future urban regions (by taxing policies, grants-in-aid to highways and institutions, housing credit practices and so forth) in what someone has called a state of absent-mindedness? How do we now achieve intergovernmental "presence of mind"?

These seem to me some of the questions we might consider after a glance at the Commission of Conservation.

THE "PATRON SAINT" OF TOWN PLANNING IN BRITISH COLUMBIA

H. Peter Oberlander

Dr. Oberlander is Director of the School of Community and Regional Planning in the Faculty of Graduate Studies at the University of British Columbia. He is an adviser to the United Nations Technical Assistance Administration on planning, education and regional development problems in the recently independent countries, notably in Africa. Currently Professor Oberlander is preparing a history of the planning movement in British Columbia.

Town Planning in British Columbia is as old as the Province itself. In fact in some ways it is even older. That may come as a surprise to those who think of town planning as a latter-day venture into fixing up cities once they are choked by traffic or lack adequate housing or suffer from widespread slum conditions. Town planning in British Columbia has a long and adventurous history.

British Columbia's first town planner was Colonel Richard Clement Moody who came to the West Coast in response to a request by James Douglas, the first Governor of the young colony. Colonel Moody came as Commanding Officer of the Royal Engineers in 1858 to perform many and varied military and engineering duties. He was also appointed Chief Commissioner of Lands and Works and his success in this capacity, although less known, ought to qualify him fully as the patron saint of present-day town planners in British Columbia, although perhaps some would question his "saintlines".

The scope of Colonel Moody's task is well described in a letter from the then Secretary of State for the Colonies to him, dated October 29, 1858:

> ... commence operations necessary for the land sales by which the expenses of the survey are to be defrayed. You will consult with the Governor as to the choice of site for a maritime town probably at the mouth of the Fraser River and for any more inland capitals to which the circumstances of the territory will suggest the most appropriate site. You will not fail to regard with a military eye the best position for such towns and cities as well as for the engineering of roads and passes and laying of the foundations of any public works.

After suggesting that the lots be sold at an upset price which was to include the price of survey, the Secretary of State instructed Moody to note natural harbours, report on gold and other minerals, note fishing possibilities and timber resources, and to test the soil for its agricultural potential. Correspondence between the Secretary of State and Governor Douglas explains why the Royal Engineers were selected for the pioneering work in British Columbia.

> By their services as pioneers in the work of civilization, in opening up the resources of the country, by the construction of roads and bridges, in laying the foundation of the future city and seaport and in carrying out the numerous engineering works which in the early stages of colonization are essential to the progress and welfare of the community ... they will ... establish themselves in the popular goodwill of the immigrants ....

Colonel Moody's duties were clearly twofold. On the one hand he was to prepare a comprehensive survey of development potential of the southern section of British Columbia. On the other hand he was to select town sites for new towns at the mouth of the Fraser and further upstream. This was a formidable task when one remembers that at the time of the arrival of the Royal Engineers in British Columbia a hundred years ago the colony was one vast wilderness where law and order had yet to be enforced, and revenues raised and collected. The entire seaboard was a huge forest separated from the interior by vast mountain ranges. The Fraser River, the great artery of the country, was difficult to navigate. The winding channels and shifting banks and shoals at the river's mouth made it difficult for larger vessels to enter. However, once inside the bar, the river was navigable for all boats as far as Langley, thirty-two miles from its mouth, and as far as Fort Hope another forty miles above that, for flat-bottomed boats. The Hudson's Bay Company was the only recognized authority in the whole area. It had established some thirteen posts at strategic points to trade with the Indians. The first one situated at Fort Langley was by far the most important since it was a supply centre. At each post, as was customary, the Company had occupied land not only for the forts themselves but also to raise crops and pasture a large number of horses.

Before Colonel Moody arrived Governor Douglas had made three visits to the mainland; the third one was on the occasion of the formal launching of the colony of British Columbia. This was in November 1858. At that time he was installed as the Governor of the new colony and selected Derby, about two and one half miles below the present community of Fort Langley, as the new capital of British Columbia. In September 1858 the same spot had been surveyed into lots by some enterprising person from Victoria. The fact that private individuals had considered the site suitable for a townsite undoubtedly influenced the Governor in his choice. He is reported to have said:

> I was guided in choosing Langley as the site of a commercial town chiefly as the partiality disclosed for that spot by the mercantile community of the country whose instincts in such matters are generally unerring.

However, another equally reliable contemporary source probably comes nearer the truth:

> It is possible that the close proximity of a large block of land held in reserve by the Hudson's Bay Company will have had something to do with the original choice.

Prior to becoming Governor, Douglas was a Hudson's Bay Company factor, with many years of loyal service to the Company. Governor Douglas felt that the site possessed great natural advantages for trade, having a good anchorage, "a cheerful aspect, a surface well adapted for building, and drainage", although having "the disadvantage of being in part low and occasionally flooded by the river". The whole site covered 900 acres of land and lots were sold by auction in Victoria late in November, under the direction of the Surveyor-General of Vancouver Island, Mr. J. D. Pemberton. About 322 lots were sold, aggregating over £15,000. Only 10 per cent of the price had to be paid as a down payment.

Governor Douglas' choice of Derby for the capital of the new colony and the sale of lots were at once questioned in London. Bulwyer-Lytton wrote to Douglas early in 1859:

> It has been suggested to me that supposing the advantages to be in other respects equal it might have been preferable to place the town on the banks of the river which is furthest from the American frontier. On such matters you now have the advantage of consulting Col. Moody, an officer of great skill and experience.

Prior to the arrival of Colonel Moody and his Royal Engineers several townsites had already been laid out. At Fort Douglas about seventy lots were occupied. At Lytton fifty houses and a population of 900 had assembled. Mr. Pemberton, the colony's official land surveyor had begun to lay out the townsites both at Fort Hope and at Fort Yale. These activities indicate that town planning—that is the laying out of townsites prior to settlement by public authority—preceded even the establishment of British Columbia as a colony.

Before leaving England Colonel Moody had studied all available maps and there is some evidence that he had already selected the approximate site for the new capital without setting foot in British Columbia. He arrived Christmas Day 1858 and soon unhesitatingly condemned Derby on sanitary, commercial, and military grounds. Colonel Moody's original report to the Governor, dated January 28, 1859, sheds interesting light on his site selection criteria for the colony's capital and his planning point of view:

> After a very careful study of the question I have now the honour to submit to your consideration that the site which appears to be best adapted for the capital of British Columbia is about 10 miles below the new town of Langley and on the north bank of the Fraser . . . . It is the first high ground on the north side after

entering the river and is about twenty miles above the sand heads. There is abundance of room and convenience for every description of requisite in a sea port and capital of a great country. There are great facilities for communication by water as well as by future great trunk railways into the interior .... There is good land for garden ground if one may judge by the forest and rich meadow land surrounding it. It is raised above the periodical flats and yet the low lands, (which will be most coveted as commercial sites, docks, quays, etc.) are close adjoining and easily made available. From the advantageous circumstances of the locality, it is easily rendered unapproachable to any enemy. As a military position, it is rare to find one so singularly strong by nature in connection with adaption as a capital of a country.

Colonel Moody then proceeds to expand upon the evident military advantages of the site of New Westminster. He considers it the only spot which could effectively be defended against any expansionist intentions of the United States. Furthermore he recognized the natural advantages that would accrue to a town located on that site:

There is deep water close along an extended line of shore: sea-going vessels of any burden can moor close to the bank, plenty of water for the supply of household purposes, and good drainage. I would wish that the upper level had not been so high as hereafter it may call for some extensive improving of the gradients of a few of the streets. The main streets for business, however, and all that may be occupied for some time to come, will be satisfactory. I might also add that any leading railway communication from the interior will pass down on the north side of the river. Politically and commercially this would be necessary.

Despite Colonel Moody's evident concern for the military advantages of the new capital he was clearly concerned with the future development of the site as a town. The site selected had obvious commercial and political advantages. Consequently Governor Douglas had to accept Colonel Moody's recommendations, albeit reluctantly. An editorial in the British Colonist of February 3, 1858, indicates the reason for the Governor's reluctance:

New Westminster is said to be the best situated in a military and commercial point of view but by removing Langley that Hudson's Bay Company's ten mile land claim will not become so valuable, and consequently Executive reluctance may be accounted for.

Colonel Moody, as Commissioner of Land and Works, was responsible for the locating, surveying, laying out and selling of town lots, as well as for the survey and sale of country land. He defined the boundaries of the Hudson's Bay Company's land, the Indian Reserves, and set aside certain land for church purposes. Apart from New Westminster as the new capital, Colonel Moody and his staff designed plans for townsites at Fort Hope, Fort Yale, Fort Douglas, Lytton and Lillooet.

All the plans are characterized by a rigid grid of land subdivision and road layout. Occasionally crescents or curving roads were introduced presumably to achieve a focus or accent in the street pattern. It seems strange that Colonel Moody and his engineers would attempt to superimpose such a relentless grid pattern on townsites which in most instances had pronounced land features and where contours and topography would have suggested quite a different street layout or lot subdivision. It must have been evident to them that a rigid geometric pattern would entail considerable engineering difficulties in building streets and laying out utilities. Adequate maintenance of these roads must have posed additional problems in areas that were almost totally undeveloped and lacked basic equipment and experience of town building, available in Europe or in Eastern Canada.

One might attempt to explain these settlement layouts in three ways. First, undoubtedly Colonel Moody's cultural background played a role: he had come from post-Georgian England where grandiose regular and geometric town layouts were the fashion and were still considered an appropriate development pattern. The town of Bath and certain new London suburbs like Bloomsbury and Kensington had recently been planned, usually in a regular grid system with circles, crescents or open squares forming carefully conceived foci in the urban structure. Second, the grid system had an obvious design simplicity; the land could easily be parcelled out in an apparently equitable manner recorded on a map and dealt with efficiently and speedily. Undoubtedly, Colonel Moody was also aware of the legal advantages of dividing the land into regular lots of exactly the same size and in rectangles. This simplified the legal description which in turn made transfer of titles relatively easy. In other words, there may have been some compelling engineering and legal reasons in favour of a grid system, particularly since little of that general area had been surveyed prior to its subdivision, and most of it not yet cleared of its first timber. Third, a land-use plan respecting contours and topography obviously requires a relatively high level of surveying skill and surveying instruments. The surveying technology in 1859 in British Columbia was indeed in its infancy. The instruments in use then were very large and exceedingly awkward to move; the grid pattern was the easiest to lay out in the field since it required the least amount of movement of the surveying instruments.

In the case of New Westminster, Colonel Moody was anxious to have the main street of the new town run parallel to the river and provide a wide and open market street and thoroughfare. All other streets were then surveyed at right angles from this main street. Serving as the base line for the rest of the land survey. The streets that resulted ran up hill and established the basic grid pattern.

Apart from site selection and layout of new towns, Colonel Moody was asked to establish land reservations for military and naval purposes, particularly on the Burrard Peninsula and along the Burrard Inlet. Two of these have achieved considerable planning significance today:

1. A military reserve of 354 acres on the south side of first Narrows, now known as Stanley Park (at least a part of it).

2. A governmental reserve for a settlement, later known as Hastings Townsite, subsequently named Vancouver, created in 1860/1861.

In addition Colonel Moody criss-crossed Burrard Peninsula with survey lines which subsequently established these lines as major roads. Granville Street is one of Colonel Moody's survey lines and so is Kingsway. In February and March of 1863 a party of Royal Engineers made a complete survey of the shore line from the "Hastings Townsite" reserve to False Creek, starting at the townsite they surveyed the south shore of Burrard Inlet laying out successively a series of lots all the way to the military reserve at the First Narrows, now Stanley Park.

The Royal Engineers have many other works to their credit in British Columbia. They established a Lands and Works Department and the first Government Printing Office in New Westminster. On January 1, 1863 they printed the first *British Columbia Gazette*, and designed British Columbia's first Coat of Arms. Their most far-reaching work however was their extensive road, bridge, and highway building as well as their explorations, surveys, and establishment of land development policies. In the hinterland of the young colony Colonel Moody predicted the coming of the railway. It was his opinion that a railway would naturally reach Port Moody, circle around the back of New Westminster and finally reach English Bay. He was convinced that a transcontinental railway from Halifax to Vancouver had to be established and made his prediction under the title of "Inter-Colonial Railway" in the *British Columbian*, March 13, 1862.

Colonel Moody was a man of many talents, great physical power, obvious personal charm, and wide experience in handling men under difficult circumstances. Although discharging his professional duties 100 years ago at a time when professional lines were not nearly as clearly and rigidly drawn as today, his approach to the critical problem of land selection for colonization for new townsites and their layout, mark him clearly a planner in the contemporary sense of the word.

THE ORIGIN OF COLONIAL SETTLEMENTS IN THE MARITIMES

Michael Hugo-Brunt

Michael Hugo-Brunt is an Associate Professor of City & Regional Planning at Cornell University. He was formerly Planning Consultant, University of Toronto, and a Professor in the Division of Town & Regional Planning. Prior to 1959 he was the Acting Head and Senior Lecturer in the Faculty of Architecture of the University of Hong Kong.
He was past Chairman and Director of the Ontario Chapter of the Town Planning Institute of Canada. He has also been a C.M.H.C. Senior Fellow, a Fulbright Scholar and a Canada Council Scholar. He has published various studies on Planning and Architecture in the professional press and has undertaken commissioned research projects in Canadian Maritime Settlements, Oriental, Portuguese and English Colonial and Georgian Planning. He lectures in Planning and Landscape History.

THE SETTING

The Maritime Provinces include Nova Scotia, Prince Edward Island, Newfoundland and New Brunswick; but this investigation was primarily confined to Nova Scotia.

The Maritime Provinces are regarded today by Canadians mainly as summer resort areas, although historically they constitute the oldest regions of exploration and settlement in Northern America. At the present time (1960's) they are experiencing a period of decline following the post-war boom, and the provincial economies are undergoing severe strain and have consequently not expanded as effectively as might have been expected.

The population of the Maritimes numbers 1,974,758 persons (according to the 1966 census), and this represents a slight gain in population since 1961, although many of the inhabitants have moved away to seek employment in the more prosperous areas of Canada in recent years. Nova Scotia functions as a minor centre for higher education and has no less than six educational institutions of importance. [1]

---

[1] The population figures given for the various provinces in the 1966 census are as follows: Nova Scotia 756,039, New Brunswick 616,758, Prince Edward Island, 108,535, and Newfoundland 493,396.

The Provinces have been traditionally associated with lumber and fish. A limited amount of agriculture is carried out, potato, apple cultivation and dairy farming being the most important activities, but the Maritimes are perhaps more celebrated because of the association of these specializations in the establishment of the Maritime co-operative organizations. Coal and gold have been mined, although the former has declined because of flooding while the latter ceased abruptly when the mines became uneconomic. Lumber is perhaps the most important industry operating at the present time.

The Maritime terrain is predominantly glacial morain, which implies that it is rugged and hilly and therefore excellent country for forestry and recreation, although poor for agriculture. The areas incorporate many picturesque lakes, well-watered rivers and numerous bays and inlets. The varied coastline affords an ideal breeding ground for fish and lobsters and is deemed to be one of the finest fishing areas in the world. The first colonisers took full advantage of the bays, inlets and creeks where they established lobster fisheries, fishing stations and shipbuilding centres.

Consequently the earliest settlements orientated themselves economically on the fur trade and fishing, and only developed major maritime industries such as shipbuilding, during the eighteenth and nineteenth centuries. Some counties have developed good dairy farming, fruit and vegetable growing. The Acadian settlers, for example, established agricultural villages along the river terraces adjoining the Minas Basin, the Chignecto Peninsula, and along the Annapolis Valley, and their small communities were associated with strip agricultural lands and dyked marshes. The remainder of the Peninsula is unsuitable for agriculture and once provided the native Indian communities, who roamed the area, with hunting and fishing.

The native inhabitants of Nova Scotia were the Micmac Indians; a pastoral and warrior people who were originally descended from a branch of the Algonquin and Iroquoian tribes. They never established any significant settlements of their own. At first when European colonisation occurred in their territories their hunting and fishing areas were not seriously disturbed but eventually they realized that these were becoming circumscribed and overworked. The situation deteriorated further when they were joined by the fleeing remnants of other Indian peoples from New England. The Indians never accepted British rule and attempted to drive their colonists out by force. The French, however, turned them into useful allies through a sensible policy and a steadfast program of Catholicism. Until the eclipse of the French in North America, the Indians functioned as a useful third force to whom each of the two nations turned in times of hostilities.

Few Indians remain in Nova Scotia today, although place names still exist which mark former Indian settlements. As early as 1820 the Nova Scotia Indians were dying out through the ravages of smallpox and alcohol. The Micmacs reared few children, for their precarious hunting and fishing economy resulted in small families consisting of two to three children.

Location of Settlements

Figure 1.

Figure 2.

Figure 3.

Figure 4.

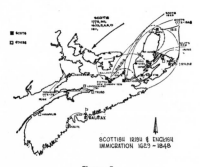

Figure 5.

Figure 6.

THE PHASES OF MARITIME SETTLEMENT, Nova Scotia, Cape Breton and Prince Edward Island, 17th, 18th and early 19th centuries.

1. Acadian, 1603–1720.
2. New England Townships, 1759–1761.
3. German, Swiss and French Protestant, 1750–1755.
4. United Empire Loyalists, 1776–1783.
5. Scottish, Irish and English Immigration, 1629–1848.
6. Military Townships, 1812.

At the beginning of the nineteenth century there were approximately 350 families consisting of about 1,500 persons, most of whom were Catholics.

The Indian tribes were organized on a family or clan system. Their tents were simple constructions of wood and skin, erected in the form of conical sugarloaves. The Chiefs were elected by vote, and during French rule they were consecrated by priests. Walter Bromley championed their repeated solicitations for reserves with some success.

THE MAJOR MIGRATIONS

Early Colonization in Nova Scotia and the Hostilities (1618-1712)

Nova Scotia was colonized by European settlers who arrived in the waves of immigration which reflected the political events in Europe and the United States. Great Britain claimed the territories, basing her rights to "Terra Nova" on John Cabot's voyages of discovery in 1497. British settlement certainly occurred in Newfoundland after 1610. Other British attempts at settlement were again made by Sir William Alexander, later the Earl of Stirling, who received a patent for the territories from King James I on the 5th of August, 1621. He called the area Nova Scotia, for as he said,

> Being much encouraged hereunto by Sir Ferdinando Gorges, and some others of the undertakers for New England, I show them that my countrymen would never adventure in such an enterprise, unless it were as there was a New France, a New Spain, and a New England, that they might likewise have a New Scotland.

This early project was similar to the plantations of Ulster and New England, being feudal in conception, and an Order of 140 Knight Baronets of Nova Scotia was established by the King to encourage colonization. Each member received a baronetcy, four miles by six miles in extent. Settlements were planted at Port Royal and in Cape Breton, but these ultimately failed.

The first actual attempt at settlement appears to have been made by the French Baron de Lery, in 1518, who landed livestock at Cape Canso, but never actually planted a community. The first French colony in Nova Scotia was developed by Pierre du Gaste, the Sieur de Monts, in 1603 at Port Royal. He took possession of the area in the name of the French Crown and called the territory New France.

The French soon expanded into the fertile farming areas of the Annapolis Valley, the adjoining Minas Basin and the Chignecto Peninsula. A primitive transportation system was developed in the line of the present road from Pictou to Truro, which was demarcated by a few scattered farms. Small fishing communities also came into being along the East Coast near Cape Sable, Chebucto, Sheet Harbour and Cape Canso. As French Canada developed there was a tendency for Acadian settlement to consolidate itself in the northern area of Nova Scotia.

Several times the New England colonies which resented progressive French settlement to their north, undertook military expeditions, and both nations intrigued with the Indians in attempts to expand their boundaries into the territory of the other. The Anglo-French wars in 18th-century Europe were reflected in this North American struggle. Hostilities commenced in the early years of the 17th century, along the line of the Kennebec River which may be regarded as the first boundary. In 1618 the Governor of Virginia, Sir Samuel Argall, organized a military expedition which destroyed Port Royal with the assistance of a disaffected French noble, Claude de la Tour. During the British occupation, Sir William Alexander attempted to plant a settlement, but disheartened by failure, he eventually granted the northern land in his patent to Sir David Kirk. Kirk, however, sold his rights back to the King of France for £5,000. Sir William Alexander then followed his example and sold his remaining possessions to de la Tour. In 1632, after the Treaty of St. Germain was concluded, Acadia was returned to France.

The French re-established their position with the introduction of new colonists, only to be dislodged from Port Royal by a force dispatched in 1654 by the Cromwellian Government, commanded by Major Sedgworth. In 1667 the Treaty of Breda again re-established French rule in Nova Scotia. In the 1690 war Sir William Phipps of Massachusetts invaded Acadia and recaptured the area. Once again it was returned, but was finally ceded to Britain at the Treaty of Utrecht in 1713.

Immigration After 1713

The Peace of Utrecht forced the British to adopt a more positive colonial policy. They decided to settle ex-servicemen in Nova Scotia, and they offered prospective settlers generous inducements which were similar to those used at first in the early northern American colonies. The significant provisions were as follows :

1. The advance and reimbursement of passage money,
2. A substantial grant of building materials for a dwelling,
3. The provision of fishing and agricultural implements,
4. The defrayment of the first year's subsistence expenses,
5. Free grants of land based on rank and family size.

This had little effect at first, and it was only after the French had constructed the fortress city at Louisburg in 1720 that the British authorities were impelled to establish a fortified settlement at Chebucto. This was planted by Edward Cornwallis in 1749 and was later called Halifax. The first colonists included New Englanders, Englishmen and Germans; it grew slowly between 1751-1761. In 1767 the Halifax inhabitants numbered 3,022 persons of whom 1,351 were American, 853 were Irish, 264 were German, 302 were English and 52 were Scots. The Acadian population of the Province totalled 1,265 persons who were all that remained after the infamous deportation of 1755.

In 1753, 1,417 inhabitants of Continental origin were transferred from Halifax to Lunenburg. Later, individual families moved to Dublin, Chester, Windsor, Falmouth and Annapolis. In 1761, a group of 100 Pennsylvania Germans were introduced by Colonel Alexander McNutt and they established themselves at Moncton and Hopewell. These settlers, the majority of whom were Hanoverians, proved to be hard-working and industrious, and the Lunenburg settlement eventually became one of the most prosperous of the Maritime towns.

The New Englanders

The New Englanders had been foremost in advocating Maritime settlement to the British authorities and they had eventually dispatched a total of 6,913 persons by 1761. As early as 1758 the Council at Halifax had issued a proclamation inviting immigration and offering:

> 100,000 acres of interval plow lands, producing wheat, rye, barley, oats, hemp, flax, etc., which have been cultivated for more than a hundred years past and never fail of crops nor need manuring, [and] also more than one hundred thousand acres of upland, cleared and stocked with English Grass, planted with orchards, gardens . . . [and] situated about the Bay of Fundi upon rivers navigable for ships and burthen.

A second proclamation was issued on the 11th of January 1759, which gave further information concerning the granting of land, the privileges of settlers and the political and judicial system of the colony. This had the desired effect and the first New Englanders arrived on the 27th May, 1759, and were granted lands in the vicinity of the Basin of Minas. The Connecticut settlers soon established the townships of Cornwallis and Horton (ville), which replaced former Acadian villages. The township of Falmouth followed soon afterwards and was granted to Rhode Islanders. Newport was later developed by them on the opposite bank of the river.

New England settlements were eventually widely extended around the coasts of Nova Scotia. There were originally two forms of township, the most important being agricultural settlements which developed about the nucleus of former Acadian villages and their associated dyked farm lands, as well as small coastal settlements whose economy depended on fishing and marine industries. The agricultural settlements developed between 1760 to 1767 included Annapolis, Amherst, Cornwallis, Cumberland, Falmouth, Granville, Horton, Newport, Onslow, Sackville, Sheffield, Truro and Windsor. Large numbers of the settlers originated from Connecticut, Massachusetts and Rhode Island. The Maritime settlements which were primarily dependent on fishing as their basic economic activity were: Barrington, Chester, Dublin, Liverpool, Port Williams and Yarmouth.

Colonel Alexander McNutt was responsible for inducing immigrants to migrate to the Maritimes from Ulster, and his colonization projects eventually resulted in the settlement of 2,165 Irish in 1761 in the settlements of Londonderry, Truro and Onslow.

A number of settlements which were founded in the mid-18th century failed. In some cases this was due to Indian attack, but the majority were badly sited, had poor communications and depended on bad agricultural land. These were: Blandford, Canso, Dartmouth and Lawrencetown. Some of these settlements were revived after the American War of Independence, by the Loyalists.

United Empire Loyalists

The United Empire Loyalists represented the moderate and pro-British section of the population who rejected the revolutionary uprising of the American colonies. Their immigration provided Nova Scotia with a hard core of much needed population which strengthened the British stock and consolidated Maritime colonization. Some were professional men [2], but the majority were artisans and agriculturists.

The first immigrations occurred after the evacuation of Boston in 1776 when about 1,000 Bostonians came to Halifax with the British Army. Between 1776 to 1783 further groups of Loyalists arrived, but it was only when New York was evacuated in 1783 that large numbers migrated to Nova Scotia. By 1784-1785 the total number of settlers was probably in the region of 35,000, although many later left to settle in Upper Canada. Some settlers were granted lands in the vicinity of some of the older New England settlements, while others established new settlements which reproduced the administrative and planning techniques put into operation after the founding of Halifax. The most important areas of Loyalist settlements were : Shelburne (1783); Barrington (1784); Yarmouth (1791); Chester (Shoreham) (1788); Digby (1783); Aylesford (1784); Wilmot (1784); Onslow (1787); Wentworth (1792); Clementsport (1784); Middleton (Gates Ferry) (1788); Parrsboro (1787); New Edinburgh (1783); and Sydney (1785).

The Scottish Immigrants

In 1773 Highland settlers arrived in Nova Scotia from Scotland. This was the beginning of a stream of Scottish immigrants to the province which lasted for 30 years. Nearly 50,000 Scots settled on Cape Breton Island, Prince Edward Island and Northern Nova Scotia. The immigration fell off in 1830. It produced a number of communities which have marked Scottish characteristics. Good examples are: Pictou, New Glasgow, Antigonish, and Inverness.

---

[2] It is believed that at least half of the graduates of Harvard came to Canada. Many Loyalists had been influential members in their colonies.

Military Settlements of 1812

After the Napoleonic Wars the British Government decided that ex-servicemen should be granted land in Nova Scotia as a reward for military services. The local administrators believed that the central area of the province could be settled, and the construction of a new road between Annapolis and Halifax was undertaken to stimulate the development. Four distinct ex-service groups were granted lands. They were the Fencibles, British Regulars, Chelsea Military Pensioners and Negro auxiliary troops. The first immigrants who arrived in 1815 were 1,800 Negroes. They were followed by veterans of the Royal Newfoundland Fencibles in 1816 and the Royal Nova Scotia Fencibles who joined them later. In the same year Chelsea Outpensioners also applied for land. An area of 10,000 acres was surveyed and divided into lots of 200 acres which strung along a 100-mile stretch adjacent to the proposed road from Annapolis to Halifax. Most of the land was made up of escheated Loyalist grants.

Preston was the first settlement and it was planted in 1815, not far from Dartmouth. Eventually it failed, although a number of the descendants of the original settlers still remain in the area.

Hammonds Plain followed shortly afterwards. Negro and Napoleonic Veterans were settled in it and many of them were employed on the construction of the Annapolis Road. The greater proportion of them, however, abandoned the settlement so that the remainder only constituted a small community which still remains.

The most ambitious of the new settlements was Sherbrooke (New Ross). About 300 ex-servicemen were established, but the region incorporated bad agricultural land. Many of the immigrants who were not suited to pioneering deserted it by 1820.

In 1817 Dalhousie was founded by the Governor, and it was considered a model settlement during his term of office. Originally there were 189 settlers who were established in 1818, but when Dalhousie retired the number had dropped to 135. At that time much had been achieved, for 113 houses had been completed, 10 were under construction, 574 acres had been cleared, and 135 acres had been chopped but not burned. The site is now occupied by a small community.

The Land System

Although the early patents granted by the British Crown in Nova Scotia were similar in form to those granted by the Northern (or Plymouth) Company in the American Settlements, these had little effect on subsequent development. [3] During the French administration, peasant colonists were granted lands. A seigneurial system was also introduced and large

---

[3] The origin of this system of feudal tenure can be traced back to the Elizabethan Plantations of Ireland.

tracts of territory were granted to minor French notables. It was similar in many respects to the James I's establishment for the baronets of Nova Scotia. This early feudal concept is of little significance, however, in the present-day land patterns.

The Maritime land system was undoubtedly derived from that of Massachusetts. It was associated indirectly, therefore, with the land system of eastern counties of England. The Massachusetts landowners subscribed to the non-conformist religion and were devoted adherents of the Cromwellian Commonwealth. Their leaders were drawn from the squirearchy, merchants groups, and also included many prosperous and educated freemen who derived their cultural and academic background from Cambridge University. Most of the Puritans came from Essex, Cambridgeshire, Hertfordshire, Middlesex, Surrey and Kent—areas where the mediaeval manorial system was different and less restrictive than in other parts of England. The East Anglian (or Kentish system), as it might be described, established itself in counties which were economically self-supporting and consequently enjoyed a higher degree of independence than most other parts of the Kingdom. The regions were wealthy and highly populated, although dependent to a marked degree upon the Continental wool export trade during mediaeval times. The counties also had extensive wool markets with the Hanseatic League and the Italians. Once the wool staple declined during the reign of the Tudors, economic decay set in. This led to universal dissatisfaction which was aggravated by the attempts of the nobility to reclaim the fen lands and enclose common lands. Their actions interfered with time-honoured precedents which, in conjunction with the economic depression, caused many members of the remaining communities to emigrate to America.

The Puritans introduced their land system to New England. The Kentish system might ideally be described as a community of shareholders who cultivated arable land, shared defined areas of pasture and meadow, and utilized waste land, woods, fens, marshes and rivers as areas for hunting, fishing, fuel collection and grazing. The pattern of lands differed from the normal open field or manorial system, being rectangular and regular in shape. It was possible for a freeman to own land in different areas for different purposes. Furthermore, mutual agreements were often concluded by the members of a community whereby they agreed to the communal division of unused land amongst themselves by impartial division.

The system was adopted in New England because the members of the new communities desired properties to be allocated on an impartial basis. An individual's wealth was not assessed in terms of personal possession or money, but was determined by the quality of his land and the manner in which he worked it. Selectmen (i.e. the elected town officials) were appointed, and amongst other duties they supervised the division of the new land so that "all contention betwixt the adventurers" was avoided.

The technique of settlement was based on that used in Ireland. A gridiron town plan was drawn up—often before the land was even seen, and each freeholder (i.e. landowner) was allocated a lot varying in size from 50 to 200 acres. Additional lands were granted as well, for each member of a family. Settlers were allowed to change their lots by mutual agreement, and could barter or buy lots from other freemen. The community as a whole was expected to provide and support certain common lots for community use, such as a church, the school, the town house, the clergyman's establishment, common lands and in exceptional cases, sawmills, grist mills or flour mills. Prominent members of the community who rendered singular service to the inhabitants were often rewarded by further grants of land. Freemen who improved their properties quickly were also granted extra lands.

In time, a new land-owning aristocracy arose who acquired their wealth through the acquisition of property by barter or purchase, and by attaining prominence through their personality, leadership or business acumen. An extremely conservative attitude developed in the settlements. Established communities resented new settlers and tended to establish them in new townships or villages—which actually occupied an inferior status to the parent town on which they depended for their initial services. The surplus population was thus removed, and many freemen of the parent town preserved lots for their own use in the new community, although sometimes they did not develop such properties but sold them after adjoining development had increased the land value.

In 1713, when Britain gained control of Nova Scotia, this system was in operation in the whole of New England. In New Hampshire alone new townships were developed on an extensive scale after 1740. Governor Benning Wentworth was responsible for the incorporation of no less than sixty-eight new townships [4]; and in all cases these towns were gridiron settlements which were laid out by surveyors. The proprietors promoted the settlements for the following reasons:

> It was desirable that there should be more inhabitants on the frontier of the Province, and more land cultivated and improved so that the Province would be better able to defend itself [and that]
>
> If there should be a war with the Indians the public taxes would be easier and provisions more plentiful and cheaper.

Admittedly, their desire for such new townships coincided with the reluctance to admit strangers into their midst, and allowed them the opportunity to invest their capital in such a manner that they did not have to undertake any of the hard, initial pioneering themselves.

Once the parent community resolved to found a new town, it divided the land into shares (i.e. 120, each of which might consist of two lots). Shares were also reserved for the clergy, the church, the school, the

---

[4] Thirty-seven of the Wentworth settlements developed in the northern parts of New Hampshire and Vermont. The townships of Nelson or Wilmington were typical examples of such conservative planning.

schoolmaster, while twenty shares (i.e. forty lots) where preserved for the proprietors. The settlers were expected to have three acres enclosed and under mowage or tillage within three years. A family dwelling had to be built and furnished at the end of six years, and the new freeholder was expected to reside there for at least three years. The freeholders, as a community, were also responsible for building a meeting house and constructing roads within ten years. If a settler did not comply with these requirements his shares and rights were escheated in favour of the proprietors. All pine trees were reserved for the Crown, while special provisions made allowances for trouble with the Indians or natural disasters. This system, it was felt, encouraged the industrious and the deserving as well as meeting the needs for religious instruction, education and local government.

When the British Government decided to establish townships in Nova Scotia it adopted the system and, in fact, became a model proprietor. As many of the early colonists were from New England their administrators believed that the settlement technique would be familiar and acceptable to them. In most cases the Government authorities (or the private developers in conjunction with the authorities) would dispatch a survey group to pick and choose the lands. These were then subdivided within a gridiron town plan upon their return, although little allowance was made for the topography, in many cases, probably because of lack of information.

The Government undertook to provide the essential needs of the early community during the early years of colonization. This was a radical departure from the New England pattern, but it was not completely philanthropic, for it was undertaken to induce and stimulate settlement. During the early years of British rule the authorities were singularly unsuccessful in inducing colonization, although they had witnessed successful projects in New England and in those territories where the French Crown had not only provided land, but also house-building material, seeds, tools, weapons, and rations. The British Government subsequently adopted the ideas of their officials and offered colonists (e.g. at Halifax) many new benefits.

The colonists, many of whom were ex-servicemen, were granted lots which varied according to their status and service. A Lieutenant-Colonel would be granted 2,000 acres, whereas an ex-soldier or private settler would be granted fifty acres on condition that he attempted to develop the lands within a stipulated period. This implied the clearing of brush and scrub followed by its cultivation or use as stock land. If the immigrant fulfilled these requirements he was eligible for a further grant. Every settler was entitled to an additional grant of land for each member of his family (usually twenty acres per head), and he was granted the necessary materials for a residence, tools, glass, seeds, weapons and rations, in addition to which he and his family were entitled to be transported to their destination at State expense.

Each immigrant became a freeholder in the new community and was expected to bear arms in the militia. He had very definite rights, although the early colonist was denied any form of responsible government until 1758. Prior to this he was expected to comply with the orders of the Governor-in-Council. He had no power of electing his own representatives except in parish affairs, although the local administrative officers appointed by the Governor were normally drawn from amongst the ranks of the settlers. Such officials were often men of rank and position, although other exceptional persons were sometimes chosen. The duties they performed included those of the justices of the peace, surveyors of highways, commissioners of markets, inspectors of produce and building materials, commissioners of lighting and paving, constables, fire wardens, custodians of the poor house and the gaol, officers and non-commissioned officers in the Militia and so on.

The Justices of the Peace of the Court of Petty Sessions were responsible for the administration and supervision of the local town government, in addition to their normal duties. They were empowered to allocate sites and levy taxes for the provision of services, e.g. paving of streets, the erection of lights, the construction of drains, the opening or closing of highways and the supervision and erection of public buildings, markets, wharfs, etc.

In the Maritime new towns the Government reserved lots for the church or churches, the governor's mansion, the court house, the green, flesh and the fish markets, the pest house, the gaol, the workhouse, the orphanage, the government warehouse, the common, the school, mills, and ferry landings or government wharfs.

Lands were allocated to the heads of families by ballot. Additional grants were usually made to wealthy individuals (i.e. merchants and shipowners) who desired waterfront areas for shipping or fishing, in which case a quit rent or a lease might be required. There were, however, clauses in all grants which required the completion of certain tasks similar to those utilized in the New England towns within the first three or four years of development.

The Court of Petty Sessions regulated the widths of public streets and their maintenance. They made no attempt at first to control building materials, although independent regulations were applied which controlled the operation and accommodation of taverns and inns. Later, after a number of disastrous fires (which the fire wardens proved incapable of controlling), elementary controls were established over buildings and materials. These were usually limited to the inspection of materials, but later building inspectors were appointed, whose duties were related at first to specific buildings. Later this task was extended to nearly all buildings. This sterilized the imaginative development of buildings which were normally erected by unskilled craftsmen, using local materials.

THE SETTLEMENTS

The Planning of the Early Acadian Settlements [5]

In 1603 Henry IV of France granted Pierre du Gast, the Sieur de Monts, a patent of settlement for all those lands lying between the 40th and the 46th degree of northern latitude. The area became known as "Acadia" and it included areas of New Brunswick and Cape Breton. De Monts attempted a settlement at St. Croix in present-day Maine. He abandoned it in 1605 and, accompanied by 120 of his settlers, he established a new trading post in Nova Scotia, adjacent to a small anchorage of great beauty. This "Habitation" was suitably located for fur-trading and fishing on the western shore of the present Annapolis Bay.

In 1939 the group of buildings was reconstructed using the drawings of the explorer, Samuel de Champlain, as a basis. These illustrated his book, *The Voyages of 1613*, and the restoration experts supplemented their knowledge with other contemporary accounts. The Habitation plan was developed around a courtyard with a well, and rooms were provided for the Governor, the officers, a priest; a store, a trading room, a bakery and a smithy, as well as a dining hall, first-floor dormitories for the artisans, and a cellar.

The complex was designed to afford protection not only against Indian attack, but also to shelter the colonists from the winter weather. Each room was built of timber and contained a large masonry chimney lined with locally-made bricks. Some roofs were constructed of boarding, while others were shingled. Windows had leaded lights or were covered with scraped and oiled buckskin or other animal membranes. The "Habitation" was eventually captured and burned by Sir Samuel Argall's expedition in 1613, and it is perhaps of more interest to the architect than the town planner.

De Monts was succeeded by Jean de Biencourt, the Sieur de Poutrincourt, in 1610. At that time Port Royal had twenty-five colonists. The new Governor concentrated on the cultivation of wheat which became possible with the influx of new colonists. He died in 1615 and was succeeded by his son who became involved in further Anglo-French hostilities.

After the return of Acadia to France in 1632, a small fort was built by the new Commander, de Razilly, at the mouth of the La Have River. He died shortly afterwards and his successor, the Sieur d'Aulnay de Charnisay, transferred the settlement to the western side of the peninsula. The new township was north of the old "Habitation" site, and was called Port Royal. It was laid out on the eastern side of the basin. The King subsequently divided Acadia into two Lieutenant-Governorships; d'Aulnay

---

[5] The name "Acadia" has been spelled in various ways; e.g. Larcadia, Arcadia, Acadia or Cadie. It was derived from Veranzzano's report to Francis I, in which he said: "We baptised Arcadia on account of the beauty of the trees".

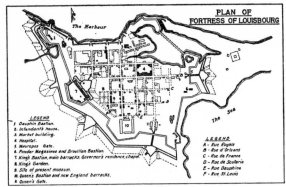

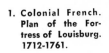

1. Colonial French. Plan of the Fortress of Louisburg. 1712-1761.

Figure 1.

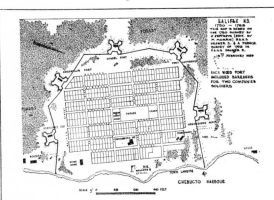

2. British Colonial. Plan of Halifax. 1750-1763.

Figure 2.

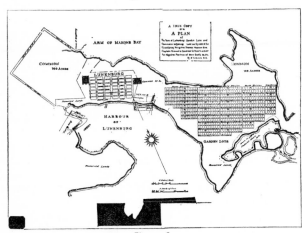

3. Hanoverian. Plan of Lunenburg. 1753.

Figure 3.

ACKNOWLEDGMENTS:

For 1.—Kathleen Maclennan, Curator, Louisburg Museum.
For 2 and 3.—Dr. B. Fergusson, Archivist, Public Archives, of Nova Scotia.

was appointed to one of these and Charles de la Tour to the other. In 1635 a fort stood on the site of the present Fort Anne, and a small village consisting of timber houses with cultivated lots adjoining them developed in the vicinity.

After the establishment of Annapolis (which might be regarded as the first garrison town in Nova Scotia) further French settlers penetrated throughout the peninsula, although they tended to concentrate in distinct areas.

A number of small villages and individual farms concentrated in the Annapolis Valley where apple and other fruit orchards were developed. This occurred after 1632, in which year Isaac de Razilly brought 300 settlers from Brittany and Tour. In 1635, fifty to sixty more families arrived under Charles de Menou and the Sieur d'Aulnay de Charnisay. These settlers became the forefathers of the Acadian population, which by 1671 totalled about 400 persons or sixty-seven families. Coming as they did from the western coast of France, they were accustomed to dyking marshes and placing the land under cultivation—a technique which they introduced to Nova Scotia.

Lands in the vicinity of the Minas Basin formed an important junction on the overland route to French Canada. The region contained the most fertile agricultural land in Nova Scotia, and new townships were soon founded in the area.

Minas, which was named after some copper mines, was one of the first villages and it concentrated on agriculture and the fisheries. It was well established between 1700-1750, and had 200 families.

Grand Pre(e), or "the large meadow", was the oldest of the fishing villages and later became famous as the centre from which the Acadian deportations were carried out. In 1680 Pierre Melanson, the Chief Officer of the Militia, moved here with his wife and seven children, and by 1688 the first church and school were built. In 1714, 1,290 Acadian inhabitants lived in the area, but their lands were eventually given to settlers from Connecticut after the deportation.

In 1703 Pisiquid was founded as a small farming community. It was later renamed Windsor by the English settlers. Another Acadian centre was Canard which was sited in the Kentville area, near the present-day Canning. This was also an agricultural village. The Church of St. Joseph was established in it, and it is said that the smaller villages of Habitant and Gasperea were also in its vicinity.

Cobequid, which adjoined the Minas agricultural settlements, was the name given to the region which lay between Minas and the Isthmus of Chignecto. The name frequently appears on the old records, and it refers to the area of shore settlements on the south of the Bay of Fundy and the northern shore of the Cobequid Basin, extending as far as Five Islands in a westerly direction from present-day Truro. It also in a rather broad manner, included Ramsheg and Tatamagouche. The designation, Cobequid, makes its first appearance on a seigneurial grant made in 1689 to Matthew

Martin, but on his death in 1724 it was decided that his territories should revert to the Crown. The inhabitants depended for their livelihood upon the exchange of produce with French Cape Breton and a combined water-road track extended to Ramsheg. This also linked up to Chignecto from Ramsheg and Tatamagouche. Being considered violently anti-British, the Acadians were deported in 1755 and a number of their farms were burned.

The Chignecto Isthmus possessed good pasture lands as well as an agreeable Indian population, factors which induced the French to establish a colony in the region in 1672, although a fishing village had been planted at Baie Verte as early as 1617. Settlement was stimulated when the French Governor of Acadia, who resided at Quebec, decided to establish seigneurial land grants which were similar to the manorial grants of the English. Jaques Bourgeois, together with four families, congregated together at Beaubassin (later Fort Lawrence) in 1672. In 1677 Captain la Vallière (an officer in Frontenac's Guard) received a similar grant and established a new community on Tonge Island. He built a manor, a mill, a stockade, dyked the marsh lands, and introduced settlers. In 1686 he built a church. The township was eventually called Chignecto and it gave its name to the area. Later, other seigneuries were granted in the area by the Governor at Port Royal. In 1740, Chignecto possessed 140 houses and two churches when Colonel Lawrence built a fort which was garrisoned with 400 men.

The Isthmus is more celebrated for the fortifications erected in the eighteenth century by both the British and French. Prior to the Treaty of Utrecht in 1713 there were a number of settlements in the area, the most important of which were Greville, Chignecto, Tatamagouche, Marstown (Cobequid village), Ramsheg, Beaubassin, Tantramar and Baie Verte. These supplied the French in Cape Breton and Canada with supplies which were transported by overland routes from Cobequid, after which they were then shipped to their destinations.

During the Seven Years War France regarded Nova Scotia as an outpost of Quebec and her military forces were based on a line which ran from Fort Beausejour (built in 1749) and Fort Gaspereaux (built in 1751) which was a temporary fortification adjoining the Baie Verte settlement. The area contained about 1,200 Acadians capable of bearing arms which would seem to indicate a population of about 3,600 persons, some of whom probably lived at Tantramar (later Upper Sackville), which had at least ninety-seven houses and a church in 1751, when the British sacked the settlement. There were also about sixty persons and twenty-five houses in the village of Gaspereaux.

In addition to the above settlements there were several dispersed fishing communities along the east coast, the most important of which was Canso, probably the oldest French colony in Nova Scotia. Canso was the largest fishery in the Province at the time, although other communities existed at La Have, Cape Sable and Meteghan in Nova Scotia and Cheticamp and St. Peters on Cape Breton. Isolated fishing families were also distributed in various bays and coves along the coast.

The Acadians were Catholic and spoke a French patois which later included English and Indian words. In 1749 the Abbé Raynal reported that they had 60,000 cattle, much poultry, and used horses and oxen for tillage. They drank beer, cider and occasionally rum, and their clothing was made from flax and sheep fleece. They also made common linens and coarse cloths. Trade was effected by barter and the settlers exchanged corn, cattle and furs at Annapolis and Louisburg. They were a simple people and their differences or disputes were amicably settled by the elders of the community. Their public acts were usually drawn up by a priest who also supervised their wills and received 1/27th of their harvest which was paid to the Church in the form of tithes. They were a society of brethren and as a man came of age the community usually built him a house, broke the land about it and supplied him with the necessities of life for twelve months. When he married his wife normally brought a dowry of animal flock.

Between the years 1749-1751 some Acadians were induced to move to French territory—particularly to Cape Breton and Quebec—and various authorities have estimated their numbers at between 1,400 to 7,000 persons. Four thousand five hundred Acadians probably lived on the Peninsula at that time and those who transferred to French territory could only have numbered about 600. Most of them were single men and as the average family size was about five persons, possibly one might have left per family unit.

In 1755 the British deported most of the Acadians to Massachusetts, Georgia and other colonies. It is probable that the deportees numbered about 6,000. Although many families were rounded up on the Peninsula, others escaped to northern Nova Scotia and the adjacent islands. Some who gained French territory later returned to France or the French Carribean colonies, but this was after the expulsion of the French from Canada in 1763, in accordance with the Provisions of the Treaty of Paris. The Acadian population before the expulsion was probably 9,000. When the census was taken eleven years later, i.e. 1766, the Acadian population totalled 1,265, but this was the worst year for the Acadian settlements as the inhabitants were still under proscription and had not yet regained the right to establish themselves. [6]

The Acadian settlements appear to have adopted a lineal arrangement. A track was developed at Port Royal which fronted the Annapolis Basin, and the first lots of land were laid out along the banks. Individual houses were built along this track. Later an additional road developed at right angles and was laid out with small farms in the same way. A fort and a chapel were erected adjoining the junction of these two roads. There was also an inn and a powder house. Agricultural lands were further away from the community, and land was divided into long rectangles which

---

[6] There were 1,056 Acadians about Halifax in 1764 of whom 700 emigrated and these figures still leave 1,735 persons unaccounted for. They probably escaped to French territory.

were 100 to 200 arpents deep and had 2,000 yards in frontage. On this land (usually dyked marsh land) maize, barley, rye, wheat and hay were grown. The house lot usually included a vegetable garden, while the owner often had an upland orchard for fruit cultivation. The houses were made of logs as were the barns for storage and stock. Most of the inhabitants also engaged in fishing and trapping.

The French Military Settlement at Louisburg, 1720-1761

The most interesting example of early French planning was the Fortress City of Louisburg whose concept represents a radical departure from any other Nova Scotia settlement. It is the only town planned to fulfil a definite function. Prior to 1713, the Louisburg area was known as "English Harbour" (Havre à l'Anglais), but when France ceded Nova Scotia to Britain in accordance with the peace provisions, their authorities decided that a new site would have to be chosen for the development of a military and naval base on Cape Breton Island (Isle Royal). Louisburg, therefore, was a fortified city constructed in accordance with the precepts of French Army engineers trained in the Vauban tradition. Furthermore, it also contained, within its periphery, a planned town which would function as a provincial administrative centre. No provision was made for a large increase in the population or accommodation densities, and the location was decided upon with little consideration of agriculture or fisheries. Louisburg was sited strategically and was designed and conceived as a military base. Yet within these terms of reference the provisions made for the town were done well and with careful planning.

As early as 1712 surveys were made of the best possible locations in Cape Breton for the proposed centre. Finally a peninsula was selected adjoining English Harbour, which was surrounded by water on three sides. It also included two ponds which were later incorporated into the defensive system. In August 1713, the French officers, garrison and 180 inhabitants sailed from Placentia and established themselves in the small fishing village adjoining the Louisburg site. The expedition commenced work on both the fortifications and the town itself. Two army engineers surveyed the site. There is doubt as to the identity of the original planner, but it is believed that the final plans were prepared by the military engineers, de Verville and Verrier who probably made the preliminary plans on the site, which were sent to France for approval and modification. Certainly the Louisburg plan was too closely adapted to the topography to be carelessly done.

The fortifications were conceived to protect Louisburg from both land and sea attack. The primary defences were ramparts manned by batteries and the garrison. These linked four major bastions, the King's (or Citadel), the Queen's, and two demi-bastions (the Dauphin and the Princess) together. Beyond these were minor fortifications, earthworks and a moat. The King's Bastion was designed as the ultimate centre of resistance, i.e. a citadel for a last stand, and it incorporated the Governor's residence, a headquarters and the chapel. Louisburg took twenty years to build, and cost 30,000,000 francs. Apart from the main ramparts which were two miles in extent, there were demi-bastions and outworks on the north-eastern and south-eastern side of the peninsula. In 1726 Governor de Broullion reported to the Crown that the fortifications were completed. Louisburg was conceived as one of the most powerful fortifications France possessed, and therefore was manned by a   garrison of 1,800 men. It mounted about 150 large calibre cannons in the various batteries.

The town was encircled by the defences and was planned for 4,000 inhabitants. It covered about 100 acres of higher ground, and was arranged on an irregular gridiron plan formed by streets running from east to west and seven streets running from north to south.

Housing adjoined the streets and large open spaces remained in the centre of each lot for gardens and grazing for livestock. Buildings were on stone foundations, with a timber frame superstructure. Fireplaces were built of random stonework or brick. The public buildings included a nunnery, a hospital and the garrison storage and warehouse units.

The private contractors were supervised by the military engineers, but the inhabitants were personally responsible for the erection of their own houses, although the authorities did supply the building materials. The town architecture was, on the whole, traditional and devoid of elaborate ornament, but the town gates, the government buildings and the Citadel were based on designs in the Louis XIV Renaissance style prepared in France.

Although primarily a military and naval station, Louisburg eventually became an important market centre for Acadian produce and developed as the centre for a small fishing industry.

The administration consisted of a Supreme Council which included the governor, the commissary, the King's lieutenant, the attorney-general, a secretary, a tipstaff and four or five burgher councillors. They were responsible for the administration and organization of the town fabric as well as the control of services, lighting and building materials.

Louisburg was overthrown by British forces twice—once in 1745 by the New Englanders under Sir William Pepperell and Governor Shirley of Massachusetts, but at the conclusion of hostilities it was handed back to France, and it was recaptured in 1758. In 1760 the Government decided that there was no reason for retaining Louisburg and it determined to demolish the fortifications. This was eventually done by blowing explosive charges under the walls. The barracks hospital and some other buildings were preserved for garrison use. When the occupation forces finally departed, 142 residences remained, although 68 were unfit for habitation, sixty required repairs and only thirteen were in good condition. None of these survived as Louisburg subsequently functioned as a "quarry" for building stone used in Halifax and Sydney. In 1782 a small number of Loyalists developed a small fishing and agricultural settlement in the area.

The British Military Settlement at Halifax, 1749

Halifax might be regarded as the first settlement planned as a whole by the British Government in Nova Scotia. The development of Louisburg stimulated the establishment, but a comparison between the two towns is not really possible because the two nations adopted an entirely different approach to planning in their settlements. A number of factors brought about the establishment of Halifax, viz :

1. The New England colonies were incensed by the return of Louisburg to France in 1745 and they expected some action to be taken to secure their northern frontiers from continued French aggression.

2. Annapolis was inadequate as a naval base. The British had hoped to establish a military and naval base as close to the United Kingdom as possible, which would also be free of ice in winter.

3. The administration wished to introduce English colonists to Nova Scotia in order to exploit the natural resources.

4. By the middle of the eighteenth century the English navy experienced a critical shortage of good mast timbers which the Nova Scotia forests could provide.

5. The Government believed that the opening up of Nova Scotia to New England immigration would meet the repeated requests from the Colonial authorities for land grants which could then be awarded to ex-servicemen in recognition of their service during the wars. Halifax and the other new settlements which would follow could then act as an additional buffer before the New England frontiers.

After the occupation of Nova Scotia in 1712, projects had been presented to the Home Government (mainly by the American Colonies), proposing the development of new townships in the area, but active measures were only taken towards this end between 1745 to 1749, when the new settlement project was undertaken. Colonel the Hon. Edward Cornwallis, M.P. was placed in charge of the operation, and unusually favourable conditions were announced to aid possible immigrants from New England, Britain and Hanoverian Germany. Transports were provided by the Admiralty while arrangements were organized for the settlers' provisions.

In July 1749 Cornwallis and 2,576 immigrants arrived at Chebucto Bay in Nova Scotia. After landing, the Military Surveyor, Charles Brewse, proceeded to lay out and survey the town. The first site proved to be unsuitable although part of it was actually cleared. It was then decided to establish the town further to the north on the side of a gently sloping hill. The settlers, aided by sailors and troops, again cleared the site and the town lots were pegged for distribution by ballot later.

The plan of Halifax was similar to those adopted in the contemporary New Hampshire townships. A gridiron plan was adopted. The insulae were 320'0 x 120'0 in size and were subdivided into sixteen building lots each having a frontage of 40'0 wide and being 60'0 deep. The streets were originally 60'0 wide, but in fact none of them were actually over 55'0 in width and many were less than this. Specific lots were allocated for the church, the governor's residence, the commissariat warehouses, and the garrison barracks. Open space was reserved in the centre.

Fortifications were constructed almost immediately after landing. The first design drawn up by Brewse was extremely restrictive for it implied a series of permanent revetments about the township. This was therefore discarded in favour of a simple timber palisade alternating with five star-shaped forts (actually timber blockhouses), which protected the town from Indian attack. Nothing was done about the naval installations at first because priority was given to the construction of wharfs and quays for merchants and the government.

Business houses established themselves in Halifax almost immediately. Some prominent New England merchants (who were also engaged in smuggling), commenced erecting stores and warehouses in the first two years. Ships' taverns and coffee-houses also appeared, and unfortunately quite a number of buildings described in the records as "disorderly houses".

In 1750-1752 many Hanoverian settlers arrived and crowded into the existing town. They were accommodated in a suburban extension to the north which became known as "German" or "Dutch" town. Their lots were arranged on a gridiron, although the area was originally reserved for market garden usage. In 1750-1751 a new line of block-houses was erected across the neck of the Halifax Peninsula to safeguard the new lots and agricultural lands to the north. Unfortunately, the topography was not really suitable for farming so that the effect of this development was transitory.

Later a number of timber and grist mills were established in the creeks adjoining Halifax. These were private projects, but were continuously encouraged by the Governor who hoped that the development would free the administration of their dependence upon Boston for lumber. The public buildings were constructed with frames and timbers which had been brought from New England. Before the first winter 300 reasonably substantial houses had been built, although Cornwallis and his Council were disappointed in the quality of the settlers, the lack of trained artisans and the lack of understanding which the English authorities manifested in his difficulties. These were climatic and financial and were complicated by the arrival of enormous quantities of supplies from Louisburg, which was then evacuated. Two regiments also arrived from Louisburg and joined the Halifax garrison.

The first administrative machinery was simple, and the early municipal functions were vested in the Court of Petty Sessions which levied taxes and organized lotteries—a favoured method of obtaining monies for paving, lighting, bridge construction and other requirements. During the administration of the Court, fish, flesh and green markets were developed, while a court house, a poor house, a gaol and a pest house (hospital) were also built. The justices also licensed and controlled the sale of liquor and the establishment of taverns and distilleries.

The fabric of the town was controlled indirectly through the surveyors of building materials, the commissioners of highways and streets, and the hog reeves. Local materials such as brick and lime were made, but these were relatively unimportant. Lumber was the major structural material.

After work commenced on the naval dockyard in 1759, Halifax changed. Not only did overcrowding cease, but the city actually proceeded to lose settlers to other settlements. The administrative hierarchy and many wealthy merchants commenced building a number of large and elaborate residences in the colonial style of New England, which might properly be described as "mansions". The first Government House was replaced, and permanent barracks for the troops were built in a style of architecture which is really worthy of study in itself. [7]

At the outbreak of the American Revolution, Halifax was a thriving and busy town possessing three churches, a naval dockyard and no peripheral fortifications other than the Citadel, together with a number of marine batteries. During the war the town experienced periods of extreme overcrowding when both troops and Loyalists encamped in the streets or wherever they could get shelter, and their privations forced them to use many buildings for fuel.

Immediately after the war Halifax dropped back to its former population, but assumed an increasingly important role as the centre of maritime activity. It was the most important port in Nova Scotia for the reception and dispatch of goods overseas. It was also the administrative centre of the Province, and during the energetic Governorship of Sir John Wentworth a new Government House, the Provincial Building and many masonry and timber-frame mansions such as Gorsebrook were constructed.

The Victorian period witnessed major changes in the central area and on the suburban periphery. A continuous expansion of the residential areas occurred along highways leading in and out of the city. This process was aggravated when the railways commenced operation in the middle of the century. The period between 1840 and 1870 could rightly be regarded as the golden years of the sailing ship. Halifax experienced a boom in trade and consequently in the establishment of business and shipping firms in the central areas. Ship maintenance and repair became important industries and supported a host of smaller activities such as carpentry and joinery shops, smithies, upholsterers, sailmakers and ship-chandlering organizations. Insurance houses, banks, clubs, restaurants and hotels also developed. All of these were row houses in solid load-bearing structures built of fire-proof materials. At the beginning of the twentieth century steel-frame structures replaced them. Land costs increased and the new buildings were devoted solely to business and commercial functions. After 1867 many new federal buildings appeared which were designed by English architects who sent their plans to Nova Scotia. The directories also listed a practising architect such as David Stirling who was responsible for the Halifax Club in Hollis Street and many other civic buildings.

---

[7] Permanent materials such as brick and stone were used increasingly, and a functional form of architecture completely devoid of decoration appeared which was used by the Army up to the beginning of the 20th century, e.g. the "Cavalier" in the Citadel at Halifax.

The Hanoverian Settlement of Lunenburg, 1753

An area near the present town of Lunenburg was formerly known as Merliguish by the Indians. The French and the English had made attempts to settle there, without notable success, although prior to the Hanoverian settlement there had been a small French fishing village. It was decided to establish the settlement at a Council meeting held in Halifax on August 23, 1750, and on May 10, 1753, Colonel Lawrence was directed to settle a town with the German settlers, most of whom came from Lunenburg in Germany. As early as 1749 Cornwallis had recommended to the British Government that more German settlers should be obtained as they had proved hard-working and industrious. The authorities had, therefore, appointed a British agent in Europe and had offered advantageous conditions of settlement to any prospective immigrants.

On the 7th of June, 1753, 1,453 settlers and 450 troops landed on the Lunenburg Peninsula. The Surveyors, Brewse and Morris, appear to have prepared a town plan similar to that of Halifax. The colonists proceeded to clear the ground which was then staked out and allocated to the heads of families by lot. The technique of settlement was similar to that employed at Halifax. Overseers were appointed from amongst the more energetic colonists to supervise building construction and clearing, and all beach rights were reserved to the Crown.

Fortification commenced almost at once, as hostilities were anticipated with the Indians. The town areas were protected by a picket fence which was made of logs sharpened at both ends and driven into the ground. The first houses built were prepared for defence, and the blockhouses followed later. The Garrison blockhouse was sited on Gallows Hill, while smaller blockhouses were erected adjacent to an old French burial ground, on the back harbour, which was subsequently called Fort Boscawen. Other blockhouses were built at Mush-a-Mush, near Upper La Have and Histler's Mills.

Justices of the peace and officers of the Militia were speedily appointed, and a site was earmarked for a church which was eventually erected at Government expense. Two thousand acres were allocated for common land and by 1754, 319 houses and ten huts had been built. A large acreage was under gardens, and almost 100 families had been settled. Four sawmills were in operation by the end of the year and barley, oats, turnips, potatoes and flax had been planted.

The town was sited on a peninsula and therefore possessed a front and a back harbour, only the landward side was protected by the fortified palisade. The gridiron plan was drawn up and, like Halifax, applied to a steeply sloping site. The community was divided into six administrative divisions each of which contained eight insulae consisting of fourteen lots, 60'0 × 40'0 in size. Every settler was granted a town lot, a garden lot, a 300 acre lot and a thirty acre lot. The first 500 lots which were drawn were recorded in a Registry Book, and each settler was expected to enclose his lot and erect his dwelling as soon as possible.

The architecture of the early houses is briefly recorded. Some were built with round poles, others of thickly-hewn timbers. Shingles and thatch were used on the roofs and chimneys were made of masonry, brick and sometimes clay reinforced with timber. Each settler received an issue of 500 bricks and a proportionate quantity of nails after arrival. Certain peculiar features soon became apparent in Lunenburg architecture. Buildings were constructed in the frame tradition of New England, but unusually elaborate decorations appeared. Many buildings were painted in black and white and the colour variations emphasized the frames, windows, doors, fascias and porches. In some cases elaborate scroll decorations were painted and carved under sills, on brackets and even beams. All churches and a large number of residences were treated in this manner.

Shops were slightly more utilitarian, but also had decoration. The standard New England plan was often varied so that the basement could be used for accommodation space: in many cases the first floor was raised 3'0 so that the basement could be adequately lighted. The entrance level was, therefore, reached by a staircase from the street. Attics were provided and were lit by dormers. In time saw-mills, ship-building and fishing sheds, as well as small factories, smithies and metal shops appeared.

The Surveyor's plan made provision for the allocation of sites to the Church of England, the Lutheran Church, the Presbyterian Meeting House, a Town House, two commons (one being seventy acres in extent and the other ninety acres), a cemetery, Goverment store-houses and two squares. In 1753 a further common of 700 acres had been added, while garden lots were laid out in five divisions on reserved lands to the north-east. These were later divided into 470 lots and distributed amongst the settlers and were quickly enclosed and worked. In 1755 farmlands in the vicinity of the town were also under cultivation.

The Lunenburg settlers were described by the Governor as:

Frugal labourers, laborious and industrious people who will not only improve and enrich their property, but pertinaciously defend it. [8]

In 1766 a number of prominent citizens applied to the Government for more lands. An unusual grant was made to Sebastian Zouberbuhler of 2,000 acres, although he had already been granted 20,000 acres in the previous year. Each councillor was also granted a 5,000 acre lot by a Governor's mandamus.

The churches were amongst the most important public buildings in the town. The first one erected was the Anglican Church which was sited on 300 acres granted to the Society for the Propagation of the Gospel, and by 1754 St. John's Church was completed. It was 60'0 × 40'0 in size, and the frame was brought from Boston at a cost of £476.16.6½. A further £224.9.9 was later petitioned of the Assembly for its repair and furnishings, but this was refused.

---

8 Col. Lawrence: Report to Council at Halifax; 1753. P.A.N.S.

In 1769 a Dutch Reformed Church was established by subscription. It was built by a Scotsman called Grant, and the plan was drawn up by a Mr. Detchman of Halifax. It cost £1,200 and later developed as a Presbyterian Church. In 1770 the first Lutheran Church was raised and a parsonage was added in 1772. It possessed a Louisburg Bell which was taken to Halifax in 1758 when the fortress was dismantled. It was subsequently purchased by the Lunenburg Lutherans. The Methodist Church dates from 1813, while a Catholic Chapel was eventually built in 1840.

After the 1763 Peace, Lunenburg produced a magnificent series of crops which established it as one of the most prosperous and successful of the settlements. In 1760 Lunenburg's population numbered 350 men and 1,114 women and children, and it continued to grow rapidly until the middle of the nineteenth century.

Lunenburg is celebrated today, not only because of its picturesque setting, but also for its cleanliness and civic beauty. It possesses a character unique in Nova Scotia towns, and has succeeded in integrating the developments of the twentieth century into its environment without causing noticeable departure from character. It is a remarkable example, however, of the imaginative application of a gridiron plan to a steeply sloping site. For it overcame the initial disadvantages by developing an elaborate architecture which possessed harmony, unity and scale when viewed en masse, and really did make the Lunenburg streets aesthetically acceptable. Fortunately, industrialization, being mainly associated with the harbour, was kept out of the residential areas and was concentrated on the coast line at the foot of the settlement.

The New England Settlement of Shelburne, 1764-65

The Loyalist towns were small and developed from earlier fishing or farming communities. The nucleus of their settlements was usually the church which was often non-conformist. In conjunction with the church, a graveyard was provided, but as the church site was often on a hill it sometimes polluted the wells of housing further down the slope, a factor which was reflected in the death rate.

Many of the small New England towns, although conceived as gridiron settlements, grew so slowly that a single street evolved with straggling houses adjoining it. Sometimes the village would have a mill on or near an adjoining stream, or, if it was sited on the coast, a small landing wharf or boat herd.

Shelburne was formerly one of the largest settlements in Nova Scotia, but like so many of the 1760 towns which were developed by New England settlers it was changed and altered out of all recognition by the Loyalists.

In 1764 the area was settled by New England immigrants sponsored by Colonel Alexander McNutt and his associates. They called this town

Figure 1.

1. New England and Loyalist. Plan of the town of Shelburne. 1783.

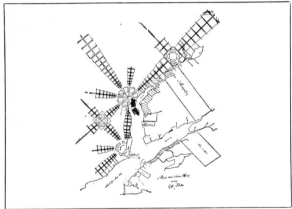

Figure 2.

2. Loyalist. Planning Project for the Town of Sydney. 1785.

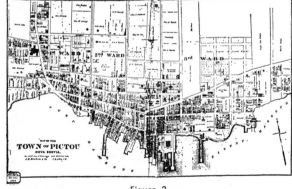

Figure 3.

3. Scots. Plan of the Town of Pictou. 1879.

ACKNOWLEDGMENTS:

For 2.—W. K. Lamb, Dominion Archivist, Archives of Canada.

For 1 and 3.—Dr. B. Fergusson, Archivist, Public Archives of Nova Scotia.

New Jerusalem and obtained grants of land from the Government amounting to over 100,000 acres. They limited their colony to a small part of the island at the harbour entrance, although a few isolated farms were built outside. Consequently large areas were escheated and regranted by the Crown after the Revolution. In 1783 Shelburne became the main centre of Loyalist disembarkation and settlement. It was then called Port Roseway.

In 1782, 120 New York Loyalists appointed a Board of Agency for organizing a settlement at Shelburne. Governor Parr agreed to grant them lands which were free of quit rents and which were to be laid out and surveyed at Government expense. Settlers were promised material assistance, artisans, and aid in the contruction of roads. They were also granted the rights of fishing and fowling in the vicinity, and he assured them that their city would be incorporated. All immigrants were free from impressement in the Royal Navy, and their acceptance of this assistance did not alienate their claims for compensation against the authorities for losses sustained in the Revolution in any way.

The Governor and his Council felt that the New Jerusalem area would be suitable for fruit farming and that it would make a "capital" port. Four hundred and seventy families immigrated in the spring of 1783. The settlers were divided into sixteen companies for the purposes of administration. Upon arriving at Port Roseway they proceeded to clear the ground and cut trees. Tents were pitched, stores were landed and three Halifax surveyors laid out the town. It was planned on a gridiron and had five long parallel streets crossed by others at right angles. The squares of ground were to contain sixteen lots having a 60'0 foot frontage and a depth of 120'0. Properties between Water Street and the shore were defined by small lanes and divided into lots. Each immigrant was allocated a town lot and a water lot in addition to receiving a grant of 500 acres in the neighbourhood for a farm. Common land was also reserved for general use.

The town was called Shelburne (Shelbourne) after the Secretary of State for the Colonies, the Marquis of Lansdowne. In 1783 Governor Parr visited the 5,000 refugee settlers, but refused to incorporate their town. At that time the community was divided into a north and a south division, the streets had been named, and squares and lots had been allocated. In 1783, 5,000 more Loyalists arrived and two new divisions were laid out on lands which had originally been reserved for later use as north and south commons. The number of streets parallel to Water Street was also increased to eleven. In 1783, 2,000 negroes arrived from South Carolina. At first they settled in Shelburne, although many eventually left.

In the following spring more land was laid out, but progress slowed down because many of the previously granted lots proved to be unusable. A site had been reserved for the erection of a Church of England, but later another was purchased which was felt to be more suitable. In 1790 the building was erected at Government expense. In 1785 the Church of Scotland received a similar lot. A workhouse, a pillory, and gallows were also built; two cemeteries were laid out—one for the northern area at the rear of the town and one in the south near a cove. These were later abandoned in favour of the churchyards. Land was reserved on the western side of the harbour for military barracks.

Dry and wet goods shops were in operation in 1793, while wharfs had been built on the sea front and ships had been purchased. In 1785 a Government bounty of 10/-per ton was authorized in an attempt to encourage local shipbuilding and it is recorded that eight vessels of between eighty to ninety tons were built. Shipyards were constructed in the northern division of the town and a 250-ton ship was launched by 1786. Most Shelburne shipping was engaged in the West Indies and coastal trades. In 1785 the first cargo of local squared logs was sent to England. Maine timber was also off-loaded from coastal vessels and later transshipped at Shelburne for Europe. A whale fishery commenced in 1784, and by 1789 cod, sperm oil, smoked salmon, pickled fish and various fish oils were transported to Newfoundland and the United States. Unfortunately, none of these activities provided employment for many inhabitants.

Shelburne began to decline in population within twenty-five years, for the town could not develop sufficient industry and the agricultural land proved incapable of supporting a large population. The roads were poor, although an attempt was made to open up a direct route with Annapolis. It was allowed to fall into disrepair, however, because it had the effect of depopulating the town. Communications also existed with other neighbouring settlements, but these were only suitable for horse or pedestrian use. Most supplies were brought in by sea, so that although fish was plentiful, meat and vegetables were scarce.

The outbreak of the Napoleonic wars in 1793 heralded a period of depression in Shelburne which suffered from disastrous attacks by privateers. This state of affairs was also accentuated by a severe storm in September, 1798, which did considerable damage to the harbour installations.

It was an error to establish a town of such size for the soil was barren and sterile. Although the Loyalist community included many settlers of wealth and breeding, they were not able to sustain themselves in a town which depended primarily on an agricultural economy. Port Roseway ultimately declined and evolved as a small maritime town. In October, 1816, there were only 374 inhabitants and many of the Loyalists returned to the United States; others emigrated to Annapolis, Horton, Cornwallis, Windsor, Newport, Cumberland and Halifax.

Shelburne still maintains a boat-building industry, but it is confined to the construction of pleasure-craft and yachts. Donald McKay, perhaps the most famous Nova Scotia shipbuilder, learned his art in the Shelburne shipyards, for between 1822 and 1870 Shelburne became one of the greatest shipbuilding centres in the Maritimes. The town was advantageously located near good lumber, and its shipwrights acquired a reputation for craftsmanship, unrivalled even by New Hampshire and Maine. In fact, when the American yards closed between 1860 to 1870, Shelburne experienced a boom in ship construction which only declined with the advent of the steamship. At the present time Shelburne has a population of only

2,337 which is primarily employed in small marine industries, the quarrying of building stone and the tourist trade. Nevertheless, it retains much of its former character. The central business area in Water Street has changed over the years, but many fine late 18th-century houses remain.

The Loyalist Settlement at Sydney, 1785

The large groups of immigrants who arrived in Nova Scotia after the American Revolution in 1785, settled in previously existing townships. New centres were also established, and Sydney was the best example of these. The town was sited on the shores of one of the finest harbours on the coast. This was once called Spanish Bay because it was much frequented by Iberian fishermen. The first settlers were from New York and they arrived under the leadership of Abraham Cuyler, a former Mayor of Albany.

Cape Breton was separated from Nova Scotia in 1784. The first Governor was the celebrated cartographer, Colonel J. W. F. des Barres who named the town Sydney after the British Colonial Secretary, Lord Sydney. He also appears to have planned the settlement and his concept of Sydney marked a departure not so much in what was carried out, but in what was proposed, and the present Sydney plan bears a faint resemblance to des Barres' original plan which he had obviously hoped to develop as one of the foremost towns in Canada. The city proper is built on a peninsula with its west side adjoining the harbour. The initial settlement was laid out on a gridiron plan and the machinery of granting lands, and the administrative techniques established, were similar to those used in all other Loyalist settlements.

Sydney was fortunate in having des Barres as its Governor, for he took a personal interest not only in the welfare of the first settlers, but also in the actual planning process. There are, in the National Archives at Ottawa, a set of Sydney plans drawn by des Barres, which incorporate a much larger area of settlement than was in fact used. Many of his ideas are similar to those postulated many years later by Ebenezer Howard in the 19th century, and the scheme might be regarded as an early Georgian interpretation.

Des Barres was probably acquainted with current planning developments in London during the 1780's and was, no doubt, aware of the town-planning projects of Wood, Dance or Nash. The forms in his plan would have produced a typical Georgian layout. The des Barres' plan was adapted to topography and the layout, now the central area of present-day Sydney, regarded as the heart of the overall plan. The use of geometrical nuclei incorporating squares, crescent hemicycles and circular forms linked together by axial streets is obviously inspired by contemporary English planning. The project indicates that this area had an axial arrangement which incorporated two circular places in the north and the south. Open space was also provided in the centre of the peninsula. South-east of the nucleus a series of boulevards radiated away to five satellite communities. Des Barres named three of these, viz, Friendstown, Ficksburg and Pittsburg.

Each satellite is circular in form and is grouped about a circular plaza. Four roads radiated from each community, and lots, which were successively larger in size, strung out and along them. The largest of these were placed on the furthest extremities and were reduced in size as they approached the township centre.

All of the suburban satellites were located outside Sydney at varying mileages. Possibly the planner conceived this as a device to phase the town growth. Friendstown was the nearest, being but five miles away. Pittsburg was four miles out, while the St. Peter's satellite was seven miles away. Each community had an inner common about one mile in diameter, and an outer common divided by crescents which were presumably designated for commercial use. Residential development appears to have been associated with large lots so that at first these would have been used as small farms. Some lots were actually granted which conform to the plan, and these adjoin the banks of the Sydney River. Two large areas of land were also reserved for Crown use.

The keynote of the scheme is controlled development. It is not possible to decide whether des Barres visualized different types of housing, land use or social grouping within these forms; nor is it possible to do more than speculate whether provision was made for industrial or other specialized use areas.

The Governor obviously intended to preserve open space between each community so that it would be available to all communities. His plan was never carried out, probably because Sydney never received immigrants on the scale which des Barres envisaged. In fact, his settlers were left without supplies, funds and assistance for a considerable period of time by the Home Government; so much so that des Barres paid for the necessary supplies out of his personal funds on more than one occasion.

Sydney was an unusual conception. If the plan had been fully executed it would have been the only imaginative planned project in 18th century Nova Scotia.

Highland Scots joined the population between 1802 and 1828, but they did not have any obvious influence on the town form. Eventually the New England character disappeared with the development of industry and the business expansion which occurred between 1840 and 1870.

Present-day Sydney is an industrial centre and it incorporates Dominion Steel and Coal Corporation (Dosco) which is one of the largest self-contained steel plants in America. [9] In the suburbs of Sydney Mines and North Sydney, coal mining, machine shops, foundries and fish industries operated. Sydney expanded greatly from 1870 to the present day and its industries received a great impetus during the world wars. Extensive residential areas have developed around the peripheral areas of the city during the last forty years.

---

[9] In the fall of 1967, the parent firm, Hawker Siddeley Canada Ltd., disclosed that it was closing down its Dosco operations. A new federal-provincial agency, the Development Corporation of Cape Breton (DEVCO) now operates the steel mill and a few coal mines, which generally are being phased out of production.

The Scots Settlement at Pictou, 1767-1773

Northern Nova Scotia is associated with Scots settlements of which Pictou is the most celebrated. Pictou was originally founded by six families of settlers from Pennsylvania and Maryland; they were sent out by Col. Alexander McNutt's Philadelphia Company and arrived at their site on June 10, 1767. [10] Previously there had been Indian and French fishing communities at Merigonish, but these were deserted after the surrender of French Canada. The town overlooks a fine harbour formed by the discharge of three rivers, and is on the site of an old Indian village.

McNutt took little interest in the proposed settlement, but the members of his Philadelphia Company were determined to proceed with their project. They had been discouraged at first by a report from their agent, a Mr. Anhill, who had represented that the country was "rocky, barren and unfit for improvement". He had also made injurious representations to the Government, all of which had the effect of discouraging intending settlers.

In 1767 the six families arrived and each was allocated a one-half acre town lot. Once this was cleared and in use, a further one-half acre was granted. Farm lots were also marked out. Shortly after their arrival the settlers opened up a track to Truro. By 1769 the township had a population of eighty four, a sawmill had been built, fishing commenced and town officials had been appointed.

In 1773 the Proprietors induced 200 Scots to immigrate, and this marks the beginning of the first effective settlement. A temporary camp was erected and the company laid out the town to a gridiron plan. Blocks were subdivided and settlers were allowed to select their lots. The Scots, however, had settled two to three miles outside and refused to accept company lands. After a dispute with the American settlers, the company then stopped their provisions, but the authorities interceded on behalf of the Scots. Many settlers were so disgruntled, however, that they left for Truro and Onslow. There is little doubt that the company was less generous than the Government in its sponsored settlement plan for it required the settlers to comply with the following conditions:

1. The settler had to clear and work at least three acres of every fifty granted within three years / or clear and drain three acres of swamp land / or drain three acres of marsh / or keep three neat cattle until such time that he had cleared three acres.

2. If a quarry or a mine was developed, and a hand was employed for three years, then 100 acres were granted.

---

[10] The McNutt settlement represented a new departure from British governmental settlement policy. The Irish speculator, Colonel Alexander McNutt, formed a company of thirteen in Philadelphia at the conclusion of the war in 1762. He was granted 200,000 acres between Onslow, Truro and Tatamagouche. This grant was later relocated between Tatamagouche and Pictou. A total of 1,600,000 acres was granted to McNutt in Nova Scotia by the British authorities, of which 100,000 acres were at Pictou.

In 1783, veterans of the 82nd (Hamilton) Regiment arrived as well as many Loyalists and 20,030 acres of escheated lands were granted to them. Governor Lawrence was not satisfied with their progress, consequently many left. In 1798 coal was worked and Pictou supplied fuel for the British garrisons. In 1825 the mines were leased to the Duke of Kent who later sold his interest to the General Mining Association, whose company then began operations on a large scale.

In 1786 the Rev. James MacGregor was appointed the first Presbyterian Minister. He sadly records his arrival in these words:

> When I looked around the shores of the harbour I was greatly disappointed and cast down, for there was scarcely anything to see but woods growing to the water's edge. Here and there a mean timber hut was visible in a small clearing which appeared no bigger than a garden compared to the woods. Nowhere could I see two houses without wood between them.

Fortunately at this time the town had a "grog shop". Two Presbyterian meeting houses were built by 1787. The town was laid out above the gut, but growth was retarded because the wily Colonel McNutt had obtained a grant of the waterfront for himself. It was eventually escheated and obtained by Walter Patterson who started selling portions of it. He laid out part of the present town which he called "Coleraine", and is now the eastern section of Pictou. Patterson also earmarked lots of a market, public buildings and a public landing wharf. In 1787 further lots which furnished a Market Street were transferred to him. A 40' wide strip was also preserved on the seafront which eventually became Water Street. Patterson subdivided his holdings into small building lots and later sold them.

Shipbuilding, chandlering and repairing commenced in Pictou between 1796 and 1812, although such activity only attained maximum potential in 1840 by which time Pictou had become a secondary shipbuilding shed. Ship construction boomed with the demand for barques, clippers, brigantines and packet ships until about 1871 when the steamship came into its own. There was, therefore, intensive development of the waterfront. Shipbuilding firms developed slipways and construction sheds on the eastern and western shores adjoining Coleraine Street. Merchant houses prospered and erected three and four-storied administration buildings. A customs house, a registry office, banks, offices, an academy, a Masonic hall and churches were built. Gasworks, an iron and brass foundry, two tobacco factories, a carriage builder and two iron works followed; and in 1879 Pictou was described as:

> Having commodious and handsome mansions, modern villas and neat cottages, all of which are unmistakable indication of the opulence and prosperity of its inhabitants. The public buildings are likewise of notice.

Nova Scotia became the third ship-owning country in the world, and the subsequent prosperity was commemorated in towns like Pictou by considerable building development. Many of the office structures remain, although they have, in some cases returned to a residential function. The Victorian and the Late Georgian architectural styles, similar to those used in Scotland, are reflected in Pictou building.

THE ARCHITECTURE

Residential Construction

Maritime architecture derives a great deal from New England. The first French settlers built small timber homesteads, but as none of these remain, it is only possible to surmise their construction. They were probably built to a simple plan which included one or two rooms as well as an attic and a cellar. Cornwallis mentioned that they built substantial log houses. The chimneys were made with brick or masonry and served for cooking and heating. Building foundations were made of local stone gathered on the site. [11]

A number of British settlers moved into Acadian houses after 1712, and military engineers erected barracks and storehouses. When Halifax was founded in 1749 residences were built and a new architectural style appeared. This New England style was typical in most new settlements, although national variations appeared, e.g. Lunenburg.

The first dwellings were of timber. Temporary shelters which had been built at first were later replaced with more substantial structures. The first plans were similar to Massachusetts "salt box". A frame structure having external clapboarding and an internal plank lining was used. Roofs were made with shingles, were pitched, and often incorporated attics which functioned as storage or sleeping units. The plan was developed around a central or end chimney and included two rooms. The "salt box" later expanded with lean-to additions and increased height to include further accommodation. Timber was produced by local mills, although frames were occasionally imported from New England. Foundations, chimneys and sometimes floors were built of local masonry.

Variations occur later and the typical colonial plan is introduced, having four rooms opening off a central hall which often included a staircase leading to the first floor. After 1761 some buildings had gambrel roofs—a form common in the New York area. Occasionally houses were built of brick and local stone. Some Halifax houses were even built with stone obtained from Louisburg. Many dwellings were large and elaborate, particularly if the owners were wealthy.

Unfortunately, few of these "mansions" remain. Good examples are Admiralty House (Halifax) or the des Barres residence (Guysborough).

---

[11] Probably "en colombage" construction was often used in the early period. The floors often had a rubble filling for hard core. Post and beam construction having various forms of braces were used in barns and chapels. Coupled trusses at 5'6" centres following the Norman pattern were also to be found. Few nails or spikes were used and joints or pins were employed in their place. Roofs were covered with boarding or hand-split shingles.

It is risky to date Nova Scotian housing by appearance for there have been extensive alterations, and many buildings erected during the Victorian period copied the Colonial and Late Colonial styles. Even today new houses sometimes emulate the traditional Colonial designs, not only in plan and exterior but also in building technique, particularly if the builder is a local farmer or fisherman.

Some residences were eventually adapted to fulfil special functions such as shops, small craft industries or smithies. Unfortunately, few of them remain because commercial structures were amongst the first buildings replaced during the boom of the 1870's. Most houses differ in detail when compared to their American counterparts. Although the structure and craftsmanship in Nova Scotia housing bears comparison with that of New England, harshness of climate, the nature of the regional economy and the restricted contact with Europe produced a stark, aesthetic expression. [12] Residential architecture between 1749 and 1800 might be characterized by brute functionalism, simple proportion and Puritan austerity.

Buildings were invariably painted in white, but there were other treatments evolved by different racial groups and traditions. The Lunenburg Germans used the same plan forms and constructional techniques, but were more Germanic and elaborate with external and internal decorative details. Black paint expressed the vertical and horizontal frames, porch and gutter fascias, windows and doors. This treatment was also introduced in New England and Loyalist settlements by German artisans. Hanoverian craftsmanship is generally conceded to be of a better quality than is to be found in most other settlements.

After 1800 stronger English influence is observed in some private residences. This was mainly an attempt to emulate official structures and taste, and it would be more accurate to describe this style as an "official" transplantation. The most progressive group were the government officials and military officers, usually transient residents, who were more closely in contact with English development.

The settlers themselves, although strongly anti-American in sentiment (many of them being Loyalists) were, nevertheless, inclined to remain American-orientated in their tastes which they saw little reason to change. Many of them had come from the intelligentsia of the former colonies and consequently identified the styles and ideas with themselves when they transplanted their lives to Nova Scotia. There was no conscious attempt to reject former traditions and turn to Europe for artistic inspiration, as was the case in the United States.

Thus, there was little noticeable difference in the Late Colonial and the early 19th-century architectural styles. Some of the most notable remaining buildings were the official residences for the Governors, military commanders and Members of the Legislative Council. Halifax is fortunate in

---

[12] In America elaborate porches, staircases, balustrades, captain's walks, external and internal decoration attained a richness and excellence in wood-carving which has not been equalled in the Maritimes.

Buildings in the Town

Figure 1.

1. Early British Colonial. St. Paul's Church and the Grand Parade, Halifax, N.S., 1751-1839.

Figure 2.

2. Hanoverian (British Colonial). Detail typical Lunenburg residence, about 1783.

Figure 3.

3. Late British Colonial (Commercial). The Shopping Unit, Parrsboro, 1814.

ACKNOWLEDGMENT:

For 1.—Public Archives of Nova Scotia.

preserving two such early 19th-century residences, viz. the Governor's House and the residence of Robert Uniacke at Uniacke House. There also remains the once beautiful residence of Gorsebrook which is unfortunately today in a ruined condition.

These buildings might be described as Palladian mansions. They were built of stone and had similarities with the Late Colonial style, although there were more extensive outbuildings. Decoration was more profuse and often in the Adams' style. Neo-classicism scarcely makes an appearance, and there is a forty-year time lag when related to similar development in the United Kingdom. Most buildings were designed and built by local contractors and had no known architects.

There was one solitary example of the Regency style in Halifax. It was the country or "suburban" residence of the Duke of Kent—a one-time Commander-in-Chief of the military forces. It had well-landscaped gardens and was of considerable size. All that remains today is a small rotunda which was used as a music room.

Public Buildings

Larger buildings for civic and religious purposes, such as churches and the court houses are well represented. Nova Scotia has particularly fine examples of timber churches which remain today as significant monuments of early settlement. The Acadian villages possessed a number of churches, although none of these survived. A reconstruction of the Chapel of St. Charles is to be found in the Grand Pre National Historical Park, and this affords some idea of the architecture. The Chapel is designed on French precedents dating from 1750 and is built with local stone and timber. It is an extremely simple building and, unlike its Anglo-Saxon successors, it possesses no steeple, but a fleche over the entrance.

Later came the public constructions in Louisburg which should be regarded in a class of their own. These were the Governor's residence (or Citadel), the hospital, the convent and the gates, all of which were drawn and were designed in the Louis XIV style. Such structures were examples of "official" transplantation, for the designs were prepared in France and sent out to Cape Breton. Military engineers and surveyors supervised the building which was carried out by local contractors.

When Halifax was planted, a number of public buildings were erected. The most important of which was St. Paul's Church (1750), and its construction established a pattern for many churches which followed. The church was based upon a typical New England plan and used a frame structure. In many Maritime towns, church frames were prefabricated and brought from Boston and other parts of New England.

All religious buildings, with the exception of the Lunenburg churches, have an austere purity. There is no decoration and the clapboarded walls were painted white. Windows are simple and often Gothic in shape. Roofs are pitched and shingled, and the only element breaking the sturdy monotony of the design is to be seen in the towers or steeples. Some of these are robust, squat and heavy in appearance, but in many of the Loyalist churches of the late eighteenth century their forms become light and in many cases gracefully elegant and even fantastic.

Interiors are as austere as the exteriors and are reminiscent of the New England Meeting House. There is never any attempt to decorate with paintings, frescoes or carvings as was the case, for example, in New Hampshire. Occasionnally unusual churches were built. The Lutheran Church (1776) and St. John's Church of England (1754) are the earliest exceptions. In the former the black and white decoration on the exterior as well as the scale and massing of the timber structure, are most noteworthy. There is a distinctive Germanic quality. In St. John's, a Georgian experimentation in Gothic is found. It is possible that Colonel Hopson, the Governor, knew something about the current architectural trends in England—for it was about this time that Gothic experiments appeared. St. John's is a fantastic building when considered in detail. The stark contrast of the black and white timber and the spires and pinnacles give an emphasis to the volume and offset the horizontality. Later another unusual church was built at Sydney by Governor des Barres for the Anglican community. St. Gorge's (1786) was reminiscent of an English parish church and is built of stone.

It was followed by the most notable experiment in church plan and construction, viz. St. George's, Halifax. The church was built in 1780 and was possibly influenced by the desires of the Duke of Kent who is reputed to have liked "circular shapes". The structure was built of timber and was circular in shape. It was more than normally high for the period, and the architect is reputed to have been Colonel F. W. des Barres. [13]

The majority of churches were built during the Loyalist immigration and were nearly always based on New England precedents. Fine examples exist of Anglican, Presbyterian and Unitarian churches at Guysborough, Shelburne, Digby and Grand Pre.

Pictou, Antigonish, and Truro offer some good examples of Victorian Gothic structures built between 1866 and 1870. The St. Andrew's Presbyterian Church at Pictou (1866) being an exceptionally fine example. Pictou also possesses an earlier Presbyterian church erected by the first congregation in 1790.

Amongst the civic structures, court houses, masonic halls, gaols and pest houses were built. Perhaps the most celebrated of these is the Province House in Hollis Street, Halifax, built in 1818. This is a three-storied Palladian building housing the Legislative Assembly. It is built of local stone and was designed by the contractor. It is not unlike the Lord Mayor's Banqueting House which formerly stood at Stratford Place in London, and

---

[13] The cornerstone was laid by Sir John Wentworth and the ceremony was attended by His Royal Highness, the Duke of Kent. It was opened in 1803, but according to Mr. A.W. Wallace of Hamilton, Ontario, it was not completed until many years later.

the designer may have received his ideas from personal knowledge of the building or through a "pattern book". The contractor was John Merrick, and an original elevation of the building is preserved in the library of the Province House. Halifax also possesses a late Georgian town clock which stands at the foot of the Citadel and which was presented by the Duke of Kent in 1812.

The long barnlike form of the Masonic Temple is a common structure in many Nova Scotia towns and it was usually built of timber. A good example is to be seen at Sherbrooke.

Commercial and Industrial Architecture

Unfortunately few Maritime commercial or industrial structures dating before 1840 remain, although some still exist in the form of early residences which were altered. In the fishing villages large timber sheds (similar to those of New England) are found which were used for the curing, preparation and storage of fish, for boat-building, and for maritime activities such as sail-making, boat-repairing and caulking, and marine metal work. Such buildings are usually situated on the waterfront or the seashore and, in some cases, on wharfs or piles projecting into the water. They were long and rectangular in shape and were often two and even three stories in height.

Shops were often incorporated into residential structures, as prior to the outbreak of the 1812 war the units required were small. The ground floor emanated from a central or side doorway, and a shop window, or windows consisting of leaded lights or Georgian panes, faced onto the street. Shop accommodation and storage was at street level and had a loading door and yard at the rear. The merchant, his family and sometimes his apprentices, lived on the second and third floors. A traditional plan appears which was an adaptation of the standard Georgian apartment plan usually found in the United Kingdom and New England.

In addition to the small shops, merchants with large businesses carried out their operations in long rectangular timber warehouses and stores, which were two stories in height and in some cases partly split in their levels. Gambrell roof structures were also used by 1760.

The commercial areas of Nova Scotia towns were transformed between 1840 and 1870. Prosperity accompanied the development of the ship-building industry, carrying trade, and the establishment of large passenger and freight lines. Larger and more commodious structures were required. Increased accommodation coupled with the persistent hazard of fire resulted in the introduction of fire-proof, solid load-bearing structures of stone and brick. Shopping or office space was often found on three floors, and buildings of three and more stories were erected with no provision being made for residential accommodation. Shop windows and entrances became larger and buildings were more carefully planned. Floors were suspended and ceilings increased in height. Gas was introduced as well as piped water and flush sanitation. Large buildings appeared in the town centres of

Halifax, St. John, Fredericton, Pictou, Antigonish, Sydney, Yarmouth and Liverpool from 1850 onwards. Similar accommodation was built for manufacturing plants such as carriage and furniture makers; stove and sheet metal, bronze or iron workers; bakeries and breweries.

In addition, banks, insurance companies, professional offices, post offices, customs houses, clubs and hotels, commenced erecting buildings in the new vernacular, e.g. the Halifax Club. This mid-Victorian development altered the appearance of the larger Nova Scotia towns. It destroyed the former urban scale and obliterated the uniformity which resulted from the use of wood. The low, two-storied skyline disappeared and the telephone and electric light with their attendant poles and wires produced an environment of chaotic abstraction.

Unfortunately, the accompanying mechanization of transportation also changed the environment and resulted in the gradual disappearance of avenues which were removed for street widening. Open spaces were also transformed into vehicle parks.

CONCLUSIONS

What conclusions may be drawn from a study of the Maritime settlements? The geography of Nova Scotia favoured four primary activities, viz., forestry, fishing, agriculture and mining. Closely associated with forestry was shipbuilding and the marine repair industry, but these activities were only significant during the era of wooden ships. Two of these potentials induced European settlement, viz. fishing and agriculture. The former was of prime importance to the British economy, while the latter was of secondary importance to the French. Neither should be overestimated. [14]

Situated as it was, Nova Scotia became a strategic no man's land between British North America and French Canada. The Province became a battleground for both factions and early settlement was primarily military and strategic in concept. Early colonisation was encouraged, but it had the most primitive intentions as far as the exploitation of the natural resources was concerned. National policy envisaged settlement as a method of subjugating the environment and providing additional resources of men and materials in time of war. France and Britain both wished to be actively entrenched in the territory as it formed a convenient buffer zone between their rapidly developing North American colonies.

Thus, although the early British and French administrative concepts were feudal and directed towards economic exploitation, by the beginning of the eighteenth century they were primarily military. The British concepts of colonisation were ostensibly military, but the pressure of public opinion in the North American colonies increasingly directed their interests

---

[14] The earliest settlements were orientated to the fur trade and trapping, while forestry assumed increasing importance as a valuable source of timber for the Royal Navy, and of course shipbuilding during the late 18th to the mid-19th centuries.

to economic exploitation. The Britsh eventually formed many settlements—numbers of which had no possible military value, but which developed the lumber resources and accommodated New England immigration. The British, having a less autocratic administration than the French, encouraged immigration and settlement, for not only did this further their influence and control in unexploited land, but it also developed valuable raw materials. Two settlement types evolved, and these were orientated towards agriculture or fishing. The techniques of land development and community planning remained unaltered and were adaptations of the British system in the North American colonies. The building of Halifax in 1749 was the first attempt to develop a settlement as a State-sponsored project since the Elizabethan period in Ireland.

Private individuals or business groups (often originating in the American colonies) also undertook and sponsored settlements with the approval of and, in some cases, the aid of the authorities. Similar techniques not unlike those developed in Massachusetts were used.

The outbreak of the American Revolution (1775-1784) brought about a crisis. Settlements were formed in the Province to accommodate refugees and to reinforce the Province against American penetration. There were still no radical departures in town-planning concepts, although the Governor of Cape Breton understood the implications of planned development and attempted to depart from the conventional planning technique at Sydney. Unfortunately his plans were not implemented. Few early settlements were outstanding successes because of the difficulty in getting the right type of immigrant, the desire to settle ex-soldiers rather than artisans or agriculturalists, and the careless selection of sites. Although often built on scenically magnificent sites in terms of location and environment, town planning was dull and unimaginative.

The predominant influence on the settlement pattern is American, and this was reinforced by the New England and Loyalist immigrations. Their architecture and the land system were therefore reproduced with modifications. The settlers spent many years in consolidation. They lived a hard life, but accepted it believing that the transitional period of utilitarian development would eventually pass away with increased economic prosperity. This never occurred because of the nature of the country, its resources, and the inflated sanctity attached to the individual ownership of property. Land represented wealth to the individual and he was unwilling to accept communal restriction in any form if it could be avoided.

Nor should climate be forgotten. Undoubtedly the overseas possessions of other European nations had more attractive settlements, e.g. the Dutch, Spanish and Portuguese. All of these races tended to emigrate to warmer areas. They intermarried with the local population and lost the desire to preserve their national identity after they had attained wealth and prosperity. The hotter climate allowed them a full annual working schedule and they were able to indulge in the luxurious living of a slave-orientated society. Their administrative officers also tended to keep abreast of the national cultural developments in the home countries because of the temporary nature of their appointments. The autocratic administrative system of their colonial society ensured that there could never be any dispute as to who would make decisions and set standards, particularly in planning and architecture.

In Nova Scotia, on the other hand, development took the form of a community of freeholders who were men of relatively limited wealth and whose achievements were wrested from an unwilling land by their own labour. They made the colony their home, and their ties with England were slight for they were more closely orientated to the living pattern of their southern neighbours. Ideas from outside were usually imposed by British Government administrators and tended to be transitory. They certainly did not effect architectural revolutions or introduce any new planning techniques. The democratic nature of an artistically inarticulate community swamped the inventive dreamer. Conservatism became the hallmark of the colonist and was easily associated with the Puritan mentality.

The development of shipbuilding and ocean trade and travel marked the first serious break with the traditional architectural forms of New England, but only made its appearance during the 1840's. The predominant character of the town up to the middle of the century was that of the village, and a sense of cohesion in the central areas and scale appears during this period of prosperity and contact. This process also resulted in aesthetic catastrophe, for technological improvements found the authorities unable to cope with the planning problems.

Gas, the telephone, electricity, television, the internal combustion and the steam engine, refrigerated and tinned foods—all of these imply new three-dimensional forms which have to be integrated into the urban complex as street furniture, shopping centres, special storage facilities, service stations, car parks and garages—in short, many of the technological improvements associated with community life today are only now being happily integrated into Nova Scotia towns which were designed for a different set of conditions. Unfortunately, most towns are weak economically at the present time, are unable to provide any radical planning solutions, and are forced to seek makeshift arrangements to remain in existence. Some which have been unable to do this are declining.

The only solution for the reorganization, replacement, preservation and restoration of Maritime towns and villages lies in the creation of a major regional planning organization, preferably financed with federal funds and in possession of more effective planning powers than exist at the present time. This could possibly be administered at provincial government level, and should be reinforced by the introduction of a department specializing in the preservation and maintenance of historical areas and monuments, and civic design and landscape.

Acknowledgments

The author gratefully acknowledges the courtesy and assistance he received in the course of his research from Dr. Bruce Fergusson, Archivist of the Public Archives of Nova Scotia; Mr. W. K. Lamb, Dominion Archivist of the Public Archives of Canada at Ottawa; the librarians and staff of the various public libraries in Nova Scotia, New Hampshire, Toronto and Ottawa; the officers of federal and provincial government departments, municipalities and other local authorities in Nova Scotia and New Brunswick; and from many members of the public. He is particularly grateful to the Central Mortgage and Housing Corporation of Canada which awarded him a Senior Fellowship to undertake the research; and to Professor Gordon Stephenson, Head of the Division of Town and Regional Planning of the University of Toronto, who initiated the project.

SOME ECONOMIC AND SOCIAL INFLUENCES ON REGIONAL PLANNING IN ALBERTA

Leonard O. Gertler

This paper was prepared when the author was Director of the Edmonton District Planning Commission, a regional planning agency in Alberta. Professor Gertler is Deputy Chairman, Department of Geography and Planning, and Director, Planning and Resources Institute, University of Waterloo.

The diverse forms of regional planning have one thing in common—they all operate within a multi-governmental area. While each unit of local government recognizes its interdependence with the rest of the area, each is reluctant to vest any of its authority in a supra-municipal or governmental planning agency. As a result there arises a serious dilemma—the planning process is split between preparation, based on the study of a comprehensive area, and implementation, based on the consent of each constituent governmental unit. The regional planning function remains voluntary, advisory and usually ineffective.

In nine of the ten Canadian provinces this basic dilemma of planning in an area of divided municipal jurisdiction has not been overcome. A recent step to resolve this problem in the remaining province, Alberta, is therefore something of a phenomenon. In terms of Canadian development, it will be useful to have some insight into the environmental forces from which the Alberta solution has sprung. To the degree that social and economic conditions in Alberta find parallels in other parts of the world, this investigation may have wider than Canadian significance.

In April, 1957, the Legislature of Alberta passed a major amendment to the Town and Rural Planning Act, which extends authority to district planning commissions, centred in cities with populations in excess of 50,000, to require local conformance to a regional plan as adopted by a two-thirds majority of a commission. This amendment represents a logical evolution of a regional planning system, established in the five principal city-centred regions of the province, which has been mainly advisory, but strengthened by the broad definition of planning regions, by substantial provincial financial assistance making possible adequate planning staffs, by control over subdivision, and by the effectiveness of local planning administration in the constituent municipalities. Breakdown, however, has at times occurred within this system because the basic dilemma of regional planning—the split between preparation and implementation—remained.

The new legislation overcomes this difficulty by identifying those aspects of land use, which transcend exclusively local concerns and are inherently regional in nature, and by making the district planning commission responsible for control of development and land use within the defined fields of development. In this way, the prerogatives of local government are preserved, and the means for dealing with common, inter-municipal problems are provided in the interest of the wider regional community.

The scope of regional planning within the newly constructed framework is suggested by the land-use zones which come within the purview of the "district plan". These are: general urban, major industrial, high-density agricultural, low-density agricultural, highway commercial, small-holding, country-residence, district recreational, and new general urban. In the two major centres, Edmonton and Calgary, where the new principles will be applied first, the size of the district planning areas are respectively 3,600 and 4,200 square miles.

A regional plan, conceived in these terms, becomes an instrument for controlling those determinants of the quality of urban environments, namely size, shape and structure, which may be decisively influenced by developments that occur far outside the jurisdiction of the central city within a region. But this instrument cannot be employed to achieve a sound pattern of growth, from a long-term community point-of-view, without coming into conflict with what appears to be a deeply-ingrained Western Canadian belief in the sacredness of private property, which includes the right to a speculative gain from the sale of land. And this makes regional planning in Alberta, with its far-reaching controls over the use of land in the public interest, all the more remarkable—and paradoxical.

Amongst the historic influences that must be reckoned with in a search for the roots of regional planning in Alberta, is the tradition of the frontier. Viewed in broad North American terms, the settlement of Alberta, which did not commence on a large scale until 1906, was the last of a series of waves of settlement into virgin frontier territory, which began with the crossing of the Appalachian Range into Kentucky and Tennessee in the period of the American Revolution.

While the major settlement of the virgin lands of the United States and Canada occurred over a period of about a hundred and fifty years, and in varying conditions of terrain, soil and climate, there were certain broad conditions common to all stages of the frontier's advance. It was a movement, en masse, of land-hungry European immigrants, and of "native" farmers from expensive and/or less productive soils to land that was free, or almost free. Thus, in Alberta, of the forty million or so acres of occupied farm land, about twenty million were originally granted by the federal government in the form of free "homesteads" of 160 acres, subject only to certain residence and cultivation requirements. The rest of the land, held by the Canadian Pacific Railway Company and the Hudson's Bay Company, was sold by these concerns at $7.62 and $12.10 per acre respectively. [1] Occupation of the major part of these lands, once it commenced,

---

[1] Wiesman, Brahm, "Town and Rural Planning," *Journal, Royal Architectural Institute of Canada.* February, 1953: p. 36.

was in the form of a number of sudden, almost explosive, population movements. The population of the province which was 73,000 in 1901, doubled in the next five years, and then doubled again between 1906 and 1911, and increased to about half a million in 1916. [2]

These conditions of rapid population growth in primaeval areas on free land, common to the frontier at each stage of westward advance, have caused a group of Canadian and American historians and sociologists to evolve what has become known as the Frontier Thesis. [3] A basic tenet of the thesis is that frontier-conditioned ideals, institutions, attitudes and habits have persisted and have become a major "formative influence" in the social and political development of the two countries. The American historian, Frederick Jackson Turner, who has been called somewhat mischievously, the "prophet" of this concept of the frontier, and author of its "Book of Genesis" has expressed the idea in this way—"Long after the frontier period of a particular region . . . has passed away, the conception of society, the ideals and aspirations which it produced, persist in the minds of the people." [4]

In Alberta, the persistence of a large measure of equality in the size of farms, provides a material basis for the persistence of frontier ideology. At the last census in 1951, there were 84,315 occupied farms in the province, of which 42.5% were between 300 to 640 acres—the minimum economic unit over extensive mixed farming areas; 30.3 per cent between 100 to 300 acres; 5.4 per cent below 100 acres; and 21.8 per cent above 640 acres. About two-thirds of the farm land is owner-occupied. Thus, in spite of tendencies to the contrary, rural society in Alberta has the aspect of an egalitarian society composed of independent farmer producers. [5]

In the context of this study, these aspects of the frontier heritage that relate to the use of land are of prime interest. And from this viewpoint, one is impressed by an inheritance of two sharply contrasting cultural traits. The duality is expressed, unconsciously but tellingly, in a letter of a mid-western pioneer to friends in the East, in which it is observed that "it is a universal rule here to help one another, each one keeping an eye to his own single interest". [6] In the conditions of the frontier, based on extensive individual farming enterprise, "society", in Turner's words, "became atomic". The individual was exalted, and "unchecked by restraint of an old social order", he had an open field to pursue his interests, without a care for the advice of paternal government.

---

[2] Hanson, Eric, *Local Government of Alberta*. McClelland & Stewart Limited, Canada, 1956: p. 129.

[3] Creighton, Donald, "Towards the Discovery of Canada", *University of Toronto Quarterly*, April, 1956: pp. 276-279.

[4] Turner, Frederick Jackson, *The Frontier in American History*. Henry Holt and Company, New York, 1950: p. 264.

[5] The Bureau of Statistics, Province of Alberta, *Facts and Figures, Alberta*. Queen's Printer, 1954: pp. 28 and 31.

[6] *Op. cit.* Turner, p. 343.

"A fool can sometimes put on his coat better than a wise man can do it for him"—it was said. [7]

But the very process of earning a livelihood and building communities under frontier conditions made the pioneer a split personality in his social attitudes. "In Saskatchewan and Alberta", it has been observed, "the entire community equipment and all the physical apparatus by which governments perform their social role had to be provided almost overnight. . . . People in haste to realize a goodly heritage found private enterprise too slow in providing some of the services commonly left to its care in older communities and they easily agreed in asking governments to furnish them." [8] Under these exigencies, individualism, on occasion, gave way to co-operation and governmental activity.

In this early period of settlement, however, the use of land was not governed by any consideration of long-term public interest. Ways were sometimes found to circumvent the requirements of the Homestead Act, and speculation was rife. "With every sign of improvement in general conditions . . . the land speculator was there in advance of the farmer, the village doctor, lawyer and store-keeper. Only too frequently he was the village lawyer or doctor or store-keeper himself." [9] And land was settled indiscriminately without sufficient regard for soil and climatic factors. In south-east Alberta, a major land-use error occurred with the opening up to settlement of a semi-arid grassland area, corresponding approximately to the province's Brown Soil Zone, of about 12.5 million acres. [10]

The crisis of the 1930's induced by depression, drought and soil erosion, created agricultural land-use problems that were manifestly beyond solution by the individual farmer. Between 1928 and 1933, per capita income in Alberta fell by 61 per cent compared to 44 per cent in the more economically diversified eastern provinces. [11] Rural land-use planning became a matter of grim necessity. It was initiated by three major enactments : a federal government measure, the Prairie Farm Rehabilitation Act (1935) providing mainly for the conservation of water, the reclamation and irrigation of land, and the resettlement of farmers on irrigated land; the Special Areas Act of Alberta (1938) which eventually placed 10,000 square miles of the most severely stricken land in south-east Alberta under direct provincial administration, and which provided for agricultural land-use survey and classification, and for grants to farmers moving to better soil and climatic zones; and the Agricultural Service Board Act (1945), empowering rural municipalities to establish special boards, served with professional advice, for the purpose of advising on all aspects of agricultural

----

[7] *Ibid*. Turner, p. 249.

[8] Royal Commission on Dominion-Provincial Relations, *Canada: 1867-1939*. Ottawa, 1940: p. 81.

[9] Martin, Chester, *"Dominion Lands" Policy*. The MacMillan Company of Canada Limited, Toronto, 1938: p. 406.

[10] *Op. cit. Facts and Figures*: p. 17.

[11] *Op cit. Canada: 1867-1939*: p. 150.

production and land use. This measure, which is perhaps the most enduring and comprehensive of the three, vests in a rural council the rather extraordinary authority to take control of land that is being neglected either from weed infestation or erosion, and to manage such farm land until it is restored to a satisfactory physical and economic condition. This authority, which is on occasion actually used, is of interest, apart from its intrinsic features, for the principle of jurisprudence it seems to reflect, namely that there is a degree of trusteeship—of responsibility to one's neighbours, if not to the community as a whole—attached to the private ownership of land. [12]

While rural land-use planning took large strides as a result of depression conditions, urban planning was one of the many casualties of that debacle. A provincial planning branch functioned from 1929 to 1933, when it was dissolved "in the face of drastically curtailed provincial revenues". Due to the efforts of that period, Alberta today is one of the few areas on the North American continent where the natural landscape is not supplemented by a terrifying procreative growth extolling the virtues of "cokes" and cars. [13]

The Depression had two additional effects—one social, one political—that form important background to the development of planning on a regional basis. It dramatized, rather painfully, the economic interdependence of town and country; contraction in farm income brought hard times to the market centres. And it swept into power, in 1935, a new political force, the Social Credit movement that, unlike its predecessor which was a farmer's party, appealed to all sections of the population and in so doing, cut across the town-country line. [14]

Since the market centre is the germinal urban unit in Alberta, the Depression experience may have strengthened that town and country unity, upon which effective planning in a city-centred region so much depends. This is a distinctive Prairie phenomenon, inasmuch as the same basis for town-country unity does not exist where the economic base of an urban community consists primarily of activities serving wide national or international markets. And further, the dominance of an urban-rural political force had the effect, at the very least, of removing an obstacle to town and country co-operation.

While the economic crisis upset the old political equilibrium and brought a new political movement into power, on a platform of monetary reform and protection against exploiters, the fundamentals of the agrarian society of "independent" farmer producers were not challenged. It has been said, authoritatively, that "the leaders . . . were prepared to fight against the quasi-colonial economic subordination of their people, but not to do

---

[12] *Op. cit.* Wiesmann, Brahm; and Hanson, Eric.

[13] *Ibid.* Wiesmann, p. 37.

[14] Jean Burnet, *Next-Year Country.* University of Toronto Press, Toronto, 1951: p. 88.

anything which would undermine the sanctity of property rights".[15] This political orientation arose, first, out of the conviction that the main source of economic disorder came from outside interests which determined the costs of production and terms of trade of the farmer; and, secondly, out of the premise that land ownership was the basis of independence, however that may be materially qualified and called an illusion by academic observers. In effect, the individualistic side of the dual personality of the independent farmer, which had its origins in the free-land period, was not seriously disturbed or qualified.

The forces of economic expansion, after recovery from the depression, played an important part in shaping the regional planning system in Alberta. The impact of oil and gas development is dramatically delineated in the changing facts of production. Agriculture is still the leading industry. But it has slipped, relatively, from a position in 1947, the year of the first large oil discovery, when it accounted for more than half the net value of production, to a position where it represented less than a third of the total. In 1947, mining, manufacturing and construction represented together 41.9 per cent of the net value of production; in 1956, they represented 67.2 per cent.[16]

These broad shifts in the economic composition of the province underlie the ascendance of the urban population. In 1946, residents of cities, towns and villages represented 44.1 per cent of a total population of 803,000; in 1956, the urban group was approximately 60 per cent of a total of 1,123,116. There has been no net gain in rural population—in fact a slight decrease—and all the population increase of the past decade has been in urban areas.[17]

Thus in ten years the economy and the rural-urban population balance has undergone far-reaching change. While Canada as a whole is in an expansive phase, the pace of development in Alberta has been unique. The Province now absorbs the highest per capita capital investment in the country, and in this respect has deviated notably from the other Prairie provinces; in 1955 Alberta's per capita investment of $793 was 52 per cent higher than that prevailing over the remainder of the Prairies. Edmonton and Calgary have the highest rates of growth in Canada for cities with over 100,000 people.

There is no doubt that the rather sudden emergence of regional planning in Alberta in 1949 was in response to the urban flood released by the rapid and large-scale development of oil and gas resources. Edmonton newspaper reports of the period bristle with comments about "mushroom growth", the city "bursting its seams", the "disgrace of fringe area development", and with many expressions of civic helplessness. The

---

[15] C.B. Macpherson, *Democracy in Alberta*. University of Toronto Press, Toronto, 1953: p. 220.

[16] Dominion Bureau of Statistics, and Bureau of Statistics, Province of Alberta.

[17] *Op. cit.* Hanson, Eric: p. 135. Dominion Bureau of Statistics, *Canada Year Book, 1956*. Queen's Printer, Ottawa, 1956: pp. 151 and 695.

establishment of advisory regional planning authorities, in this period, in broadly defined, city-centred regions was an attempt to deal, in an orderly and economic way, with all those uses that are generated in the city but invade the open country. From this rather limited concept of town and country interdependence, with its strong urban bias, there has been a gradual evolution of a regional planning program that embraces the total land resource, so that urban and rural land-use planning, which have different origins in Alberta, and have always been separated, are moving towards their necessary and natural union. [18] The recent transformation of district planning powers from advisory to executive status with respect to inherently regional aspects of development, represented a far-sighted response to the deficiencies exposed by experience. "We are convinced", wrote the members of a Royal Commission on metropolitan problems, "there can be no orderly development in any area [where] . . . the dissent of one member municipality alone could disrupt the entire plan". [19]

While the means for the achievement of a regional plan, conceived in the best community interest, have been greatly improved, all the problems of implementation have not been eliminated by a single legislative stroke. Ultimately, planning is either voluntary, by common consent, or there is no planning—at least no planning that is worthwhile or workable. There is an abundance of experience suggesting that an imposed plan is made unworkable by the weight of public antagonism and inertia. If this is correct, then we are left with the relationship between the traditional individualistic concept of property rights and the objectives of the regional plan. Are the two reconcilable? Lewis Mumford in *The Culture of Cities* has taken a rather doubtful view. "As long as individual ownership is regarded as sacred", he writes, "the most important needs of the community may be balked, and its most vital plans may be mangled". And he goes on to assert that "without decisive control that vests with collective ownership . . . working for the common good, regional planning is an all but impossible task". [20]

Mumford's view, which if accepted literally might force us to throw up our hands in complete frustration and resignation to the "inevitable", suggests the need for a different formulation of the problem, along the following lines—Is there any possibility that in a country with both democratic and private enterprise traditions, that the critical importance of land to human life, and its unique qualities as a resource, can change the concept of property rights—to the point where the ownership of land is commonly regarded as a public trust ? This formulation does not lend itself to a categorical answer. Considered in the context of Alberta, it can only be said that there are some conditions favourable to the postulated change,

18 For an example of this integration, see Edmonton District Planning Commission, *A General Plan. The Municipal District of Stony Plain.* Edmonton, 1956.

19 *Report of the Royal Commission on the Metropolitan Development of Calgary and Edmonton,* Queen's Printer, Alberta, 1956. Chapter 5, p. 54.

20 Mumford, Lewis, *The Culture of Cities.* Harcourt, Brace and Company, New York, 1938: pp. 328, 329.

some unfavourable and some indefinite. There is space for only a brief reference to these.

Favourable factors are the co-operative side of the frontier inheritance; the hard lessons of the depression, greatly intensified by the misuse of land; the opportunity to learn from the errors of the older cities of the continent; the open-mindedness of a society, only half a century of age, which "questioned the older order of things and made innovation its very creed" [21]; and finally the positive and flexible attitude of the provincial government to the problems of rural and urban land use.

Factors unfavourable to a basic change in the concept of individual rights in land ownership are the individualistic, rugged and irresponsible side of the frontier inheritance; the conservative tendencies of the western farmer, in good times at least, based on his assumed independence as an entrepreneur; and the speculative bias of both country and town—the farmers who, as Veblen expressed it, "have been cultivators of the main chance as well as the fertile soil"; and the market centre, whose municipal affairs, civic pride and community interest, Veblen observed, "converge upon its real-estate values, which are invariably of a speculative character, which all its loyal citizens are intent on 'booming' and 'boosting'—that is to say lifting still further off the level of actual ground values as measured by the uses to which the ground is turned". [22]

Finally there remains a set of imponderable factors which will loom large in future years, arising out of the indicated changes in the economic and population composition of the province. In the nature of things, one can assume that politics do not operate in a vacuum, and that ultimately the significant economic groups will find satisfaction of their interest through government. Recent Canadian studies indicate that the rapid transition from a predominantly rural and agricultural society to an urban and industrial one, has been accompanied by a high degree of concentration of economic power. [23] In Alberta, a new urban and industry-based power structure is in the process of formation. The new groups [24] will be concerned with land, primarily, as space rather than as a means of production, and there is a possibility that they will regard fringe lands, whatever their agricultural productivity, simply as a convenience waiting to accommodate houses or factories or junk-yards. In Alberta, the problem is further complicated by a significant degree of absentee ownership and control of resources and industries, from Montreal, Toronto and New York.

From this assessment of the factors affecting the concept of property rights, it can only be concluded that the maintenance of effective regional planning in Alberta, will for some time be very much a matter of conscious and relentless striving—politically, administratively, and educationally.

---

[21] *Op. cit.* Turner: p. 355.

[22] Thorstein Veblen, "The Independent Farmer", and "The Country Town", *The Portable Veblen*. Viking Press, New York, 1948: pp. 400 and 407.

[23] John Porter, "Concentration of Economic Power and the Economic Elite in Canada", *Canadian Journal of Economics and Political Science*. May, 1956.

[24] See Hanson, Eric, *The Dynamic Decade*, for the role of the oil industry.

2. *The Background Ideas*

THE FUNDAMENTAL AIMS OF PLANNING

A. Benjamin Handler

*The author is Professor of Planning in the
University of Michigan. An economist by
training, Professor Handler has done much
work in housing and urban planning.
Amongst his numerous research activities,
he was director of the study on High Cost
of Housing for the Joint Committee on
Housing of the United States Congress. His
Canadian roots go back to Kingston, Ontario
where he grew up, and attended as well as
lectured at Queen's University.*

We may readily agree that at certain stages in man's development the
city came into existence to make life possible. And we may just as
readily agree that it continues to exist to make life good. (It is important
to note that Aristotle in this formulation was referring both to the urban
area proper and the surrounding countryside, which together comprised
the City-State.) But it is a far cry from the justification or purpose of
the city—what it ought to achieve—to what it actually accomplishes.
Life in most cities is only partly good, and for some it is downright bad.
If urban planning has any fundamental aim at all, it must be to move from
the existing state of affairs to something more desirable, namely the good
life.

Having said this, we can proceed to dismiss it on three counts.
Presumably most, if not all, of human endeavour is directed towards the
good life, and planning cannot arrogate to itself the whole of the human
task. Nor can an objective stated in such general terms be of any earthly
use as a guide to anyone. Unlike sin, everyone is for it. Even if we were
to elaborate and make it more specific, we would still have to depend for
its attainment on a proper utilization of means. Ends and means go hand
in hand for each depends on the other. The failures of classical antiquity
may be attributed to an outlook or cultural preconception which neglected
method. We widely blame the failures of contemporary western civilization
on our intense preoccupation with method, with processes and ways of
doing, to the neglect of human needs and essential values.

Now planning, by its very nature, must be concerned with both ends
and means simultaneously. It cannot, on the one hand, adopt idealized
solutions utterly lacking in realism. And it cannot, on the other hand,
rest content with an attitude current in the social science which says in
effect : let someone else specify the ends, we are only concerned with means.
I am not maintaining that planning must not be tinged with utopian
idealism, nor grounded in technique. Every planner must have a little
of the visionary in him and a high degree of technical competence as well.

It follows that we cannot state the aims of planning exclusively either in procedural terms or in normative terms. Planning aims at certain ways of doing things and at the results of the doing. For urban planning (or any other kind of planning, for that matter) to achieve its objectives, it has to meet three main requirements. It has to be comprehensive, have proper focus, and have an organizing principle.

COMPREHENSIVENESS

One of the most often repeated platitudes in current discussions on planning is that it must be comprehensive. Any planner maintaining that planning need not be comprehensive would probably be treated with suspicion, and rightly so.

What seems to be emerging from current discussions is a new concept of comprehensiveness. Until quite recently comprehensive planning meant being only partly comprehensive. It was comprehensive in the sense that it concerned itself with the whole as distinct from a part of a given geographical area. But it lacked comprehensiveness in that it failed to treat that area from all relevant planning viewpoints. At first the designer, the engineer, the decision-maker tended to identify planning with the kind of focus resulting from his own particular approach to the problem. Then when it was realized that other foci were necessary, each tended to regard his as dominant, as constituting the essence of planning, with the others playing a subservient or secondary role. There seem to be indications that even in academic circles planners are ceasing to indulge in such "fun and games". Circumstances are developing a strain of planner ready to welcome all the required foci equally in tackling the problem at hand in a co-ordinated manner.

As opposed to no planning, any planning at all, no matter how lacking in comprehensiveness, can result in improvement. But to the extent to which it is lacking in comprehensiveness, it tends to be a mere drop in the bucket, falling further and further behind the sheer quantitative impact of rapid urbanization with its increasing profileration of problems. For example, from eastern Massachusetts to northern Virginia, for a length of over 600 miles, stretches a continuous urban system—a Megalopolis with a population close to thirty million and a unique concentration of industry and commerce. Other smaller and less intensive consolidations are developing from Cleveland to Pittsburgh, and outward from Detroit. And there seems to be a tendency for them to merge with each other. A map was published recently showing that not too many decades hence practically the whole of the United States is likely to be covered by a continuous network of metropolitan areas. In the face of such vast and complex growths, no partial planning can work.

An awareness of implications has been forced upon planners. They have had to watch the reverberations of partial planning solutions throughout the urban structure. In one instance occurring in the area in which I live, a school board and a city council independently located a junior high school, a main thoroughfare and a large shopping centre contiguous to one another. The eventual inconveniences, hazards and costs were detrimental to both and to the whole community. Location and design of a through-highway can have all sorts of consequences for municipal growth and liveability. As they have become increasingly aroused to the consequences of partial planning, the ideal of comprehensiveness has possessed planners. Because solutions through one approach point immediately to other approaches without any apparent end, planners do not quite know where to stop. Planning is no longer a neat, tidy thing but a strange amorphous beast galloping wildly in all directions.

This is so because comprehensiveness in planning is one of those unexamined notions which means different things to different people. It sounds fine to say that planning must extend its horizons beyond particular goals and values to the co-ordination of ends themselves, must see things whole and reach towards meaningful unities, treat parts only provisionally as ends in themselves but ultimately as aspects of a wider whole, deal with complex and aggregative interrelationships, with the simultaneous analytical decomposition of systems into components and their integrative recomposition into wider wholes, and achieve a multi-purpose co-ordination of means and ends. (This is practically a verbatim paraphrase of something I wrote not so very long ago.) Does this mean the same to you as it does to me or to the planner across the ocean ? I strongly suspect that to many school planners, for instance, it refers to the school system only, and to many physical planners it means comprehensive urban design, while for others it may also encompass administrative co-ordination, for still others economic interrelations as well, and perhaps social interaction, too. The range of interpretation can be very great and the degree of inclusiveness extremely varied.

How then can we formulate this ideal of comprehensiveness to give it some precise meaning ? Here again we must go to current discussions on planning. Two notions seem to emerge : balance and structure. The first is variously phrased as the need to search for a balance, to establish certain balances between functions, to maintain a dynamic balance. There is an emphasis on internal consistency and in linked programs. Equally significant is the stress on such matters as a theory of structure, community structure, the structural relationships of an area. What we really have here is an accent on form, on the arrangement of parts as distinct from an exclusive preoccupation with the parts themselves. Let me hasten to add that form here cannot be taken to refer solely to shapes and visual relationships. It can only be regarded in some such sense as that developed in Lancelot Law Whyte's philosophy of science, or perhaps in the morphological sense in which Goethe used it. What these ideas, currently in the air, mean is that if we are to tackle problems in a comprehensive manner, they must be handled structurally or in terms of form. If planning is to be comprehensive, some form or system of structural relationships must knit together its many facets and the various kinds of problems with which it deals. This is not a matter of superimposing form on content.

The two must be integral and the treatment of each conditioned by treatment of the other. Thus the content of any planning analysis of needs and requirements, and the mold in which it is cast, depends on the fact that it must ultimately go to design. Conversely, the design must satisfy all the conditions indicated in the analysis. Financial, legal and control considerations have to be satisfied. They in turn exercise a determining influence.

Let us now see if we can arrive at some notion of the content of comprehensive planning. One formulation of what constitutes comprehensive planning seems to me to incorporate both the relational considerations we have just discussed and to indicate the general character of its content. It states that comprehensive urban planning is the harmonious utilization of the possibility of a city. Herein are contained the ideas of balance and structure (harmonious utilization) as well as a hint of the kind of content (possibilities of a city) with which planning has to deal. Moreover, attention is fixed simultaneously on means (possibilities) and on ends (their harmonious utilization). It implies that urban planning must aim to develop the resources of a city to the utmost so that they work well in conjunction with each other. Comprehensive planning is thus both a resource development and a resource use problem, having as its twin objectives the capacity development of resources and their integrated use. It means that the more a city's resource potentialities are developed and the better their use is co-ordinated, the better off we are. Planning can concentrate on one of these facets rather than the other only at the expense of human welfare.

This raises the question : with what kind of resources is planning concerned ?

FOCUS

To give a content to comprehensiveness in planning and thereby make it work, a focus is needed for it. The problems of planning are increasingly becoming more pressing. To solve them, planners need to know precisely what they are dealing with. We require a new, more inclusive focus to supplement (not replace) the several foci of partial planning, such as physical configuration, human needs, or legal controls. If we look upon each partial emphasis as a system, then what we need is an inter-system focus which, by bringing them all together, will clearly define and circumscribe comprehensive planning. This can only be done if there is something common to them all. If we cannot find something common to them all, then planning will not be able to overcome the discontinuities and lack of co-ordination which plague it today. It will lack form and structure and be unable to achieve a harmonious utilization of possibilities. It will, in short, not have the prerequisites for comprehensive planning.

The one thing common to all kinds of planning is a common subject matter. This is what makes it possible to bring them all into an inclusive focus. If we survey all aspects of urban (and for that matter, regional) planning, we find that they all deal with the same kinds of things—physical improvements. True, each planner deals with improvements in his own way. The designer handles their placing and arrangement. So does the engineer, but with a greater emphasis on technological determinations. Others, operating generally within the area known as the social sciences, consider how much of what improvements should be put where and when. Still others, primarily concerned with administrative management and control, consider how physical improvements should be used and transformed during their useful life. Regardless of the particular angle from which any one planner approaches his subject matter, the attention of all focuses on physical improvements. These are the products of the construction industry—developmental construction like roads, water supply and sewage disposal; facilities used by consumers, such as houses, schools and hospitals; productive facilities like factories, commercial buildings, utility structures, transportation and communication networks.

Before we pursue some of the implications of giving planning this focus, let us examine other attempts at providing it with a focus. Widely accepted is the view that planning deals with land use. If this means that the focus should be on land, it can readily be seen that not raw land but what is done to or on it is the important thing. If it means that the focus should be on how land is used, then this is primarily a matter of what improvements are made to or on the land and how these improvements are used. What, after all, are land-use maps and studies if not maps and studies of actual or desirable physical improvements ?

Another attempt at focus is in terms of a geographical area. According to this view there are two kinds of planning, urban and regional. This means a dual rather than a single focus. It is doubtful whether such a duality can be maintained in practice. City, metropolitan area and region are so interrelated, that their problems can only provisionally be kept separate. If they are to be handled adequately a common focus is required. There is, however, a basic reason why any attempt at a focus in terms of geographical areas must fail. It still does not define what constitutes the business of the planner within that area. Planning does not deal with every single thing within an area. It certainly does not encompass every field of human endeavour. The question still remains: What aspect of an area is the concern in planning if not physical improvements ?

Similar considerations apply to attempts to focus planning around the decision-making process. True, planners are inevitably concerned with decision-making. But so are all sorts of other people. The difference lies in the kinds of things about which decisions are made. The question still remains : about what kinds of things do planners make decisions if not physical improvements ?

Attempts have been made to see planning as focused on development. It is stated variously as : ordered growth, development and conservation; desirable and possible development; guided programs of development and redevelopment; remaking a city and directing its growth; making decisions about development; co-ordinating and integrating physical improvements and developmental activities. Now the growth and development here referred to can only be achieved through physical improvements. What is lost if we substitute physical improvements for development in any of these phrases, except imprecision ? We know better what we are talking about when we speak of : ordered accumulation and conservation of physical improvements; desirable and possible physical improvements; guided programs of physical improvement, expansion and replacement. Developmental activities can only refer to those connected with physical improvements.

These several attempts at giving a focus to planning fail through being too diffuse. They leave the planner still unsure of the exact nature and scope of his activities. The common ground—physical improvements— provides him with the necessary precision.

To say that planning is concerned with physical improvements does not mean that it has exclusive and proprietory rights. Though all planning deals with this class of things, every activity connected with them is not necessarily planning. If it were, then engineers, architects, economists, public administrators and a whole host of others would automatically be planners when their activities led them to deal with physical improvements. It is not the fact of dealing with such improvements, but the kind of activity carried on with respect to them that differentiates planning. The activity of planning is not concerned with the technical processes connected with improvements. There is nothing, of course, to preclude technical experts from being planners as well. To engage in planning they have to go through the process of making decisions about the creation and use of physical improvements. This does not refer to the techniques whereby they are produced, installed, and their use enforced and controlled. It refers to the prior decisions in accordance with which the technical processes are carried out.

Planning is thus the decisions man makes about the kinds, amounts, location, arrangement, and use of the physical improvements with which he surrounds himself. All manner of persons are constantly making decisions of this sort. Presumably they are engaged in planning of a kind. Yet we would be very hesitant to call much of this kind of activity planning. The reason is that it is not comprehensive. To be effective (for that is, after all, what we are after), planning must satisfy both conditions : be focused on its proper subject matter—physical improvements—and seek to develop and harmoniously utilize this kind of resource to the utmost extent possible.

In order to achieve such harmonious utilization of physical improvements, planning must approach the problem of making its decisions from three main angles:

1. Analysis of requirements. This is the determination of how much of what improvements should be put where and when. It involves forecasting the requirements for physical improvements and setting up capital improvement programs for meeting them, all in the light of resource pos-

sibilities. Essential to this process is a balancing of requirements with each other and a balancing of requirements with resources. Otherwise the capital improvement program will not bear a proper relationship to possibilities or to requirements.

2. Physical configuration. This is the determination of the positioning and arrangement of the physical improvements. It involves proper placement with respect to the natural environment, relation to each other and environment to facilitate the movement and functioning of people and things as well as to achieve satisfactory visual results. Essential here is an integration with environment, a co-ordination of technology with function, and a harmonious relation of improvements to each other.

3. Management and control. This is the determination of how the physical improvements should be used and transformed during their useful life, and when liquidated or replaced. It involves the proper use of legal, administrative and management devices in order to ensure that the possibilities inherent in the improvements are utilized in a co-ordinated manner.

Each of these approaches may be very well integrated internally, and still fail to achieve a harmonious utilization of physical improvements. They must, in addition, be integrated with one another. Facilities' requirements, for instance, have to be balanced against how they are likely to be used. What is put in place and its physical configuration have both to be balanced against resource and legal limitation. A complex of physical improvements may work well functionally, but because they prove costly to use and maintain, or because in their planning insufficient attention has been paid to other requirements, they may never function as intended. Legal and administrative co-ordination of recreational and school facilities may be perfect, but their physical relationship may make it ineffective. Conversely, their physical co-ordination may be excellent but not realizable because of legal difficulties. Zoning does not guarantee that an area will function well or even that it will be used at all.

The job of planning, however, is not confined to a balanced use of physical improvements. Planning also involves getting as much of such improvements as possible. This is not a matter of competing for available resources, but of participating in the balanced development of resources. Perhaps an example will help make the point clear. A few years ago two of my colleagues at the University of Michigan went on a United Nations' mission to assist and advise the Indonesian government on housing and town planning. Though architects, they were given the title of socio-economists, and very proud indeed they were of this title. They found in Djakarta the kind of conditions with which we are all familiar and which are present in most large cities of the East. The tremendous influx of population had rapidly filled the interior of the blocks with housing of a sort. Shacks occupied all the front lawns, the sidewalks, and extended into the broad avenues, leaving only a narrow way down the middle. In this kind of situation what kind of planning is possible? It makes no sense to talk of balanced use of physical improvements. Laws with respect to them are unenforceable, requirements cannot even be approached, and physical planning is impossible. The problem becomes one of resource development, first an ability to accumulate capital and then to make decisions on the forms in which it is stocked. Without the ability to accumulate, no planning of any kind is possible. With it we can begin to make decisions about the kinds of capital to be accumulated, their respective quantities, and the uses to which they are put. In any given geographical area, no matter how large or small, the need for "foreign" balances for required "imports" have to be balanced against needs for durable goods, and both against physical improvement needs. What is possible in the way of improvements can be increased by enhancing the ability of the area to accumulate. With a given accumulative ability, what is possible is conditioned by the necessity of achieving a balance among the various kinds of capital.

Normal planning operations embrace such matters as road, harbour and port development designed to increase the accumulative ability of an area. To the same end they seek to encourage the migration of productive facilities into an area through the creation of a favourable physical environment. The development of recreation facilities to attract tourists is designed to increase this accumulative ability in a different way. Planning also involves participating in decisions about the distribution of accumulations among the various kinds of capital. Its claims for physical improvements have to be balanced against and co-ordinated with the city's claims for machinery and equipment. Planners, too, are involved in making decisions about how much of the taxpayer's accumulative ability shall be devoted to physical improvements and how much to other uses, both private and public.

It is clear that, even with a definite focus, planning cannot avoid being somewhat complicated. Multifarious connections have to be made among the various planning approaches—analysis, design, control. Similar kinds of balances have to be established between the ability to accumulate capital, the extent of its allocation to physical improvements, and the way in which this allocation is used. In order to handle all these interrelations, translation from each aspect or facet of planning to the others has to be facilitated. Without some organizing principle, comprehensive planning is too complicated to be manageable.

ORGANIZING PRINCIPLES

I know of two devices for organizing the subject matter of comprehensive planning; the master plan and the capital budget.

Let us take the capital budget first. Basically it is a future plan of action with respect to physical improvements. Designed to exercise foresight and control over recurring needs, capital budgeting must be a continuous process subject to periodic review. It consists of an ever-extended long-term program of: (1) the types of improvements to be undertaken, (2) their timing, location and cost in the light of changing needs, and (3) a co-ordinating program of the methods by which they are to be financed in terms of the financial capacity of the community. To be really effective as a planning tool it must be profoundly and precisely rooted in human needs and values. In its monetary aspects, it is made up of three ingredients: the cost of putting each of the planned facilities in place, the annual amounts of income receipts required and the sources of these receipts; annual expenditures to be made for interest on loans, for principal repayment and directly for capital outlays. This, however, is merely the accounting mold into which the results of capital budgeting are cast. Capital budgeting is far more than this. It is a complicated process of policy determination, program analysis, and administrative co-ordination. These comprise the crux of capital budgeting. Upon their adequacy depends the success of the capital budget as an integrating device for comprehensive planning.

Capital budgeting covers the whole gamut of decisions that have to be made by planners in balancing needs and demands with resources. Because it reaches conclusions ranging from amounts to financing of physical improvements, it is able to reveal many kinds of imbalance that may occur between requirements and resources. When, for instance, it shows a long-range inability to meet needs with resources, it helps reveal where administrative consolidation or co-ordination is required. It also permits attention to be focused sharply on an unbalanced distribution of physical improvements in meeting needs. Not the least of the merits of capital budgeting is that the act of integrating within a formal mold requires justification of what goes in. This helps to promote the development of an adequate background of knowledge, thought and information for effective planning.

Where the capital budget deals with the analysis of requirements, the master plan deals with the physical configuration aspect of planning. Yet the master plan has a very definite relationship to the capital budget. For it, too, deals with kinds, location, and amounts of physical improvements. If the quantities of improvements in the capital budget do not include amounts of land required for them, the master plan has to translate improvements into area. Apart from this, they treat their common subjects differently. Where the one deals with flows of physical improvements into stock, the other deals with the stocks themselves at periodic points in time. Where the one traces the process of arriving at a certain state of physical improvements, the other depicts that state itself. In order to clarify the relationship between them, let us imagine ourselves making a map of a city showing the location and amounts (including associated land areas) of the various kinds of physical improvements now in existence. To this let us add the kinds and amounts recommended in the capital budget, and subtract whatever the budget indicates is to be eliminated. We begin to approach a master plan. The result, however, is still not a master plan. What is needed in addition, is a recommended arrangement of improvements and their associated areas with respect to each other. The master plan thus retains the balance of the capital budget and adds a new kind of balance. The two are now well related. The master plan, too, shows what functions should impinge, overlap and extend beyond the city. Hence it helps to reveal where administrative co-ordination is needed.

Undoubtedly the master plan is a necessary organizing device for comprehensive planning. But it must be flexible and susceptible to change when needed. Otherwise it may rapidly become obsolete and be a hindrance rather than a help. It can be integrated with capital budgeting, which undoubtedly is also a necessary organizing device. Whether they are sufficient cannot be known until both have been used correctly and in conjunction with each other.

CONCLUSION

In the course of this discussion I have tried to keep to the main highway of what is fundamental to planning. I have carefully avoided such interesting bypaths as the differences between urban, regional and any other kinds of planning we can think of. The similarities seem to me far more significant. We today tend to be fascinated by differences. Perhaps it is due to the high value we place on variety. Whatever the reason, if we are not to be overwhelmed by the uninformed and see unsundered chaos return, we must find structure, focus and modes of organizing the endless diversity around us. These are the fundamental aims of planning.

SUBURBS: MYTH AND REALITY

André Saumier

> Mr. Saumier is at present Assistant Deputy
> Minister (Rural Development) with the
> Federal Department of Forestry and Rural
> Development.
> This paper was written in 1963 when the
> author was Research Director of the Can-
> adian Council on Urban and Regional
> Research. The paper was presented at the
> University of Montreal as a contribution to
> the discussion on a book by Mr. Humphrey
> Carver, Cities in the Suburbs.
> Before his present appointment, Mr. Sau-
> mier held an executive position with the
> General Investment Corporation of Quebec.
> He also lectures on urban sociology at the
> University of Montreal.

The suburbanization phenomenon, like the spectre of Banquo, does not haunt us without enabling us to discern its origin and history. Purists will even assert that it is nothing recent. Weber, in his classical study of 1899, *The Growth of Cities in the XIXth Century"* [1] had already noted the population exodus towards the outskirts of several big cities at the end of the last century. And do we not have the striking example of London where, since 1861—date of the first census that can be used to this end—one notes clearly a more rapid growth on the outskirts than in the center?

The conventional trend, conventional at least in the ethnocentric out-look of American and Canadian sociologists, for the trend is not universal, (see, for example, the studies of Pierre George on the suburbs of Paris [2] and those of Dotson on Mexico [3], seems to develop in two steps that I woud like to detail briefly. First, we observe the urbanization process, typical of the nineteenth century in the USA and Canada. If we want to harden our definitions, we may say that this process has four character-istics: first of all, one notes the multiplication of population concentration points; meanwhile, one observes a constant increase in the number of in-habitants in each of these points; besides, this concentration is such that an always increasing proportion of the total population of the country or of the area being urbanized is found in these concentration points. Thus, in the USA and Canada, despite the fact the total number of urban and rural

[1] Adna F. Weber, *The Growth of Cities in the XIXth Century*, Ithaca, Cornell U. Press, 1963.

[2] Pierre George et al., *Etude sur la banlieue de Paris*, Paris, Armand Colin, 1950.

[3] F. and L. Dotson, *Ecological Trends in the City of Guadalajara*, Mexico, Social Forces, Vol. 32 (1954).

inhabitants has continually increased, we observe that since 1870 and 1871, the growth of the urban population has always been greatly superior—sometimes ten times more rapid—from decade to decade than the increase of the rural population. Finally, a fourth characteristic, as crucial as these three others, will allow us to differentiate the above-mentioned urbanization from these dense settlements in the alluvial plains of Asia: the majority, if not the totality of our urban people devote themselves to activities which have nothing to do with agriculture and production of food necessary to their own survival. We obtain thus economic dimensions which give colour and a special flavour to urban life. In brief, urbanization leads to the appearance of the city, in the noble and strict meaning of the word, in the meaning of Mumford, if you want: the city as "magnet" and "cointainer".

To this stage succeeds a second one: suburbanization, a phenomenon we all know about, sometimes from painful experience. We may define this new stage by calling on three elements, which directly affect the characteristics of organization that we have just mentioned. If we take the urbanized zone as a unit, one first notes that the population grows more rapidly on the outskirts of the zone than in its centre and secondly that these outlying areas themselves account for an increasingly greater part of the metropolitan population. These two phenomena have been known for many years. The American census refers to the notion of metropolis as early as 1910 (we will have our "greater cities" beginning with the 1931 census) and one finds out that starting with 1930, the outskirts grow faster in the United States than in the urban cores. Suburbanization also presents a distinctive economic component: one notes the appearance of a very complex division of labour inside the metropolitan area, undoubtedly bearing the stamp of interdependence, as Gras [4] observes, but mostly bearing the stamp of the central city, documented, for example, in the studies of Vernon [5] on New York.

This ecological evolution has also struck a popular note. Even though the pre-war works, such as the classic *Urban Society* of Gist and Halbert [6] have shown much insight in their descriptions and analyses of the phenomenon, nevertheless the global and unitarian concept of suburbs has become commonplace for the public and has finally—there would be a fascinating sociological study of science to be undertaken—overwhelmed the perspective, it appears to me, of the investigators themselves. This mythology has found its eloquent and caustic bards in Whyte and Spectorsky, to say nothing of our own *Crestwood Heights*.

Will I confess to you that I find traces of it in the work of Mr. Carver, particularly in his three laments: "Muddle", "Uniformity" and "What isn't there?", the eloquence and imagery of which are in no way

---

[4] N.S.B. Gras, *Introduction to Economic History*, Harper & Brothers, New York, 1922.

[5] *New York Metropolitan Region Study* (Raymond Vernon, director), Vols. 1-10, Cambridge, Harvard University Press, 1959-60; see particularly E. M. Hoover and R. Vernon, *Anatomy of a Metropolis*.

[6] N.P. Gist and L.A. Halbert, *Urban Society*, New York, Thomas Y. Crowell Company, 1933.

inferior to the ironic acidity of Whyte and Spectorsky. I note in particular two components of the myth: the suburbs would generally be inhabited by the upper social classes and, therefore, their average income would be higher than those of the core inhabitants.

Those two statements were and are still so well embedded in our unconscious concept of the suburbs that several recent books [7] and articles formally take them to task. I will point out, most particularly, a series of articles published in 1962 and 1963 in the *American Sociological Review* [8], in which the American sociologist Schnore sharply criticizes these concepts. The first article states that the thesis according to which the suburbanites have higher average earnings than those living in the central zones (this is the median earnings by family) is valid only for the metropolitan areas with a population of more than 300,000; yet the metropolitan areas having a smaller population include some 49 per cent of the total metropolitan population of the USA. The second article, more ambitious than the first one, seeks to establish a sort of linear theory of the structural dynamics—I mean the socio-economic classes— of cities. The recognized theory of the suburbs being superior to the cities they surround, from a socio-economic standpoint (based on income, education and occupation), is now greatly modified by the investigation of socio-economic data on American cities and their suburbs, provided by censuses taken between 1900 and 1960. It is clear, especially upon examination of the 1960 census, that this hypothesis is verified solely in the most heavily populated areas (i.e. over 100,000 inhabitants) and particularly for the oldest settlements. A more thorough examination shows that age of settlement is the fundamental variable accounting for the socio-economic differences between the suburbs and the urban centres. Thus, unlike the older cities, the younger metropolitan areas are concentrating their social and economic wealth in the central zone.

If I reminded you that the 1960 census has shown that the well-known negative correlation between population and fertility which has quite recently received additional documentation by Duncan and Reiss [9], has now lost much if not all of its validity, would you be inclined to come to the conclusion that the suburbanization era may be nearing its end?

Then may I say that you would not be the only ones to have asked yourselves such a question. Back in 1960, Anselm Strauss [10] published an interesting and keen analysis of the evolution of the conception of the American city through the mass media. Strauss defines three phases: the rural-urban dichotomy, the suburban-urban dichotomy and finally, rising

---

[7] See for example: B.M. Berger, *Working Class Suburb,* Berkeley & Los Angeles, U. of California Press, 1960. W. Dobriner, *Class in Suburbia,* Englewood Cliffs, Prentice-Hall, 1963.

[8] Lea F. Schnore, *City Suburban Income Differentials,* Vol. 27 (1962), *The Socio-Economic Status of Cities and Suburbs,* Vol. 28 (1963), American Sociological Review.

[9] O.D. Duncan and A.J. Reiss, *Social Characteristics of Urban and Rural Communities,* New York, John Wiley & Sons, 1956.

[10] Anselm Strauss, *Sociological Quarterly,* 1960.

on the horizon, the "strip-city", this Megalopolis which Gottman [11] has recently been heralding with hammering authority.

And in fact, the particular economic structure of the city-suburb complex, which I have already mentioned, seems to be in the process of disappearing, at least in the case of New York City. A voluminous survey undertaken by the Franklin National Bank of Long Island and published in late 1962, shows that Long Island is now an economically autonomous zone within the New York metropolitan area. The Long Islander is no longer a suburbanite working in New York and coming home at night to his dormitory-suburb; quite the contrary, he works on the Island itself, in the vast air-craft-building shops of Republic Aviation for one, and instead, it is the New Yorkers who go to work daily in Long Island. This proposition is heavily documented in the course of the survey by a series of examples that leave one wrapped in thought. You might also reflect upon the thesis that Boskoff [12] has developed in a recent work: the city and its surroundings now constitute a "super-community" and the basic analytical concept is that of the "community", made up of interdependent groups living within a given area, each having its own institutions; this thesis is also brought forth by Greer.

Allow me to draw from all this a few conclusions, though they may be slightly far-fetched, that may be of interest to Canada. I believe they are optimistic and favourable to the establishment of the "Town Centres" which Mr. Carver describes with visionary and poetical enthusiasm.

Canada is a country whose urbanization followed that of the USA, and we can state with confidence that the subsequent phase, that of suburbanization, is not as advanced here as it is in the United States. Thus, from 1941 to 1951, four of the fourteen Canadian metropolitan regions were still in the urban concentration phase, while ninety-four of the ninety-nine USA metropolitan regions had already reached the deconcentration phase between 1940 and 1950. On the other hand, our metropolitan regions generally have relatively low populations and their access to this privileged statistical status is rather recent.

Then, would it not be possible to reverse the suburbanization process, particularly its detrimental aspects: such as the decaying of the central zones and the exodus of the elite towards the suburbs? It seems to me that a rational and systematic effort towards urban renewal of the centres of our cities might have good chances of succeeding, if the hypotheses I have just outlined are correct.

I therefore yield the floor to the town planners.

---

[11] Jean Gottman, *Megalopolis, New York,* Twentieth Century Fund, 1961.

[12] A. Boskoff, *The Sociology of Urban Regions,* New York, Appleton-Century Crofts, 1962.

PLANNERS' CONCERT

Humphrey S. M. Carver

This paper is the unrevised text of the presidential address to the Town Planning Institute of Canada (T.P.I.C.), held at Halifax, Nova Scotia in June, 1964. While some of the specific references have already been overtaken by events, the issue raised—changes in the development of our cities and regions and their impact on planning practice and education, are currently of great concern in Canada, the U.S.A., and the United Kingdom.

Mr. Carver is author of several works on planning themes, including Cities in the Suburbs, *and he was Chairman of the Advisory Group, Central Mortgage and Housing Corporation, Ottawa, until his retirement in December 1967. In 1966, he was elected a Fellow of the Town Planning Institute of Canada.*

How different we planners are! Different as people and in professional backgrounds and in the kind of work we do. In our approach to community planning some are romantic virtuosos like violin players, some are technical specialists who, like the oboe player, appear but briefly to make the critical intervention, and some are good at banging drums and blowing trumpets. And yet we all manage to play in the same orchestra and enjoy an astonishing unanimity in what we want to accomplish for Canadian cities and for the people that live in them.

This diversity within unanimity, this concert of planners, is a good starting point for taking a look at the situation now faced by town planners in Canada.

Perhaps it would be too strong a word to say that the TPIC is now faced by a "crisis". Nevertheless I think it's probably true that what we do to give shape to this profession during the next year or two, may well be critical for the long future of planning in Canada. We've got to try and build a profession with new skills and very diverse talents if we are to keep out in front of rapidly changing urban technology and show the world how to build great cities. (Incidentally one aspect of this crisis is that you can't expect to keep pace with events in an organization that only meets once a year.) To explain the nature of the crisis I will try to establish what is, I believe, the logical connection between

1. Changes in the nature of town planning itself;

2. Possible changes in our own professional organization;

3. The relationship of these changes in Education for Planning.

These are the particular considerations of this 1964 meeting of the Town Planning Institute of Canada, and within the brief span of a two and a half-day conference it's not easy to grasp the connections between the different subjects of discussion.

1. As to a shift in the orientation of town planning, are we not coming out at the end of a long historic period of town planning that has been preoccupied with the aim of sorting out and separating out the constituent parts of cities? This kind of planning was a response to the confusion of the nineteenth century industrialization of cities and all the consequent multiplication and overlapping of city functions, the mixture of work-places and living-places. For more than half a century the efforts of town planners have been dedicated to cleaning up this mass mess by separating, segregating and prescribing the uses of each area of land. Town planning claimed to be scientific because it was engaged in the process of classification.

This was a complete change from the previous period dating from the Renaissance, during which planners were concerned with the classic form, the visual and symbolic arrangement of civic elements and their composition in relationship with one another. This period had its dying kick in what we call the City Beautiful and Beaux Arts schools.

But now one can perceive a third phase in which the idea of integration appears as a theme of the planner's work. This urge to integrate or weave together the fibre of the city is a response to the separation and segregation which was, in its turn, a response to the industrial confusion. In this sequence of responses we now feel the need to blend some of the elements of the city together into much more dynamic and lively compositions.

I'm sure you will recognize what I mean by this. But let me cite a few examples:

(1) There is the obvious example of the great central-area developments like Place Ville Marie in Montreal and the proposed Cornwallis Centre in Halifax and a number of comparable schemes in North American cities. Here is an entirely new and exciting aim to put together into single integrated compositions a whole range of city functions including offices, hotels, shops, theatres, restaurants, car-parks, and all the supporting arrangements for traffic and communications. The imagination and the enterprise and the planning that have gone into undertakings of this kind belong in a sphere of thought quite different from that of the separating, segregating land-use planner.

(2) Then there is that interest in the diversification of housing that was partly stimulated by the Jane Jacobs attack on planners and their segregationist effects. Instead of acres of housing stripped of all the supporting apparatus of life and its social relationships there is now a move to build into apartments and housing groups things like restaurants and

shops and swimming pools and clinics and professional offices and other features that add to the pleasure and convenience of living. This is integration in contrast with the sterilizing effect of land-use segregation.

(3) In the field of urban renewal we are trying to move away from the crudities of "Projectitis", the phase in which planners aimed to remove slums and put back big segregated chunks of public housing. Planners are disenchanted with this process and now hope to remould the existing city with a much more sophisticated blending of the old and the new, perhaps with diversity of economic classes side by side, with high-rise and low-rise building forms and some flavour of the character of the old city, in its streets and architecture and smaller open spaces. This is the integrating spirit of the new amendments to the National Housing Act with money provided for rehabilitation and conservation as well as for clearance and rebuilding.

(4) I must mention my favourite subject: Cities in the Suburbs. This is the idea of grouping together the principal social features around which suburban communities gather—the shops and schools and churches and recreation centres and libraries and parks—to form the nuclei for new suburban development, as the centres of the British New Towns form the nuclei for those satellite communities. For this purpose a suburban town centre site should be reserved for an integration of community uses, blended into a total composition in the same sense in which my first example (of the Place Ville Marie type) is a blending and integrating of centre-city functions.

(5) Then there is the very interesting prospect of reorganizing the distribution of population and community services within non-urban regions. In regions of the Prairie Provinces and of the Maritime Provinces, where populations have been scattered in agricultural and forest and fisheries employment, how can these areas now be focused upon regional centres that can provide community services comparable with those available to city people? Here, at a regional scale, it is necessary to bring together the equipment for higher education, for hospitalization and health services, for shopping and for the housing of old people. This might well be one of the most exciting prospects for planners—in Newfoundland, in New Brunswick, Quebec and Saskatchewan.

(6) And as a final example of integration, what about the future prospects of the new clean automated industries that are as sanitary and wholesome as the refrigerators in our kitchens and the TV sets in our living rooms? In response to the dirty behaviour of industry in the coal and steam era we separated and segregated work-places from living-places. But now a number of industries are as immaculate as the original suburbs and have an amenity value in their cosmetic architecture and dainty landscape that most of us can hardly live up to.

2. In what way could this new orientation of town planning affect our views about the planning profession and about the organization of the TPIC?

Perhaps it is true that these examples of integrated planning are only incidents within the general framework of a city plan and that it will always be the principal business of town planners to set out this general land-use structure, in some kind of master plan to guide the direction and intensity of development. But once these general structural plans have been laid down perhaps the process of integrated development will really be the main job of planners. If members of the TPIC are going to be the "in" people on this process they will have to be more specialized in their skills, far beyond the simple procedures of determining land use. There will have to be market analysts to validate the proportions of the diverse elements in the various kinds of integration or "mix". There will have to be urban designers and housing specialists and people with knowledge of recreation and community facilities and a great deal of know-how in traffic and transportation systems. In the language of the Willis Report there may have to be far more planning "specialists" in proportion to the number of planning "generalists".

Now we're not a very large urban population in Canada to support a force of planning specialists. So if we're going to try and do a sophisticated job of city-building in Canada we will have to regard the whole country as the professional market area in which such people can make a livelihood and a career. We've got only half-a-dozen large cities and a dozen middle-sized cities in which to accumulate technical experience. In Canada there are few enough top jobs in the general direction of planning, not so many more second and third echelon jobs and only occasional opportunities to assemble teams of experts.

If this is a correct view of the situation it's clear that we've got to work for a "common market" for planners in Canada. We simply can't afford to chop up Canada into a lot of little market areas with professional tariff boundaries between them, if we're going to try and move out of the "land-use segregation" period of planning and enter a new "integration" phase. Canadian planners must be able to regard the whole country as their universe of professional advancement and opportunity. We ought all to have a passing knowledge of all Canadian cities, sharing and accumulating our collective experience. That's why we need a national organization and that's why we are holding this meeting in an important Canadian city, instead of withdrawing to a rustic retreat as we have done for so many of the annual conferences of the TPIC.

As a national institute we are now presented with a crisis by the appearance of separate provincial bodies to give statutory recognition to the professional status of planners. We appreciate the motives of those who have run for the cover of this kind of legal protection of planners in Quebec, in Saskatchewan and wherever else this problem has been discussed. But obviously we have to be extremely careful that we don't buy this protection at the cost of something far more valuable : the opportunity to develop in Canada a substantial professional force of diversified skills that can be brought into action in all parts of the country and that couldn't exist without this national field of practice.

I'm sure that the protection of provincial statutes and the existence of a national organisation and a "common market" are not mutually exclusive benefits. Our difficulty in this dilemma is that we need not only statesmanship and common sense in the TPIC Council and the provincial groups, but—what is harder to get—it will require many tough hard man-hours of work to engineer the compromises, if we are to avoid being chopped up into a lot of little compartments. Unfortunately, we are all busy, income-earning people. It is extremely difficult to find the time and the money to gather one meeting of the TPIC National Council. It is hard to be statesmanlike without money or time. This is the toughest problem for an incoming President.

If you can accept my general proposition that there will have to be a greater diversity of specialists within the family of planners you might agree upon two major policies for professional organization :

(1) To support a professional market for planners in general and for specialized planners in particular, we must be able to cross the fences of provincial protection.

(2) We ought to recognize a diversity of special qualifications for admission to membership in TPIC, beyond the qualifications of the generalist planner who can claim to be a candidate for any middle-of-the-road planning job.

I think you will have to agree with me that it would be much easier to deal with the qualifications of specialists to enter a single national organization than it would be to write the terms of this diversity into ten provincial statutes. This leads me to wonder whether we could work out a two-storey form of membership, in which the provincial recognition was applied only to the generalist planner who would thus qualify as a full member of TPIC—and that the various forms of specialist could be recognized as associate or affiliated members of TPIC; they might also carry on their professional titles the indication that they were architects or urban-design planners, or that they were economists or traffic experts or resource specialists. In this way they could be active and valued members of our planning fraternity without becoming involved in the difficulties about the right to "practise" planning in the general sense.

3. I now turn briefly to the third aspect of this whole subject. How does education for planning fit into this new orientation of town planning and into the future form of professional organization ?

The first thing to be said on this subject is that there has been an extraordinary advance in our educational position, corresponding with the rapid growth of the TPIC itself; in a few years we have grown from a scratch collection of about 100 members into a substantial professional body of about 500 members. Only a few years ago our university courses were cliff-hangers, clinging rather desperately and precariously to the outside edges of university establishments, and we were using CMHC* fellowships to recruit a handful of people into one-year courses. Now

---

* Central Mortgage and Housing Corporation.

there is a total enrolment of about eighty in the graduate schools, most of them proceeding through two-year M.A. courses and amongst them some people of first-class academic record.

Four years ago, in 1960, the TPIC held its annual meeting in the University of Montreal to encourage the founding of a new school. After some of the painful experiences of birth-pangs and infancy, this school is now a going concern with a full two-year graduate course which is attracting some first-rate people. We all hope this school is going to make a tremendous contribution to the exciting social revolution and urbanization that is taking place in Quebec. Our best wishes go to the Director, Mr. Alaurent, and to our friend Benoit Begin, for the future success of this great undertaking.

This is the occasion also to congratulate John Dakin on the establishment of the two-year M.A. course at the University of Toronto. By any reckoning this is now one of the biggest planning schools in North America and, with this opportunity for a higher level of scholarship, it is no doubt going to win laurels as one of the great planning schools.

Meanwhile UBC, the first Canadian school to establish a full two-year M.A. course, continues to attract excellent students who are taking their place in our Institute and in planning jobs.

Harold Spence Sales is the pioneer of Canadian education for planning and his school at McGill and the subsequent developments at Toronto, Manitoba and UBC all grew up without any formal connection with the TPIC. It was not until Professor John Willis conducted his Inquiry last summer (his report has now been published) that there was any attempt to bring about a confluence of these two parallel developments—the growth of an educational system and the growth of a professional organization. The immediate practical outcome of Professor Willis' report was a confrontation meeting held in February 1964, at which for the first time the Council of the TPIC met the heads of the five Canadian planning schools for a two-day seminar discussion in Massey College, Toronto. The discussion to take place at this 1964 Annual Meeting is a continuation of this same dialogue.

In the concluding section of his Report, as the first item in a list of "highlights", Professor Willis says : "I have noted in several connections the dual loyalty that these schools, being both university schools and professional schools, owe. I assume that the universities, the schools, and the profession will continue to respect both the 'university idea' and the 'professional idea'! He explains this in greater detail on page 11 of the Report. "The interest of the university which is in 'educating' planners, lawyers or doctors or engineers or architects and so on, is always and inevitably opposed to some extent to the interest of the profession which wants 'trained' graduates. Whether you call this conflict 'theory versus practice' or 'principles versus technique' or 'Lady Why versus Madam How' does not matter—for the conflict is there and it is a real one."

Now I don't want to anticipate this afternoon's discussion; I only want to complete the circle of my line of thought about the reorientation of town planning and the consequent direction in which the TPIC might shift its form of organization and membership. This line of thought leads to some possible conclusions about educational policy.

(1) On the professional training or "technique" side there is a case for strengthening the common elements or "core" subjects in the curricula of the five schools, having in mind that graduates are being prepared to work in all parts of Canada, as the common market for professional careers. (Toronto and UBC graduates are just as likely to get jobs in the Maritimes or in the Prairies as in their original home territory.) With this in mind, could the schools and the TPIC get together to work out some written text material that would be available in all the schools, as the basis for teaching technique and practice? I picture a series of technical papers that would accumulate in loose-leaf form and be changed from time to time, in the light of new legislation and the introduction of new techniques.

This core of material on planning practice would not in any way trespass on the academic or "educational" freedom of universities in dealing with theory and principles.

(2) Then there is the question of specialization. To some extent specialization will arise out of the somewhat different emphasis in each school, even though they are all turning out what they regard as planning "generalists". One school is likely to be stronger on the economics and resource side and another stronger on engineering or design. This is presumably a good thing and helps planning directors in looking for staff to round out the specialisations in a planning team.

However, in using the expression "planning specialist" I think of people who have made a more intensive and concentrated study of some particular sector of planning work. The so-called "expert" in transportation or market analysis or urban design has usually achieved that reputation through a series of jobs he has done; and usually he is not a person who started with professional training in planning. I am suggesting that we need to draw from within our own professional ranks some people who can be both planners and experts. This might be done by a system of more intensive specializations within the universities. Perhaps it is most likely to occur through the development of university research programs that deal with "special" subjects and so produce some real technical experts among planners.

(3) As as special item among specializations I would like to note specially the field of "urban design". If I am at all right in my idea about "integration" being the theme of reorientation in planning, then obviously we are going to need many more planning designers than planning policemen. Somehow we must bring it about that the people who are going to do the design work, in the important process of city integration, are in the same camp with us planners. We don't want to find that all the creative work is done by another profession and that members of this Institute are simply cast in the role of policemen and administrators who are always thwarting the imaginative aims of urban designers.

Finally, may I return to the observation that we have a crisis on our hands. Fortunately it's a crisis in strength, optimism and riches rather than a crisis in weakness and poverty of resources. The facts are that we're in for another great surge of urban growth, but this time we have an established force of 500 trained town planners and behind us we have a really superb opportunity for intellectual strength in our five university schools. Nevertheless it's a crisis because our Institute is threatened with provincial balkanization, our schools have not worked out any scheme of co-ordination and the ordinary Canadian costs of communication make it extremely difficult for our members and councillors to meet and take action.

3. Land, as Resource and Space

"RESOURCES FOR TOMORROW", THE BACKGROUND PAPERS

John Dakin

> *Professor A.J. Dakin is Head of the Department of Urban and Regional Planning, University of Toronto. He is a former Assistant Provincial Town and Regional Planner in the Provincial Administration of Natal, South Africa. Dr. Dakin has a special interest in inter-disciplinary work between the social sciences, planning and building. He has undertaken studies on housing conditions in Ontario, and is at present engaged on a study evaluating planning in Metropolitan Toronto. In this review paper, Dr. Dakin presents an evaluation of the studies that were prepared as background to the "Resources for Tomorrow" conference, 1961. The conference was a country-wide assessment of the role of renewable resources in Canada's development.*

The preparatory papers of the Conference are impressive in their bulk : 1,061 pages; 80 papers ammounting to 850,000 words.

At ten dollars these paper-backed volumes will find a place on many bookshelves in Canada and elsewhere. They present a sustained and successful attempt to bring together the work of many experts in widely different fields, making available a synoptic view of resource problems for those varied interests concerned to record, assess and act in the complex operation of resource development.

Some will read the whole. Others, probably the largest group, will pick out those subjects which are their special interest. Yet others will use the volume only for reference.

Perhaps the most valuable service this assessment can perform is to address itself to the last two categories of reader. I shall therefore attempt to give description and comment on the various sections, and evaluate from the point of view of the planner.

THE HISTORICAL PERSPECTIVE OF THE CONFERENCE

This is the title of the opening paper. It contains so much contextual material important to an understanding of the present Canadian approach to resources that a very brief resume is essential.

The Conference was called to deal with *renewable* resources. In North America the key idea in the approach to resources has been that of conservation—understood as the efficient use of renewable resources without despoliation. The motive of conservation, and therefore of an enquiry into renewable resources, is strictly the wise economic use of the nation's substance in productive long-term development : resource management in face of the threat to the supply of the resources.

Toward the end of the last century the impact of human activity on forest and water began to cause alarm. Theodore Roosevelt called a conference in 1909 to discuss a conservation program for Central and North America. In Canada the first Forestry Convention had been held in 1906 when the relationships between forestry, agriculture and irrigation were discussed. Canadian thinking had therefore been stimulated toward conservation before the 1909 American Conservation Conference opened. This conference agreed on principles to be used in approaching problems of public health, forests, waters, lands, minerals and game.

The Canadian Commission on Conservation was set up in 1909 with the aim of protecting renewable resources by sound conservation practices. The Commission had committees for: forestry, lands, fish and wildlife, water, minerals and fuels, and public health. It paid attention in its studies to urban and rural planning and brought Thomas Adams to Canada. Its most important contribution was in the ecological emphasis it gave to subsequent Canadian thinking in stressing the need to respect the natural balance of resources and the necessity of looking at all resources together as a single complex problem. The Commission was disbanded in 1921. Effective liaison between the many agencies working in resources died with it.

The Prairie Farm Rehabilitation Act of 1935, the next important step, dealt with forest, soil and water resources, aiming to promote greater efficiency, economy and diversification in farming practice. The Second World War had its effect on the working of this Act and in 1943 the Advisory Committee on Reconstruction was set up to study all aspects of the socio-economic life of Canada. The resources subcommittee of this organization proposed the establishment of a National Development Board, and urged that conservation measures be taken to protect the renewable resources. A Dominion-Provincial Reconstruction Conference, held in 1945, endorsed the idea that the Federal Government should be responsible for basic surveys and research on a national scale for "the conservation, development and management of natural resources".

THE AGRICULTURE AND WATER PAPERS

Agriculture

Five of the twelve papers have interest for the planner : those covering demand and supply, the *Appraisal of Canada's Land Base for Agriculture, Land Use Planning and Development,* and *Resource Adjustment in Agriculture.*

"Agriculture can expect in the longer run to enjoy the almost forgotten privileges of an expanding industry." But coupled with this is a warning that the next ten years will probably be difficult. There is stress on the danger of increasing agricultural productivity faster than domestic and export demand. "The harmonization or meshing together of national policies of production and marketing and international programs of distribution and economic aid is the great problem of agricultural policy which will challenge the ingenuity of the policy-maker in the years ahead." Implicitly rather than explicitly these papers bring out the need for adequate planning at all levels of government : that national economic planning must be properly related to regional land-use planning.

The present trend toward regional specialization in agriculture coupled with a tendency toward fewer and larger farms will reduce the farm labour force to half a million by 1980, producing a major problem of employment for the surplus farm population who must become part of the urban two-thirds of all Canadians.

Land Base for Agriculture gives the planner a useful overall picture. The total land acreage of Canada is 2,272 million acres. Of this two-thirds is too cold for agriculture and 100 million acres is improved. The census figures show a steady rise in improved land but this is diminishing in the East to the gain of the Prairies, where the future agricultural development is expected.

Two very important factors are stressed in the study on *Land Use Planning.* First, that there is a need to correct mistakes made earlier by way of faulty land settlement : to see that land is indeed used efficiently for the benefit of the whole economy .... "the co-ordination of detailed objective studies of the economic and institutional forces which are primarily responsible for the determination of land use". Secondly, there is the vital importance of land-use planning *before* any contemplated development takes place, and therefore the indispensability of adequate study. This is an agricultural expert speaking, not a planner.

Placed in the agricultural group, this paper gives the impression of suggesting that land-use planning is an agricultural matter. Land-use planning and development should always be understood to embrace all uses to which we put land, and future governmental responsibility must be for all uses. We should no longer be thinking of land settlement, but in terms of full regional development.

The truncated view of land use perhaps stems from the fact that responsibility for national resources is scattered in ten or more Federal departments. The *Resources Adjustment* paper points out the importance of fitting the various responsibilities into a workable organization which will include adequate Federal-Provincial co-operation. Although the management and sale of national resources is a Federal responsibility under the B.N.A.*, in practice resources adjustment depends on Provincial machinery created for land management. The paper goes on to stress the need to recognize in legislation and administration the advantages of multi-use development based on the river basin as a major element in the organization of resource adjustment, and underlines the need to adapt the present assortment of legislation to this end.

In addition to the five papers mentioned, the *Social Effects of the Evolution of Canadian Agriculture* should have notice because there is so little sociological study of this kind. The paper applies values other than economic efficiency standards, even daring to suggest that perhaps some farmers ought to be kept on the land although inefficient, and that we should control the evolution of our agriculture, centering our policy on social rather than on predominantly economic considerations.

Water

Water as a Basic Resource, and *Water Management Problems and Issues* are of interest to planners. The first of these contains useful maps and tables; the second stresses the regional basis of water management and the importance of recognizing the river basin as the basic unit of planned development. The writers suggest that multi-purpose action in basin development should be undertaken by both Federal and Provincial governments. Illustrating from recent British Columbia experience, they stress that no agency has the responsibility for assessing the various alternatives so that maximum long-term benefits can be assured. Clearly the planner has a most important role to play in this context.

The paper on the *Administrative Framework for Water Management* contains comprehensive graphs of the distribution of responsibility for management.

Perhaps the most valuable paper for the planner in this group is *Objectives and Organizational Arrangements for Multi-Purpose Development and Management*. This important paper has the excellent feature that it takes into account the basic facts of cultural and technical change and attempts to predict their effects on water development, the authors carefully considering the likely effects of the increasing importance of leisure, education, recreation, etc.

Predictions concerning the nature of the emerging society, and therefore of the kind of life people are going to live, are conspicuously absent from these papers. We have here quite starkly the difference between the planner and the technical expert. It is the planner's specific contribution to be aware of all the factors in his attempt to meet the predictions of the experts. That is why, in the long run, we may question whether successful

---

* The British North America Act, Canada's Constitution.

river basin development can be achieved by a water agency. Must it not be done by a planning authority capable of taking into account all the factors: use of water, land use, degree of urbanization, communications, likely cultural pattern and developing technology? It is these last two items which will make increasingly unworkable the single viewpoint approach, whether via water, agriculture, mineral extraction or urbanization.

Benefit-Cost Analysis and Project Evaluation is a useful follow-up. Describing the process, it draws attention to the problem of choices at national level. This is a tool which planners will be using with increasing frequency.

The next group of papers gives examples of river basin development in Canada, the *St. John River Basin, Multi-Purpose Development of the Fraser River,* and the *Water Resources of the Nelson River Basin.* These are of general interest.

Ontario's Experience with Conservation Authorities is of interest to planners. The paper describes the organization and financing of an authority, its aims in terms of land use, and water management. There would appear to be a good field for comparative research here.

FORESTRY, FISHERIES, AND WILDLIFE

The papers dealing with these subjects and those on recreation, comprise the second volume.

There are nine papers on forestry covering *Demand Prospects, Potentialities, Multi-Purpose Use, Management of both Public and Private Forests, Taxation and Tenure, Research, Development of Forest Industries,* and *Policies Review.* I have to confess to not reading them all; this in no way reflects on the quality of the papers but only on the stamina of your assessor.

In 1959 Canada produced 55 per cent of all world newsprint excluding the Communist countries, the forest industries accounting for the largest class of Canadian exports. The market is expected to grow but the need for competitive production is stressed. The potential of the land under forest is about four times the present output. This lack of impetus in the industries dependent on forests is apparently due to Canada's high-cost economy.

The paper on the multi-purpose use of forest areas stresses the importance of safeguarding the economic value of forests whilst at the same time allowing forest areas to be used for recreation to an increasing extent. Careful planning and new agencies for co-ordination of effort will be necessary to interlock the demands of wildlife, fish, expanding agriculture, and recreation.

Development of the Forest Industries is of interest because of the changes that have taken place in the post-war period. Regional relationships are particularly significant and so is the fact that the one-time advantages of Canada in the forestry products field can no longer be regarded as automatically present in any given situation.

"The fisheries will no longer play a leading and active role in Canadian economic development" is a provocative statement. To a layman, it seems a curious irony of the human situation that perhaps half the world starves, whilst the other half cannot make it worthwhile to continue to harvest the sea. The comments in the *Role of the Fisheries in the Canadian Economy* bring out the extreme complexity of the physical and cultural environment of the fishing industry. The fisheries group contains papers covering the economic role of the fisheries, the *Demand Outlook, Productive Capacity, Effects of Man-made Changes on the Environment of Fisheries, Survey of Legislation, Research, Extension Work in the Atlantic Fisheries,* and the *Management of Atlantic Salmon.* These papers would make valuable reading for those concerned with areas dependent on fishing. A paper on new ways of using the sea for food production could have been usefully added.

The wildlife papers have a pleasant flavour of releasing us from the normal constraints of the work-a-day world, and make pleasant reading. I suppose most planners feel a little indulgently toward this subject, or perhaps it is that people who devote their lives to trout or moose are a special breed.

The hunting pressure is increasing faster than the human population, and there will be heavier demand for day-use recreational activity in relation to wildlife. There is useful information about who hunts and who fishes: over twelve years of age 10 per cent of the population hunts and 18 per cent fishes in the U.S.A. Canadian hunters spend annually about $100 million.

Wildlife in Perspective relates factors of this kind to the emerging cultural pattern of our society and shows that we must expect a demand for activity related to wildlife of an order far beyond our present thinking. This paper is one which all planners should read.

Other papers—*Economics of the Fur Industry, Legislative and Administrative Limitations on Wildlife Management, Problems of Management, Research, Migratory Waterfowl, Pesticides,* and the *Policy* are for the specialist. *Wildlife as a Recreational Resource in the Atlantic Provinces* is a straightforward statement of the facts in a specific area, with suggestions for improvements.

RECREATION

"Canada is unique among western nations in its failure to give positive guidance and support to a national policy of recreation." Sad. "In our development of work and destructive potential we outshine every civilized era in history. We are the great creators of leisure. We must now face the task of creating a capacity to use that leisure." *The Social and Cultural Aspects of Recreation,* a stimulating paper informed by a broad concept of what our life could be, makes some tart remarks about addressing ourselves to leisure with the same degree of light-hearted gaiety we bring to Monday morning, and stresses that we are not paying enough attention to recreational requirements in the next decade or so. Most planners would find this paper informative and stimulating.

Culture and Recreation in Montreal is a lively account of the city's efforts to provide cultural activities for the citizens and the citizens' children. *La Roulotte*—a mobile theatre in which children act—sounds particularly intriguing. The city spends $1.5 million on recreation, devoting $100,000 of this to cultural activities.

The Forces Shaping Demand for Recreational Space in Canada is an important paper. Demand is growing very fast because of rising personal incomes, greater leisure and mobility, and the increase in population. Not only are cities going to gobble more land for immediate accommodation but they will make heavily increasing demands on the neighbouring and distant countryside for outdoor recreation. Land is limited but the demand is not. The great lack of research is pointed out, particularly in terms of the prediction of demand. The 1985 mean use of some Canadian areas of recreation may be 18 times that of the 1955 figure. Some areas in the U.S.A. will have an increase of 30 times. The Canadian rate of annual increase of attendance at National Parks is 12 per cent. Planners should read this paper.

Assessing and Allocating Renewable Resources for Recreation contains a statistical statement of the problem and analyses the reasons why we have given over so little land to recreation on a public basis. The Federal and Provincial public developments are carefully evaluated. There is much useful information of a specialized nature in this paper, as there is in the paper *Reservoirs in Recreation* which stresses the importance of planning the recreational side of reservoir development from the start and with high status. All water engineers please read.

Recreation loses out when in competition with other land uses. *Problems and Techniques of Land Acquisition* points up this problem, noting that Canada has almost no tradition of public rights of passage over private land and suggesting that it is perhaps time to develop a tradition of this kind. This paper reviews the present procedures for the reservation of lands for public purposes, the recapturing of private lands, the winning of parklands through development control, and the provision of public access to water. It is a useful synoptic contribution to a subject which must inevitably become more pressing on all planners, urban and regional.

The social planning aspects of recreation are dealt with in the *Organization of the Field of Recreation in Canada;* and *Tourism in Relation to Natural Resources* draws attention to the rising importance of this activity.

The Hierarchy of Government and Public Agencies in Park Development tells how parks are administered, and shows how there are difficulties because of lack of definition of function between the various tiers of government. Difficult as the provision of municipal parks is because of financial problems, local government attitudes and Provincial policies, it is in the sphere of regional park provision that our greatest deficiencies lie. The need to relate recreational programs to other programs is stressed and the paper makes a plea for a clearer definition of all regional functions and for the setting up of a second tier municipality responsible for regional planning.

The papers on recreation offer much of interest to the planner. Read as a group, they suggest that we are probably not taking the coming recreation explosion seriously enough. New York State has recently approved a $75 million bond issue for land acquisition for recreation.

THE REGIONAL PLANNING PAPERS

The stage is set with the *Regions of Canada and the Regional Concept*. Beginning with a brief discussion of the characteristics of a region and the methods of procedure, the authors offer a regional analysis based on a resources approach. Population and settlement patterns are a major factor for the delineation of regions since human beings have created regions by congregating closely together or by settling areas thinly. Regions, so delineated, are primary to the Canadian scene and are notable for their dynamism and tendency to rapid change. Because of the great importance of this analytic method of approach the paper could with advantage have been expanded with a statement of the resource characteristics of the regions.

The analysis by *topographical* criteria gives the Cordilleran, Appalachian, Innuitian (Ellesmere to Prince Patrick), the Interior Plains (between the Shield and the Cordillera and reaching up to the Arctic Ocean), Great Lakes-St. Lawrence Lowlands, Hudson Bay Lowlands, and the Arctic Lowlands.

The next analysis is *climatic*: tundra, subarctic, temperate, the humid micro-thermal of parts of Ontario and Quebec, mountain climate in the West and so on. There follows a grouping by soils and vegetation.

This leads us to the *geographic* regions. Using all the factors already mentioned the attempt here is to delineate on the basis of distinctiveness and homogeneity: the Arctic, Yukon Basin, Mackenzie Lowlands, Central Forest Region, Pacific Transitional Zone, Western Transitional, Eastern Transitional, Southern British Columbia, the Prairies, Great Lakes-St. Lawrence Lowlands, and the Gulf.

A strong plea is made for an improved statistical base for resource information, so that data can be related to the homogeneous geographical regions. Given an improved basis, it would be possible to use the data for input-output relationships between the factors within a region and between region and region. This is the key to an intelligent long-term appraisal program for Canadian resource development and the paper gives the criteria for such a system.

The paper cites the advantage of the U.S.A. State Economic Areas and suggests that we could have about 400 such divisions in Canada, geared statistically to the geographic regions, Census Districts, etc. The problem is how to reconcile the structural (geographic), and the legislative and functional (economic) elements in a regional delineation. Clearly the efficient use of resources and the satisfactory working of the political-administrative unit depend on the efficiency with which the region can be delineated.

Few attempts have been made in this direction. The units in use now reflect the Economic-Administrative Zoning of Canada, 1954. They are based on the zones of the Department of Defence Production giving sixty-eight structural-functional regions (broken down into 265 smaller zones), combined for purposes of the Conference into the physiographic regions already listed.

Considerable progress has therefore been made in organizing statistical information on the structural and the functional bases. The aim now is to reconcile these, to achieve a delineation allowing resource development to be tied to regional and national programs in a meaningful way.

To the planner this is a very valuable paper for the clear way in which it states the methodological problems of the regional planner as they present themselves in the basic approaches to the subject.

Mapping for Renewable Resources is a useful paper stating the problems involved, sketching the likely demand and indicating new developments.

Regional Planning and Development makes a strong case for focusing attention on the urban-centred region, looks at the problem of goals, discusses organization, and suggests that the interlocking network of urban-centred regions may be a basis for large-scale regional programs.

The paper uses the regional structure of human settlement as its key. There are important reasons for this choice : we are most ignorant in this aspect of regional planning; there is great difficulty in gearing resource development, seen at national level, with actual detailed development at local level; as population grows in any given area it is particularly land and water which are vulnerable in their renewable capacity; it is in the region defined by the structure of human settlement that the whole purpose of resource development—the improvement of man's condition of life—is worked out.

The urban-centred region is to be regarded as the basic planning unit because it is formed by the geographic concentration of people, having personal contact and interrelations—commercial, recreational, political and social. This implies a regional community having its focus in the central city. Whilst precision of boundaries is not possible, such a region provides an opportunity for society to struggle toward an optimum relationship between community development, resources, and economic development. Examples in Canada are the Capital Region around Victoria and the Planning Districts of Alberta.

The chronological phases of regional goals are next examined : first, defensive to prevent breakdown; second, the attempt to protect land by creating a climate of opinion—a "regional morale"—to sustain land as a social value. It is pointed out with good reason that awareness of our resource base tends to diminish in proportion as the chain of dependence on technology lengthens. The third phase of goals is positive : the move to optimum resource use compatible with acceptable environment. We need a balance between our economic development and our social life and both must have reference to our resource base.

The first and second phases of goals are straightforward : traffic congestion must be reduced, the journey to work must be shortened, disorder in land uses needs correcting, land must be protected against undesirable commitment. But the third phase of goals confronts us with words like "optimum", "harmonious correlation", and a distinction between ends and means in our civilization.

The writer's brave expedition into this semantic muskeg is commendable. It shows clearly the difficulty we have in identifying the goals of positive regional planning. We must, I think, regard these words as hopeful rather than precise, because of the absence of any stated standards of values against which we can measure "optimum" or "harmonious". In a democracy "optimum" can be only in terms of efficiency in achieving what the majority want. All of which may give an anything but satisfactory regional development. And there's the rub.

Phase four is the integration of the regional plan with broader planning activity. The urban-centred region is part of a network of such regions, which must fit into an interregional framework. This implies that there must be planning at national level. A brief discussion of the organization of regional planning follows.

This paper deals with some of the toughest and ultimately most important aspects of regional planning. What is regional planning when viewed as an activity transcending the negative aim of preventing obviously bad things ? For planners this is the most important paper in the section on regional planning, for we cannot effectively press the claims of regional planning upon government unless we have clear ideas ourselves. The paper sums up our position in this regard and gives many pointers for further thought.

Trends in Industrial Location in Canada is an economist's expert appraisal of the present tendencies : the persistence of the high concentration in Ontario and Quebec; the declining density of manufacturing in the Atlantic Provinces; some decline in B.C.; the only significant density increase has been in the Prairies.

The author points out that during the last twenty years the smaller cities of Canada have, on average, grown as fast as the larger ones. Dispersion of manufacturing has taken place so that a smaller fraction is now located in the major industrial cities than before the war. Massive suburbanization of industry has occurred, but change in location over the broad region has been small. It can be deduced that a process of centralization is at work in the location of non-manufacturing city-forming jobs.

Because of the improvements in medium distance transportation the area that can be integrated into the metropolitan industrial complex has been enlarged. Therefore the smaller town tends to lose out to the larger. This is coupled with the increase in the demand for services—a process which together with the growth of governmental activity has reinforced the trend to centralization. The idea that the large agglomeration offers to industry a better hedge against the uncertainties of industrial and commercial life than does the smaller city or town is also noted.

The paper concludes with a brief reference to the difficulties of policy formulation for industrial location, the author taking the view that specialization of effort by region is the most rational form of industrial development: the specialized exploitation of the underlying economic advantage of the region rather than "buy local". The crucial factor in location is identified as the problem of encouraging industry to fit in with some pattern of overall development decided at a political level at which all factors—social as well as economic—are taken into consideration.

This is a useful paper. I would have liked more on the subject of location policy, because this is an area in which the regional planner needs much help, particularly in relation to the planned distribution of population.

The last of the general papers on regional planning—*Environment as an Aspect of Regional Planning and Development*—deals with the physical environment as a resource, the idea being that the man-made cities, towns, villages and rural areas are a renewable resource.

The factors which have contributed to the formation of the Canadian environment are briefly examined: the natural landscape, the variety of cultural backgrounds which man has brought to bear, the developed land-use pattern, and the degree to which conscious planning has been applied. The cities and towns as developed in the post-war period are seen as having failed to achieve an acceptable standard of physical environment, but it is suggested that this failure is now beginning to be critically examined.

The second half of the paper consists of a sequence of twenty-two annotated illustrations showing many Canadian scenes illustrative of the physical urban and rural environment. These form a useful collection, showing many good and bad features.

As far as the physical environment in planning is concerned, the important requirement is a statement of the criteria against which the damage, or otherwise, likely from resource development can be evaluated —an exceedingly difficult assignment, because the standards must vary according to the pressure of population, real wealth, technical ability, and the inherited cultural patterns of the society.

No doubt for reasons of space the historical formation of the physical environment in Canada is touched on only obliquely in this paper. Yet this would appear to be a very important aspect of the subject since the inherited value is built up cumulatively over the decades, thus this is a subject which would seem to be suitable for the historical method of approach.

In reading both the planning and the specialist papers in these volumes the reader not infrequently meets the notion, implied or stated, that the adequacy or acceptability of the physical environment is the criterion against which regional action is to be judged. Industry cannot be located freely according to economic requirements, but may be permitted only within the framework of a physical environment suitable for a fuller life; resource development must stop at the point where it is conceived that damage will be done to an ideal concept of physical environment.

This notion of an ideal balance between the use of resources and the adequacy of the physical environment as a concept of regional planning implies, I think, an undue restriction of aims. It smacks of absolutism in an age outstanding for its understanding of relativism, it ignores the way in which resource development is inevitably dependent on the level of technological mastery (the greater this is the greater is the freedom not to develop some resources), and it fails to take into account the declining marginal utility of further increments of adequacy after a certain level of acceptability in the physical environment has been reached. Crystallization of the physical environment at or a little above this level might be very seriously inhibiting to any society.

There is no obligation on society to get the maximum out of its resources. This is a notion characteristic of the acquisitive West. Resources are there to be used, or not, as society sees fit, and perfectly reasonable regional development can be obtained with small resource exploitation. The selection as between various resources for intensive exploitation is very important: society may elect to develop only one minor resource in an area, or may decide to exploit resources extensively in one region to satisfy needs in others—the whole point of specialization. A concept of regional planning to be valid must therefore be framed in terms of the whole social process in any given place and at any given time. For certain purposes we may agree to have the physical environment less satisfactory in the interest of winning benefits at some other point in the social process. The social environment or the pattern of culture, with its exaggerations (e.g. acquisitiveness) and illogicalities is therefore the chief area in which we must search for our goals and criteria. Even the spring mattress of a satisfactory physical environment will never confine human life, seen as a regional activity, to the Procrustean bed of optimum resource development.

THE REGIONAL EXAMPLES

The Kitimat Region, The Edmonton District, The Thames River Valley, The Lac St. Jean, The Niagara Peninsula, The Peace River Region, The Prairie Agricultural Region, The Avalon Peninsula and *The Atlantic Provinces as a Region.* These papers discuss various kinds of regions. None is an example of a regionally planned area in the full sense, but limited planning activities are described.

The Edmonton paper, which describes a city-centred multiple-resource region is important because of the positive approach to regional planning made possible by the Alberta legislation on the basis of the district. A clear picture is given of how the present regional pattern, which includes new towns, came into existence. The economic stimulus coming from oil and gas appears in the planning situation of the region, not in the light of resource use but as a series of problems, arising once removed, in the field of population and urban growth. These problems and their attempted solutions show clearly the needs for a planning agency having a role between that of the municipality and that of the province. Most planners will read this paper for its value in indicating a possible way to effective regional planning.

The Thames River Valley gives a brief description of a river valley development program based on the need to control a river. Flood control, storage dams, reforestation, wet lands management, recreation and research have been undertaken. The ways in which the provisions of the main acts, Conservation, Planning, Water Resources Commission and Highway Needs have been used are usefully described.

The project shows what can be achieved given the major impetus of the need to control a difficult river: co-operation between municipalities, collaboration with provincial road programs, control of the urban fringe, provision of recreation space and solutions for the water problems. But this must not be confused with a regional plan for the upper Thames Watershed. Perhaps it is by way of major compulsions of this kind that public opinion and governmental action will be moved increasingly in the direction of regional planning.

The Niagara Peninsula is a very substantial paper, very well documented with good maps and tables. Only 6 per cent of the land in Ontario is devoted to agriculture and this is being eaten up for urban and speculative purposes at the rate of 12 square miles a year. Careful examination of land use is imperative, and the Province (Community Planning Branch) therefore undertook a thorough study of the Peninsula: population, manufacturing, service industry, transportation, recreation, agriculture and planing organization.

A popular misconception was revealed—that the Peninsula is mostly peach trees. Actually only 5 per cent of the area is orchard. The annual value of fruit, however, is $10 million—about half of Ontario's total. Changes in the agricultural uses will not cause major change in the settlement pattern, but changes in industry will. This is important because the future of the area probably lies increasingly with secondary industry.

This regional study, while not yet leading to a regional plan, has been of great service in helping various agencies to clarify their problems. A regional development association has existed since 1957, a conservation authority since 1959, and a large part of the Peninsula is covered by a planning authority of some kind.

This type of study, embracing most aspects of the region's life, is the essential base for any serious regional planning. It is to be hoped that provincial governments will increasingly realize the importance of full documentation and that they will not wait to be driven by the pressure of circumstances before initiating comprehensive research at regional level. At its present stage, regional planning could justify itself almost entirely on its ability to record and examine the facts of regional activity.

The *Peace River Region* gives much useful material clearly stated. The aim for the region should now be the orderly development of the agricultural lands, and the realization of all its resources. This requires planning, but neither in B.C. nor in Alberta is there a single co-ordinating governmental agency for the Peace area, and conflicts between the various levels of government cannot be satisfactorily resolved. The plea is for Peace regional development comprising a development plan and a regional capital budget. The establishment of a special regional authority is not favoured, rather planning should be done through a provincial planning agency, which should be established in the Peace Area.

The author stresses that the "relationship between resource development and the institutions and policies of government requires perception and understanding of the major resource use relationship spatially", and rightly comments that although many studies are done within the framework of a region, it is rare to find the whole complex of resources treated together in the combined way required for regional planning.

The paper goes on to describe the physical setting, the past, present and future development of the region in terms of agriculture, population, oil, hydro, etc., and discusses regional planning. There may emerge a serious conflict between resource plans and city plans because resource planning, as at present practised, gives little thought to the pattern of industrial development or population settlement. The contents of the physical plan are briefly indicated and the regional capital budget is considered. The TVA independent authority method is rejected because no regional plan can in the long run be fully effective unless well tied in with the federal, provincial and municipal programs. The proposed planning agency would not, therefore, be confined to the Peace, but would cover other regions as well.

The short paper on *The Avalon Peninsula* keeps resources well in mind. This is an example of a city-centred region faced with the problem of how to promote a fuller use of the local natural resources. The present uses are examined and some suggestions such as new use for bogland are put forward. Regional planning is called for as essential to efficient resource development.

The Atlantic Provinces as a Region discusses the decline in employment requirements in the resource-based export industries of the region. New employment in service industries and construction has not been enough to counteract underemployment. The future development of the provinces is thought to depend on a further expansion of the resource-based industries but it seems unlikely that this will eliminate unemployment and underemployment. It will therefore be necessary to encourage manufacturing industry. The present condition of these Provinces points up the importance of viewing all regional development from the federal level so that differentials of development as between regions can be appreciated. This paper also shows obliquely the importance of knowing the demographic facts—a field of knowledge missing in most papers.

THE CANADIAN NORTH

Of the four papers, the first deals with *The North as a Region.* The North is a whole complex of regions; the Cordilleran, the area of the sedimentary lands, the Pre-Cambrian Shield, and the Eastern Arctic mountains. Minerals, oil and gas are examined as economic possibilities, but the extent of firm knowledge is not clear from the paper. Agriculture is described, and the forest, recreational, game and fur resources are listed. At present there is a great need of small industries to provide a cash income to the inhabitants of these areas; this will probably be met later by the exploitation of the non-renewable resources. Attention is being paid to improving knowledge on this subject including the question of adapting the methods to the cultural patterns of the people. There is a useful section on the human factor in Northern development, describing the problems of the Eskimo in transition.

Transportation is one of the most difficult problems in the North. *Transportation as a Factor in Northern Development* has illuminating things to say about the viability of the various kinds of transportation. The bulk moving of petroleum, asbestos and fish is likely to be required before 1980, and base metal transportation presents a growing challenge. North of Lat. 60° N. these will probably move by water, whilst high-value, low-tonnage materials may go by other means. There is a good description of the Mackenzie River system and the possibilities for railway development are examined. As the Alberta tar sands represent the biggest reserve of fuel in the world, railway activity in that area may expand. Highways, oil transportation and air carrying are also considered. Ground-resistance machines are thought to offer possibilities for bulk transportation, provided they can operate at costs not greater than those of trucking. It is thought they have no significant place if their costs come between those of the truck and those of the plane. Most planners would find this paper of interest.

Cultural Adjustment in Relation to Northern Resources Development, I found a refreshing paper. Why do we admit the need to call in the anthropologist when dealing with a culture different from our own, but forget him when inside our own cultural system?

The great social significance of adjustment to small numbers and mobility is stressed in Eskimo life. The new pattern may retain the mobility but will be radically different in terms of numbers. Contrary to what one might expect, the most striking adjustments are not those of man to nature but those of people meeting changing institutions. This is important because the values of the tribal society will tend to be carried over into the new urban large-scale society. It recommends that the Eskimos and

Indians should be given as large an area of self-determination as possible to help the transition.

This is a very clear paper containing much sharp observation and wise comment.

Northern Research Review and Forecast surveys the administrative responsibility for Arctic research, the personnel, the use of the research material, the finance, the research contribution by Northern Affairs, the Department of Transport, National Health and Welfare, the National Research Council, the universities, private industry, defence research and the Arctic Institute of North America.

It discusses in detail some trends in Northern research: in the physical sciences, the biological sciences, the social sciences, linguistics and oceanography. The paper concludes with a plea for an assessment of work waiting to be done, and a determination of priorities. Activities in Arctic research are unco-ordinated, and there is a shortage of both research and researchers.

This paper gives the layman an enlightening synoptic view of the state of knowledge and problems in Arctic research. It is clear that there are some extremely serious gaps such as the absence of any chair of Eskimo linguistics in Canada. It is also a most disturbing matter that the future of the Northern population is apparently being determined by present administrative policies largely formulated without basic research studies.

WHERE ARE THE RESOURCES ?

In general there is a serious lack of information about where the various resources are located. The several authors of the papers are doubtless well informed on this subject, but hardly any of them thought to provide simple maps giving this basic knowledge. An atlas of the renewable resources would be worthwhile.

Some papers were markedly deficient in maps, and many maps were reduced in scale so that the wording is difficult to read; and some maps lack any indication of scale.

PEOPLE

Many papers touch on the distribution, growth and density of population but no paper looks at resources specifically from the demographic point of view. It is understood that in preparing the framework for the papers this was considered and rejected because the size of the subject indicated it should be covered by a separate conference. If adopted, this suggestion would give the opportunity of combining demographic and social studies in relation to resources. Nevertheless in these two volumes one paper might beneficially have been dedicated to the demographic side, perhaps specifically in relation to pools of skill.

In terms of sociology and social anthropology the human being fared better. There are several papers in this field, but not enough since resource planning, like any other planning, can be meaningful only within a social framework explicitly stated. For our epoch it is of particular importance to know the nature of our society resulting from the rapid advance of our technology: what kind of a society are we expecting to be reciprocally related to our resource potential?

May we look forward to a second conference dealing with man in all his relationships to resources?

RESOURCE PLANNING AND REGIONAL PLANNING

Renewable resources have played a conspicuous role in the development of Canada and the idea of resource development and planning is well built into our society's system of values. This is not so in all countries and it may lead to a special way of approaching regional planning in Canada.

It is notable that many authors of specialist papers call for planning almost as though this were a new idea. It is good that they call for it, but the suggestion of novelty is disconcerting. It appears often not to be appreciated that the planner takes over where the agricultural, water or other specialist leaves off. It also seems that some specialists see themselves playing the planner's role. This could be dangerous.

For planners, an interesting question emerging from this material is the role of resource planning in relation to regional and national planning in the present social context. On the one hand, there is social capital in the fact that resource development and conservation have been in the public mind in Canada for a number of decades, and have therefore become accepted channels of action for certain regional purposes. On the other hand, regional planning is not well established as an accepted activity of government and there may be a danger of regional planning coming to be carried out by special interests. An extension of thinking from a beginning in conservation, for example, may be the only politically possible way of achieving any regional planning in a given area; but because of its narrow approach this is not to be accepted with equanimity. The same goes for trying to plan regionally through the operations of agricultural or water agencies. Planning for resources is to be accepted only as an activity which logically leads to overall regional planning, it being thereby made explicit that what may be best for the development of a resource may have to give way to what may be necessary, or preferred, for the good of the nation as a whole.

The planning papers would have gained by making this attitude clear, and a most important service would have been performed if a paper had been devoted to putting the contributions of the specialists into their correct perspective. Such a paper, included in the planning section, would have been of benefit to government, specialists, public and planners, and would have helped disperse the great cloud of misunderstanding about planning which hangs over many of the papers.

CONCLUSION

In abbreviated form the following points appear to be of importance:

1. There is a great deal of available information about renewable resources in Canada, but there is a very great lack of co-ordinated action at the information level among the various departments of government and among the various agencies collecting information.

2. The status and role of resource policy and development is not properly examined in relation to regional and national planning. The concept of resource planning is assumed as a value. In its present form it may be just the opposite.

3. There is much ignorance, even among experts, about the role and work of the regional planner. The erroneous impression exists that regional planning is simply one among many activities to do with resources, when in fact it is the one operation which embraces all others.

4. Regional planners must think hard about their aims, since they will be increasingly pressed by experts, whose specialities have the inestimable practical advantage of easily definable goals.

5. These papers must stand as incomplete until the compensating material in demography and the social sciences is available, because resource use depends in the last analysis on the cultural characteristics of the society.

Some of the papers are excellent; many are good; a large number are of value to the planner. A most important service has been performed in bringing together the contributions of experts in the many fields of Canadian resources. The papers which are to come will be awaited with interest and read with attention.

Those who have been responsible for organizing the writing of these papers, for ensuring their reasonable balance, and for assembling them into a coherent whole are to be congratulated on having carried out a most exacting task in a workmanlike way. They have provided a powerful stimulus to future thought and action.

RESOURCE PLANNING AT THE FEDERAL LEVEL

J. L. Jenness

> *Dr. Jenness is Chief of the Research Division, Department of Energy, Mines and Resources, Ottawa. This paper was written in 1961, in the period leading up to the "Resources for Tomorrow" Conference. It serves to give an overview of federal resource planning policies at that time, and as such fills an essential niche in Canadian planning history. At the time of writing this paper, the author was Economic Adviser, Department of Northern Affairs and National Resources.*

Planning, as we all know, has become in our society an established and recognized professional field. Individual planners come into the field along a variety of routes. An architectural background, for example, is a very frequent avenue of approach; but some planners start out in engineering; others in economics or geography or some other social science; and yet others take their preliminary training in law or public administration. Graduate schools of planning provide a sort of melting pot, out of which emerge the city and town planners, the land-use and regional planners, the highway system planners and so on. Generally speaking, the title held by a professional planner provides, even for the layman, a reasonably good idea of the kind of work that he is engaged in.

The word planning, however, also has a much broader meaning than the one customarily used by the planning profession. In a broad sense, anyone who plans anything is a planner; and any devising of a scheme of action or of procedure or of arrangement is planning. Thus, we speak of ourselves making plans for the future, for example; or of the general who plans military strategy; or of economists who plan future economic development for a region or nation.

For precisely the reason that planning means different things to different people, we have, in government at the federal level, a situation in which a great deal of planning goes on, yet little of it calls for the services of the professional planner. This is due primarily to the kinds of planning with which national governments tend to concern themselves.

A recent news despatch out of Washington will perhaps illustrate this point:

> President Kennedy has pledged his administration to carry out a comprehensive program of natural resource development and to spend whatever is justified to meet rising demands for water, hydro-electric power, minerals, and forest products. His stand

switches the emphasis from development through private enterprise (which prevailed under the Eisenhower administration) to
long-range federal planning and public development.... To lay
the ground work for long-range planning, Kennedy is authorizing
the Council of Economic Advisers to study available resources in
relation to future needs and economic growth.

Of course, a federal government's responsibility involves more than just
stimulating resource development. The government must also perform
other kinds of economic duties, as well as discharging political, social,
cultural, and other functions on behalf of the people of the country.

It must, for example, formulate and carry out plans which preserve
our national sovereignty; which protect our rights and our liberties; which
maintain and if possible improve our standard of living; which support the
aged, the sick, and those without work. At the same time, the government
is expected to shoulder heavy international responsibilities. Together with
other like-minded nations, it is constantly striving to devise some plan, some
formula, that will bring conditions of peace into our uneasy world. Without
peace, quite conceivably, not too much of anything else that is worthwhile
will survive into the future.

There are many kinds of planning going on at the federal level. In my
department—Northern Affairs and National Resources—we concern ourselves with fulfilling certain federal responsibilities towards resource management in the country at large, and more particularly, with administration
and resource development in the Northwest Territories and the Yukon. This
statement will be directed towards resources, or towards facets of government planning that bear upon resource development and management.

AEROMAGNETIC SURVEY PROGRAM

It is axiomatic that an adequate inventory of available resources is
essential to sound resource development planning. We still don't have this
inventory in Canada. The country still contains great unsurveyed areas,
particularly in the Northwest Territories and the Yukon, but occupying also
large portions of the northern parts of all the provinces outside the Maritimes. We, therefore, have only a very limited knowledge of the mineral
and other resource potential of a very large part of Canada. It is perhaps
not going too far to say that nine-tenths of the country is still inadequately
known.

The Federal Government gives a high priority to inventorying the
country's renewable and non-renewable resources, but the area to be covered
is vast and the equipment and manpower available for this purpose are
comparatively limited. Even a superficial inventory covering the whole of
our national territory is still many years away from being realized.

To help speed up the process in the geologically most promising areas,
the Federal Department of Mines and Technical Surveys recently initiated

a new program, involving aeromagnetic surveying of unsurveyed territory in the Canadian Shield. The program according to the Department,
is the largest and costliest ever undertaken on behalf of Canada's mineral
industry. It gets under way this summer, it will take twelve years to
complete, will cover an area of some 1,800,000 sq. miles, and will cost
altogether about $18 million. Two-thirds (or $12 million) of this expenditure will go towards aeromagnetic surveys in the provinces, and here the
costs will be shared by the Federal and provincial governments concerned
on an equal basis. The remaining $6 million will be used for similar surveys
in Shield areas in the Northwest Territories and the Yukon; but the cost here
will be entirely federal since resource development in the Territories remains
a national responsibility.

The governments concerned naturally hope they will uncover significant mineral deposits in the areas being surveyed. Quite possibly, their
optimism will be rewarded. It was just such aerial surveys as are now planned, although carried out on a much smaller scale, which brought to light
the Metagami base-metal deposits in western Quebec and the large iron-ore
deposit at Marmora in south-eastern Ontario. Even if the program gives
Canada no more than a picture of the mineral potential of the surveyed
areas, it will have accomplished a great deal. With reasonably good luck,
however, the survey program should be an investment with a profit. With
luck, it could have far-reaching effects upon the future development of
mining in the Canadian Shield; and by this means upon the growth and
importance of the entire mining industry in Canada.

The program was originally proposed by Mr. Comptois, the Federal
Minister of Mines and Technical Surveys, at the Provincial Mines' Ministers
Conference in Quebec City, late in 1960. It obviously made a great deal
of good sense despite its costliness, and the provinces were unanimous in
accepting it. When co-operation exists between federal and provincial
governments—as in this case—it is evident that soundly based planning and
carefully executed action can materialize, to the ultimate benefit of the
nation as a whole and of its parts.

"ROADS TO RESOURCES" AND
"DEVELOPMENT ROADS" PROGRAMS

The Shield areas to be surveyed under the new program, and the
whole of the northern Territories, are still far out on the frontier. They are,
in the main, devoid of established arteries of transportation; and they are far
removed from Canadian and foreign centres of commerce and of industry.
In economic terms, these areas still lag in development far behind the
remainder of Canada.

Distance creates frontiers. If you can somehow decrease the distances
and lessen the remoteness of the isolated North, you bring closer the day
when its resources can be exploited and when industries and townsites can

come into existence and flourish. With this fact in mind, Federal planners have long regarded transportation as the key to northern development.

The Government in Ottawa is therefore trying to break down the barriers created by distance in order to foster more rapid economic growth throughout the northern frontier. It is building ice-breakers, for example, and using them to open up navigable channels along the Arctic coastline; it is constructing airstrips strategically spaced in different parts of the North; and it is carving roads and highways through hitherto unexploited wilderness in the northern interior part of the continent. Construction will soon be started on the first railway to enter the Northwest Territories from southern Canada. Among other means of encouraging a more rapid pace of development in the North, the Government is involved in power projects, in training the indigenous people for gainful employment, in constructing schools, hospitals and townsites, and in other programs which—taken all together—will integrate this frontierland more firmly into the remainder of Canada.

Most widely publicized, perhaps, of all the Government's northern development programs are the road programs which it enunciated and embarked upon three years ago. These programs fall broadly into two categories: first 'Roads to Resources" which are being built in every province in Canada; and second, the "Development Roads" Program in the Northwest Territories and the Yukon. The formula being used, particularly in financing the roads, is rather similar to the Aeromagnetic Survey formula.

Under "Roads to Resources", the provinces take on the primary responsibility of planning, constructing, and maintaining roads which come under the program. The Federal Government, of course, conceived of the program and can take credit for so doing. Its remaining, and larger function is that of a catalyst. It has a say in what roads get built, and it pays half of the cost of these roads. By participating in this way, it encourages expenditure by provincial governments on resource roads in more remote areas.

The Federal contribution towards each provincial program is $7.5 million, conditional in each case upon Ottawa being satisfied that the proposed roads have definite resource development merit. All such roads when completed, therefore, will help to bring some kind of resource into production. This may range from encouraging tourism in some parts of the Maritimes to opening up areas of commercially exploitable timber or of minerals. Wherever possible, the program has encouraged multi-purpose roads that will stimulate interest in a variety of resources.

The Northwest Territories and the Yukon, being even more remote than the northern parts of the provinces, have a narrower range of resources that will be susceptible to early development. If any substantial development is to take place here in the foreseeable future, it must come about chiefly through exploitation of mineral and energy resources. The "Development Roads" Program in the Territories is therefore oriented primarily towards opening up the most favourable mineralized areas. Roads built under this program should, at least, lend encouragement to exploration; but those who plan them naturally hope that these roads may stimulate mine development and lead to mineral production.

In its program in the two territories, of course Ottawa must assume responsibilities which elsewhere would be shared between federal and provincial governments. It must do the planning, the engineering, and the building of the roads, and in addition, it must provide 100 per cent of the financing.

By and large, federal planners anticipate that these territorial roads will yield returns in the long term rather than in the short term. It is only being realistic to assume that the roads may at first seem less dramatically successful than some of the "Roads to Resources". However, in at least one instance already, the Government is assured that its road will bring about a tangible benefit.

A recently discovered valuable mineral property will be coming into production as soon as it becomes accessible by road and thus can commence moving its concentrates away from the minesite. This new mining property is located in the remote mountainous area on the Yukon-Northwest Territories boundary, 130 miles from the nearest surface artery of transport. The company that has examined the property has established the presence of a substantial orebody, but in order to develop it into a mine, there must be a road. Air transportation costs in the North are extremely high—in this case too high—to allow the company to reach markets with its concentrate at a competitive price.

The mineral in question is tungsten which, as you probably know, is a strategically important metal, used particularly in pure form in the electronics industry and as a high-temperature alloy with steel and copper. There are no mines producing tungsten in Canada at the present time. This makes all the more significant the fact that this prospective new mine in the Territories contains a proven tonnage of ore that is equivalent to 12-15 per cent of the known free world resources. The tungsten-bearing deposit is apparently susceptible to being mined at a rate of some 100,000 tons per year, thus giving the mine a potential life of at least twelve years even if no further reserves are discovered.

The Federal Government, earlier this month, concluded an agreement with the company concerned whereby a road will be built to the minesite on a cost-shared basis. One million dollars of private money has already been spent by the company on its property. The new road agreement will now allow it to go ahead with additional expenditures, amounting to several millions of dollars in the next two to three years, to place its mine in production. I have every confidence that there will be tungsten shipments from the Northwest Territories to overseas markets by the end of 1963, if not earlier.

As this project illustrates, the Federal Government believes it can work closely with industry when obvious benefits will accrue to both of the parties involved. The mine itself lies in a very interesting, mineralized geological area. The government naturally hopes that its road will lead to further discoveries and ultimately to the development of additional mines.

THE NATIONAL OIL PICTURE

Consideration has been given to inventorying resources and encouraging new resource development. Government planners and policy advisers commonly must deal also with problems which arise after resources have been brought into production. The well-being of the Canadian petroleum industry brings up a situation of this kind.

For several years, petroleum companies in Western Canada have been striving to find larger markets for their Alberta and Saskatchewan output. One of their major difficulties is that Canadian oil is not now competitive on world markets where it must match the prices of low-cost producers in the Middle East, in Venezuela and elsewhere. In the end, oil from our Western provinces is entirely confined to Canadian outlets or, in comparatively small quantities, to outlets in oil-poor areas in the United States close to the Canadian border. In end result also, the oil wells of Saskatchewan and Alberta are chronically producing at levels that are far below their rated capacities.

Even within Canada, Prairie oil is not able to command the whole of the market. In 1960, Canadian production of oil amounted to 518,000 barrels per day. Of course, about one-fifth, or 113,000 barrels, were exported to the United States, but an amount three times as large was being imported. 1960 imports amounted to 343,000 barrels per day, of which 260,000 or almost 80 per cent of the total, went to the eastern Canadian market centred on Montreal. All of Montreal's oil requirements are being met at the present time by imports.

Independent Canadian oil companies and the large international companies occupy quite different production and marketing positions. The latter have access to foreign as well as domestic production; also, they have a strong sales position in all parts of Canada using oil from one of their sources or the other. The independent Canadian producer, on the other hand, finds himself squeezed into a restricted marketing position and sees no prospect of escape from this squeeze as long as current marketing arrangements continue. The independents, therefore, have been clamouring for assistance; one of their most insistent requests is that the Federal Government build a petroleum pipeline from Western Canada into the Montreal area. The international companies with their present arrangements for supplying the Montreal area are quite naturally lined up against the proposal.

The Federal Government must, of course, safeguard the national interest. In this particular matter, it is obviously faced with an extremely difficult and complex problem, one that already has become strongly controversial and that could easily become more so before it is resolved.

In October of 1957, the Federal Government reacted to the then mounting national oil dilemma by setting up a Royal Commission on Energy, with Henry Borden as Chairman. The Commission made its first report a year later. Among a lengthy list of recommendations was one which advocated the establishment of a National Energy Board; and as you know, the Federal

Government has since brought this Board into existence. In a second report, the Commission gave the government its advice on the Montreal pipeline. It said, in effect, that the government should call upon the refining companies to expand their use of Canadian crude voluntarily or become liable to having an increase made mandatory. The Commission also suggested that if voluntary methods seemed to be failing, the government should then restudy the Montreal pipeline and decide whether it would be in the national interest to build it.

Since the publication of the Borden Commission Reports, a great deal of behind-the-scenes planning has been going on in Ottawa. This has included, among other things, a study of the economics of the pipeline, made by the newly created Energy Board. Then early this year—also as a follow-up of Borden Commission recommendations—the terms of a new oil policy for Canada were announced by the government.

In this new oil policy the petroleum industry is being asked to give full support and co-operation, without formal regulation, towards a Canadian production target of 800,000 barrels a day of oil and natural-gas liquids, to be attained by the end of 1963. This roughly speaking is the production total which the government believes would be realized if the Montreal pipeline were to be brought into existence.

Mr. Hees, Minister of Trade and Commerce, announced the new policy in the House of Commons on 1 February. He expressed the belief that the 1963 target could be reached if (1) Canadian oil is substituted for foreign crude in domestic markets west of the Ottawa Valley; (2) refining capacity in Ontario is increased to handle the large quantities of Canadian oil that will be moving into these areas; and (3) provided there is some expansion of export sales to present U.S. markets that are accessible through existing pipelines.

The government has instructed the National Energy Board to evaluate and report periodically on the progress being made, and upon the extent to which individual companies are co-operating, towards the attainment of the government's production target objectives. The government is now also on record as saying that if the desired results are not produced by voluntary means, further action will be taken to ensure that its policy objectives are achieved.

In the meantime, the Montreal pipeline remains in the background, shelved for the time being, but not necessarily a completely dead issue.

CANADA MINING REGULATIONS

The present situation in our oil industry points up an even larger national dilemma. Can our economic freedom and a meaningful national identity be maintained when we rely so heavily upon foreign capital in developing our basic resources and industry? Just about 65 per cent of the Canadian oil industry, for example, is now owned outside of Canada and the percentage is almost as high in mining and manufacturing.

It has become government policy to try to provide Canadians with a greater opportunity to take part in the ownership and development of the country's resources and industries. This policy is reflected in the Canada Mining Regulations passed in April 1960. In the provinces, of course, mining is a provincial responsibility and federal regulations cannot be enforced here; but for the remainder of Canada the regulations are federally originated. The Canada Mining Regulations are therefore binding and enforceable throughout approximately one-third of the total area of the country.

These Regulations have been basically revised, during the past two years, for the first time since the early 1930's. As issued in their new form they are of course designed to encourage mineral exploration and production; at the same time, they now contain features which call upon Canadian individuals and companies to assume a larger responsibility towards the development of mining. This is being done through Section 42 of the Regulations; the so-called Canadian Participation Clause, under which only Canadian citizens or corporations incorporated in Canada with Canadian ownership will be permitted to obtain a lease to hold or produce minerals. Under this clause, an individual seeking a lease of mineral rights must be a Canadian citizen; a corporation applying for a lease must be incorporated in Canada; if the corporation is private, it must also be at least 50 per cent Canadian owned, and if it is a public corporation, it must at least be listed on a Canadian Stock Exchange. Canadians must also be given an opportunity to participate in the financing and ownership of any corporation engaged in the development of minerals in areas which come under the Regulations.

Note, however, that the Canadian Participation Clause applies only to leasing. The government issues both permits and leases and the former is all that is needed to prospect for minerals or carry out exploration. Foreigners can still invest freely in the exploration stages of mining without being subject to the new Canadian Participation ruling. They may continue at this stage to enjoy any special tax benefits which they previously had. However, if an individual or a company wants to hold onto a mineral property for a prolonged period of time, or if it wants to bring it into production, then the government requires it to take out a lease. It is at this lease stage that the new Regulations insist that Canadians be allowed to participate.

The Canada Mining Regulations therefore, insofar as they apply to ownership and control, are intended to provide incentives to Canadian investors and to give Canadians more opportunity to benefit from mining operations going on in Canada. The Regulations were framed, if you like, to protect the rights of Canadians. Much early newspaper reaction has suggested that the Participation Clause discriminates against foreign companies and foreign investors. To whatever extent this may be so, it seems to me that the discrimination is being directed, as it should be, towards those foreign companies who prefer doing their business in Canada in ways that contribute little to our national interest.

DISCLOSURE LEGISLATION

This question of foreign control does not just apply to our extractive industries, but to the economy generally. It is, as you know, a subject that has generated much controversy. One reason for this is inadequate information. At present no one has enough facts to measure accurately the degree of this control. Such measurements as are possible are based primarily upon Dominion Bureau of Statistics data, supplemented by whatever can be gleaned from company annual reports and from other less readily available sources. However, there are many gaps. While much can be learned about the way some companies or enterprises conduct their businesses very little information is obtainable about others.

On February 17 of this year, the government presented Bill C-70 to the House of Commons for first reading. Its purpose is to require that more information be made available about the operation of some of the country's biggest businesses and labour unions. This is apparent from its title which reads as follows:

An Act to provide for the Furnishing of Financial and other Statistics relating to the Affairs of Corporations and Labour Unions carrying on Activities within Canada.

Under this new law, all but the smallest foreign-owned companies or subsidiaries of foreign-owned companies must divulge to the government such facts as to how much they have earned, how much they have sold, who are their directors, and how much these directors are paid.

Canadian private companies and purely Canadian unions are to be exempted from the new legislation. It is abundantly clear that the purpose of the Act is to provide the government with a precise measurement of the degree to which foreign corporations and labour unions have been and are penetrating into the Canadian economy. The objective is to have the factual basis for taking such remedial measures as may turn out to be warranted.

"RESOURCES FOR TOMORROW" CONFERENCE

This reference to future planning leads naturally to an important federal project oriented entirely towards planning for the future.

In October of this year (1961) several hundred recognized experts will come together in a national conference to discuss "Resources for Tomorrow". This is, in fact, the name being given to the conference. Its main focus will be upon methods of achieving improved management of Canada's renewable resources. It will also examine, in a general way, the kind of economic setting within which this improvement can be brought about.

There have been resource conferences held previous to this one, both nationally and provincially, but the "Resources for Tomorrow" Conference —in terms of both size and coverage—is going to be without precedent in Canada. It will also have a quite different pattern from the usual federal-provincial conference. It is not going to be a conference to which the provinces come as a group to bargain with the federal government. Instead, eleven Canadian governments will be sitting down together on an equal footing and discussing with business and with other non-governmental groups a range of resource problems in which all share an interest. Together they will be attempting to reach a common understanding on how best to initiate desirable courses of action.

A great many months of planning have gone into arranging the "Resources for Tomorrow" Conference. Out of an idea attributed to the Honourable Alvin Hamilton a Steering Committee was formed, consisting of the Federal Minister of Northern Affairs and National Resources and the Resources ministers of the ten provincial governments. The Steering Committee then got together and drew up terms of reference for a Secretariat for the Conference. The Secretariat was then formed. As one of its first steps, it assembled groups of specialists from all over Canada— "National Advisory Groups" as they were called—for a series of meetings in January and February of last year. These specialists and the Secretariat discussed how the various resource topics might be tackled at the Conference. Topics covered included water, forestry, recreation, fisheries, wildlife, and agriculture, and regional and northern development, all of which have since become embodied in the Conference program. From these Advisory Group meetings also, persons were selected to prepare background papers on specified topics, these papers, to be published before the Conference convenes and to serve as reference material for those who will be taking part.

The Conference will be held throughout the week of October 23rd to 28th, at the Queen Elizabeth Hotel in Montreal. It will be attended by invited participants from each of the provincial governments, from the Federal Government, from universities and other scientific bodies, from resource industries and from related organizations and societies.

It will consist of a number of plenary sessions, open to all participants, but the larger part of its time will be devoted to workshops oriented towards the various specified resource sectors. As each sector is to be treated from several vantage points, a great many different subjects will be involved in total, and each of these is to receive thorough discussion. Topics will include, for example, such things as river basin development, and how this development can be planned; how maximum power, recreation benefits, and water can be obtained for cities, industries, and irrigation; and so on.

All the signs point, therefore, to this being a thoroughly interesting and extremely valuable conference. It also seems virtually inevitable that a variety of follow-up programs will be planned and initiated at its conclusion.

The "Resources for Tomorrow" Conference approaches most nearly to the kinds of planning that are practised by professional planners. In fact, planners are sprinkled through the Conference's "National Advisory Groups", and they have also been invited to become participating members. From the planner's viewpoint, then, it seems to me that the Conference can be looked upon, among other things, as a sort of forum at which the Federal Government and the planning profession will be drawn more closely together. Certainly, the Conference will be devoting itself to matters in which federal interests, regional interests, and the planners' interests all overlap.

RECREATION AREA PLANNING :
SOME PHYSICAL AND ECOLOGICAL REQUIREMENTS

Eugene Mattyasovsky

Professor Mattyasovsky, of the Department of Urban and Regional Planning at the University of Toronto, teaches recreation area planning as part of his subject "Physical and Ecological Bases of Planning". This article is based on a study, sponsored by the Canadian Council on Urban and Regional Research, and conducted by Dr. Mattyasovsky. It appeared in Plan Canada *in 1967.*

SCOPE OF THE PROBLEM

Our rapidly growing cities, with their varied land use demands, create a complex planning task in the selection and provision of suitable land for these uses. "Suitable" can mean different things. The criteria used in determining the effectiveness of various uses change over time in response to changes in technology and ideals.

Among these land uses outdoor recreation is increasing rapidly in significance. The demand is growing much faster than the population because the per capita demand is also increasing. According to some U.S. experts, in twenty years from now four times as much area will be needed per capita as in 1967.

The "planning" of these areas has many aspects: sociological, ecological, economic, legislative-administrative, transportational, etc. All are important; we need the help of all of these perspectives for selecting, developing, and maintaining outdoor recreation areas.

Recent research sponsored by the Canadian Council on Urban and Regional Research and conducted by the author concentrates on the problem of "establishing physical and ecological criteria for site selection and maintenance" of outdoor recreational areas outside a city. To translate this into everyday language, the research tries to provide answers to the following questions:

1. What are the basic physical and ecological criteria for selecting and planning regional recreation areas?

2. What are the specific ecological questions connected with water?

3. What are the multiple uses? Compatibility of different uses?

4. What are the positive steps such as erosion control, flood control, preservation of vegetation covering, etc., required to be taken?

5. How to establish and maintain a so-called "partial ecological balance" or at least a "natural state" within the areas?

6. What "intensity" or "use density" of the various uses may be permitted?

As an experimental research area for studying the questions on the "ground", the outer areas of a fifty-mile radius from Toronto were selected. The existing and potential recreation areas in this belt were examined, excluding city parks, high-density use recreation areas, sports fields, and other specific recreation uses. Outdoor recreational areas of fifty acres and above in extent with at least partly natural settings and mixed active and passive uses were identified for research purposes.

The reason why this belt and this group of recreational areas were selected is that they are typically the most difficult to obtain and reserve, and the most urgently required, not only in Canada, but everywhere in the western world, since it is the population of rapidly expanding cities that have the greatest need of recreation space.

A necessary first step was to obtain an overall picture of the present situation in the fifty-mile radius belt, including the more or less accepted working assumptions of the different authorities. Unfortunately no such compilation was available in comprehensive form so a map had to be made (1:50,000 scale) showing all the land categories which have any outdoor recreational significance, such as provincial parks, "conservation areas", larger private and municipal parks, hunting and fishing preserves, etc.

The data of the map and inventory were compared with the existing and expected 1980 population. Without going into details, what is really interesting for us is the overall picture; how the existing recreation areas relate to the users and what the picture will be in 1980, adding proposed future recreation areas.

The areas used as a basis of comparison in this study did not include presently proposed lakeshore recreation developments or city parks (High Park, Island, etc.) and the Niagara Peninsula, but include the following categories with recreational relevance:

(1) existing conservation areas for public recreational use,
(2) proposed conservation areas,
(3) proposed reservoirs,
(4) existing provincial parks,
(5) proposed provincial parks,
(6) private parks (above 50 acres),
(7) municipal parks (above 50 acres),
(8) special areas with recreational significance,
(9) proposed provincial hunting areas,
(10) private hunting preserves,
(11) private fishing preserves,
(12) proposed river valley green belts,
(13) proposed public access to fishing.

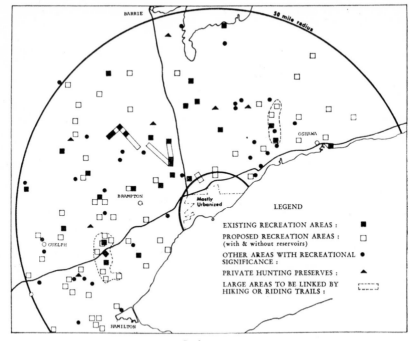

Study Areas

These areas are within a fifty-mile radius, beyond which are extensive recreational areas utilized by the same population.

The existing areas give approximately 6.5 acres per 1,000 population or 6.1 acres if Hamilton, Kitchener, and adjacent towns are included as "users". If the existing recreational areas and those at present projected are taken in relation to the anticipated 1980 population the respective figures per 1,000 population would be 11.4 and 11.2 acres.

Considering that these areas are limited to the fifty miles radius and exclude some important categories such as lakeshore development, etc., the overall picture is not altogether unfavourable. As some U.S. reports show, it compares well with that of many North American cities (Bartholomew: *Land Uses in American Cities*, etc.) and is much more favourable than that of most European and Latin American metropolitan regions.

But all this is a kind of one-sided and quantitative picture.

Admitting the importance of the quantitative side, our emphasis was on the qualitative aspects, such as:

(1) the differentiation and suitability of areas for different recreational uses;

(2) aesthetic, historic value of the land in question;

(3) physical and ecological aspects of the outdoor recreation areas.

Number (3), above, particularly interested us.

In a selected natural setting the following aspects can be considered relevant from physical and ecological points of view :

(1) size,

(2) physiography, soil, geology,

(3) water,

(4) vegetation covering,

(5) animal life,

(6) management, maintenance practices, recreational demand sought by the public, etc., as far as they are connected with points (1) to (5).

THE "PROPER SIZE" OF RECREATION AREAS

The most valuable existing outdoor recreation areas in the fifty miles radius belt are larger than 400 acres. Many are in the 400 to 600-acre range.

In a typical area in the 400 to 600-acre range 15 to 30 per cent of the total acreage is made up of more or less artificially manipulated lands, such as parking lots, headquarters or other buildings with their immediate surroundings, picnic areas, swimming pools, sport and play fields, etc. Also a characteristic feature of many of these parks is a 50- to 150-acre open area adjacent to the entrance.

The remaining and greater part is intended to be kept in its natural state, with a network of nature trails.

It appears reasonable to approach the physical and ecological consequences of the size of a recreation area by attempting to establish either a minimum or an optimum size. The minimum size would be an area where a more or less complex biological community, characteristic of the original setting, can be preserved; and optimally where this community can be preserved in a "balanced" or "self maintaining" state. Unfortunately, the term ecological "balance" may only be vaguely defined and does not answer the question of whether there should be a "balanced" state at all; the concept cannot be used at the present time as a precise basis to determine size. Where it has been determined for practical reasons (as in some cases by provincial authorities dealing with natural parks or game reserves) it was determined in a rather arbitrary way.

So our attitude should be : many different sized areas have to be accepted for practical reasons, and the ecological considerations should be adjusted to the actual size. This implies a very far-going compromise. But to create a possibility for this compromise, "ecological balance", or rather "natural state", is one of the goals of the research.

Of course, even if we accept, in principle at least, that all sizes are acceptable, there are important items to consider :

Certain 40- to 120-acre lands needed for facilities, etc., are not easily reducible, which means that in a less than 400-acre area the remaining "natural" part becomes so small that it is nearly impossible to maintain as "natural". The relative length of boundary with adjacent areas becomes proportionately so great that it is increasingly difficult to protect the land from outside threats.

With smaller than 400- to 600-acre areas it would seem better policy to change the character rather than force compliance with a general pattern of providing these areas with all the conventional outdoor recreation facilities in a reduced space. There can be exceptions in specific areas such as the Cold Creek Bog where these characteristics can be preserved even in a relatively small area. The Department of Lands and Forests also considers 500 acres about the minimum size in which an interesting complex biological community can be preserved and shown to the public, where plants with a wide variety of physical requirements can provide habitat to animals with wide territorial ranges. This is unfortunately difficult to secure in a well-settled human world, so in this belt at least, considering all factors, the more medium-sized parks serve better an overall recreational purpose than a few very extensive ones.

An immediate reaction of the reader may be that a compromise could be the answer : one or two extensive areas and more medium-sized areas. Even this is questionable as a practical possibility. Looking at the map and considering the possibilities given by nature, there are two possible areas within the fifty-mile belt, namely the Campbellville and Chalk Lake districts, where there are still extensive scenic areas, relatively undeveloped, and where the acquisition prices are perhaps not prohibitive. Even in this case the relative value of a very extensive wild land area near a city can be questionable. A reasonable policy appears to be to connect these extensive scenic areas with hiking and riding trails. Both types of trail are rather neglected in eastern Canada. The connecting can be done by buying rights from land owners of the intermediate areas. Much of the trails would go, of course, on the publicly owned recreational areas. These measures are strongly advocated in some American plans. The following areas or recreation area groups seem to be suitable for such linking :

(1) the Greenwood-Claremont-Glen Major series,

(2) the upper Humber parks (proposed and existing ones) up to Glen Haffy.

VEGETATION COVERING IN RECREATION AREAS

Usually the most conspicuous feature of an outdoor recreation area is its vegetation. In this respect the outdoor recreation areas within the fifty-mile radius belt show certain common characteristics :

1. The forested and partly forested areas appear to have been given preference in selecting areas for parks in Ontario.

2. The vegetation covering in most cases is varied by age, species of plants, percentage of actual coverage, etc. Generally the appearance is less monotonous than, for instance, in reforestation areas or in some European parks.

3. Although the plant communities in most of the areas are disturbed, they give the appearance of "naturalness" to the visitor.

4. Most of the areas contain previously cleared farm lands.

On the negative side of the picture some further observations can be made :

5. There are practically no remnants of the original forest cover of the area which might give some idea of the vegetation of the pre-colonization period. Some of the white cedar dominated areas, and some other exceptional spots can be considered the nearest to this.

6. Very few unique plant communities are contained in the existing outdoor recreation areas. Examples are : Cold Creek Park, some lakeshore sections, and marshes or "lagoons" along the Ontario lakeshore, etc.

The vegetation covering of an existing or prospective recreation area can be examined from the following aspects :

(1) general character as it stands;

(2) the interest, or "demand" of the visiting public, and its relation or effect to certain recreational uses—wildlife, fishing, hiking, etc.;

(3) management practices : possibility of manipulation; policy of management.

The first two can be seen together, or the first can be examined from the point of view of the second.

In a passive-type outdoor recreation area the public is looking for a varied, scenic vegetation which gives a natural appearance. The aim is to be "with nature" or to have the illusion of being with nature.

Varied vegetation implies variation in coverage. Open areas vary with patches of dense forest, or with scattered trees and bushes, some water-edge vegetation, etc. Differences in age and size of the trees can add to variety and scenic value. Such variety of coverage actually exists in many of our areas; the problem is one of preservation, rather than of conscious manipulation.

The case is different where previously cleared farm land is to be integrated into a recreation area; this will be discussed in the "Management" section.

Variety in floral composition also adds to the variety of appearance and general scenic value. The following objectives and general management policies seem desirable in this respect :

1. Preservation of the flora found on the establishment of the recreation area should be attempted in whatever serial stages they are found, with a minimum apparent sign of manipulation.

2. Specific consideration should be given to plants with value as food for wildlife or other unique importance for the whole ecology of the area.

3. Preferably, the introduction of too many exotic species should be avoided.

4. Specific attention should be given to strongly diseased or susceptible trees (elm, etc.) and to some water vegetation.

MANAGEMENT PRACTICES AND VEGETATION

There are different views as to the extent to which the natural vegetation should be manipulated within a recreation area.

Extreme "non-interference" can be a workable policy in certain types of recreational parks with the expressed intention of preserving a piece of undisturbed biotic community, although non-interference is an ideal rather than an achievable reality. Some compromise has to be made when human access is allowed.

In other kinds of recreational areas the degree of manipulation of the vegetation varies with the type and intensity of use.

Generally speaking, management practices regarding interference with the natural state or development of plant cover are less conspicuous in large passive types of recreation lands. On the other hand it can be rather artificial in some "high density" city parks. Some observations connected with the management practices in existing recreation areas would be germane.

The predominantly natural vegetation is interspersed with manipulated, "trimmed" sections providing picnic areas, playgrounds, etc., for the public. Though it is sometimes strongly criticized, it is a necessity and a certain degree of artificiality in appearance is unavoidable. One of the most conspicuous interferences is the establishment of lawn or grass covering with its corresponding permanent mowing. Unfortunately the public is inclined to forget that without this mowing the same area would be covered by aster, solidago, etc.—"weed" jungle in only a few years. For these areas the interference is a necessity, the only consideration being how far it should go.

Besides mowing, the use of herbicides can be questioned. This objection is sometimes justified : it depends on the kind of herbicide. Their use may have far-reaching consequences which are sometimes not fully understood. This would suggest a policy of avoiding their use as much as possible.

Another problem is the question of what to do about diseased trees and plants, parasites and plants that are harmful or not desirable from a recreational point of view. It is a subtle question, depending for an answer on how we define our goal. The standard treatments (for example, D.D.T. for elm diseases, etc.) can save the tree but at a certain expense to the whole biotic community. To define the desirability of their application is not as easy as in forestry practice. There is much to be said for the view that removal of the diseased trees rather than the saving of them by chemicals is, in most cases, the proper policy to pursue.

The removal of fallen or dead trees and branches is strongly objected to by those interested in animal life. They are important elements of the habitat. The distribution and density of certain animals is strongly affected by this seemingly simple operation of keeping the area "neat".

On the other hand, barren branches extending out of green, healthy vegetation can disturb the aesthetic and scenic value of the area, especially in a conspicuous spot. A proper compromise could be the removal of the dead trees or branches in exposed places (picnic areas, edges of open meadow), but to leave the fallen trees where they are in other places, with some exceptions for nature trails and highly used areas, or adjacent to pools and streams.

Probably the most important plant management problem is how to establish or re-establish a "proper" covering in previously cleared or other barren areas such as graded or eroded banks, etc. There are many areas of this kind and some are quite extensive. They arise from previous agricultural use, or from other sources. A policy for correcting or re-establishing vegetation covering should include the following elements :

(1) similarity or harmony with the original vegetation, "natural" appearance;
(2) fast-growing, undemanding components;
(3) variety, coverage, floral composition, "skyline";
(4) food plants for animal life;
(5) scenic value;
(6) in some cases, provision for erosion prevention;
(7) specific consideration of water and water-edge vegetation;
(8) and—where it exists—provision for preservation and accentuation of the natural historical interest of some feature.

We do not have too much experience with this kind of planting. Foresters, landscape architects, recreation area planners, can jointly work out some measures. These measures should fit the specific conditions of the area. On the other hand, if worked out individually, there will not be a widely applicable measure in all cases. The ideal solution would be to work out a few general patterns, and the choice, with perhaps some modification, would be left to the expert applying them in a specific recreation area. No such general patterns or measures were found in the literature presently available. There are proven forestry patterns such as erosion protection, wildlife cover, and landscape architectural forms, but none filling all the above requirements has yet been developed. Perhaps many of the forestry, wildlife, and other patterns should be integrated in recreation areas.

Some suggestions can be offered for achieving this integration :

1. A "natural landscape plan" should be worked out beforehand.

2. To fulfil the above plan, more expensive methods and material can be justified such as (1) use of trees or bushes of more advanced age at transplanting; (2) soil cultivation, fertilizer application, irrigation or other cultivation practices should be considered, of kinds normally never used in typical extensive forestry practice, because of much higher initial costs. The application of other cultivation methods would accelerate the growth rate of trees.

ANIMAL LIFE IN RECREATION AREAS

The questions connected with animal life in the existing parks can be discussed from the following aspects :

(1) faunal (species) composition;

(2) their permanency in the area (permanent, transient, migratory; etc.);

(3) their ecological role, density, fluctuation;

(4) habitat and other factors affecting their existence, natural and man-made;

(5) desirable policy of management (to encourage, discourage, their increase or presence, and with what measures);

(6) game animals.

The composition of "species present" is the easiest and most frequently found "check list" in the published conservation studies. This check list sometimes also briefly refers to permanency or migratory habits, etc. We never know how reliable these lists are. Are they really checked or is this just a list of animals that "should" be there ?

The "check lists" give an interesting but limited picture of animal life. We are equally, or even more, interested in their relative density, and their role in the biotic community. Also very interesting, for the same reason, is the role of some prominent insects or other "lower" animals.

The ecological role, density, and fluctuation, of numbers of different animals in our parks is to be viewed for our present purpose as an animal ecologist sees them but modified with some comments on the recreational aspects. In other words, the park can be viewed as a piece of undisturbed nature—actually this is what the visitor seeks—or if disturbed, the degree and direction of disturbance may be acknowledged. Some of these disturbances are unavoidable for the maintenance of our parks but fortunately can be managed in a way that does not appear "disturbed" or "unnatural".

The most important representatives of animal life in the parks are the "small" animals. They are present in the greatest numbers and it is easy to interfere with their density, at least with small mammals, but this is less true with birds.

There is very strong interest in the larger animals—the deer—on the part of visitors. Unfortunately, they are, in many cases, transient.

The role of the nature trail is partly to give an opportunity for animal watching. The opportunity for the visitor to watch animals is much less than their actual frequency or density would suggest. Only diurnal animals can be observed by the average visitor; and as many of the mammals are nocturnal, the impression is that there are fewer animals in the parks than there actually are.

Another reason why the users of nature trails are disappointed in their contact with animals is the behaviour of those users who are less interested. On the other hand, the animals are surprisingly quick in adapting to the presence of man. It is questionable, however, whether in small parks this "taming" of animals should be encouraged. As a result, non-territorial species or species of wide range, such as deer, become easy victims of hunters in lands outside the parks. With properly regulated use, the nature trails are also the best places to give opportunity for bird watching.

The factors affecting the population-density of different animals inside the parks are similar to those outside the parks. Some of these factors are :

(1) use of chemicides within the parks,

(2) danger of irruptions in the case of certain species,

(3) prohibition of hunting,

(4) effect of adjacent lands,

(5) effects connected with management practices and recreational use.

The danger of population irruptions of certain animals always increases in an area highly protected from external interference where the usual regulating factors are disturbed, and the area is limited.

Considering the complexity, interdependent and mutually regulating character of biological communities, what is actually more interesting from an ecological point of view than the few observed irruption cases, is the lack of these irruptions.

There is some increase in deer population but nowhere similar to that in some larger parks in the U.S.A. Only in a few exceptional cases has damage caused by deer to foliage been observed, thus :

1. The intensive temporary use of parks (week-end use) apparently does very little damage to habitat. No evidences of adverse effects were observed.

2. The food sources of the habitat are scarcely used up in any trophic level in the Southern Ontario parks (as compared to same cases in the U.S.A. parks). The observations show just the opposite.

3. One very efficient habitat manipulation observed in many parks was the synchronizing of hay or other plant cutting in open areas with the breeding and nesting time of certain mammals and birds.

Other observations of park personnel and ourselves pertaining to factors affecting animal life within parks were collected. Most of them point to direct threats to animal life. Some of these are :

(1) farm practices in adjacent areas;
(2) boys with an inclination to disturb birds, or as "conservationists" just collecting birds' eggs;
(3) stray cats, especially where the land is immediately adjacent to residential areas;
(4) stray dogs, mostly in remote areas not adjacent to residential areas;
(5) highways with considerable traffic adjacent to outdoor recreation areas;
(6) hunting in adjacent areas;
(7) vandalism, frequently mentioned by park personnel.

WATER

Every recreation survey emphasizes the importance of water. It was found that in most U.S.A. and Canadian parks some form of water proved to be the most critical single factor used or enjoyed by 70 to 80 per cent of park visitors.

To provide water in a recreation area implies many requirements about its physical, chemical, and biological conditions.

The following aspects may be examined :

1. The "forms" of water for recreation areas (flowing water, ponds, reservoirs).

2. The quantity of water.

3. The quality of water for different recreational uses such as swimming, fishing, boating and wild life habitat.

4. Pollution.

5. Compatibility of the uses in item 3.

6. Manipulation, regulation, etc. for the above purposes.

"Forms" of Water for Recreation

The area around Toronto is exceptionally well endowed with different forms of water available for recreation. In this respect it is one of the best endowed areas in the North American continent. Many of these water bodies are within a very short distance of the city.

All the main "forms" of water such as flowing water, lakes and reservoirs are equally well represented; perhaps the reservoirs will be more dominant in the future than they are now.

Of the different categories of water the following aspects have recreation significance :

1. The quantity and seasonal distribution of water flow. In the case of lake water tables : permanency and other seasonal changes.

2. Quality of water. Chemical and biological characteristics from a recreational point of view. Question of temperature.

3. Characteristic shore or bottom features, not directly water characteristics but relevant for the potential recreational use of the water itself.

These quality and quantity aspects can only be discussed in the broadest outline characterizing mostly the differences between the different "forms" of water.

The *rivers* emptying their water into the Great Lakes are relatively short water-courses with small to medium flow.

Although all have some potential recreational value they differ greatly according to :

(1) seasonal and minimum waterflow,

(2) temperature of water,

(3) chemical and biological properties of water,

(4) degree and kind of pollution affecting the above properties.

The Lakes (Other than the Great Lakes)

There is hardly any other great city on the North American continent better endowed with lakes than is Toronto. Not only lakes but all kinds of lakes, of every imaginable size and quality are available within a 100-mile radius of Toronto and all have some kind of recreational relevance.

An evaluation of them for recreational use implies a review from two approaches : from the point of view of what is appropriate for both the lakes themselves and the users of the lakes.

The user side, here, means the subjective evaluation of preferences, biases, what a body of water should be, etc. These preferences and biases can be dealt with when evaluating the different lakes.

What kinds of lakes are there in Southern Ontario, and how can they be evaluated for recreation ?

The ecologist makes a convenient distinction between "oligotrophic" (poor in life) and "eutrophic" (rich in life) lakes. This categorization explains many things, but needs amplification.

1. The "oligotrophic" lakes are mostly outside our 50-mile radius but their recreational value is so important that they cannot be neglected here. These are the typical lakes of the Shield. Their characteristics are : transparently clear, cold, deep water, generally poor in nutrients and life. Their further characteristics and dynamisms are thoroughly described by the pertinent literature. Nearly all of their main characteristics have recreational relevance, such as :

(1) Their real and apparent clearness appeals to those swimmers who are enthusiasts of the "crystal clear" waters;

(2) temperature affects their value for swimming in a negative way (being usually cold, warming up late in the season and localization of warming to shallow bays, etc.);

(3) their characteristics do not affect boating practices but do have some affect on water skiing (as for swimming);

(4) the natural low productivity of the water adversely affects fishing. (Although some favourite sportfish species such as trout and small-mouthed bass thrive well in these waters, their number per acre of surface water is necessarily low.)

2. The lakes within the 50-mile radius mostly belong to the "eutrophic" group. Their assets or disadvantages are roughly the opposites of the "oligotrophic" category. Swimmers frequently criticize their apparently "unclear" water (opaque because of microscopic algae or other organisms); fishermen object to their excess of coarse fish; and boaters dislike their frequent shallowness and dense water vegetation. On the other hand, the water is warmer, warms up earlier in the season and potentially can maintain a much higher fish population.

Great Lakes

There is extensive literature on the Great Lakes which deals not only with general lymnological, ecological and physical aspects but also their recreational value. The last-mentioned has become especially prominent in recent years due to new attention directed toward them as a source of great, barely tapped, recreational potential.

Here are only a few general comments on the Great Lakes :

1. They show great differences not only in their general characteristics but also in their recreational value. Temperature, degree of pollution, productivity, and shore features, make Lake Ontario, Lake Erie and Georgian Bay quite different for recreation.

2. There are great differences of opinion about their recreational value. These range from the highest enthusiasm to the most pessimistic view, expressed by authors of different papers.

3. There is an unquestionable trend toward a continuing deterioration of recreational value of waters, mostly in Lake Erie and near great population centres in other lakes. For example, Lake Ontario around Toronto.

4. The most prominent recreational problems are temperature and pollution.

The whole "deterioration" problem of the Great Lakes is one of the main concerns of the surrounding areas. In spite of the tremendous efforts of different institutions, commissions and government agencies, there seems to be an irresistible trend toward decline. One cannot even say that the problems are not thoroughly studied (sufficient evidence may be assembled through reference to the extensive literature : *Lymnological Survey of Lake Erie,* technical reports of other authorities, etc.). But even where the processes are rather well understood it is difficult to improve them : all the more difficult because the "use pressure" on these waters will rapidly increase in the next few decades. On the other hand, with proper technology the harmful effects can be greatly reduced. The relatively satisfactory situation in the Ruhr Valley waters shows what can be achieved—if we really make the effort.

Reservoirs

We previously pointed out how well-endowed the Toronto area is with lakes. Knowing this, it sounds curious that so many reservoirs are planned partly or mostly for recreational purposes. Quite a few considerable-sized reservoirs are planned within the 50-mile radius. They are flood control reservoirs, with about equal emphasis on recreation. Many are double reservoirs, the upper one acting as a regulator for the lower one. They are not, at least the lower ones, draw-down reservoirs; the levels are kept adequately high even in the late summer when other reservoirs are usually at their lowest.

On examination of the visitor statistics and their trends, there can be little question that these reservoirs are needed and will be well patronized. They are also flood control reservoirs but their multiple use aspects are not discussed here.

From a recreation point of view a reservoir has many advantages :

1. The quality of water can be manipulated.

2. The temperature also can be well manipulated.

3. In the case of a non-draw-down reservoir the shoreline is more or less stabilized and can be developed for recreational purposes.

4. The whole biota can be manipulated.

The most important possibility for manipulation is connected with sport fishing. By a small change of water level the whole species composition can be affected.

The Quality of Water

Requirements for swimming :

The ideal "swimming water" is clear, has equable pleasant temperature, is the proper size, and has comfortable bottom and shore conditions. These requirements can be found only in an artificial swimmnig pool. Many of these qualities, such as clear, sterile water, are not compatible with other recreational uses. Consequently swimming water is always a compromise, defined by minimum requirements, rather than absolute criteria. These minimum requirements are mostly connected with health hazards to the user. Unfortunately there does not exist an overall well-defined set of standard criteria. Most authorities, municipalities and health departments follow different "standards". Water is generally considered unsuitable for swimming if the count of coliforms is in excess of 2,400 per 100 milliliter or if any coliform samples show raw sewage discharge in the water and five-day B.O.D. does not exceed 4 ppm.

This is a somewhat meagre and debatable standard. "Coliform" refers only to the form of the organism, and does not necessarily imply pathogenic qualities. Even a smaller count than 2,400 coliforms per 100 mill. may contain virulent pathogenic organisms. There is no escape, as all natural water contains coliform bacteria and can be used without much health risk. Other criteria of such publications as the *Objectives of Water Quality Control* are rather imprecise and undefined. It puts in general terms only what should not be present in the water such as "highly toxic wastes" or "deoxigenating wastes" (whatever they are). Exceptions are "phenolic type wastes" where exact criteria are given, by not exceeding an average phenol content of 2 ppb. and a maximum of 5 ppb.

There is usually no consideration of the condition of the bottom (broken glass, metal sheets, etc.) or speed of current and other health hazards except sometimes around dams.

Possible proposals are :

1. More uniform standard requirements should be worked out and generally accepted.

2. The artificial swimming areas should be handled independently from the natural ones, applying a much stricter system of standards.

3. Other criteria and "minimum requirements" should be applied in addition to the coliform bacteria count made by the authorities.

Requirements for Boating

The quality of the water itself is less important for boating considerations. The boater's interest connected with water is rather (1) the size of the body of water, (2) certain bottom features (rock reaching the surface, etc.), (3) water vegetation conditions, (4) interference with other users, (5) existence of certain features necessary for the use of boats. These requirements are of a higher order in the case of powered boats than hand-propelled boats.

The basic problem with boating, with particular emphasis on power-boating, is the question of its compatibility with other recreational uses. Boating is a space-demanding use. Its claim for water, where the area of water is limited, can interfere seriously with other users. This and many other aspects of boating, especially motor boating, make the recreation area planner less concerned with providing the needed space than with protecting other users from interference caused by boats. More correctly : to establish a fair equilibrium between the different demands.

All observations would seem to justify the adoption of policies for the different types of boating in recreational water to be held to well-defined *zones.* This means that high density uses of water such as swimming must be given preference, and boating should be confined to areas where it interferes less with these uses. In some cases where water sources are limited, power-boats may be excluded altogether.

Sport Fishing and Ecological Criteria of Water Used for Sport

According to statistics, approximately 17-22 per cent of recreation area users are fishermen.

But there are different kinds of fishing. Their physical and ecological requirements also differ widely.

To provide and maintain this habitat we have to know our goals. There are also many prejudices and preferences, involved. The so-called "quality" fishing, "coarse fish", etc. notions already express something of this prejudice. To make it more complicated, these prejudices and preferences are most strongly held by those who manage and direct sport fishing activities.

To choose the right habitat, or to manipulate the available ones to provide the most satisfying sport fishing, outdoor recreation area planning has to consider :

(1) The water quantity, quality and temperature requirements of fishing intended to be established in the area and its relation to the available water.

(2) The bottom, shore and other physiographic features of the water course or lake bed.

(3) The manipulability of the water.

(4) Access to the water.

(5) Compatibility of other uses, including other recreational uses, for the same source of water.

It is extremely difficult to define "water quality requirements" for sport fishing generally. We know a lot about the specific requirements of different sport fish, especially about some of the preferred ones such as trout. A logical approach would be to provide these conditions and assume that everything will be all right. Unfortunately the problem is much more complicated. What can be done with great effort and expense is not always the most desirable thing. Certain changes and trends are going on irresistibly as consequences of our intensive use of the environment. To reverse them is getting more and more difficult and eventually will be practically impossible.

Changes in the fish habitat are not only due to pollution but also to many other factors which we cannot reverse. The best policy would be to recognize this and reckon with the factors concerned. They probably create a constellation of conditions in terms of which different policies can be accepted. I have in mind :

(1) circumstances where the improvement of conditions for certain desirable fisheries are feasible and will be the right policy;

(2) other situations where there should be strong efforts made to improve or reclaim conditions to a certain degree but at the same time to adjust sport fishery to a changed environment;

(3) where the main concern is to adjust the fishery to the changed conditions and make the best of them.

At the present time point (1) reflects the general attitude. This is right so far as it is aimed at improving existing waters, fighting against pollution, etc., where there are reasonable hopes of achieving these goals.

The first attitude is perfectly well justified in many cases, such as in dealing with middle and upper sections of streams, recreating or preserving the habitat for cold-water fish and fighting pollution. In many cases proper management of these waters needs only stricter implementation of existing legislation, or some very inexpensive improvements, and proper measures to control the use of these waters. The work (and partly the purpose) of the conservation authorities includes these jobs. And, as the results show, most of them do it very satisfactorily with co-operation from the Department of Lands and Forests and other authorities.

It is, of course, outside the scope of this study to try and debate technical questions. These lie in the fields of lymnology and fish management, well worked-out areas (although never adequately), and well known by the responsible authorities.

The water requirements differ according to the species of fish, and are connected with the quality, quantity, oxygen content and temperature of the water.

In spite of some uncertainty, some generalizations can be risked :

Temperature : The requirements are very different. Some fish tolerate a wide range (so called eurythermal), others only a narrow (stenothermal) range. In the case of sport fishing, for fish in the Salmonid group, the problem is to have cold enough water. An important indirect effect of temperature is that it is connected with the amount of dissolved oxygen.

Another aspect of the problem is the temperature required for spawning. This factor can be used in reservoir water-level manipulation to influence the fish species composition. For example, pike spawn when the temperature reaches 10° C, perch 12° C, carp above 18° C.

What are the criteria relating to water quality requirements of water organisms, primarily for sport fish ? It sounds incredible that after consulting concentrated and substantial pertinent literature one cannot give a quite definite numerical figure about these requirements. Even more discouraging is the summing up of the situation by one of the most authentic experts, Clarence M. Tarzwell, in 1962 in the publication *Development of Water Quality Criteria for Aquatic Life*. Although he himself risked giving some criteria in 1956 he now appears to be less sure, emphasizing rather the uncertainties of their selection. He states : "There is a need to know more about the maximum concentrations of dissolved toxicants and the minimum concentrations of dissolved oxygen that fish and other aquatic organisms can withstand for short periods and to what level water temperature may be raised for short or extended periods without adversely affecting aquatic life".

A very generalized set of criteria can be suggested in the following form :

Oxygen content : dissolved oxygen should not be less than 5 ppm. Some warm-water fish tolerate even 2 ppm. for a considerable period of time. An overall level of 5 ppm. can be suggested as a minimum.

Carbon dioxide: In lakes, reservoirs, and other more-or-less standing waters the free CO_2 concentration can be toxic and at least temporarily harmful for certain organisms. The tolerance here again varies with the species. Generally 5 cc. per litre can be considered as maximum. Other sources give 3 cc. per litre as the higher limit.

Ammonia : The decomposing organic matter—the main source of nitrogen compounds or rather the recirculation of nitrogen—contains a considerable amount of ammonium compounds. One of these ammonium compounds, ammonium carbonate, has a relatively high toxicity for many aquatic animals. In natural circumstances in unpolluted water, the ammonium carbonate is well below the toxic level.

Suspended solids : The two main sources of the most frequent inorganic suspended materials are : (1) erosion, (2) effluents from earthworks and other industrial enterprises. The latter appear to be a growing danger which can—and actually do—destroy aquatic life on considerable sections of water courses.

Consequences of Pollution for Recreational Uses of Water

The general term "polluted water" covers a wide range of quality conditions, according to the causes of the pollution. The effect of various pollutants on aquatic life is also widely different.

Possible categorization by origin of the wastes can point the direction of necessary measures. These may include the following :

(1) domestic sewage;

(2) industrial wastes, chemicals;

(3) industrial wastes, suspended inorganic material;

(4) hot water from power plants, boilers or other sources;

(5) washed-in chemicides from adjacent agricultural use;

(6) chemicides used in the water for mosquito control;

(7) oil products from motor boats;

(8) washed-in toxic material from dumped wastes along the water course.

CONCLUSION

In this brief summary, we have tried to find the necessary physical and ecological criteria for the outdoor recreation area planner.

The planner's task in these fields is extremely complex and needs the contribution of specialists and special knowledge. This in itself is not new. Nearly all planning tasks are complex by their very nature. In this case the importance of biological sciences such as ecology came out with strong emphasis. The problem is that most of our planners are not too well prepared in this field. In many respects the best outdoor recreation area "planners" are at present some of the members of the pertinent Authorities; (Metropolitan Toronto Conservation Authority, Department of Lands and Forests, River Valley Authorities, etc.). This is "right" to a degree and not unexpected, but as recreation areas are becoming one of the most important land uses around metropolitan areas, their development and control cannot be separated from the overall planning view.

A Selected Bibliography of Outdoor Recreation Used for the Study

Brockman, C. Frank: *Recreational Use of Wild Lands;* McGraw-Hill, New York, 1959.

Clawson, Marion: *The Crisis in Outdoor Recreation.* Reprint No. 13. Resources for the Future, Inc. Washington, 1959.

Conservation Council of Ontario. *The Need for an Outdoor Recreation Survey of Ontario;* Brief presented to the Prime Minister of Ontario, April 5, 1963.

CONSERVATION AUTHORITY REPORTS

Farina, J.: *The Social and Cultural Aspects of Recreation.* pp. 941-950.

Glikson, Arthur: *Recreational Land Use,* in *Man's Role in Changing the Face of the Earth,* ed. by W. L. Thomas, Jr., University of Chicago, 1956, pp. 896-914.

Hardy, E. & McGilly, Frank J.: *The Hierarchy of Government and Public Agencies in Park Development.* pp. 1037-1046.

Hunting in the United States—Its Present and Future Role; 105 pp. Department of Conservation, School of Natural Resources, Univ. of Michigan.

Land for Recreation. In *Land for the Future* by Marion Clawson, R. Burnell Held, and Charles H. Stoddard; published for Resources for the Future, Inc., by the Johns Hopkins Press, Baltimore, 1960, pp. 124-193 (Chapter 3).

Metropolitan Regional Council and Regional Plan Association, Park, Recreation and Open Space Project of the Tri-State New York Metropolitan Region. Regional Plan Association, Inc., New York, 1960.
    1. Shirley Adelson Siegel: *The Law of Open Space.*
    2. Marion Clawson: *The Dynamics of Park Demand,* RPA Bulletin No. 94.
    3. William A. Niering: *Nature in the Metropolis.*
    4. *The Race for Open Space:* Final Report of the Project, RPA Bulletin No. 96.

Meyer, Harold D., and Brightbill, Charles K.: *Community Recreation: a Guide To Its Organization* (Englewood Cliffs, N.J., Prentice Hall Inc., 1956), p. 38.

Multiple Use of Land and Water Areas, 29 pp., prepared by John Shanklin.

Our National Parks in the Year 2000. National Parks Magazine, Vol. 33, No. 142, 1959, pp. 2-7 and 11.

A Positive Approach To Open Space Reservation. Journal American Institute of Planners. Vol. 28, 1962, pp. 124-129.

Perspective On Outdoor Recreation—A Bibliographical Survey, R. I. Wolfe, Department of Highways, Ontario.

Recreation in the Age of Automation, Annals of the American Academy of Political and Social Science, Vol. 313 (Sept. 1957).

REPORTS OF THE OUTDOOR RECREATION RESOURCES REVIEW COMMISSION,
WASHINGTON, D.C.

Volumes 1-27

1. Public Outdoor Recreation Areas—Acreage, Use, Potential, 193 pp.
2. List of Public Outdoor Recreation Areas—1960, 161 pp.
3. Wilderness and Recreation—A Report on Resources, Values and Problems, 344 pp.
4. Shoreline Recreation Resources of the United States, 144 pp.
5. The Quality of Outdoor Recreation: As Evidenced by User Satisfaction, 87 pp.
6. Hunting in the United States—Its Present and Future Role, 105 pp.
7. Sport Fishing—Today and Tomorrow, 119 pp.
8. Potential New Sites for Outdoor Recreation in the Northeast, 123 pp.
9. Alaska Outdoor Recreation Potential, 51 pp.
10. Water for Recreation—Values and Opportunities, 65 pp.
11. Private Outdoor Recreation Facilities, 146 pp.
12. Financing Public Recreation Facilities, 85 pp.
13. Federal Agencies and Outdoor Recreation, 68 pp.
14. Directory of State Outdoor Recreation Administration, 134 pp.
15. Open Space Action, 107 pp.
16. Land Acquisition for Outdoor Recreation—Analysis of Selected Legal Problems, 55 pp.
17. Multiple Use of Land and Water Areas, 29 pp.
18. A Look Abroad: The Effect of Foreign Travel on Domestic Outdoor Recreation and a Brief Survey of Outdoor Recreation in Six Countries, 72 pp.
19. National Recreation Survey, 387 pp.
20. Participation in Outdoor Recreation: Factors Affecting Demand among American Adults, 83 pp.
21. The Future of Outdoor Recreation in Metropolitan Regions of the United States (three volumes).
22. Trends in American Living and Outdoor Recreation, 250 pp.
23. Projections to the Years 1976 and 2000: Economic Growth, Population, Labor Force and Leisure, and Transportation, 424 pp.
24. Economic Studies of Outdoor Recreation, 158 pp.
25. Public Expenditures for Outdoor Recreation, 150 pp.
26. Prospective Demand for Outdoor Recreation, 49 pp.
27. Outdoor Recreation in the U.S.: Its Literature and History, 129 pp.

Resources For Tomorrow, Vol. 2, Ottawa 1962.

Sport Fishing—Today and Tomorrow, 119 pp., prepared by the Bureau of Sport Fisheries and Wildlife, U.S. Department of the Interior.

Tilden, Freeman: The National Parks: What They Mean To You and Me. New York 1951, revised 1954.

Tilden, Freeman: The State Parks: Their Meaning In American Life, New York 1962.

Wilderness and Recreation—A Report On Resources, Values, and Problems, 344 pp., prepared by the Wildland Research Centre, University of California, Berkeley.

Williams, Wayne R.: Recreation Places (Reinhold, N.Y. 1957).

LAND SPECULATION: ITS EFFECTS AND CONTROL

R. W. G. Bryant

The author is an Associate Professor in the Department of Geography, Sir George Williams University, Montreal, former member of the Faculty of L'Institut d'Urbanisme, and currently instructor in L'Ecole d'Agriculture at the University of Montreal. He writes on the subject of land speculation with a background of extensive British and general European experience.

The problem of speculation in land may be compared to an iceberg, only a small part of which is visible above the surface. The general public is hardly aware of the extent to which it pays tribute, in the form of increased land prices, to people who have contributed nothing to the communal good in return for their gains. It is odd how home-owners resentful of increasing taxation, often say little about speculators, who in the economic sense are like fleas on a sheep's back.

Land speculation is a deeply entrenched feature of American life, and most North Americans have not yet reached the point of seeing anything immoral or improper, in making profit out of land deals. The point is well made in a recent excellent study of American planning practice by a British civil servant. [1] As the author says—

> Quick fortunes are still made on the land market. Land in Houston (Texas) that was bought ten years ago for $400 an acre can be sold today for $4,000, or in some parts of the city for $40,000. One of Houston's pioneer families still owns a 60,000-acre ranch which now lies within the city limits and is being released in calculated amounts for development. Speculation in land has been a tradition in America, and was in fact a major motivating force in opening the West. It was not the prerogative of the rich (none of the great American fortunes derived from real estate) but in an underdeveloped country was available to all comers. This speculative bent still colours American attitudes toward the land, and is a factor to be reckoned with in attempting to control its use.

The phenomenon of soaring land prices is, of course, not peculiar to North America; it is universal in market economies, and with world-wide trends to urbanization, land values round great cities everywhere afford golden opportunities for people able or willing to take advantage of the situation.

---

[1] John Delafons, *Land Use Controls in the United States*, Harvard/M.I.T. Joint Center for Urban Studies, 1963.

The Houston figures just quoted are parallelled by trends in Britain. A 64-acre estate in Surrey, on the fringe of greater London, sold for £25,000, in 1958, and it was resold for £210,000 in 1961. The City of Birmingham in 1961, had to pay £1,500 an acre, where it had bought adjoining land only five years previously at £400 an acre. In Hull, land valued at £70,000 only four years earlier cost the city £500,000 in 1960. [2]

In Copenhagen, the post-war expansion of the built-up area was originally planned to follow a "finger plan", providing for expansion in the form of five fingers along main lines of communication, separated by broad green wedges. This plan had to be abandoned owing to the intense pressure for development. The steep rise in land values had made it impossible to prevent development in the "green wedges", since Denmark still had relatively primitive arrangements for the control of land use, compared with those say in Sweden or the Netherlands.

The whole question of land speculation must, in reality, be looked at as part of a much greater whole, namely, the matter of control of land use. If it be accepted that the operation of normal market processes is the proper determinant of the proper use of land, and that individual proprietors have unrestricted right to develop their land in accordance with their personal calculations of profit, then any attempt to curb speculation, and control prices of land becomes next to impossible. Price control is not applied to other sectors of the market save as an emergency measure, commonly in time of war, and it must generally be accompanied by some other control mechanism such as rationing.

Such measures are accepted as necessary in times of emergency, but direct control of prices is generally abandoned on the conclusion of the emergency as quickly as possible. The reasons for this are good and sufficient, and based on elementary economic laws. Prices are determined by the interaction of supply and demand : any attempt to interfere artificially with the operation of that basic mechanism is bound to lead to distortions and inefficiences. Commodity speculation can be curbed by various means—but the fundamental way of holding prices down is to increase the supply in relation to demand.

With land, especially land on the fringes of cities, this cannot be done, for the simple reason that the supply is fixed and limited by nature. This alone is good and sufficient reason for regarding land as a very special commodity which cannot be left to the free and uncontrolled operation of the market. The ordinary market mechanisms simply do not produce the right answer in this field. Even in free enterprise North America this fact has been recognized for a very long time. The very existence of zoning by-laws is evidence thereof. Even the early colonial towns with their subdivision amongst settlers, had to provide themselves with regulations governing and controlling development, in the interests of the community. [3]

The ideology, typically, was that of the community of freeholders—the manor with its aristocratic ownership of large tracts took root to some

---

2 *Signposts for the Sixties*, p. 19.

3 See Carl Bridenbaugh, *Cities in the Wilderness.*

extent in Virginia and further south, and in the Hudson Valley, but is not typically American. In Quebec, the old seigneurial system has been profoundly modified.

Today, with modern technology, conditions of life, and sheer pressure of numbers, conditions are infinitely more complex than 300 years ago. The land problem is likewise infinitely more complex in respect to public control of its use, and to its market relations.

The old system of individual freeholds, established by the early settlers, is still solidly entrenched in the social fabric, but it looks less and less adequate as a satisfactory basis for a modern society. On the one hand, complex and difficult issues surrounding the public control of land use have an urgency unknown to our ancestors. On the other hand, the ordinary operations of the market produce anomalous results, especially on the fringes of cities where pressure for development is great, and each piece of land has several, and often conflicting demands for its use.

West of London (England), for example, in the Thames Valley, there was an exceptionally fertile market-gardening area, the Middlesex brick-earth area. Apart from its intrinsic fertility, its productivity had been built up over the centuries, by fertilizer produced by the city. It was an irreplaceable national asset. Yet in the 1930's, the whole of it was built up, its value for that purpose being even greater than its value as market garden land. At that time, there were no mechanisms of control to stop such developments; under present-day British legislation such an area can readily be preserved from development. Canada has a similar problem with the peach-orchard area in the Niagara Peninsula—the peach orchards are irreplaceable, but their market value for development is even greater. Unfortunately, the relatively primitive system of land-use control existing in Ontario does not permit any effective check on development of the peach lands.

These two examples both illustrate the fact that the play of the market forces may be very far from producing the best use of a given area of land. Public interest is in conflict with private profit, and it is very often so—one could multiply illustrative examples. Yet attempts to reconcile the two, or to set the public interest first, are often met with the familiar appeal to the rights of the individual proprietor to do what he pleases with his own property. Land speculation is the outgrowth of this habit of mind.

The common attitude has a sophisticated basis, evident in the writings of American economists in the field of real estate. Two important American works, one by Weimer and Hoyt, the other by Ernest Burgess [4], both accept as natural and proper the economic determination of the use of land. There is a large mass of American writing, based on this assumption; after all, it is in line with the prevailing climate of economic thought. The Americans study most conscientiously the impact of this or that freeway

---

[4] Arthur W. Weimer and Homer Hoyt, *Principles of Real Estate*, 1954; Ernest W. Burgess, "The Growth of the City"; in R. E. Park *et al. The City*, 1925.

construction on real estate values. Clearly the interaction of land values and land use is very clearly appreciated.

This stands in strong contrast to British practice, wherein development plans are drawn up often with only the vaguest notions as to the effect on land values. The point is, of course, that in Britain under the 1947 Town and Country Planning Act in its original form, local authorities were able to plan the best use of the land in the public interest, without regard to financial considerations. Even if this is no longer true, the attitude still remains. (See N. Lichfield, "Economics of Planned Development", *Estates Gazette,* London, written on and for British conditions.)

But one finds few American voices ever raised to ask whether it is right and proper for private owners of land to make profits out of improvements built at public expense. This important question of "betterment" is rarely faced in America. It is usually taken for granted, that if a freeway or a bridge or any other man-made modification of existing accessibility is brought about, then private individuals have every right to make windfall profits out of it. This is a question of morality and social philosophy as well as of practical ways and means. Attempts on the part of the public authorities to recover "betterment" due to public works undertaken by them, have seldom been successful. Few in America have even got around to asking the fundamental questions which brought about the Uthwatt enquiry in Britain more than twenty years ago.

Of course, a certain amount of betterment is recouped by public authorities by means of taxation, provided that the assessments keep pace with increased market values. This leads to another point altogether, namely the possibility of levying taxation on "bare site" values rather than on the buildings and structures thereon. It would certainly bring about certain shifts in the market values, as between one piece of land and another, and it might be more equitable than present forms of real-estate taxation. But its effectiveness as a weapon in curbing speculation is still not proven.

Be that as it may, North America in general sticks to the play of the market, in determining both land values, and land use, and to the right of proprietors to any increase in value which may accrue for whatever reason. The operation of the zoning by-laws has been conceived as a means of conserving and protecting property values, just a much or even more, than as a means of promoting good and harmonious community development. This much is made clear time and again in public hearings on zoning questions—the public are interested in the impact on their own property of this or that zoning or re-zoning, far more than in general issues. And a re-zoning, say from low to high density, or from residential to commercial use may very generally mean presenting the proprietor concerned with a handsome financial windfall. This too, is "betterment", just as that produced by expenditure on a new autoroute or freeway. This is yet another aspect of the argument that development values in land due to the right to develop, or the potentials for development, should be regarded as public property, since they are created by public action and owe little to the initiative of the proprietors involved.

It is strongly urged that no satisfactory solution to the problem of speculation in land can be found unless a proper attitude is taken to these development values. There is, unfortunately, little evidence that the general public is anywhere near ready to do that.

Here we must take into account attitudes and modes of thought as a background to suggesting a policy. But policy-making is the art of the possible, and a policy must depend on public opinion.

The prevailing attitude of mind is not unnatural in a society which regards the profit motive as the proper mainspring of economic activity. Therefore to change public attitudes must necessarily be a long and delicate process. It involves the questioning of assumptions that the vast majority of people simply take for granted.

The value of land falls into at least two quite distinct and separate categories—firstly, the value for its existing use, and secondly, its value for development. This is, of course, why 100 acres of farmland in New Jersey are worth much more than 100 acres of equal fertility in Vermont. This may seem elementary, but it is an essential point of principle. It was clearly grasped, for example, by the British enquiry in 1942 (the Uthwatt Committee).

A strong case can be made for holding that the element of development value in land should not be regarded as private property, since it accrues out of the general development of the community. This in fact was the logical basis of the proposals of the Uthwatt Committee. If it be held that the element of development value in the land is the property of the community, then of course it follows that the owner cannot claim compensation in respect of being refused permission to develop.

The expert committee under the chairmanship of Mr. Justice Uthwatt was set up to consider :

1. The payment of compensation and the recovery of betterment in relation to public control of land use.

2. The possible means of stabilizing the value of land to be developed or redeveloped.

3. An equitable basis for the acquisition or expropriation of land by the public authorities.

The final report, of September 1942, may be summarized as follows :

1. Local authorities should be given far wider powers of expropriation than hitherto, not only for specific public purposes such as schools, but also to ensure that land would be developed according to the provisions of a town plan. They should have the power to acquire and develop land themselves if private developers failed. Local authorities should retain the ownership of all land in their possession—where private enterprise develops thereon this should be a leasehold basis.

2. All unbuilt land outside urban areas should be subject to a "development rights" scheme, involving public acquisition of all such land when the time was right for it to be developed. The government would

develop the land itself or lease it to a private developer. (In this way, the public would itself recoup the development value.) A global value would be placed on the development rights of the whole country, and this sum would be shared out among owners as compensation. This would obviate over-compensation and eliminate the element of "floating value", for example : all owners of land on a given sector of urban fringe are apt to set a value on their land in the hope that development will take place on their particular land, whereas it will in fact settle on certain areas only. The sum total of "development values" is much greater than is actually warranted—something clearly perceived by the Uthwatt Committee.

3. In urban areas, the value of all sites should be ascertained every five years, and there should be a levy of 75 per cent of any increase in value over every five-year period.

The Committee suggested that the logical solution to the problem would be public ownership of all land, but refrained from suggesting this on the ground that it would be too controversial. But even so solid a journal as the *Economist* (March 18, 1944) thought the Uthwatt proposals too timid in this respect.

The Uthwatt proposals were rejected as such, although the basic ideas were the foundation of the subsequent very important White Paper on the Control of Land Use (June 1944), which formed the basis of post-war policy in this field. The only one of the Uthwatt proposals to be accepted in toto (and embodied in subsequent legislation) was that for the definition of "reconstruction areas" of war damage or obsolescence, within which local authorities should have powers of expropriation. A drastically amended version was incorporated in the British Town and Country Planning Act of 1947, but the system was intensely disliked by the then Conservative Opposition, and the Conservative Government dismantled it in 1954, with disastrous results, in the spiralling cost of building land.

SUGGESTED POLICIES TO CURB SPECULATION IN LAND

Legal Controls

One course is regulation of sub-division and development, to confine development in defined areas, with possible agricultural zoning of the areas not to be developed, either in the near future, or at all (as in Santa Clara County, California).

This method, of course, depends entirely on the willingness of the municipalities concerned to follow a firm and vigorous policy of channelling development, and one is not aware of much willingness to do this in general. Where such powers are available, if they are vigorously utilized they are an effective tool for regulating the extension of an urban area.

On the other hand, whereas such a policy firmly applied may discourage speculation in land not zoned for development, it cannot entirely obviate it, because there is always the hope that it will later, and eventually, become available. Moreover, such regulation would tend to drive up prices of land zoned for development—the "floating value" of Uthwatt would settle in the zoned areas. However necessary in the interest of securing orderly development the weapons of legal control may be, they cannot be deemed of prime importance against speculation. There would no doubt be loud and bitter complaints on the score of interference with private property rights.

Here we are intimately involved in the question of the extent to which the community has the power and the right to prevent development on this or that piece of land. Public opinion is not always ready to accept that an authority is justified in refusing permission to develop. There would be formidable problems of compensation—and these in turn lead very directly into the question of the ownership of development rights. It would involve great discrimination between owners of land on which development is permitted, and of that on which it is not. If the former is serviced, and demonstrably apt for development in the public interest, and the latter is not, the discrimination can be objectively justified.

Delafons, for example, quotes the controversy which arose in Santa Clara County, California, around agricultural zoning. Wm. H. Whyte had written an article in *Life* magazine warmly commending it. The city councillors of San José were so affronted that they protested officially to Time, Inc. The city manager wrote that "the green belt in our booming society is an anachronism". In North America as a whole, the conservation of agricultural land is not a problem, rather the problem is one of farm surpluses. But in Santa Clara County there are some of the richest fruit farms on the continent, and a very strong case for preserving them from development. How much less acceptable would it be to attempt to operate a green belt policy in urban fringe areas where land is of less superlative agricultural value?

The question of physical controls of fringe development involves enormous difficulties, however necessary they may be to secure proper development. But the real answer to the problem of land speculation is to be found on other lines more directly concerned with the financial aspect.

A lesson may be drawn from Swedish practice. Under Swedish town-planning law, the country is divided into two zones—the countryside where scattered development of rural character is permitted, with but the simplest of controls, and the urban and urban fringe areas of "close" development; in these, control is very firm. Swedish law lays down, not that the land-owner in the urban and urban fringe areas may develop as he likes, but that he may develop only in accordance with the master plan. The plan specifies not only the type and location of development, but also the timing of it, in accordance with the availability of services and so on. No compensation is payable for refusal of permission to develop. In other words, development rights, and accordingly, development values are profoundly modified. Clearly there is much diminished scope for speculation in land under such conditions—apart altogether from the common Swedish practice of municipal land ownership.

The Fiscal Weapon

A certain amount can be done to check land speculation by judicious tax administration.

The idea of levying taxation on site values has been extensively discussed, and recommended as a discouragement to speculation. On the other hand, actual experience with it in Western Canada does not bear out the claims made for it by its more enthusiastic exponents.

Another fiscal measure would be a capital gains tax, imposed on increasing land values; assessed at periodic intervals. But apart altogether from the practical difficulties of assessment, to single out one particular form of capital gain for taxation would be to discriminate against owners of one particular form of investment, and this might very well be offensive to public opinion in spite of the special conditions that apply to land. In any case the practical difficulties of assessment are enormous.

In connection with "agricultural zoning" in California, it has been pointed out that assessment practices tend to encourage sale of farm lands for development, inasmuch as farm land in suburban areas is assessed for tax purposes at values based on its actual market value. It would be easier to resist pressure for development, if land zoned for agricultural use were to be assessed for taxes at an agricultural value; obviously, farming is discouraged if the land has to pay taxes at an urban, or suburban level, for the support of services required by neighbouring residents.

Where land is zoned for agricultural use, or for greenbelt, one might contemplate a system of partial tax remission on farm land in suburban municipalities, arranging for such land to be taxed at "agricultural" values so long as it remained in agricultural use, but liable to pay arrears of taxes at full rate, with compound interest, as from the date of sale as soon as the land is sold for development.

Clearly, this would be a powerful weapon for preventing urban sprawl and would also, to a certain extent, discourage the holding of land for purely speculative purposes. It needs more detailed investigation, but the matter is of necessity dismissed more briefly in this paper than its intrinsic importance warrants.

The following section does not set out to be an exhaustive summary of an exceedingly contentious and complex issue. Considerable material is already available, for example, the brochure *Site Valuation as a Base for Local Taxation,* reprinted by the Canadian Federation of Mayors and Municipalities from the report of the 1961 Conference of the Canada Tax Foundation. Research Monograph No. 4 of the Urban Land Institute, written by Mary Rawson, *Property Taxation, and Urban Development,* is a comprehensive study of probable effects of a shift to site value taxation in Burnaby, B.C. The literature cited in these two works is large—much of it in the form of official reports, American, British, Australasian, and South African.

The relationship of land speculation with land taxation keeps cropping up in all discussion of the matter. For example, a pre-war investigation by a Commission on Unemployment appointed by the Ontario Government advocated site value taxation on the ground that "a reform of the present system of taxing land appears indispensable to lessen the evils from speculation in land which contributed to the recent industrial depression".

The four speakers at the 1961 Tax Conference, whose speeches are set out in the brochure mentioned above, expressed widely divergent views. Mr. Eric Beecroft declined to be dogmatic, either for or against, but emphasized the need for further objective study.

The system appears to work well in Australasia. On the other hand, the kind of difficulties associated with urban fringe development and land speculation have by no means been obviated there.

It is claimed for a system of taxation based on site value rather than on buildings and improvements, that it would greatly reduce the social evils of speculation in land, whereby owners of idle land reap an unearned increment as their land appreciates in value.

In fact a great deal depends on the extent to which tax assessors' valuations of property approximate to the true market value. Under-assessment is chronic. Opponents of site value taxation often emphasize this point. On the other hand, very many parcels of vacant land remain undeveloped, even in the heart of mature built-up areas. If the owners had to pay taxes thereon based on their true market value they would be less likely to leave them undeveloped a day longer than possible. To this extent, sprawl on the outskirts would be discouraged, and redevelopment to a higher standard encouraged.

The Committee of Enquiry into the Design of Residential Environment set up by the Royal Architectural Institute of Canada (Report of 1960) stated (para. 185) "The Provinces, at no great expense, can ascertain for Canadian conditions the benefits or disadvantages of a general change from taxes on land and improvements to a system of real property tax on site value only. The difference in these assessment methods clearly has great import for the quality of the huge residential areas we shall have to create and maintain in the years before us."

Acquisition of Development Rights

The abandonment of the British experiment is not really conclusive. It is possible that a comparable scheme might be successfully operated. The lessons of the British experiment could be applied to working out an improved version. The important things are firstly, simplicity of administration; secondly, acceptance and understanding by the public; thirdly, retention by the private owners of a proportion of development rights, in order to retain the ordinary economic incentives to development. To assess the "development charge" at 100 per cent of the development value over and above value for existing use was perhaps the biggest mistake in the British scheme.

When all is said and done, however, any such scheme is bound to be rather cumbersome. The Uthwatt Committee of 1942, suggested this approach only as *faute de mieux* as compared with full public ownership.

Another interesting approach is that adopted in Oslo (Norway), where the city acquires servitudes in many cases rather than full title to land, in order to prevent development, for example in areas needed for watershed or recreational purposes. In effect, the city acquires the development rights in the land, separating them from the land itself. But one does not need to go as far as Norway. Professor Raymond Vernon [5] mentions this practice in connection with the acquisition of land for public purposes as follows: "An old concept is being brushed off and re-examined with considerable interest for its possible application to the current planning problem. This is the notion that the authorities which are responsible for planning the use of land should have the power not only to zone the land, but also to buy various kinds of property rights short of outright ownership. This property right could be an easement for limited public purposes: it could be a development right which excluded certain private uses from the land; or any one of half a dozen other forms of interest."

The relevance of this for measures against speculation is clear.

Another approach is to "freeze" land prices—a form of confiscation applied to development values, but it is clearly so obnoxious as not to warrant further discussion.

Public Ownership of Land

The best and most effective means of stopping speculation in land is unquestionably for land to come under public ownership. It is worth all the zoning by-laws and planning controls in the world, as a means of securing properly organized development. This is perfectly well understood in some European countries.

In North America, the general attitude to land ownership is much less sophisticated and mature—if maturity in a democracy is to be judged by the extent to which public good is held to override private profit seeking. Even so, it is surprising how even in the U.S.A. legal powers exist for public acquisition of land, and how large a proportion of the country is owned by public agencies of one sort or another—over a third of the whole. Something like half the total area of California is still owned by the state or federal government, or local authorities. But this doesn't help the battle against speculation round the fast-growing cities, for the reason that these vast public holdings of land are predominantly in the sparsely settled regions.

---

[5] Raymond Vernon, *The Myth and Reality of Our Urban Problems*, M.I.T./Harvard Joint Center for Urban Studies, p. 39.

An interesting monograph by Robert A. Sigafoos [6] on the subject of making land available for industry, contains references to existing American legal powers enabling municipalities to acquire land. "In Pennsylvania, municipalities have the power of eminent domain . . . to assure ownership, to control the disposition of property which is foreclosed upon for taxes. . . ."[7] But the municipalities generally have no policy or program for the review of tax-delinquent properties, selling them, with the absurd result that many authorities will probably be buying back at top prices, properties they once held temporarily on tax foreclosures. Only in Pittsburgh, parcels of land are held for one year, to give city staff time to consider possible requirements of land by public authorities and to prepare recommendations.

In 1958, the New York State Legislature granted to its cities the power to condemn land not actually blighted but at present predominantly vacant—but subject to its being badly subdivided and ill-serviced. Cities are thus permitted to assemble large tracts for sale to private developers, but on the condition that the sale price must equal the cost of acquisition and site planning. [8]

In Wisconsin, municipalities have power to borrow to finance purchase of property, in their own or contiguous areas, for use as industrial sites.

In California, the enormous pressure for development, exemplified by a monthly intake of 30,000 immigrants, is expected to involve doubling the present population of the state in eighteen years. In 1962, therefore, the governor set up a high-powered Advisory Commission on Housing Problems (the Eichler Commission), to report on housing and land problems on a state-wide basis. One of the Commission's recommendations is that the familiar urban renewal formula, namely, assembly of land by public agency, should be extended to cover operations on vacant land, both inside and outside cities. A public authority, state or local, would thus assemble suburban land, make proper plans for its development, and sell appropriate tracts to private developers. [9] (In Canada, of course, this is the federal-provincial land assembly procedure.)

Clearly, even in the U.S.A., there is a discernible trend towards public participation in land development on lines already very familiar in Europe. Not only does it abolish speculation, but it also affords the opportunity to organize development in a rational way. There is very general dissatisfaction with the ugliness and inefficiency of North American cities, and the evil consequences of urban sprawl. Land speculation is only one part of this greater problem. To tackle the whole problem is also to solve the part problem. Here is one of the challenges as yet unmet, namely how to make our cities comely, and convenient and economical places in which to live. The problem is not insoluble—the Swedes have solved it superbly

[6] Robert A. Sigafoos, *Land for Industry—the Pennsylvania Case*, Institute of Public Administration, Pennsylvania State University.

[7] *Ibid.* p. 57.

[8] *Ibid.* p. 64.

[9] Charles Abrams, *Architectural Forum*, Sept. 1963, pp. 104-169.

in Stockholm, the mere existence of which is a standing reproach to the inchoate mess that so often results from the combined operations of individual developers, speculators, and zoning by-laws. The basic difficulty rises out of the archaic system of subdividing land into lots—it is fearfully difficult to achieve satisfactory development under this system. It is, in fact, an unfortunate hangover from pioneer times. In modern conditions of advanced and complex technology, we should be ready to reshape our ideas, and system of land tenure, so that good development is not made so difficult.

Good development on lines as up-to-date and excellent as that of the Stockholm suburbs, can be achieved where the owners of large tracts of unsubdivided land are prepared to engage competent city planners to produce a master plan for the whole, as is happening for example, in long Beach (California), and Reston (Fairfax County, Virginia), but this happens so seldom, and this point does not cover the problem of speculation. The Eichler Commission in California came up with the only truly effective suggestion for obtaining that, namely, public ownership.

In North America, one so often hears slogans such as "a city should not enter the real estate business". To European ears this seems quaint, because so many European cities do precisely that, as a matter of course. Partly, this is a matter of long-standing tradition, partly a matter of deliberate modern policy.

Stockholm owns an area greater than its administrative area. This policy of acquiring as much land as possible, when it comes on the market, has been a main feature of Stockholm municipal policy since 1904—it antedates the present Social Democratic government by many years. The following figures are taken from the article by Sven Markelius in Kidder Smith's book *Sweden Builds*. The city now owns approximately 61,750 acres, of which 10,000 are within the city limits. The municipally-owned land, in fact, is greater than the area of the city. Much of this land is leased to private developers on building leases of between fifty and seventy-five years. Most of the post-war development has taken place on city-owned land, by various organizations working on land leased from the city. This is the key to the dynamic and successful execution of the Stockholm metropolitan plan—and in this respect Sweden is a long way ahead of North America. Where the city wishes to have a green belt or a forest reserve, the land can be protected from development without paying ransom to speculators. And "cluster" development, at relatively high densities, keyed in with the transit system, is undertaken without the sort of arguments that characterize North American zoning procedures. The cluster satellites are built where it is judged best to build them, in accordance with the master plan—not simply that this or that land owner wishes to develop, and can get his land zoned accordingly. The whole procedure is so infinitely more effective in producing an agreeable and convenient environment than is common in North America, that it deserves careful study as a model—and municipal ownership is the key.

The city of Coventry, in England, owns about a third of its area. The reconstruction of the war-damaged area has been done on a basis of expropriation. But the municipal land holdings in the city centre are small compared to the very large ones on the outskirts. Coventry practice differs from that on the continent of Europe, in that the city-owned "fringe" land is not leased for development, but is used for municipal purposes. In terms of area, the two most important uses of this land are firstly, municipal housing, secondly, schools, and their associated playing fields, thirdly, deliberate retention in agricultural use, to preserve land from development and to maintain the green belt. The municipal aerodrome and its approaches are a special case. The play of the market applies to the values of private land subject to the particular British conditions described elsewhere in this paper.

The city of Coventry derives enormous benefit from this municipal estate. Much of it was purchased many years ago, so that its cost to the city was a fraction of its present value. If the city continues to grow at the present rate, and a radical revision of the green belt becomes necessary, then the city already possesses considerable reserves of land, at present farmed, which can be made available at low cost.

The British are now seriously considering public acquisition of urban fringe land, to solve fearful problems of rocketing land prices, due to the adandonment of the 1947 scheme. It is very probable that a Labour Government in Britain will undertake some form of nationalization, or public ownership of land on the outskirts of cities.

In Britain, the conception of development by private enterprise on municipally-owned land is old-established. In cities like Birmingham and Liverpool, municipal holdings of land have been managed for very many years according to the best principles of estate management, through the granting of long-term leases to private developers. Not only does the city retain complete control over the type and quality of development but also, the continual increase in the value of land, due to the general growth of the community.

Two Canadian examples may be cited, Red Deer (Alberta), and Saskatoon (Sask.). In Red Deer, city-owned land on the outskirts is sold to builders according to a paced and organized program, in accordance with a general plan, and with public services properly arranged. It is understood that this procedure is eminently satisfactory from the point of view of the house-builders, who can plan their operations in the knowledge that serviced land will be available at a reasonable cost, as and when required. In Saskatoon, likewise, the opportunity afforded by municipal ownership of considerable suburban tracts taken over for non-payment of taxes before the war, was utilized to ensure orderly development, after the war. In neither case does it appear that the device of leasehold was used —the land has been or is being sold outright.

In the Netherlands, municipalities use real-estate transactions as an instrument of policy in securing good development, and have done so since the turn of the century, when the country began to experience industrial expansion and intense pressure on its very limited land area. Where 11,000,000 people are crowded into an area two-fifths as big as Maine, land is too precious to be misused.

We are not here concerned with the Rotterdam policy of expropriating land in the war-devastated city centre, but with policy in relation to the whole of a fast-growing city, which occupies a key position in relation to the whole of the Common Market.

The following information is taken from an article by Mr. J. Rutgers, Director of Development and Reconstruction, in Rotterdam, originally published in the Belgian periodical *Habiter—Wonen* in March 1960, and summarized in the *Journal of the Town Planning Institute* (London), Dec. 1960.

In January 1950, Rotterdam set up a separate land service organization to acquire and manage municipally-owned land. Capital is provided through the ordinary Municipal Loan Fund, at a predetermined rate of interest (about four per cent in 1960). Unavoidable losses, through holding land temporarily idle, are covered from the normal city revenues. It is policy to release land for development at its "book value" i.e., at prices sufficient to recoup these losses. If the returns from a particular block show a profit, that is turned into a general reserve to cover losses on other blocks.

In 1958, the City Development and Reconstruction Department submitted 161 proposals for acquisition of land. Most sites were purchased by agreement but some expropriation was necessary.

If land is included for acquisition in an approved development plan, a compulsory acquisition decree can be proclaimed by Order. The interests of the owner are safeguarded by reference to an independent tribunal.

The city acquires all land to be developed, carries out site works, with service, and either sells or leases the land to developers. This gives exact control of the timing of development, and obviates speculation. The cost of making land available for development is arrived at by adding together:

(1) cost of acquisition,

(2) cost of site works entirely chargeable to the development,

(3) a due part of the cost of site works partly chargeable to the development.

Values are set, and made valid for one year from the date of reservation of the land, but to prevent speculation, land is not handed over until building has started.

Why not adopt the California suggestion for fringe land on the outskirts of cities now under heavy pressure because of the demand for development? The thing has already been done in development areas. Is there any logical reason why it should not be extended in scope?

A version of the California procedure in the opinion of the writer, represents the only reasonable approach to the problem of land speculation, subject to the proviso that public land ought on no account ever to be sold outright, but leased to developers.

WAYS AND MEANS

If it be accepted that withdrawal of urban fringe land from the operations of the market is the only effective means of preventing speculation in land, it remains to consider how best to arrange for public ownership, and under what conditions. It is a question of whether it is better to set up an ad hoc organization to acquire land, or whether to use existing authorities. Are municipalities willing or able to enter the real-estate business? In view of prevalent attitudes, this seems doubtful. It would necessitate a good deal of propaganda and public relations work to put the idea across to municipal representatives. On the other hand, it would probably be easiest in precisely those areas where the problems of speculation are most acute.

On the face of it, it seems that the best way of securing public control of land development is through machinery at state level. The existing expropriation procedure may be applied to land for general development, just as in the case of land required for highway works.

It cannot be too strongly argued that once land is taken back into the public domain, or "resumed" as they say in Australia, it should on no account be sold outright, but should be leased to developers on long leases, of varying length, for example from eighty to ninety-nine years. The advantages of this are manifold. The public authority retains ultimate control of the land, and of the development, which is to take place thereon.

The kind of controls that can be written into a deed of lease are worth all the zoning by-laws in the world. More than that, the only owning authority retains the plus-value, and on the expiry of the lease, it recoups the value and can grant a fresh lease on more advantageous terms.

There is nothing revolutionary in this, it has been done very often elsewhere. It is simply a question of adapting familiar procedures, and making vigorous use of powers and machinery often already available. This must be coupled with a campaign of education and information, to gain the backing of public opinion.

4. Developing and Planning the Regions of Canada

OBSERVATIONS ON CANADIAN CITIES, 1960-61

E. T. Rashleigh

> *Mr. Rashleigh is a community planner with an academic background in Sociology. His planning work has been in Ontario and British Columbia, where he was Director of the Community Planning Association of Canada, B.C. Division. This paper is the product of a two-year cross-country personal survey of the cities of Canada.*

Over the past ten years, any planner working in Canada has been kept constantly aware of the rapid pace of urban growth, particularly in the larger centres. Everyone takes for granted that this growth will continue to typify the expansion of the country, and no one, to be more specific, seemed to question the validity of the 1980 predictions made by the Royal Commission on Canada's Economic Prospects five years ago. What was surprising was, that if no one questioned the prospect of feverish urban growth over the next twenty-five years, few seemed very concerned about it. Yet it was my impression, as a working planner, that the larger metropolitan centres which were expected to more than double their populations in thirty years, had not, so far, demonstrated any remarkable prowess in city building, and had ignored several fundamental problems which would become critical as the rapid urban build-up continued. After well over a decade of post-war building, the most we could point to were isolated successes across the country: a good neighbourhood subdivision here, an inoffensive highway approach to the city there, a block of slum clearance somewhere else.

Until recently, much of this was supposition based on the author's own experience in Toronto and hasty or second-hand impressions of other cities. Over the past two years, however, the writer has spent time in most of the metropolitan centres of the country, becoming familiar with their layout while keeping in mind the future forecast for them. This paper is, in large part, a product of this tour. It is a critical commentary on what is on the ground today, not so much in any city in particular as in the larger cities generally. The author must apologize beforehand because most of the observations will be familiar ones, and many have already been set down in one publication or another. Perhaps, though, it is worthwhile to reaffirm, on the basis of a personal survey, that certain characteristic failings of Canadian urban growth still persist.

THE VITAL CORE

It would be wrong to describe the typical form of growth exhibited by the central commercial cores of Canadian cities, without first recognizing that they differ from each other in many respects. By this I refer not only to such obvious qualities as the old-world charm of Quebec and the maritime orientation of some cities, but to the fact, for example, that Quebec and Ottawa have developed two cores instead of the customary one, each with a different function; that the core of Regina displays an emphasis on serving not just the city, but the surrounding farm population, whereas Windsor has a relatively small downtown core because Detroit lies just across the river, and because another section of Windsor, once a separate municipality, still maintains a flourishing shopping district; and, of course, that each core reflects the character of its original townsite layout.

The Typical Pattern

Nevertheless, one can generalize to a considerable extent on the manner in which all cores are growing at the present time. The traditional heart of downtown still prevails in most cities as a hard core of better retail outlets extending for several blocks along a street that connects directly with the main roads out of town. The less-than-best outlets try to get as close to this centre of gravity, on the same street if possible, or on other main intersecting streets. Thus, the retail area acquires a strip or vertebrae shape. When it grows, it tends to be attracted by the main arteries more than any other single factor. But the medium-sized cities of Canada cannot sustain a hard retail core much more than four or five blocks long without low-rent, low-density gaps appearing, and it is also apparent that a core will stretch only so far along the main street before it loses its "downtown" quality. However, because there are so many streets on which the core may deepen, the small businessman does not like the gamble of locating on a side street or losing a direct connection with the existing retail core, so premium retail development does not usually occur behind the main street unless there is a large office building, parking garage or big store to establish the pattern. The usual deepening process starts on the side streets crossing the heart of the core, which build up until the back street, running parallel to the old main and between these streets, can be built up. This second main street is a fairly recent feature of core development. Edmonton and Calgary have one that built up in the typical piece-meal fashion, while the Wellington Square enclosed mall in London is a deliberate attempt to deepen the core en bloc.

Around the hard core are other functional segments of downtown. Specialty stores must be near the heart of the core. But in trying to locate cheap space they help give a new direction to retail expansion. The cheap outlets may locate anywhere on the periphery, or out along a main street, but they also may congregate, in the retail core of a bygone era, as a skid-row near the railroad station, and so on. Cities with a farmers' market, like London, Windsor and Ottawa, have a special retail dimension to one side of the main street: regrettably, this element has almost disappeared in Hamilton and will probably be removed in Windsor. Most cores contain groups of related businesses, such as wholesalers, banking and insurance companies. This tendency to congregate has been repeated in recent years with the building up of prestige office streets, although rather than establish a completely new pattern, they tend to capitalize upon an existing, well laid-out and attractively landscaped street. A prominent exception to this is the complex of new oil company office buildings in Calgary, which is several blocks removed from the old core; here the transformation has been so rapid that a nineteen-storey building virtually rubs shoulders with a two-storey frame house. In many cities the retail core has acquired, in recent years, a sprawling backside of parking lots and other automobile services so that it stands isolated in a no-man's land of asphalt, the inevitable result, under present circumstances, when large cities have a high incidence of automobiles.

Influences and Inadequacies

Having generalized on the pattern of the core, I now turn to the effect of this pattern. By and large, most cores possess cacophony and at the same time monotony, a relentless regularity in plan and chaos in elevation, an anaemia of content and a chronic lack of intentional emphasis. Where this description does not apply, it usually means that the major factors which shape the core have been offset. These are: a rigid adherence to the past, a jealous retention of property rights, and an absence of a unifying hand.

Literally underlying every development is the pattern of streets and individually owned parcels of land, which were designed in a different era for a completely different purpose. These remain, extremely resistant to either modification or reorganization. The grid-street system creates the overall mould of uniform blocks. Narrow lots break the blocks up into small parcels which were laid out with no appreciation of the fact that retail operations require a different layout from residential properties. So stores and office buildings have long since had to make maximum use of the land, leaving the task of circulation wholly to the public rights-of-way. Efforts to improve traffic conditions immediately run into both the expense of acquiring intensively built-up frontage, and the difficulties of changing traffic flows when nearly every street constitutes the only access to a block of properties. The pattern is equally hard for new private construction to break. The assembly of a parcel of adjoining properties is so difficult that instead a patchy, jagged-tooth facade builds up; even where assembly has been possible, the new development is still designed as a two-dimensional facade, because it is so much more difficult to assemble a parcel running through the block between streets. Thus, the old format is reaffirmed and the old errors duplicated at higher densities. Not only do these rigidities inhibit improved site development; they also obstruct the logical expansion of the various functional parts of the core. A stubborn owner, an old business which has become an unsuitable neighbour, a type of development which creates dead frontage, all can isolate a portion of a block, prevent an area from redeveloping logically, and even drive expanding businesses to other parts of the core, or outside the core, or even outside the city.

Forces other than business produce the colourful elements in the core: business is too much a creature of the national and international world, and too much motivated by a self-interest which stops at property lines to create anything more grand than a building, or to add anything unique to the street scene. The municipality is the major co-ordinating influence in the core, but so far, few have acted vigorously, partly because there are so many interests which place a great value on the downtown. But the municipalities must share the blame more directly. Most seem to have a very narrow conception of the core's function: it is expected to move cars and store them, contain stores, offices and factories, and provide pedestrian access to them. It is hard to believe that municipal authorities regard their downtown as a place to enjoy, to relax in, or to look at. So for this reason, too, innovation, experiment and imagination in new growth is rare: most of the pleasant features, the idiosyncrasies, the surprises are inherited from the past. Also one gets the impression that dollars and cents alone are deciding the fate of the core as the main centre of non-business activities.

This restraint on the part of the municipality manifests itself in a number of shortcomings. In several cities, the future direction of core expansion is not at all clear, as though it is being left to work itself out through the push and pull of individual decisions. Public institutions are scattered through the core and outside it, sometimes in unsuitable locations; too often the question of whether to decentralize the auditorium, art gallery and museum, or to organize them into a centre is being decided on the basis of land costs alone. Existing historic public open spaces are respected, but rarely appreciated to the extent of being duplicated. There are few vantage points where one can step aside to watch the activity of the core, or, in maritime cities, to get a panorama of the harbour. Nature is excluded from the core, or at best, found around its edges. The retail core is an introvert structure, preoccupied with its business and ignoring its surroundings: few efforts are made to relate it to adjoining parts or take advantage of the natural assets of the setting. (One example of this is downtown London which ignores the river at the end of its main street; but maritime cities can be accused of the same indifference.) Lastly, contemporary building, with its anonymous face, is wiping away much of the old character of the central city. Just one example of this: St. John's is the only large city in Canada where you can walk along the main street and at every intersection see the water's edge a few yards away; this perfect symbol of the city's economy is to be eradicated by a truck access route.

Surely it is now obvious that, as the core is one of the most intensively used parts of the city, there must be comprehensive planning if it is to improve. There must be a unifying power able to set the design "theme" of the core, which will link and draw together its elements, and work out the pattern of expansion. This requires less of the uniform restraint of the zoning by-law, but more emphasis on restraint, and a greater direction of new growth by the municipality.

Acceptance of this degree of intervention by both business and the municipality, is the stumbling block, but there are a few hopeful signs: new city halls have involved several municipalities in so heavy an expenditure that they are taking special care to encourage suitable surrounding development. Perhaps Windsor has gone furthest in this direction: it has started pushing a boulevard through from the civic square to the waterfront, and may eventually link up with a riverside park that was recently created at the foot of the main shopping street; this has already become a focal point for an auditorium and a local museum. Too often, though, municipal improvements stay within the traditional limits of responsibility. Too often, costly street improvements are unaccompanied by a reassessment of the organization of adjoining land or by an equivalent concern for the needs of the pedestrian. The closed-street mall is a useful solution to these problems, because it causes a minimum of disturbance to the status quo of property ownership. In many cities, though, the main shopping street is also a main artery which cannot be closed; if, instead, an adjoining secondary street is successfully converted, this could shift the centre of shopping activity. However, the closed-street mall will not work in all cities; moreover, it is a hesitant compromise which does not overcome the inadequacies of the grid-street and lot layout. If substantial improvement of the core is to be achieved, the mall, or any other concept, will have to be a component of a master plan which predetermines the redevelopment of each block, and has the power to co-ordinate the use of the constituent properties.

No special case is being made here for any one form of core revitalization: on the contrary, the hope is that every core will continue to typify the city and region it serves, and can overcome the strong tendency to make it look like every other core. Also, I hope there will be less preoccupation with getting maximum use out of the land and more determination to develop the core as the most colourful and most human part of the city.

URBAN TRANSPORTATION : THE BEST MEDIUM HAS STILL TO BE CHOSEN

There is no need to describe at length the problem posed by the automobile: present traffic, and improvements to handle it, are cutting ugly strips and patches across every city, affecting properties and choking streets. Every city is tackling these problems, usually with a greater vigour and sophistication of technique than is applied to other urban problems, and, in the smaller cities especially, the auto is still an efficient and popular method of transportation. Nevertheless, I am satisfied that the automobile is the most un-urban method of carrying people, and as cities grow, its use will have to be curtailed. The importance of the automobile as an urban carrier will vary with the size of the city. In the smaller metropolitan centres, it will continue to be a major element, with public transit providing a minimal service to a limited clientele. But beyond a given size, public transit should be favoured, by creating special lanes, subsidizing fares, building peripheral parking lots, and so on; and at a larger size, the major investment of transportation should be in a rapid transit system that will virtually replace the private automobile in the central city.

There is little evidence yet that most municipalities are trying to do much more than cope directly with the rising volume of vehicular traffic. At the present time, the automobile is permitted and given privileges at the expense of something else, if crowded downtown sidewalks and sheared-off front yards are any criteria: already highway improvements that are amenable to their surroundings cannot be afforded. Municipalities will probably continue to build bigger and better roads, for although token acknowledgement is sometimes paid to the need for public transit, plans for road improvements have the greatest popular support. The present danger is that medium-sized municipalities will commit themselves financially, and by policy decision, to improvements that have only short-term efficacy, thereby incapacitating themselves for later improvements. By this process, urban transportation will always be out of date.

LIVING THE GOOD URBAN LIFE

Some parts of a city dictate the type of land and layout they require, or are not influenced too strongly by natural conditions, but residential districts suffer and benefit from the conditions which affect the city as a whole. In Saint John the ground is so irregular in most parts, it will never permit an even expansion of the city, but will probably ensure that open space, useful or otherwise, will always be plentiful. In extreme contrast, Regina has so flat a site that development in any direction is unimpeded. London is properly called the Forest City, and for most of its life has had to be more concerned with clearing away natural growth than with replanting. Regina again presents the opposite situation of a city where every tree has been planted by man. Canadian cities also differ in their inheritance of past growth. The railroads chopped up cities like Winnipeg, which grew rapidly during the boom of that era, while Hamilton, which developed as a heavy industrial centre, acquired street after monotonous street of mass-produced housing. A large portion of Saint John was destroyed by fire and rebuilt at a time when it lacked prosperity and, in the opinion of some, architectural taste. Past growth has also bequeathed particular problems to each city: Windsor has an extensive root-like form of outer development which is very difficult to fill in and rationalize; pre-war Quebec includes numerous rabbit warrens of high density; the Prairie cities possess large old grid subdivisions still only sparsely settled.

These inheritances give shade and emphasis to the contemporary residential growth and problems of each city. But if there are differences, there are also common prospects facing the cities. All should recognize that as they grow to metropolitan dimensions, the range of types of housing that their populations need and want extends in the direction of higher densities: it is more likely, however, that the experimentation and even the permissive atmosphere necessary to produce the new forms will not appear because of ignorance or prejudice; certainly, many examples of multiple family housing reflect a failure to understand the requirements of higher density housing. It must also be recognized that the process by which neighbourhoods are now built is considerably different from that which prevailed before the war. If earlier subdivision pushed far beyond actual need, it also tended to create odd-shaped lots and leave vacant land in most neighbourhoods, which later were taken up as parks, or filled in with houses of a different period. The end product, the older districts of the cities today, display diversity and contrast as a result. Post-war subdivision, on the other hand, leaves little to chance and less to future decision. Irregularly shaped land is no longer neglected, but made usable by the bulldozer. The building process is not left to the different tastes of different times, but carried through by one developer on a full-block basis. Open space in a neighbourhood has been reduced to the minimum parkland required by the municipality. Thus modern subdivision development is more orderly and efficient, but so far also tends to be more sterile and characterless.

The Good Neighbourhood

When walking through the many different areas where people live, one realizes that each district, regardless of calibre, has benefited if certain qualities are present and suffered if they are lacking. These qualities are described below as a basis for the appraisal of different types of residential areas.

An atmosphere of community. Some districts are more successful than others in binding individual properties together as a larger whole. With them, the stranger senses, first, that he is entering an area, then, with some embarrassment, that he is an intruder. Here the home life of the resident does not stop at his frontyard; it takes in the activity of the street, the local store at the corner, the church and the playground. And over all these things there is a feeling of ownership which only the residents can possess.

This feeling of community is strongest in the older, more densely built-up districts of the Eastern cities. There the inside of the house is often worn and dark, and the yard space negligible. The street is the communal frontyard where children play and men fix their cars, while the rest of the family sits on the porch watching the world go by. Of necessity, such people must participate more in the local community, and for all its failings and ugliness, there is a homely feeling to the street which better-class apartments in suburban districts rarely possess. A sense of community, perhaps not as intimate as in the poor areas, also prevails in the old areas which once were separate communities: the district in Edmonton which once was the municipality of Strathcona, and the old centre of Sandwich, now part of Windsor still retain a unity and spirit which sets them apart from the surrounding development. One of the most carefully structured residential districts is Walkerville, also in Windsor, which was created to house employees of the Hiram Walker distillery, and in layout reflects the socio-economic differences of the residents.

This sense of community is not simply a product of age; a study of these communities reveals that physical layout, though often natural, and unintentional growth over the years, is responsible to a considerable extent. If, therefore, one observes that few recently built districts possess a sense of community, it implies a criticism of their design.

Good neighbourhood design. Without attempting a detailed discussion of principles and techniques, we may acknowledge the importance, in this period of mass housing programs of subdivision design that is comprehensive and sufficiently detailed to build a community that is efficient, visually pleasing, suited to the particular needs of its residents, includes the elements needed to make it complete, and has qualities conducive to producing a sense of community. Some of the more important elements of good design are the subject of the next five sections.

Protected isolation. Perhaps one of the most obvious and universal truths about residential properties and neighbourhoods is that they stay in better condition and have a longer life if they are cut off from surrounding non-residential areas and activities. Houses on a dead-end street are better off than those on a through road; a residential district several blocks wide stays in better repair than a street of houses within a non-residential area; a pocket of residential blocks located on one side of a main artery keeps in better condition than a district lying between two arteries. There are numerous examples of old, poorly built districts, with no open space or other community amenities, that nevertheless are able to retain their integrity and good condition because they are not subjected to a daily pounding from through traffic, or riddled with non-residential uses. While conditions of protected isolation prevail, the neighbourhood serves a useful residential function, but if, as the area declines, it is opened up to any kind of potential development, the majority of housing is doomed, not to extinction unfortunately, but to continued misery.

Visual contrast. This rudimentary principle of design must be emphasized because contemporary residential growth is so persistently uniform, in type of house and its setting, in the facade of its streets, in the evenness of its development, in the appearance of its shopping centres, and so on. The forces producing uniformity are so powerful, that if a greater diversity is ever to be achieved, a deliberate effort will have to be made to plan residential areas so they look different.

A community centre. Even more important than a clear-cut boundary is the centre about which the neighbourhood clusters. It is a point of identification for the neighbourhood; one of the few places where all the residents come together; the place where the local community comes to a head. Most community centres in Canada have grown naturally, along a main road and usually at an intersection, but the more successful ones, from a planning viewpoint, are much more than a line of stores. From these it can be generalized that a good community centre is not just a retail centre, but the place where most of the institutions serving the community are concentrated, and therefore the main centre of local community activity. Like the neighbourhood as a whole, the centre has identifiable limits and a point of focus. The latter may be a municipal building or a park, though usually it is a main intersection. The centre should be sufficiently well organized that people can get to it and move around it easily. Lastly, although it may never be an architectural triumph because it is the product of many hands, it must attract attention and must be a human setting, not one dominated by the automobile or the symbolism of national corporations.

Open space and landscaping. Open space and landscaping are probably more underrated than any other feature. The trees and landscaping of a district can mark its boundaries, establish its character, soundproof it, cool it, and create its contrasts of colour and light intensity. A district is improved more by attention to plant and tree growth than by adding to the value of the houses. This is demonstrated by the better residential areas, which invariably have open space as a major feature. Much of the luxury atmosphere of Rockcliffe Village in Ottawa, for instance, is achieved by keeping properties very large, and the roads very narrow, so that the whole district is dominated by natural growth: the houses are largely hidden from view. The same result is more consciously achieved in Wildewood, a middle-class district in Winnipeg, which is one of the best Canadian examples of the Radburn principle of fronting properties on a common central park and hiding the roads behind the houses. And again most of the poorest areas on the outskirts of cities, if they have nothing else, enjoy empty lots and open fields. It seems as though the rich and the poor can have good open space, but the middle-income groups, whose housing needs are catered to on a mass-production basis, have to get along without it—for the first ten years at least.

Subordination of the auto. When the private automobile is treated as an all-important factor in the layout of a residential area, it becomes objectionable. It confines the neighbourhood design to the few alternatives which enable the car to get right up to the house. It requires most of the land which can reasonably be set aside for public use. It dominates the landscape and introduces an accident hazard precisely where small children most frequently play. It adds significantly to development costs through the installation of pavements, curbing and dual sidewalks. In short, in the moderate cost subdivision, the dictates of the automobile can be satisfied only at the expense of other features of residential life. If any residential area, new or old, is to be improved, the convenience offered by the automobile must be subordinated to the other needs of the neighbourhood.

Minimum standards for family districts. Cities in Western Canada are generally built at lower densities than those in the East; this includes their central residential districts which, though old and poorly built, manage to keep gardens and a bit of grass. Largely because of this, these areas never seem to reach the level of nastiness and disrepair that can be found in the cities further east. At a time when so much private building seems to have the objective of getting as much floor space on a lot as will be tolerated, and with the need to rejuvenate old housing increasing every year, it is necessary to recognize that there are minimum standards for building and rehabilitating family housing areas, which, if undercut, destine a district for premature decline. Setting a maximum gross density is not enough. There must be standards of light, air and privacy for each dwelling unit, and there must be space for recreation and other activities in the neighbourhood. The closer development approaches the minimum standards, the more cleverly and precisely it has to be planned: so it can endure intensive use; so different parts do not conflict (children's play areas with houses, for example); so public areas can be kept clean and tidy; so that boundaries are well defined; and so well-used areas are durable as well as good looking.

These seven qualities of good residential districts lead to one important conclusion: to have stability and be pleasing to the eye, a residential district does not have to have a picturesque topography or costly housing, but it must have a sensible density, a street system suitable for the land, variety, and contrast in layout, a proper balance of neighbourhood facilities, and an imaginative use of open space and natural growth. Without these qualities, well-designed housing is mediocre; with them, the simplest housing can form a healthy attractive neighbourhood.

The Shortcomings of Suburbia

Criticism of post-war suburbs has almost become a national sport, perhaps because, in the part of the city least restricted by the dead hand of the past, modern city building has regularly produced the trite and the obvious. One can criticize suburban architecture, which from coast to coast follows the strawberry-box school, and continue with a detailed critique of the street and neighbourhood. But perhaps the failing of suburban growth can be reduced to two main faults.

First, suburban neighbourhood design is dominated by an indiscriminating desire for space. This has produced lots of space for all things and between all things. The typical residential street is dominated by an expanse of road, boulevards, sidewalks, and front yards, against which the single-storey house offers insignificant contrast. This low line of houses is occasionally broken by a square of park, but rarely by more imaginatively planned open space designed to contrast with the street. The shopping centre stands in asphalt isolation from the surrounding development, typically a bald line or "L" of low stores. Other components of the suburbs—school grounds, community centres and the like—add to the expanse. Largely because of the developer's scorched earth policy, there are few trees and bush growth to fill the void; instead the popular standard of lot layout—front lawn, back lawn, path to front door, driveway to one side of lot, low hedge if any, not much garden, a picture window unobscured—contributes to the visual monotony.

The second failing of suburbia is that it has few of the unifying features that the term "neighbourhood" implies. One area runs into the next, divided only by main roads and roadside development. The methods used to protect and isolate the houses are half-hearted and only partly successful. In Edmonton, much of the new subdivision has service roads and grass boulevards between the main arteries and the residential properties, but in other cities, the curvilinear road design alone is usually relied upon to discourage non-local traffic, with few attempts made to add a buffer. Also, in every city there are countless examples of houses fronting on main streets, and shopping centres or gas stations flanking a row of houses. The average suburb is without a centre, too. Rather, development is turned inside out, so its shopping centres are on the edges and oriented toward the road. Besides, the shopping centre fails as a community centre because, being organized strictly to do business, it has no space or time for other community needs; and unfortunately the other community facilities are only occasionnally combined with the shops to form a well-rounded neighbourhood centre.

It is perhaps too obvious to conclude that improvement will only come with more detailed neighbourhood planning which relates the essential components to each other, and, more than anything else, minimizes the influence of the automobile over neighbourhood design.

Post-war building has been little concerned with the need for low-cost housing; presumably, under existing conditions, this market offers little or no economic incentive. It is therefore worthwhile noting that certain pre-war and wartime efforts offer examples of how low-cost housing can be built. The economies are realized by reducing subdivision standards and services to their minimum. Wartime housing projects illustrate one approach which has been successful enough to keep them in good condition up to the present time. Lots are only 35-40 feet by 120 feet, but by building two-storey houses, the yard area is kept as large as possible. Other savings in land come from reducing the local road to an 18-foot width of pavement and running the sidewalks right alongside them. The compactness of this layout is relieved by open spaces which sometimes are the focal point of the subdivision. It is indicative of the quality of the layout that many wartime subdivisions turn their backs on surroundings through roads and even include a perimeter buffer strip. Older subdivisions which filled in gradually during the Depression years, demonstrate that a residential area can get along quite well without many of the niceties now insisted upon. Roads and sidewalks can be gravelled, ditches can take the place of curbs and storm sewers, even building standards can be cut to the bone. The district produced may never become a model of middle-class suburbia, it may even be slightly more costly to maintain, but it is one way for low-income families to occupy their own homes instead of subsidized housing. In a society which places great value on home ownership, surely this should be an important objective.

Preserving the Old Districts

A report of the Advisory Commission on Reconstruction, published at the end of the last war, roughly estimated that, in 1941, 40 per cent of the dwellings in urban Canada were thirty-one years old and over, with the greatest volume of residential construction having taken place in the Twenties. [1] Numbers of these dwellings have since been demolished, but

---

[1] Subcommittee on Housing and Community Planning, *Final Report*, Queen's Printer, Ottawa, 1946, p. 29.

it is obvious that in every city there are still large areas of houses which are now forty to sixty years of age. Despite old age and deficiencies, these districts include centres and pockets of development which have built up and elaborated over the years, so they now are among the more interesting and characterful sections of the city. At the same time, much of it is not good housing: three-storey houses achieving high densities are common, especially in Ontario; many of the smaller houses are of simple frame construction which soon deteriorates if neglected; some were jerry-built; some streets of houses are wedged tightly between older developments; much is dull and monotonous.

This old housing is being subjected to pressures and strains created by the post-war growth of the city. Central districts lie in the path of the expanding core, which under speculative development, tends to open up more area than it needs. In a similar fashion, institutions which previously were reasonably compatible with their residential neighbours, want to expand their plant and parking space, while more institutions try to locate cheap central quarters among the old houses. Small industries which never were compatible grow into bigger industries. The old mansions of a city create a problem because they were designed for a particular use of a past era; obsolete and expensive to maintain, the owners seek to put them to any use that is economical, with the result that they, more than small houses, are in danger of being overused and misused. And all residential districts close to the city centre are incapable of handling either the volume of traffic to and from the downtown area, or the automobiles their residents now own.

If the old houses of the central city were destined to disappear in the near future, their present living conditions would be of passing interest, but it is inconceivable that the majority of them will be taken over by non-residential operations or replaced by new housing. In fact, the old districts will probably continue to supply a wide range of accommodation—single rooms, flats, and low-cost family housing; they will remain the customary locale of ethnic settlements; and they will increasingly reflect a tendency, apparent so far only in the larger cities, for some middle-class families to live in the central city.

It is surprising how well this housing is being maintained on the whole. But the owners are labouring under disadvantages which only the municipality can overcome, and yet the older districts seem to be less protected by municipal policy than are the new suburbs. Zoning is the typical defence, a negative safeguard with legal non-conforming loopholes that have particular significance in this part of the city. Slum clearance projects have removed relatively small amounts of deteriorated housing, and could not cope financially with much larger areas; even if possible, it is debatable whether a large amount of public or subsidized housing is desirable in the central city. What is needed are broad, continuing municipal programs to protect and improve the integrity of the older houses and their neighbourhoods. The appropriate action would have to vary with the particular need of the area: a decision not to widen a heavily used road, or to close it;

punching a hole in a tight block of houses; the removal of non-conforming uses and houses in bad condition. The appropriate action should also take into consideration the attitude of the residents: in districts displaying local pride, it might be logical, and economical, to give indirect public support (e.g. a supply of house paint at cost) rather than undertake public works. Lastly, the appropriate action will have to maintain the existing use of housing, or provide for a transition to another use; if the objective is to assist but not eradicate an area of low-cost housing, it will be important to avoid removing or driving away such features as the corner store, cut-rate shops and space to work on the car.

Rehabilitation on a large scale has not yet been faced by Canadian municipalities. Because it involves new expenditures, extra administration, and a degree of community improvement not yet practised, municipalities will likely resist assuming this responsibility, especially if already committed to expensive slum clearance projects.

The Good Life at High Densities

The number of apartments built varies a great deal from city to city, but on the whole they are one of the most distressing products of post-war urban growth. The buildings are usually of a trite plan design, sited with a minimum of imagination and landscaping. Much of the fault stems from a preoccupation with achieving a maximum density on a lot designed for low-density use, complicated by the need to provide off-street parking space: the end-product is necessarily a structure which hogs a site surfaced in large part with asphalt. When several apartment blocks are built side by side, the effect is so arid one wonders why any man, whose wife is less than very loving, bothers to come home at night.

Up to now apartment sites have been selected more on the basis of the advantages of the site than in accordance with an overall plan; zoning is the main regulator, but in some cities this has limited significance in the older districts. Properties that are deep and wide are invariably sought out, and this has resulted in the replacement of many old, but nevertheless handsome mansions, as well as the filling in of irregular parcels which previously had been neglected. (What will happen, one wonders, when the supply of large lots is used up? Will apartment standards drop, rents go up, or will land values go down?) Apartment developers usually ignore areas in need of reconstruction, preferring to capitalize upon the attractiveness of well-landscaped, stable districts. As the apartments appear, that charm disappears, and too often the stability of the district is weakened. In the new suburbs, apartments are cramped on the land at higher densities than the surrounding houses but with no compensating features: frequently they lie alongside a main road or butt up against a shopping centre. In some instances one is led to conclude that these buildings are intended to be sound barriers rather than housing. In the other districts, the introduction of more intensive housing brings drastic changes to the existing pattern of development. At present, the allocation of land for high-density housing is still treated as a zoning matter, and the implications of introducing larger buildings and more people into an area are substantially ignored. It is difficult to see how any improvement can be made here without assembling properties in accordance with a plan designed to prepare a district for high-density use. Obviously, to do this a fair degree of public participation will be necessary.

Post-war building trends substantially ignore the fact that many families, particularly in Eastern and Maritime cities, live in multiple unit buildings of one kind or another. Row housing, duplexes and the like, permit a moderate increase in density over the single-family unit, but to compensate for this gain, they require a skilful site layout. Because this is a characteristic failing of Canadian building, there are many bad examples of multiple unit buildings across the country, which probably accounts for the strong resistance to new efforts in this direction. There are some good examples though. A street of row houses in Walkerville, Windsor, some approaching the charm of ivy-covered cottages, comes to mind as an example from the past. Among the recent products, public housing projects seem to represent the best we can do. The rows are not built too long to be monotonous, the street system and siting of the buildings create a diversified scene, even though they have a straighforward design. The project site is large enough that the buildings are oriented away from the main road, and interior roads are kept to a minimum; instead foot paths and stretches of grass run between many of the units. Parking space is organized on a communal basis.

Nevertheless, the projects have several common failings. Invariably they are devoid of trees and shrubbery. Perhaps this is a maintenance economy, but it does much to establish an impersonal institutional and in the summer, oven-like atmosphere. Open space is not usually segregated, and inevitably the children play around the houses; at these densities there is a need for at least one organized recreation area removed from the houses. Perhaps the most striking omission is that there is no outdoor privacy or any demarcation to show that certain grounds belong to a particular unit. As a result, each unit is never more than an anonymous part of the institutional whole, bound together by unbroken stretches of open space. Surely each resident should be given the opportunity to enjoy a feeling of possession, if only to encourage his responsibility for maintenance.

WIDENING THE SUPPLY OF OPEN SPACE

No feature of contemporary urban growth suffers more than open space from our insistence on accounting for every scrap of urban land. The error lies not only in inadequate provision, but also in an oversimplified concept of its form and use: open space has become a parcel of land set aside for use as a park or a playground, which means it is either equipped for sports, or is a square, perhaps a triangle of land, levelled, grassed and cleared of all growth except for a selection of trees, shrubs and neat beds of plants. Somehow, the lessons offered by the past have not been taken to heart, so that with very few exceptions, we must still look at pre-war products to appreciate the wide range of open space it is possible to have.

In a sense, the largest open space is that which offers panorama. This may be a view of the sea, a river, a section of the city, or one of its features. The City of Edmonton has a well-established policy of developing, as public boulevards, the lands overlooking the broad and deep South Saskatchewan River valley. Regina has no opportunity to look down or up, so early in the century, the creek running through the city was dammed to make a lake, and extensive parkland was planted with trees. This now forms a very cool setting for the provincial government buildings, with ample space for even socialist government expansion. Other cities have inherited similar bounties, but too often—in the East more than the West it is my impression—they are not adequately preserved or developed. Fort Howe, in Saint John, for example, affords an aerial view of the city and harbour which Toronto would give its eye teeth to possess, yet it is undeveloped and neglected. Even more common is a failure to have adequate points of public access to the sea or riverfront, especially in the older parts of the city: the railroads are a frequent obstruction. Every city has at least one major, developed park which is its pride and joy. To my knowledge, all are inheritances from the past. A surprising number were military holdings originally. Others are ravines and valley lands, unsuitable for intensive development. But clearly, some cities have been more methodical than others in parkland acquisition and preservation. For example, Edmonton has four golf courses, two municipally-owned, close to the centre of town: compare this with the Shaughnessy Golf Course in Vancouver now close to being subdivided, and the shortage of golf links common to most large cities. One other form of major open space is a connected system of parks, public grounds, boulevards and paths. A good example is in Calgary, where a boulevard runs along the top of the Bow River valley from a park overlooking the valley, to the grounds of the Jubilee Auditorium about a mile and a half away. With an emphasis on variety, an ability to utilize a wide range of types of land, and an effect of tying a district together, this is one of the most potentially useful concepts of open space.

It is not necessary to recite the standard need for local parks, but the all too standardized approach should be pointed up. Too many parks look as though they were surrendered under the subdivision regulations rather than included as a component of the neighbourhood design; their original lack of justification perhaps explains why they remain open stretches of grass, clearly labelled "Park", and set apart from their surroundings. Some of the better subdivisions use space as a visual breather, or to preserve a natural feature, or as a setting for the houses : again, the Wildewood subdivision in Winnipeg, with a winding park as its central theme, provides an exceptional example. Occasionally, too, one comes across a juxtaposed shopping centre and park which hints at a way to create, within a park setting, a community centre of shops and local public services. An obvious scheme perhaps, but how rarely is it attempted.

The attitude of keeping open space in its place also prevents it from finding its way into the downtown core. I am tempted to generalize that one of the main design inadequacies of Canadian cores is caused by an ignorance of the value and versatility of open space. Traditionally, central open space is limited to that which is immediately utilitarian or obviously decorative. Most fall into one or more of these categories :

the commemorative square,
a green space set apart for people to rent,
a natural feature that has been preserved,
a setting for a public building,
open space geometrically positioned in the original town plan,
an outdors business activity, most frequently a market.

The more successful open spaces, if measured by intensity of use or aesthetic appeal, are areas which have outlived their original function and been allowed to convert to a more casual use. Quebec within the walls offers several examples : Dufferin Terrace, once a battery site commanding the St. Lawrence, evolved into the main promenade of the city, and the two squares nearby that are focal points of the tourist city, previously functioned as a parade square and a market.

These represent a type of open space that only recently has received adequate recognition : an area of public activity which functions as part of, or is physically related to, the main function of the core. The sidewalk and the public market are the traditional versions, the mall is recent. Such open space does not have standard dimensions or layout; it can use the odd, left-over scraps and corners, the pieces that are most readily surrendered for such a negative use. But if more is to be done in this direction, we must have a better appreciation of the social psychology of open space in the core. We must learn that people like to watch people, to see them act, and to get into the act themselves. The citizen comes to see what is new with his fellow citizens, and to take part in the daily performance of the human comedy : as glamour girl or undeniable romeo, superior observer or lonely isolate, humanitarian or proselytizer. The people create the drama, but the planner-architect must first create the setting. Good central open space of any size has transition and contrast in its middle, and ends that lead somewhere else. There is unity, but also diversity in colour, design and surface texture. Sound is controlled; the noise and activity of auto traffic serves as a background to open space, not an intrusion. In some places, people are properly crowded together, but there should be quiet sidewaters as well even within the same space. Whatever is done, the objective is to give the users maximum freedom to make of the place what they will, by creating a setting which suits them and the environment : for all its appeal, Piazza San Marco should not be imported.

The supply as well as the quality of open space varies considerably from city to city. The quantity seems to increase from east to west, but it is probably true that every city has a shortage of open space and, in addition, under prevailing conditions of compact development, needs a continuing program of parks acquisition to anticipate future requirements. One can easily become pessimistic about this being done. Some cities have never been overly concerned about open space, others have enjoyed such an abundance within the city and without, that the need to prepare for the time when the population will outgrow the natural supply is not taken seriously. In fact, all cities are too close to their small town and frontier days to appreciate what they are in the process of losing. Besides, open space is never regarded as the most pressing need : how many cities have even stopped polluting the waterways within their boundaries ? The prospect of a wider, more intelligent use of open space is gloomiest of all in the core, for, in the part of the city where land values are highest, what chance is there for a land use which cannot be judged by sound business principles ?

THE CITY AS A "COLLECTIVE WORK OF ART"

[The city] is a conscious work of art, and it holds within its communal framework many simpler and more personal forms of art. Mind takes form in the city; and in turn, urban forms condition mind.... The dome and the spire, the open avenue and the closed court, tell the story, not merely of different physical accommodations, but of essentially different conceptions of man's destiny. The city is both a physical utility for collective living and a symbol of those collective purposes and unanimities that arise under such favouring circumstance. With language itself, it remains man's greatest work of art. (Lewis Mumford, *The Culture of Cities*).

The previous paragraphs have followed the customary planning approach of looking at each functional part of the city separately. This overlooks, or at any rate underemphasizes, a quality of all contemporary urban growth which should be primary cause for concern among planners.

From one viewpoint, this can be described as a lack of visual diversity. The development patterns of Canadian cities have basically two origins. Some cities have grown naturally, coping with land conditions piecemeal, following original trails and growing at the whim of individual developers. Victoria, St. John's and old Quebec are good examples. But more often, city growth, including parts of these three cities, has adhered to, and up to the post-war period extended, a grid system. Thus, order and regularity prevails in the layout of most cities, but contrast, change and surprise are rare, and what does exist is not a product of forethought, but of chance and gradual evolution. Planning removes the element of chance in urban growth, but so far has not often been successful in introducing intentional contrast, and recent building has only consolidated the regularity of urban design.

The growing tendency to urban uniformity may also be expressed as a loss of local and regional differences in urban growth. In terms of founding dates and site conditions Canadian cities probably represent as wide a range as will be found in any country. It is still possible to see these cities as the products of several generations of people who have a historical background that still influences their attitudes, their values and their tongues, who make a living in particular ways, and who have adapted their way of life and their city to the weather, land form, changing technology and external pressures. But the image of each city is blurring. More and more they are coming to look alike, as new construction reflects national and international patterns : gas stations are identical in appearance from coast to coast; roadside development on the outskirts of every city uses identical building and advertising techniques; basically the same subdivision and house plans are adopted across the country (because, one is tempted to believe, they are most likely to be accepted by, often were designed by, the federal mortgaging authority); office buildings reflect international architectural styles and use module-dominated, standardized building techniques and materials. No doubt there is something to be said about these tendencies being desirable or unavoidable, but there is much to be said, and little being done, about preserving and encouraging individualism in Canadian cities. It is naturally repugnant to the average resident if he is told his town looks like many others, or has no character : it implies the same may be said about him, and certainly there is an interaction between a city and its people which shapes both. It may well be that the universal urban forms that are imported will eventually prove unsatisfactory under local conditions, or worse, will work to obliterate the identity of the residents. The planner, who presumes to rationalize the building process, will be increasingly challenged by this wholesale depersonalization of cities, and be confronted with the aesthetic issue of contemporary urban growth : whether, with such an impoverished background of conscious urban design in this country, the strong tendency to regularize development can be overcome.

WILL IT BE AN ERA OF PLANNING ?

These are the major issues I see cropping up in all metropolitan centres during this period of rapid urbanization. Some are inheritances from the past to be overcome. Some involve foreseeing the long-range needs of the future. All are intensified by the present rapid pace of growth. A sound planning program is essential if we are to cope with these problems; more to the point, more effective planning is needed than now prevails. This is less a criticism of Canadian planning talent and more a concern about the atmosphere the planner works in today. Will cities face the issues that arise as they grow to metropolitan stature ? There is no final answer except a *post factum* one, for no form of development, good or bad, is inevitable. Fortunately many of the important decisions have still to be made, but we must admit that one pedestrian mall does not represent a revolution in downtown design, nor one Don Mills a major breakthrough in suburbia.

The planner must recognize that Canadian society has ingrained attitudes and values which are inimical to the truly urban way of life, and particularly the planning action it entails. It might be well to summarize these.

First, many older Canadians (some now in positions of authority) grew up on a farm or in a small town, and if younger adults did not take part in this way of life, many inherited a family background that did. Moreover, a generation ago our largest cities were small enough and sufficiently loose-knit for the countryside to be near at hand. There was land to spare, and people displayed a frontier-like indifference to what was done with it. Roderick Haig-Brown describes how each of the resources of British Columbia was, of necessity, ransacked in order to open up the province. [2] With Canada still a country of wide-open spaces, the traditional attitude to the land has been carried over to the urban setting, where, as in earlier times, the cost of indifference is not yet fully realized.

Second, this heritage, along with a failure to import other than the most straightforward planning concepts when the cities were laid out, has resulted in Canadians having almost no first-hand knowledge of the more sophisticated and architecturally interesting forms of civic design.

Third, in this country, the social value of land ownership is high, while tenancy and public ownership is held suspect. Private land ownership is so sacrosanct in public opinion and law, that it can question the propriety of planning proposals and defeat legitimate community objectives. One of the most effective limitations it imposes on planning comes from the extreme stability it gives to property lines, even when they divide the land into parcels unsuitable for modern use.

Fourth, the municipality is expected to provide the necessities of public life, but its responsibility for community pleasures is limited. Compared with European cities, municipal responsibility in Canada for promoting the arts is small and uncertain. Several metropolitan cities do not have a public auditorium. Many art galleries and museums are privately organized operations billeted in old houses. The preservation of local history has only recently started to receive public support. City halls are singularly lacking in outdoor space for civic celebrations. A hard thing to generalize upon certainly, but I am tempted to conclude that, on the municipal level of government no great responsibility is accepted to propagate the cultural and social pleasures of the people. Nor does the populace, in turn, either expect these pleasures or hold them in very high esteem. The attitude toward city building is that it be concerned with the pioneer tasks of supplying a roof over your head, an adequate supply of water and other basic necessities, and rarely are there aggressive demonstrations of public dissatisfaction with an urban setting that is

---

[2] R. Haig-Brown, *The Living Land*, Macmillan, Toronto, 1961, Chap. I.

visually trite or ugly, or unable to provide the finer, non-essential things of urban life.

Fifth, there is a widespread reluctance to subordinate the ideas and wishes of the individual to any plan designed to meet the needs of the community as a whole. Whether explained as human nature or a continuation of the pioneer spirit, this attitude in its extreme forms directly opposes the basic premises of planning. The attitude "We have no right to tell a person what to do with his land" still prevails, and a fear of flouting public opinion and private interests which hold this view can be read into municipal hesitation to undertake new planning programs.

The criticism of these social values is not that they are inherently wrong, but that they are out of date as far as city building is concerned. The period of exploration by rugged individualists is over, and we are confronted in our cities with a version of the world problem created by our growing population : determining to what extent man must submit to common objectives and common operations in order to survive. We are at the stage of urban growth in Canada which requires, not grudging recognition of the need to plan in the trouble spots, but positive recognition of the value of taking everything into one's ken, of knowing, when you pay Paul, how much you are liable to rob Peter. The alternative is to have, not collapse, but mediocrity and inadequacy in our cities.

This problem is still being resolved, and the planner regularly finds himself in a dilemma. On the one hand he is better aware than most of what must be done, but on the other hand, every day he hears opinions expressed and decisions made which prevent the community growing sensibly and efficiently. Should he play a more active part in putting plans across ? Some will point out that the municipal planner is a professional servant of the people and thereby limited in his public behaviour; the planning profession as a group in Canada has tacitly pursued a policy of not taking a public stand on issues. Others say the task of gaining acceptance of planning is lengthy and painstaking : much is still to be done, but much has already been achieved. But the nagging question persists : How much time do we have before the city of the next few generations is built ? Too often the answer seems to be that it is half built already, in all its archaic splendour; the planner is rapidly becoming the person who should have been listened to. So to the question : Should the planner work at putting planning ideas across ? the answer often seems to be, Who else ? Who better ? There is also a selfish aspect to this answer. Planning, like any creative art, must be marked by achievement; frustrated planners turn out handsome reports, but happy planners see their ideas implemented by a sympathetic community. Surely this is an important part of the adventure of planning.

FLEMINGDON PARK, A NEW URBAN COMMUNITY

Macklin L. Hancock

Mr. Hancock is President of Project Planning Associates Limited of Toronto, which undertook the basic planning for Flemingdon Park, an integrated residential district of some fourteen thousand people which has been built up over the past six years. The author writes with the perspectives of both a landscape architect and a city planner.

INTRODUCTION

Planners everywhere will be thoroughly familiar with the factors that have led to the planning and now the development of the Flemingdon Park project. The basic concept is that of creating, in a desirable location, a new community of much more urban character, correcting in part the formless, sprawled peripheral sectors of the Metropolitan Toronto area. It is hoped that it can also act as an example that will turn at least a large segment of our population back towards the city, as opposed to non-city or suburban life. It is inspired and necessitated by the same urban pressures that caused the building of Fresh Meadows, Vallingby and Roehampton.

To understand the context within which the Flemingdon Park development has been planned and designed, it is necessary to review the growth of Metropolitan Toronto and its environs since World War II.

The spectacular growth of the area over the last fifteen years, with the surging population increase and rising use of the automobile, placed the formerly rural municipalities adjoining Toronto under great pressure. There ensued the development of the ubiquitous low density subdivisions of single-family dwellings, punctuated by the continuous ribbons of automobile-directed commercial facades of the major concession streets, these having acquired pavement, increasingly heavy hydro-electric poles and transmission lines, and neon. With mortgage financing favouring the single-family dwelling and the nation's people experiencing rising incomes, the warning of the planners and others concerned for the welfare of our vital urban plant went unheeded. It appeared that the outward flow of suburban nebulae would carry on unstemmed.

The three large suburbs of Etobicoke, North York and Scarborough were most affected by this growth. Prior to 1948, North York, the municipality within which Flemingdon Park is located, was a substantially rural township undergoing a modest amount of urbanization on a low density basis in sporadic development contiguous to the built-up areas of the City of Toronto and also at older community focal points such as Willowdale. Between 1948 and 1950 a rash of new, large, and unrelated

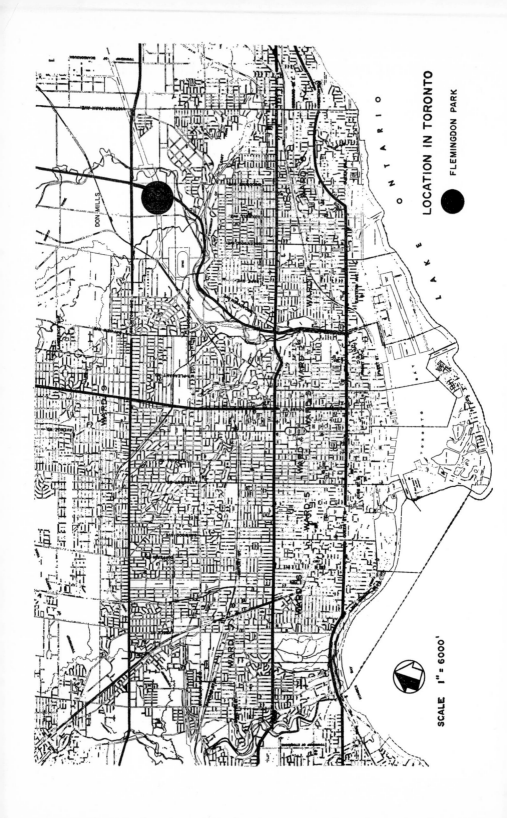

LOCATION IN TORONTO

● FLEMINGDON PARK

SCALE 1" = 6000'

housing areas appeared, characterized by continuous gridiron street patterns for the most part, with artifice occasionally shown through the provision of looped and broken circulation routes. Shopping, schools and cultural foci were placed usually on through-streets where traditional land use dictated they should be.

In 1951, following a period of careful private land assembly and influenced in part by the new town examples of Great Britain, the Don Mills integrated community was proposed. Here the first of a number of satellite communities of the Township was planned, illustrating the next evolutionary step in the growth of the municipality as a part of the Metropolitan complex. That this evolution occurred too late to be of much value in the build-up of the aspiring urban complex of Greater Toronto is shown by the vast expanse of open land that has been swallowed up for the dormitory deposition of families, whose sustenance is derived from employment obtained to the extent of more than seventy per cent of the total in the central urban core. In the main, the new communities were planned, designed and developed with the residents, financial institutions and planning boards appearing to fully sanction them. The difference with the Don Mills type of development was the creation of an integrated, balanced and unified segment of the township almost as a single townsite, rather than a scattering of parts of the urbanized sectors of Toronto pushing out into the Township.

Except for certain isolated developments, such as the McLean-Hunter publishing firm, some smaller industries in the Jane-Wilson area and at de Havilland, North York was largely barren of industrial development. With the advent of Don Mills, a complete industrial estate became an element in the township's growth, attached in a concerted way to a total community plan bounded by the twin valleys of the Don River. Regardless of improvements achieved, the community still appeared with a considerable emphasis on single-family housing and with insufficient urban character.

Development proceeded apace with a number of these more complete subdivision developments adding in large increments to North York's expansion. Now over 250,000 persons reside in the Township and an increasingly significant portion of the Metro industrial base lies there. Thus, over the last decade the Township has changed from a rural one with some urbanization to that of an urban township with blocks of undeveloped land awaiting the movement of the bulldozers, and it is apparent that the remainder of the Township will become completely urbanized within the next twelve to fourteen years, assuming the present growth trends.

In the burgeoning expansion of the Township, the Don Valley area had escaped initial urbanization, owing to poorly developed concession roads through the valleys to the plateaus in between the two branches of the River and to the difficulty of extending municipal services from the City of Toronto or adjoining built-up areas of North York. Development had followed lines of least resistance, pushed northward up Yonge

Street and through the East York and Scarborough areas, and had moved out the Danforth and Kingston Roads. With existing circulation routes, and, owing somewhat to chance, the Don Mills development had emerged to the north of the Canadian Pacific's main line, leaving the bulk of the Fleming Estate south of the railway in a single remaining parcel. It was accessible initially by Don Mills Road.

The only development south of the C.P.R. was the large International Business Machines Ltd. plant. Plans to extend the Eglinton route through the two Don Valleys south of Don Mills, long in the planning stages, were finalized by the new Metropolitan Corporation. The Don Valley Parkway, an early goal of the new Metro government, was proposed to be built, carrying up the east branch of the Don past Don Mills to connect with the newly-opened (1954) Highway No. 401. The Fleming estate, sitting astride these routes, surrounded by Leaside, East York and Scarborough's Golden Mile development, with the completing of Don Mills to the north, could not long escape its destiny as urban land.

The potential of the site, acknowledged by many, was unrealizeable for most developers, owing to the rapidly rising land values. The Robert McClintock Limited firm of builder-developers made a successful bid for the strategic prize and purchased the Fleming estate south of Eglinton Avenue late in 1955.

The firm, engaging a planning consultant, analyzed the area and proposed that the new Don Valley Parkway, rather than passing around the plateau overlooking the river valleys, should be made to carry on through the centre of a very large industrial estate. Overpasses would connect the two industrial sectors as formed across the Parkway and a small portion of the land would be devoted to some multiple-family dwellings overlooking the valley in the southern part of the site. They coined the name Flemingdon Park.

It was necessary for application to be made to the Township of North York to amend its Zoning By-Laws and request the Minister of Planning and Development to amend its Official Plan, to permit a change from the existing residential to industrial lands. This the municipality eagerly agreed to, in its ever-conscious search for much needed industrial assessment to balance the, by this time, preponderance of single-family subdivisions. Approved subsequently by the Minister and the Ontario Municipal Board in 1957, these changes clarified the location of the Don Valley Parkway.

In the spring of 1958 Toronto Industrial Leaseholds (1957) Limited, an affiliate of Webb and Knapp (Canada) Limited, acquired the Flemingdon Park site and engaged Project Planning Associates Limited as planning consultants for the development of these holdings.

From the outset, it became evident to the new owner and its consultants that, due to an enormous rise in land costs, a reduced demand for industrial land, and other matters related to development, a review of the existing plan was necessary.

The main, specific reasons for the production of a new plan were brought to the attention of the Township Council and Planning Board. The Township's Planning Director was apprized of the problems.

The high cost of land in the general area of Flemingdon Park precluded the prospect of any large-scale industrial estates with the common established low ratio of building coverage of about 7- to 10 per cent. This had been the result achieved within Metro Toronto during the period from February 1953 to January 1955. It is apparent that this ratio can only be used on lands of relatively low cost. The cost of land, therefore, dictated a much higher coverage for lands to be allocated for industry, but this type of coverage and its high land cost is only attractive to a limited sector of the industry, such as head offices, regional sales offices and prime distributors. A requirement for the type of industry willing to pay for expensive land is the attractive, strategic location of its site for identification, and a high level of visual character of the neighbouring uses. The former plan allocating about 160 acres for industrial purposes was not considered feasible under the prevailing market circumstances. It was felt that only a much smaller area with choice locations for a type of select industrial development could be achieved.

Sketch conceptual plans were prepared, discussions ensuing with the Planning Commissioner of Metropolitan Toronto, who along with the consultants viewed this as a possible example of the more urban integration of industrial and residential communities within the Metropolitan fabric. The relatively untouched lands of the Don Valleys indicated a considerable potential for a series of distinct, new and contemporary communities. The proposal was for the areas of land within the holding to be utilized to produce a well-planned grouping of neighbourhoods within identifiable, balanced community sectors. It is felt that the master plan accomplishes this by allocating approximately 180 acres for residential uses, 140 acres for greenbelt and internal open space uses, leaving about 35 acres for industrial purposes. Between Don Mills and the new Eglinton Crosstown Highway, a large undeveloped acreage held by the Fleming estate remained. It was the consultants' advice that this be added to the project to more effectively permit cohesive development of a substantial industrial estate or park. Negotiations were, therefore, immediately undertaken to complete the land assemblage on this basis.

In analyzing exact plans for site land use in relation to the overall concept for Metro's development, it appeared desirable to achieve the more rectangular profile of London's development rather than the triangular profile of the usual North American cities. Thus, high density of development was believed to be a necessary goal, consistent with attaining adequate open space areas for human amenity.

In Toronto, the main source of employment remains in the central city area while many new manufacturing and assembling industries are locating nearer to the outer suburbs. The establishing of residential belts of higher densities between will greatly enhance the ability of the conurbation to be served by the public transit system and directly relieve congestion on the main transportational routes within, and leading to, Metro. In examining the conservation of urban land and its potential in North York, the subject area is among the most strategic, and has some of the greatest values. Of course, the land is ideally situated for industrial purposes at the junction of Metro's first cross-town route and its new limited access parkway. However, the juxtaposition of the site with the two valleys render use for industrial purposes primarily, a waste of land. This area is ideally suited to more continuous human enjoyment, and fulfilment, which is after all the prime goal of our work.

A planning and technical report was then prepared for thorough understanding of the principles and design characteristics of the plans in a physical and three-dimensional sense, and augmented by means of a topographic and structural model. The model was employed in subsequent meetings with the respective planning agencies, Metropolitan Technical Committee, Metropolitan Executive Committee and North York Council.

The planned relocation of the Don Valley Parkway was a fundamental consideration and fruitful negotiations indicated the intrinsic value of the location of the route in a positon circumferential to development, overlooking the river valley, and permitting the artery to become primarily a parkway, rather than an industrial-fronted route. The industrial contact is achieved to the north of the Eglinton Avenue route where the proposed radio-television centre was located, a type of development compatible with the attendant park, parkway, industrial and residential land uses. This proposed relocation was perused by the Department of Planning and Development, Metropolitan Roads Committee and the Municipal Planning agencies, eventually being approved by Metropolitan Council, prior to expropriation, on the route suggested by the Parkway and developers consultants in May of 1959.

While there was great interest in the Flemingdon Park plans and proposals at administrative levels, the elected representatives in most cases were apprehensive about the character of development for such a location, primarily owing to a lack of suitable examples in North America. The consultant planners advised that only at the Roehampton development in the London County Area, and at Vallingby, the new residential quarter of Stockholm, could similar community planning, and physical design be experienced. The reeve of North York, the local councillor, the Municipality's planning director, engineer and clerk were instructed in a noteworthy step by Council to study these developments at public expense. Enlarged to include the Metropolitan Planning Board Chairman and Planning Commissioner, the developer's general manager and legal adviser, the group embarked on a six-day inspection of developments relating to urban and suburban growth in England, Denmark, and Sweden. In late April, the consultant planner having arranged the trip through English and European professional contacts, accompanied the group to examine Harlow, Basildon, Roehampton, Golden Lane and Crawley in the London area; Bellahoj and Arne Jacobsen's housing in Copenhagen; Vallingby, Farsta and central area redevelopment in the Stockholm area. The municipal leaders were able to discuss the problem with Sir William Holford, Dr. Thomas Sharp, L.C.C. officials and elected representatives in London, and Sven Markelius, J. Siedenblatt, Per Holmgren and others in Stockholm.

Considerable debate ensued in the weeks following the trip, but the realization came that the proposals were necessarily related to the development of the modern city. Hence, although the decisions were not unanimous, the Planning Board and Council of North York gave assent to the Flemingdon Park plans and technical report in July of 1959, and application was made to the Minister of Planning and Development for amendment to the Official Plan.

In the interim, site plans were prepared by the consultant planners for implementation of the housing and space relations studies in the report. The planners recommended to the developers that a selection of several architects skilled in housing, shopping centre, school and industrial design be employed in the first phases of development. These were to work in conjunction with landscape architects to establish the basic concepts of the master site and development plan of the technical report. The municipal planning directors and legislators concurred with this *modus operandi*. In 1959, North York Council amended its Zoning By-laws and applied to the Ontario Municipal Board for ratification. The draft plan of subdivision as required by the Planning Act was approved by the Minister on November 30, 1959 and the final plan was subsequently deposited with the Registry Office.

LAND USE CONSIDERATIONS

The Site

Location and Site Characteristics—The Flemingdon Park land parcel forms one of the largest undeveloped sites in the urban portion of Metropolitan Toronto, and occupies a position of strategic importance and natural beauty.

Flemingdon Park is located between the east and west forks of the Don River, overlooking their confluence, with the almost 30,000 population of the Don Mills area to the north. On the west is the community of Leaside with its heavy concentration of industry and carefully planned streets for homes and community facilities, laid out in 1915. On the east are the rapidly growing areas of North York adjoining the Golden Mile and Eglinton Square of Scarborough. East York on the south is characterized by industrial concentration and densely built single-family homes bordering on O'Connor Drive. The holding is just to the east of the geographical centre of Metropolitan Toronto.

Topography, Geology and Soils—The site itself consists of a flat almost table-like plateau with an elevation of 410′ m.s.l.* at the southern

---

* m.s.l. mean sea level.

limits rising gently to 425′ m.s.l. at Eglinton Avenue. On the west at its southern limits the site is nearly 415′ m.s.l. Similarly, at its northern limits the site varies but slightly, within the contour of the 425′ m.s.l., extending almost from Don Mills Road to the eastern limits of the Don Valley Parkway cloverleaf.

The eastern portion of the site, however, drops abruptly into the valley of the east branch of the Don River, which flows tortuously past the upper plateau at an elevation of over 100′ lower than the plateau. The river itself is approximately 15′ below the adjoining bottom lands.

The large plateau area hereinafter described is deeply incised by a ravine cutting through the site from north to south, slightly west of centre, with its lower end meeting the elevation of the Don River at approximately 300′ m.s.l. It tapers to the north, with minor subsidiary ravines and channels serving to drain the flat plateau, gradually reaching the surface approximately 1,400′ south of Eglinton Avenue.

West of the site, and on the opposite side of Don Mills Road, lies the deep valley of the west branch of the Don River. This plateau land, between Don Mills Road and the ravine bank of the west branch, varies in width from 400′ on the north to 40′ at the midpoint of the site and back to 300′ at the southern limit of the site.

The geological morphology of the site consists of a glacial till plain with layers of outwash sand and gravel partly affected by the lacustrine action of former Lake Iroquois. Bedrock lies at an elevation of from 90′ to 135′ below the surface in the upper plateau and is occasionally exposed in the lower regions of the Don, east and west of the site. The upper profiles of soil consist of 3′ to 5′ of varied overburden overlying the plateau of the site, with the upper horizons consisting of sand, sandy clays and silty soils. Below this profile lie sand deposits interspersed with layers of fine gravel.

Vegetation—Parallel to Don Mills Road for a distance of approximately 800′ is the previously mentioned deep ravine which is heavily wooded with the exception of the hydro right-of-way. Trees here consist mainly of elm and maple, some oak, birch, poplar, and black locust.

The easterly third of the site, which is marked heavily by the eastern branch of the Don, is mostly wooded, particularly on the steep slopes of the ravine. Here the natural surface cover has been preserved as farm woodlots with stands of native beech, oak, elm, ash, basswood, hickory and maple predominating, interspersed with isolated stands of white pine and hemlock. Some birch also give interest in colour. The slopes to the south present the same type of vegetation.

Circulation and Access—The site has a frontage of 3,700′ on Don Mills Road which forms the westerly boundary. Don Mills Road is a major Metropolitan road connecting with O'Connor Drive, the old route to downtown, approximately one and a half miles south of the property. Eglinton Avenue moves through the northern boundary of the site as it crosses between Leaside and Scarborough's Golden Mile spanning the west

Flemingdon Park—General Features

The model portrays a distinct community of diversified housing accommodation in parklike surroundings. Industries are located at Eglinton Avenue; and golf course, motor hotel, C.B.C. project to the east of the Don Valley Parkway.

Development in progress, January 1961.

and east branches of the Don River. This route provides a major connection between Highway No. 27 on the western fringes of Metropolitan Toronto and Highway No. 2 on the east. At the intersection of Don Mills Road and Eglinton Avenue a grade separation with a ramp interchange is proposed.

The Don Valley Parkway, a six-lane arterial route, is now under construction and can be expected to be the most important north-south artery in Metropolitan Toronto. On the south it will connect the Gardiner Expressway, paralleling the north shore of Lake Ontario, with, on the north, Highway No. 401, the four-lane controlled access, inter-provincial highway, which cuts across the upper portions of Metropolitan Toronto to link the City of Windsor with the Quebec border.

The Don Valley Parkway route skirts the southern boundary of the site and cuts northward through the Don Valley within the limits of Flemingdon Park. It emerges upon the plateau just south of Eglinton Avenue. At Eglinton, a grade separation is provided to carry the proposed route over the cross-town route. Further to the north the Don Valley Parkway is depressed beneath the Canadian Pacific Railway right-of-way to cross the east branch of the Don River and pass through Don Mills. A full cloverleaf interchange is to be provided at Eglinton Avenue. The Don Valley Parkway is expected to be completed northward to Eglinton Avenue in 1961. It will reduce the driving time to the downtown areas of the city by one-half.

CONCEPT OF THE MASTER PLAN

Land Use

An unparalleled opportunity exists for a completely new type of model community to be established in relation to the major artery and open-space systems of Metropolitan Toronto. A chain of distinguishable integrated community elements could be constructed up the Don Valley in incremental units. The first of these would be Flemingdon Park, established to the south of Eglinton and cradled by the two branches of the Don River. Don Mills would be the next to the north with the lands lying between the two communities adjoining the C.P.R. and Eglinton Avenue comprising the industrial zone. Again, to the north of Don Mills would lie another industrial parcel where the C.N.R. meets the interswitch track from the C.P.R. North of this would lie another complete community immediately south of Highway 401 and overlooking the valley of the river. To the north of Highway 401 and again contained by the Don Valley Parkway extension and the east branch of the Don River would be another complete community. It would extend up to Steeles Avenue which is the northern limit of North York, and would be in two sub-communities. This would carry on into Markham Township to the north in the same fashion.

"A serious attempt will be made to produce a completely mixed form of development with town and row houses, terrace and maisonette units, high rise slab and tower apartments and point blocks."

General Layout

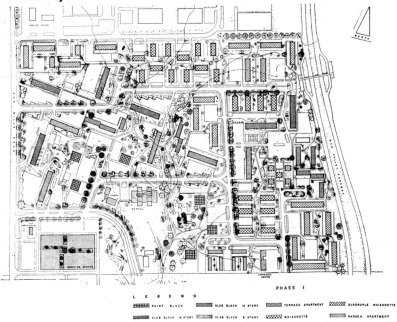

NORTH NEIGHBOURHOOD: community shopping centre, public school, church, community centre, convenience centre, as related to open space flow and housing elements.

Analyzing the relationship of communities of this type to Metropolitan Toronto, an almost perfect arrangement of circulation network related to open space and recreational patterns exists. Firstly, the interprovincial highway passes through the upper regions of Metropolitan Toronto in the form of Highway 401, crossing the east branch of the Don River at Oriole. It then connects with the Don Valley Parkway which will take circulation from the province into the heart of Metropolitan Toronto and its central urban core and also into the upper reaches of York County and Lake Simcoe.

The communities to be designed, and also Don Mills, would then attach themselves, in identifiable elements, to the west side of the Don Valley Parkway, in all cases overlooking the recreational and open-space assets of the east branch of the Don River. Thus a continuum of regional open space would move past, from south to north, and this would be crossed by the interprovincial highway and paralleled by the regional highway.

In addition, Metropolitan arteries of cross-town character would move between these elements. To the south of Flemingdon Park is O'Connor Drive; in the north Eglinton Avenue, stretching from east to west in Metro. To the north of Don Mills is York Mills Road and Ellesmere, and, to the north of the community, Highway No. 401. Beyond Highway No. 401, Sheppard would separate the next major community and to its north lies Finch Avenue and Steeles Avenue.

The first and most southern of the identifiable units would be Flemingdon Park situated on the peninsula of land immediately south of Eglinton, and almost an island surrounded by recreational open space. To the west are the proposed Metropolitan Conservation and Parkland areas of the Don Valley and Wilket Creek. The arterial open space pattern of the Parkway is on the south, along with other uses currently being laid out and designed by the Don Valley Parkway consultants as a completely planned, continuous parkway element. To the east, on land leased from the Metropolitan Conservation Authority, is a golf course, closely linked with the proposed Flemingdon Park motor-hotel unit.

North of Eglinton Avenue more valley lands open up which could be used as an extension to golf facilities. To the north of the C.P.R. main line lie the recreational lands of Don Mills, the ski club facilities, and now the country club development in embryo.

Flemingdon Park thus is planned to gain advantage of these circulatory, recreational and open-space assets. Two neighbourhood elements are designed, each around its own elementary and adult educational school plant. The focus of each of these neighbourhoods is towards the elementary schools and inner-park system which acts as a continuous pedestrian link separated from vehicular movements, running from north to south through each neighbourhood and in turn connected to the centre of the townsite as a focus for the neighbourhoods. The two neighbourhoods are drawn together by means of a major boulevarded artery. Strategically and centrally located on Don Mills Road and within the main collector road, are the community shopping centre, offices, medical and dental facilities, restaurants, meeting rooms and other nucleus-type facilities.

One of the main governing features of the layout of the community is the small highly attractive ravine running from the central shopping hub as the spine of the park and walkway development. Stretching up from the valley lands to the south and woven completely through the resultant community of multiple-family dwellings, the space systems are developed within each neighbourhood, to move continuously inward towards this green lung, separated from vehicular movements, that flows to the centre of the community.

The major collector street, Gateway Boulevard, connects with Don Mills Road, the major north-south feeder street. A continuation of the collector extends from the west of Don Mills Road through Thorncliffe Park. It continues eastwards as designed, into the community, to pass the school site at the heart of the first neighbourhood and then turns and parallels the ravine to extend into the north neighbourhood. Connecting with the community shopping centre, the road then proceeds to the west and meets Don Mills Road at a point overlooking the valley of the west branch of the Don River.

In turn, sub-collector roads are directed towards this main collector and an orientation toward the shopping centre and other central community amenities is achieved. In addition, the street patterns internally are specialized in the form of secondary, tertiary roads and courts.

A continuous movement occurs in each neighbourhood towards the central school facility. Integrated into the parks and circulation system are the two elementary school sites, of a size and form to adequately serve the developments on the north and south sides of a power transmission right-of-way. A complete pedestrian walkway link focused towards schools and churches, permits them to become definite hubs in each neighbourhood.

Not only are the school site and school plant to be employed for the education of the younger children, but they will also become social and cultural nuclei for the varied patterns of community and neighbourhood life. These are to be supplemented by adequate community centre sites which will eventually be built as complete cultural and recreational units. Continuous pedestrian links again focus towards the community shopping centre.

Each neighbourhood is to be developed into sub-neighbourhoods attached to the sub-collector roads, with a maximum of visual open space achieved through the careful siting of buildings. The groups of Flemingdon Park buildings will be diverse in type, height, and space relationships, with visually attractive surroundings for all the inhabitants, and a definite choice of type for all sectors of income level. Laid out in this way, the site takes maximum advantage of views into the Don Valley.

To the east of Don Mills Road high-rise dwellings related to shopping and transit facilities will be placed in landscaped areas with the additional amenities of swimming pools and recreational use areas, overlooking the scenic Don Valley. This situation again occurs on the south where views will be obtained from the high-rise dwellings into the area at the confluence of the branches of the Don River. Close to the perimeter of the Don Valley, the buildings of low elevation and child-family type will be closely

POPULATION AND HOUSING—FLEMINGDON PARK

Families by Number of Children at Home—Census, 1951 and 1956

METROPOLITAN TORONTO

	1951	%	1956	%	% Increase
Total no. of families	301,381	100.0	360.904	100.0	19.8
No children at home	122,349	40.6	140,993	39.0	14.5
1-2 children at home	144,122	47.9	168,983	46.8	17.8
3-4 children at home	30,493	10.1	44,512	12.4	14.6
5 and more children at home	4,417	1.4	6,416	1.8	14.5

Composition of Dwelling Units, Family Size and Estimated Future Population

Dwelling Unit	No.	% of Total	Family Co-efficient	Population
Bachelor	368	7.7	1.1	405
1-Br.	969	19.8	2.2	2,088
2-Br.	2,719	55.5	3.0	8,157
3-Br.	788	16.1	3.3	2,600
4-Br.	40	.9	4.5	180
Total	4,884	100.0		13,430

Composition of Dwelling Units

	Bachelor Units	1-BR Units	2-BR Units	3-BR Units	4-BR Units
Point Block		306	612		
16-storey slab block	210	315	630	210	
12-storey slab block	88	152	264	88	
S. storey slab block	70	105	210	70	
Double maisonettes			638	280	
Maisonettes			208	104	
Terrace apartments		91	157		
Garden apartments				36	
Town houses					40
Total	368	969	2,719	788	40

Total 4,884

tied and related to the valleys of the Don. In this way, taller buildings will not obstruct views from residential precincts of buildings of low elevations, while at the same time the slab and tower apartments gain sweeping views over all.

Land adjacent to Eglinton Avenue and on the west side of the cloverleaf at Eglinton Avenue and Don Valley Parkway are set aside for a very high type of industrial and business development with a high ratio of coverage, each industry maximizing the potential of highway identification. This industrial estate will complement the industrial build-up of Leaside west of the west branch of the Don, and the parcels to be developed on the north side of Eglinton Avenue which are zoned for industrial purposes and which will be developed to be compatible with the noted plant of International Business Machines. The estate will also conform with development further to the east on Eglinton Avenue, at the location of Scarborough's Golden Mile. Variety of design and building heights will be achieved to produce an attractive layout with a proper orientation of parking areas to building functions, and with a continuum of landscaped open space.

Building Types

The Master Plan envisages a variety of dwelling units to satisfy requirements for each type of rental accommodation, with an optimum relationship of dwelling unit to open-space areas and the park systems. The siting of buildings will achieve safe and convenient traffic conditions, and employing suitable topographic, microclimatic and orientation conditions, will result in achievement of healthful and sanitary environs, augmenting the long-term values of the development. The building types will be safe, sound and economical contemporary construction, with good circulation, privacy and flexibility to provide for family growth and the changing life cycle of the community. A serious attempt will be made to produce a completely mixed form of development with town and row houses, terrace and maisonette units, high-rise slab and tower apartments and point blocks. Wherever possible, underground parking is to be employed to conserve land for open and activity space, and relieve the landscape of the ever-present automobile. The composition of dwelling units, family size, and future population are indicated in the accompanying tables. It will be seen that the accommodation provided within Flemingdon Park, i.e., Bachelor or 1-Br., 2-Br., units amount to 83.0 per cent of the total, while the percentage of population requiring such accommodation, i.e., families without children and families with one and two children, amounts to 85.8 per cent. The allocation of dwelling types in Flemingdon Park very closely relates to the Metropolitan household characteristics.

Flemingdon Park Accommodation		*Metropolitan Household Composition*	
Bachelor units	7.7 per cent	1 person household	5.8 per cent
1-Br. and 2-Br. units	73.3 per cent	2-3 and 4-5 person household	76.8 per cent

Garden apartments (with underground parking) their spacing and relationship to high-rise apartments.

The scenic Don Valley East, the location of a golf course now under construction.

High-rise apartment in spacious surroundings.

Education

Flemingdon Park is planned to have two elementary school sites located respectively in the two neighbourhoods. The school sites are interlocked with the walk and park system for the safe and convenient circulation of the school children. At the two elementary schools, provision will be made for kindergarten facilities. Day nurseries will be accommodated according to request and demand in various apartment blocks at ground level. High-school facilities have to be provided in the environs of the community preferably, and a site is considered at Overlea Drive and Don Mills Road.

A future school population of 1,400 pupils is anticipated and schools with seventeen classrooms at the school north, and twelve classrooms at the school south are proposed. Both schools will have a kindergarten.

Recreation—Parks

Recreation plays an important part in the life of any community. To produce a balance of recreational facilities for each age group for the physical and mental well-being and the development of self discipline, sportsmanship, and community spirit, provision was made for tot lots, play lots, play grounds, play fields, recreation areas and parks, community and recreation centres and golf course, athletic field or stadium. Ready access, safe approach, a maximum of sunlight, air, circulation, spaciousness, quality of appearance, screening against traffic and bordering uses, are factors governing the location and shape of recreational facilities. Consideration was given to the inter-relationship of schools, cultural and social agencies and recreational activities. Full advantage was taken of the existing natural features of the site and its environs. The major ravine traversing the community site, together with various small depressions will form the structural spine for the major interior park and walk system of the community. Within the superblocks, tot lots and play lots will be related to the buildings and incorporated in the open-space system of these blocks. The natural conditions around the community, i.e., the table lands to the east of the Don Valley Parkway are perfectly suited for the most imaginative system of play and recreational activities, active and passive. The proposed motor hotel south of Eglinton Avenue and east of the Don Valley Parkway in conjunction with the golf course will greatly enrich the social and recreational activities of the community. Societies and similar organizations interested in nature and outdoor life will have every opportunity for exploration in the vast valleys of the Don River branches within walking distance. Present Metropolitan plans are for the west branch of the Don and Wilket Creek sectors to become parkland similar in concept to the New York Central Park.

The major park system traversing the community connects all major functions of community life. The interconnecting walks system is linked to the parks system and safe pedestrian circulation for children and adults is achieved.

In addition, negotiations have been carried out with the power company for the usage of their centrally located lands as play and park areas.

Social and Cultural Activities

In the formulation of the master plan, care has been taken to provide areas for institutions devoted to social and cultural activities. Within the community shopping centre, provision will be made for the establishment of a theatre, bowling alley, and other social and cultural facilities. Private clubs can also be accommodated within this shopping centre. Two churches and a community centre are integrated with parts of the neighbourhoods and the community. Readily accessible, and interconnected to the walk and parks system, they will produce a sense of oneness and will provide amenity for the leisure time of all age groups, broaden the social contact and be instrumental in developing cultural interest and standards. It should be noted here that in superblocks, accommodations will be provided for social and cultural clubs.

Community Services

In the community shopping centre a medical centre will be established, while in the two smaller shopping outless medical offices are planned. The postal unit will be at the community hub.

A library will be located in the central area of the community. Other additional libraries, if the need should arise, can be related to the churches or schools.

Shopping

Three shopping areas, an automobile service centre and a motor hotel are planned.

The community shopping centre is located at the intersection of Don Mills Road and the main collector road north of the power transmission right-of-way, with access to and from Don Mills Road and the main collector. It is intended to become the focal hub of the community.

The community shopping centre will offer a wide range of convenience merchandise. Second-floor areas are planned for office space near the medical centre.

A local shopping facility is planned at the intersection of Don Mills Road and the main collector road south of the power line for walk-in trade in the south neighbourhood. A drug store, tobacco store with stationery shop, a combined restaurant and delicatessen, and dry cleaner's store will be included in the building group. The second floor, if needed, may be used for office or medical suites.

Just north of the transmission line and west of the main collector road a second local shopping facility similar to the one described above is also contemplated.

Motor Hotel

South of Eglinton Avenue and east of the Don Valley Parkway, a motor hotel, serving transients and local population alike is proposed to take advantage of the natural assets of this site. The motor hotel will be part of a golf course development to the south within the Don Valley.

Transportation

Success or failure of any large-scale development in Metropolitan Toronto depends upon an adequate road within the site itself and the relationship of the development to the Metropolitan road system. The anticipated increase in population with a greater increase in movements of persons and goods on already congested roads will accentuate the seriousness of this problem. It is hoped that the long-range program of Metropolitan Toronto will improve the situation through a concentrated effort in the construction of subways, expressways, and possibly the incorporation of existing railways into the comprehensive transportation system.

Flemingdon Park is strategically located in relation to the existing employment areas of the central core, of Leaside, of Scarborough, and the northwestern industrial areas of the Metropolitan area, and is as well located for future expected development areas north of Highway No. 401. Distances are short and access to these areas is, and will be, comparatively easy. The nearness to the central core makes future transit practicable. The Metropolitan Planning Board, Transportation Division has undertaken a study of the traffic problems resulting from the development of Flemingdon Park. Its findings, taking into account future development to the north, show that the existing and planned lanes of Don Mills Road, Eglinton Avenue and the Don Valley Parkway will be sufficient for the traffic created by the project.

Services

Water—The main water supply for the project will be furnished by a 30″ trunk supply main on Eglinton Avenue and a 12″ main on Don Mills Road. The internal system will be looped into these two proposed mains.

Sanitary Sewerage and Garbage Collection—The north-south ravine within the subject area provides the location for an effective sanitary trunk collector to be connected to the existing Metro sanitary trunk in the Don Valley. The installation of incinerators in the units will greatly reduce the amount of garbage and disposal problems.

Storm Sewers—The topography of the land creates four catchment areas with convenient and rapid outfalls into the two branches of the Don River to the east and west.

Hydro-Electric Power—It has been agreed with the municipal power agency that within the limits of long-term economical maintenance and supply, all of the distribution wiring will be buried.

Gas—Existing gas lines on Don Mills Road and Eglinton Avenue provide sufficient supplies of gas consumption within the project.

Staging

A project of this size has to be developed in stages, extending over a number of years. The consultants have forecast its substantial completion, based on present trends, by 1968.

The first stage, under construction now, consists of the area just north of the power transmission lines, the industrial area south of Eglinton Avenue, and plans for the community shopping centre at Don Mills are in preparation. Ground has been broken for the school of the southern neighbourhood, to be ready for use in Spring, 1961, at which time about 600 dwelling units will be ready for occupancy.

SOCIOLOGICAL CONSIDERATIONS

The following is a resumé of excerpts from a brief attached to the original "Provisional Planning and Technical Report for Flemingdon Park", prepared during planning in 1958 by Project Planning Associates Limited. [1]

The fundamental responsibility in an undertaking of such scale places upon the prime movers the building of a "community" rather than a mere collection of housing structures and ancillary facilities.

The purposes of a modern, functional residential development may be summed up as follows:

1. The primary function of private family living is recuperation. The main purpose of modern residential housing is informal relaxation and recuperation from the demands of the world of work upon the head of the household and the demands of family life upon his spouse.

2. Comfort is stressed rather than efficiency of production; convenience is stressed rather than high standards of performance.

3. The recuperative functions of indoor and outdoor living are moved into juxtaposition to each other; they are planned to supplement and interpenetrate each other.

4. Gregarious patterns of home life are given preference over requirements for privacy, specialization of activities, and individual isolation inside the family home.

The attainment of these fundamental objectives of modern functional residential development involves the following series of propositions:

1. The neighbourhood or community must be designed, planned and developed as a whole. The wholeness of philosophy in conception implies both consistency and variety.

---

[1] *Social Aspects of the Flemingdon Park Project*, by Dr. Albert Rose, Professor of Social Work, University of Toronto.

2. Consistency implies a harmony of purpose in the nature and quality of the residential and other structures and in the siting of such structures within the project.

3. Variety implies that the entire range of the cycle of life will be both possible and present among the residents of the community. It is essential that there be both young people and older people; that there be newly formed families without children, families with young children, and families with older children.

4. It is essential, as well, that there be variation within the income groupings among the families in the neighbourhood, insofar as this is possible in relation to the costs of construction and the rental or shelter-cost schedules which will be determined.

5. Planned variation through differentiation in the size and availability of dwelling units and their availability in a variety of forms—for example, within apartment blocks, maisonettes, terrace apartments and town houses—will tend to overcome the charge of "conformity" levelled at most suburban communities. Conformity begins with and becomes rooted in lack of variation implicit in a preponderance of families of a specific age and income grouping. The single-family dwelling on the wide lot in suburbia is the single most important stimulant to conformity.

6. A community is far more than a collection of dwellings. It is a grouping of persons and families who require not merely physical accommodation but the satisfaction of many other fundamental needs. Some of these needs may be provided for through the conscious design and siting of other amenities and facilities—shopping facilities, schools, churches, recreation centres, open space.

7. There are, however, some persons or families in every community who will choose to satisfy these needs outside the neighbourhood and often far beyond it. Their group associations and friendships for the most part have already been created elsewhere in the broader society and they seek fewer of these facilities and opportunities within their residential neighbourhood. They must be permitted to meet their needs in their own way.

8. Nevertheless, for the majority of the residents, there is a demand for a close relationship between indoor and outdoor living, for a home life close to the heart of nature.

9. Recuperation from the world of work requires, as a *sine qua non*, a reasonable distance between home and the place of employment, and modern, efficient, regular transportation facilities, both private and public, to bring home and work together in their appropriate relationships.

10. Recuperation implies, as well, the most efficient physical facilities within the dwelling unit as are consistent with costs and the income of prospective residents. The performance of basic family functions—shopping, eating, sleeping, dressing, decision-making, educational and spiritual development—must be possible of fulfilment with a reasonable expenditure of time and effort.

One writer has summed up this entire argument in the following paragraph which appears within an article entitled "Architecture of Family Living".

Housing is made of stubborn material. Residential structures are customarily designed to last at least half a century. But while housing is a stubborn material, so are family customs. The consequences of deficient home design and construction have a lasting quality. As long as the dwelling unit stands, its walls are not apt to give way and its design is not readily changed. It is the family that will find itself frustrated in the performance of routine activities; it is the family that will have to eliminate those activities or to transfer them to community facilities; it is the family that will have to suffer from undue congestion and from the interference of different home activities; it is the family that may have to move; and it is the family that may lose its members to commercial entertainment outside the home if the dwelling unit does not permit joint occupancy without friction.

Flemingdon Park as planned has a "garden" quality, since an area of about 35 per cent is dedicated to parks and open space.

The community is conceived at this time as one of rental accommodation solely. This unusual feature provides a variety in housing accommodation throughout the entire range from bachelor apartments to four-bedroom town house apartments. If an appropriate rental schedule can be developed, this will ensure occupancy by family groups in every stage of the life cycle. Only during the past two years has rental accommodation in Metropolitan Toronto assumed an important share of total housing completions.

There are perhaps 375,000 dwelling units in the Metropolis; until very recently no more than 50,000 were in the form of multiple dwellings, that is, with six or more units within a single structure. Almost none were in the form of row or terrace houses or maisonettes. More than 31 per cent of the accommodation in Flemingdon Park will be provided in these types.

Although there has been a considerable addition of rental accommodation in apartment buildings during the past two years, almost all of this addition has occurred within single structures built without relationship to each other or within the concept of a single planned community. The first and most fundamental advantage of Flemingdon Park development is the wholeness of its conception and planning. Its single and singular ownership and the consistency and variety of its conception should provide Metropolitan Toronto with a sorely needed and magnificent community.

An equally important and fundamental advantage of the Flemingdon Park project is its location within the Metropolitan area of Toronto. The development is "strategically located at the focus of three important routes". Within a huge metropolis of some 240 square miles, it is located no more than seven miles from the heart of a highly concentrated industrial city.

Some Significant Cautions

There are always and inevitably serious dangers inherent in the creation of a community, particularly a residential community of rental accommodation within a metropolitan area. The first and most important danger is the possibility that "too much" will be planned and provided for within the community.

Provision for some commercial facilities, for some recreation facilities, for schools, and churches and parks is absolutely essential. Nevertheless, it must be recognized that there are extreme positions in the philosophies underlying the development of such communities. On the one hand, there are those who contend that the residents of the community should be encouraged and enabled to find every aspect of individual and group association within the boundaries of the project. On the other hand, there are those who contend that the residents should be encouraged to look outwards from the residential community for the satisfaction of many personal needs through group association.

Some balance must be found between these opposing points of view. If the inhabitants of the community find few or none of their friends within the project area, there is the very real danger that the development becomes merely another dormitory within a metropolitan area. If, on the other hand, the philosophical wholeness of the conception of the community is translated into the provision of facilities and encouragement for the satisfaction of all personal needs within the confines of the development area, there is the very real danger of community isolation and stagnation as a self-satisfied enclave within the metropolis.

The essential nature of the balance which must be sought is therefore encompassed within the phrase "sufficient consideration, but not too much". The phrase, it is clear, is much easier to utter than to define. The key to the puzzle lies in an understanding and consideration of the importance of group membership in our society. "Social life, inter-personal relationships, and membership in groups are important aspects of persons' lives because so many goals and satisfactions are obtainable most easily in groups and in some cases, only through association with other people." [2]

Certain group memberships are involuntary. For example, one is born into a specific family, into a specific ethnic group, into a specific religious group, and generally remains a member of these groups. What so many community planners, architects and social planners have not taken fully into account is the fact that living in a house also means involuntary membership in a community. The residents of a community will find that to a large extent their group memberships are imposed by decisions of the professional persons just mentioned.

There is one further major problem to which attention might well be given. This is the question of the maintenance of stability in a substantial

---

[2] Albert Rose, "A Design of Social Change", *Business Quarterly*, University of Western Ontario, Vol. XXIII, No. 4, Winter 1958.

development like Flemingdon Park which is conceived solely as rental accommodation. (It is of course, realized that there may ultimately be a certain degree of home ownership.)

It is possible that this community will face problems somewhat akin to those of a Settlement House in a downtown area, where certain families are constantly on the move up the social and economic ladder, while other "newcomer" families very quickly replace them but soon thereafter move on as well. This leads the writer once more to the view that the development of this project should not take, as its basic assumption, the provision of all possible neighbourhood facilities within its boundaries. There may be some considerable value in providing the site upon which some group of residents will carry out a plan to finance construction of their own community facilities.

It is not suggested for a moment that community facilities in Flemingdon Park should be inadequate; nor that the absence of such facilities will guarantee stability. The essence of the argument is that a substantial development of rental accommodation, howsoever well conceived and planned does not in itself guarantee stability among the residents. The writer would argue that the kind of stability which some analysts seek in emphasizing the value of friendships and group associations within a neighbourhood, may not be a desirable goal at all.

We do not have any real experience with developments of this kind conceived and planned on this scale. We do not really know what is going to happen. We do not know whether couples or families with children will find this community a desirable place to live. There is every indication, from the arguments put forth earlier in this memorandum, that most persons and families will find the location remarkably convenient; will find the dwelling units consistently efficient; will find the site plan and arrangement of the building satisfying, particularly in the relationship between outdoor and indoor space; will find that there is a consistency of philosophy and a variety of living within this development which will make them want to remain as residents. This memorandum sets out some of the basic considerations which may help to ensure these results and some of the possible dangers which must be anticipated.

NEIGHBOURHOOD PLANNING IN TORONTO

M. B. M. Lawson

This paper which was written in 1962 deals with an aspect of the planning process developed by the author during his term as Commissioner of Planning for the City of Toronto Planning Board, 1954 to 1967. Mr. Lawson, whose training is in both civil engineering and planning, is presently working on a book dealing with the process of urban development, particularly in Canada.

One of the fundamental problems in planning is to decide how to go about doing the job for the city or area for which we are responsible. Faced with a community of great complexity, knowing that everything we study or propose will have many ramifications, how should we organize our approach to understanding and planning the city? What plans are appropriate? What procedures should we follow? How can we not only study the facts we believe pertinent but also achieve the necessary public understanding, participation and decisions. Various methods have been tried, from a comprehensive fully-structured and organized approach at the one extreme to a catch-as-catch-can picking up of issues and projects as they were most pressing. At some time or other, most offices have to face this problem and decide how they will proceed.

In 1955, the planning office of the City of Toronto Planning Board was being completely reorganized and this was one of the big issues to be decided before effective planning work could get under way. As a first step, the types of jobs which were the responsibility of the planning office were listed and reviewed. In this connection, I should point out that in Ontario the legislation permits municipalities to set up planning boards which will be advisory to the local council. The board, in turn, may set up a planning staff and receive a budget from the council. It is a pure form of advisory planning board, with a professional staff to assist it in its work. In practice, the professional staff works closely with the other departments of the civic administration and is responsible for interpreting all the policies and conclusions of the board to the city council and the civic administration. In addition to spelling out the permissible form of planning organization, the Planning Act stipulates the major responsibilities that the planning boards must accept. Briefly speaking, the planning board is made responsible for carrying out necessary planning studies, for consulting with the public on these studies and the proposals arrived at, and for the preparation of official plans which are then submitted to city council for adoption as statements of the official policy of the council. In addition, council may ask the planning board to do such other planning work as it chooses and the provincial Minister and other provincial agencies may also ask the planning board to make studies.

The first conclusion arrived at from the examination of the Toronto Planning Board's responsibilities was that the planning office should be organized in three professional divisions. The first of these, called the Long Range Division, is responsible for studies and preparation of proposals on all broad planning issues. The second, called the Projects Division, is responsible for specific design projects in the implementation of the general plans and policies developed by the Long Range Planning Division. (Redevelopment projects and high-way design would come under this Division.) Thirdly, the Current Operations Division is responsible for the day-to-day issues, such as zoning amendments, which constantly come before the Planning Board; its reports and recommendations are in line with the plans and policies developed by the Long Range Division.

At this stage, it became evident that is was necessary to have a review of planning issues in Toronto to decide how to proceed with the organization of the long-term program of work. With this in mind, an Urban Renewal Study was undertaken in 1955. Despite the fact that this study had a slant towards residential redevelopment, it was primarily a review of the situation in the City of Toronto and an attempt to decide on the range of planning issues confronting the city. The study exposed issues in all parts of the city that called for the establishment of clear plans and policies and the integration of the planning process over a long term with municipal development policy.

It was concluded that the best approach to planning for the City of Toronto would be to organize it at two major levels. The first level would be city-wide. Broad issues, such as total amount of housing, commercial and industrial development, transportation and traffic movements, would be studied and suitable policies developed, together with generalized plans setting out the broad structure of the city. We have explored these issues in our publication *The Changing City*. However, on this city-wide scale, the city having a population of about 680,000 and an area of about 35 square miles, we found it was impossible to comprehend a great many issues in different parts of the city. Therefore, it was decided that there should be a second level. The city would be divided into districts, for each of which detailed studies would be undertaken, making it possible to tie all the broad city-and region-wide issues, together with local problems, into a comprehensive plan.

Having adopted the policy of establishing planning districts, the first problem was to define them. We decided that these districts should be small enough that they could be understood in some detail; they should observe significant natural boundaries wherever possible; major groups of commerce or industry should be encompassed within one district; and for purposes of study their boundaries should coincide with census tract boundaries. Since we were using statistical methods to a considerable extent, we felt they should be large enough for the statistics to be used with some reality. On this basis, the city was divided into twenty-five districts.

Having drafted proposed boundaries, we then discussed these with other departments and agencies, including the Metropolitan Planning Board and the Social Planning Council. There were some modifications and we finished up with a set of districts which were adopted also by these other agencies for purposes of organizing their studies and information.

On the face of it, the processes of studying a typical planning district are quite straightforward. To begin with, all the pertinent data is collected. This includes the usual information on population, properties, transportation, traffic, etc. In our case, we are able to organize a good deal of this information readily since, in addition to the normal census and other statistical sources, we have a property inventory with a data sheet and punch card for each property in the city, coded and cross-referenced to the planning districts and census tracts. In this way, most of the important data can be prepared and mapped before the professional staff starts to study the district.

When this data has been digested and a preliminary appraisal made, we reach the various citizen organizations within the district. These include rate-payer associations, church and social groups, welfare agencies, clubs and others that can be expected to have a substantial membership or interest in the district. It is usually known in advance that we are going to carry out the study, since we report it in our annual "Programme of Work", but if people do not know we tell them about the study and the plans to be prepared. We then ask them for their views about the district. When these have been obtained and checked against our own impressions, we follow up by asking for reactions to various problems that we have already identified, so that at these meetings we not only collect information and impressions of the district but also get a preliminary reaction to the most important problems and, in certain cases, to possible policies that might be adopted by the city to meet them.

All of this material is used in the preparation of a draft plan. This focuses, first at all, on identifying the concept of the district and its future role in the city and goes on to elaborate the way in which this should be achieved through zoning, redevelopment, street improvements and other public measures. Where appropriate, attention is drawn to private action which may be necessary. When this has been thoroughly examined by the staff and turned into a draft report, it is circulated on a confidential basis to those other officials who will be most concerned with the proposals and, together with whatever modification may be called for, sent to the members of the Planning Board for confidential review. Once it has been reviewed, the report goes to the Planning Board and is released to the public.

This report is called an "Appraisal" and presents the most important supporting material as well as the proposals themselves. Enough copies are produced so that they can be sent to all the members of the executives of the more important organizations in the area, as well as to all official departments and agencies, members of Council and other boards. Some copies are available for private individuals.

At the same time we prepare a summary of the "Appraisal". This is produced in quantity and a copy sent to every individual listed on the Assessment Rolls for the district, whether as owner or tenant. This report, called the "Plan", gives a cursory review of the main analysis and concentrates on the proposals. Along with it is sent a notice of public meetings.

Before these public meetings are held we try to meet with the executives of the organizations in the district. There we explain any points that may be misunderstood, obtain reactions to the proposals, and in certain cases, amplify our arguments in support of them. In this way we obtain a fairly comprehensive reaction to the proposals and are able to concentrate on the more contentious points when the public meetings are held.

In practice, we have found it necessary to hold several public meetings in each planning district and have divided the districts into sections for this purpose. The meetings are held in the evening at the most convenient local school. A program of each meeting is prepared and handed out to everybody attending. We have found it useful in the more complex districts to hand out also an extract from the "Appraisal" covering the particular section of the district.

Following a brief presentation of the proposals, the meeting breaks up into about five groups, according to areas described in the program. This is to allow more people a chance to ask questions and to give more opportunity for discussion about local problems. Each group goes to a separate classroom and in each of these classrooms we have a local chairman and two members of the Planning Board staff, one of whom is there to answer questions and join in the general discussion and the other to make notes. Our main objective is to get reactions rather than to justify our proposals.

We do not look to the public meetings for the reactions of the major organizations and associations in the district. We expect to receive briefs separately from them and we generally do. In the public meetings we are more concerned to get the reactions of the individual resident or owner. We also invite written submissions and usually receive quite a number.

These written submissions, together with the minutes of all the group discussions (as many as thirty in certain districts) are gone over carefully by the staff and the original proposals reviewed in the light of the various suggestions made. A Supplementary Report is then prepared. In it all the suggestions are outlined, together with the staff conclusions on whether or not there should be any modification to the original proposals. This goes to the Planning Board, together with the original "Appraisal", and it is at this stage that the Planning Board makes its decisions and recommendations to Council.

When Council receives these recommendations it has discussions of its own, first to understand the proposals and then to give citizens and organizations a further chance to address it directly on any of their views. Having heard these representations, Council then makes its decisions as to the necessary by-laws and amendments to the Official Plan and initiates whatever works may be called for.

Obviously there is a tremendous amount of work, both professional and administrative, in doing a comprehensive job of this sort. For example, in the Deer Park Planning District it took the time of three planners for about a year to make the studies, prepare the plan and write reports, even with the assistance of a typographer and professional report writer. The population of the District is 22,000; we mailed over 600 copies of the "Appraisal" and 11,500 copies of the "Plan". Senior staff attended more than twenty-five meetings with local organizations, including five rate-payer associations. There were six public meetings with a total attendance of over 1,400. Each meeting was attended by twenty-two staff members including twelve planners. There is a great deal of correspondence and supplementary administration.

All of this costs a considerable amount and takes a lot of time and it is doubtful whether it could be undertaken without an adequate organization. But as a planning process it seems to us to be extremely fruitful. It is difficult to see any other way of adequately examining all areas within the city and preparing plans which will be a satisfactory basis for long-term policy. We are satisfied that in the long run it should prove to be an effective way of keeping planning up to date with the needs of the city. Obviously there are a great many problems quite apart from the difficulty of doing the job. Even coming down to the district level, it is still not possible to deal with the detail necessary for redevelopment or improvement projects. The best that can be done at the district level is to establish policies for more detailed work on specific projects. The district plan would provide the necessary context for the project plans. Many planning issues run beyond the boundaries of the district and it is essential that these are adequately studied and become part of the city-wide plans and policies.

Even with our system of distributing copies of the "Appraisal" beforehand to those who are most involved and most likely to be able to disseminate information within the district, then sending out the short "Plan" and then holding public meetings, it is still difficult to explain adequately the proposals and the reasons behind them. This is particularly true where there are few local organizations. Where there are existing organizations with many contacts it is easier to convey your thinking to their membership. When there are few organizations, the residents of the district have to judge from the written documents; and although many of them ask us questions it is not sufficient to dispel doubts and confusion. As a result, it is sometimes hard to keep public discussion of the issues from becoming rather wild.

There is no question at all about the intense public interest and the extent to which people feel that they are vitally concerned with the proposals. In the districts we have so far dealt with, we have had a turnout at public meetings of about 15 per cent of the numbers listed in the Assessment Rolls. The discussions are certainly lively. A great many people have obviously gone through our reports quite carefully and have definite opinions to express—all of this in addition to lively sessions with the executives of the organizations in the area, particularly the rate-payer associations. I would not suggest that, as a result, all the policies we recommend as being sound for the city are accepted by residents of a district, since public interest quite often runs counter to the individual's private interest. But at least there is a considerable degree of understanding at the end of the process and the issues can be faced squarely.

Ultimately, of course, the proposals go to Council. Naturally, Council pays a great deal of attention to the views expressed by the local citizens and their organizations. But it is an advantage that Council also has a complete explanation of the situation and knows that the issues have been thoroughly discussed in advance. Views are well understood and revisions can be made more readily. There is no doubt that Council itself has to understand the situation fully and to take a position on policies which otherwise would not be faced up to, even if they were ever formulated. Having gone through this process and having made decisions, Council has been prone to resist subsequent changes from the "Plan". Throughout the period, following the public meetings, the Planning Board must try to keep the public informed, an arduous job, and one we have not yet solved satisfactorily.

In summary, I would like to reiterate my belief in the value of this technique. It involves an immense amount of work and requires great concentration but when it has been implemented thoroughly it gives us confidence that we have a foundation for the future planning of the city. In the long run, we hope that our approach will lead to a comprehensive understanding of the city's development proposals and will form the basis of city policy in all matters affecting development. With any luck, this approach to neighbourhood planning could even become the core of city action in a wide range of fields, taking as its focus the future physical form of the city.

METROPOLITAN MAN, SOME ECONOMIC AND SOCIAL ASPECTS

Murray Jones

The author, President of Murray V. Jones and Associates Ltd., Urban and Regional Consultants, is a former Commissioner of Planning for the Metropolitan Toronto Planning Board. This paper is the revised text of an address to H.R.H. The Duke of Edinburgh's Second Commonwealth Study Conference, held at Toronto in May, 1962. The author has recently served as Special Commissioner of the Local Government Review in the region of Ottawa.

By way of introduction, let me try to put Metropolitan Toronto into a sketchy context : how it started—why it keeps on growing—where and why people live and work in the Metropolis.

Toronto came into being as a "meeting place" of the Huron Indian, at the point where the portage route to the Great Lakes of the north met the east-west water route formed by the St. Lawrence River and Lake Ontario. From this point canoes went up the Humber River and up a short portage across the divide down the Holland River to Lake Simcoe, from where the Severn River flows into Georgian Bay. The first French explorers noted that this place was also endowed with an excellent natural harbour. The British built a fort at this location, Fort York. The settlement of traders which developed under its protection became known as the Town of York.

This combination of a key situation and a favourable site has remained and has been consistently developed as a primary basis for the economic life and growth of Toronto. Toronto Bay, protected from the stormy waters of Lake Ontario by a spit of land, now known as the Toronto Islands, has been developed into a modern harbour for ocean-going ships. The routes to the north and along Lake Ontario have been reproduced time and again with every change in the mode of transportation. When horse-drawn carts replaced canoes, Governor Simcoe, the first Governor of the Province of Upper Canada, supplemented the road to Kingston and Dundas at the eastern and western ends of Lake Ontario, by a new road north to Barrie at Lake Simcoe. Under the name of Yonge Street this road has become the main street of Toronto. When steam engines replaced the horse, the first railroad was built, in 1855, to Collingwood on Georgian Bay—to be supplemented, one year later, by railroads following the shores of Lake Ontario and the St. Lawrence River west to Hamilton and east to Montreal. When motor vehicles supplemented the railroads, expressways were built in the same directions : Highway 400 north to the west shore of Lake Simcoe, where it now connects with the Trans-Canada Highway which follows the eastern and northern shores of the Great Lakes; and the Queen Elizabeth Way and Highway No. 401 along Lake Ontario.

Thus Toronto has constantly strengthened and developed its position as the junction point between the developed lowlands of Southern Ontario and of the Atlantic beyond and the huge territories of Northern Ontario. Today the city is a financial and administrative centre for the development of the vast forest and mineral resources of that area, as well as a trade centre for the entire Province of Ontario.

BACKGROUND—THE TORONTO ECONOMY

When the rebellion of the thirteen colonies disunited British North America, the capital of Upper Canada had to be moved away from the threatened border, and Toronto was the natural choice for the seat of government of Upper Canada. The presence of the government and of professional people attracted by it also gave rise to educational and cultural institutions. The need to supply the population of the town and of its developing and expanding hinterland soon led to the establishment of industries such as food processing, building materials, paper, printing, and metal working. Thus the economic base of Toronto at an early stage developed the diversity characteristic of genuine metropolitan areas, each function supporting the others. In subsequent years, as manufacturing, trade, government and business administration, educational and cultural institutions have grown to serve the growing population of Ontario and of Canada, the population of Metropolitan Toronto has expanded at an even faster rate.

Why and How Metropolitan Toronto Keeps on Growing

The many and varied employment opportunities attracted and continue to attract people. The volume of people and purchasing power creates a big market, and their variety of skills offer an unparalleled labour supply, both of which attract and create further enterprises. Thus growth feeds on growth. As specialization increases, more and more functions, accounting, selling and purchasing, negotiating, financing, researching, and consulting, are divided out of the manufacturing enterprises. These "business services" are growing and proliferating even more rapidly than manufacturing. Similarly, with growing real incomes, more and more functions, formerly performed by each household for itself, become specialized into an ever growing variety of consumer services. The many and complex threads inter-connecting this multitude of enterprises, gainfully employed persons, and their consuming households form the unique web of life of the great metropolis, in which each element is dependent on daily contact with many others.

Today, Metropolitan Toronto is the prime centre of secondary manufacturing in Canada. No one industry dominates; most manufacturing establishments are of medium size. The largest plants are located outside the boundaries of the municipality of Metropolitan Toronto, as are also the few large primary industries. By contrast, most small enterprises, dependent on each other and on outside business services and frequently also on cheap rented space, which they can find only in old buildings, locate in the old inner areas of the city. This area thus performs an important function as incubator of new and pioneering enterprises.

While manufacturing continues to grow, other urban activities, summarized broadly as "services", are growing much faster. While manufacturing accounted for 39 per cent of all employment in 1950, this percentage is now about 35 per cent and is expected to be no more than 30 per cent in 1980. The fastest growth is occurring in the services which both private enterprise and government supply to a wide region. But only slightly less rapid is the growth of the services which the people of this area perform for each other; probably about half of them make their living by thus "taking in each other's washing".

To perform all the work required by these economic activities, the area has drawn on people from outside. Only one-third of the area's population growth during the last fifteen years came from natural increase; the balance is due to migration, both from other parts of Canada and from abroad. The variety of background, training, and experience of the in-migrants has greatly enriched the economic and cultural life of this metropolis. It may even have been a factor in softening the rigid injunctions of Toronto the Good against having fun on Sunday and against stimulating one's soul by spirits other than divine.

Where People Live and Work in Metropolitan Toronto and Why

When, in 1834, the Town of York was incorporated as the City of Toronto, most of its 9,200 inhabitants probably lived above or alongside their workshops, stores and offices, and frequently all members of the family shared in the work. Today, this is a rare exception. Normally, the individual travels from his home to work; and if several individuals in a family work, they travel to different places.

As long as the vast majority had to perform their journey to work on foot, they had to live close to the centre of town, where practically all the work places were. When factories were built in some village in the environs, it drew its workers from that village and from the surrounding farms; some walked to work for an hour or more, on six or seven days of the week.

With the development of public transportation, notably electric streetcars, this limitation was broken; population now spread out in ribbons along the streetcar lines, primarily along Yonge Street. Within the area served by streetcars, some new industrial districts developed along the railroad lines. Subsequently, with the widespread adoption of the automobile as a means of private transportation, a much wider area was opened up to the choice of residence. The population has spread out farther and farther. As the supply of land increases at the square of the distance from the centre, it is used less and less intensely. Population density falls off fairly regularly from the centre towards the periphery.

When industries found that they could attract workers, commuting in their own or in pooled cars, to outlying locations, they also availed themselves of the ample supply of outlying land to acquire larger sites. Of the "service" industries, many of the retail and consumer services have followed the population. However, office employment is still largely concentrated in the central business district. Employment in manufacturing, retail, and other services is also not as strongly decentralized as visual impressions may lead one to believe. A survey undertaken in 1954 showed that a central area of 12 square miles—one-twentieth of the area of Metropolitan Toronto containing one-quarter of its population—contained almost two-thirds of all jobs. With the growth of employment, as well as of population, in outlying areas, this percentage has certainly decreased. But it is safe to predict that a new survey, which is presently being made by the Metropolitan Planning Board, will still show the majority of all jobs concentrated in this relatively small central area of twelve square miles.

Within this central zone there were over 2.5 jobs for every resident worker—and jobs of all kinds. Nevertheless, one-quarter of these resident workers commuted "out" to jobs located in one of the seventeen other zones into which the 240 square miles of Metropolitan Toronto had been devided for the purposes of this survey. Of the residents of these seventeen other zones less than one-sixth worked within their own zone. Even where one of these zones contained many places of employment, the picture was substantially the same. In zone "3", which comprises the municipalities of East York and Leaside, there were three jobs for every four resident workers. But only 15 per cent of these residents worked in their own zone, and only 20 per cent of those employed in the zone lived there.

It is obvious that the desire to shorten the journey to work is only one of many considerations which determines the choice of place of work and of place of residence. Decentralization of both employment and residence certainly can decrease the necessity for commuting over long distances, but it does not eliminate it. In fact, workers commute over long distances to outlying industrial employment. For instance, in 1955, of the 4,000 workers of the Avro-Orenda plant, located at a distance of about 14 miles from the centre of Toronto, 22 per cent commuted over 15 and 55 per cent over 10 miles; less than 6 per cent lived within 5 miles of their place of employment. In the industrial districts of Leaside and the "Golden Mile", located at distances of 4 and 6 miles, respectively, from the centre, few of such extremely long journeys to work were found. But even here about 45 per cent of all workers were found in 1955 to live at distances over five miles, though tens of thousands of dwellings of all types and price and rent ranges are located closer to these industrial districts.

This widespread cross-commuting may appear as thoroughly irrational at first glance. However, these commuting workers respond to the deeper rationality of the large metropolis, whose very *raison d'être* it is to offer the widest possible choice. Without this wide choice there would be many more square pegs in round holes, resulting in serious loss both of productivity and of personal satisfaction. In a small town a worker who cannot find a satisfactory job has only the choice of accepting an unsatisfactory one—or none at all—or pulling up stakes and trying his luck in another town. It is one of the great advantages of metropolitan areas that a man can change his job without changing his residence. It is too easily forgotten that the journey to work, long, costly, and onerous as it may be, is often a substitute for the far longer, more costly, and more onerous journey from one town to another.

In fact, a majority of workers in Metropolitan Toronto do not spend more than half an hour on their way to work. While the journey to work has certainly increased greatly in terms of miles and of money, it is far from certain that it consumes more time today than it did forty or eighty years ago, when most people walked to work.

In 1955 only one person out of forty walked to work. All others travelled either by public transit or by private automobile. The share of public transit decreases regularly as one moves from the high concentration of places of employment at the centre to their scattered location at the periphery. Travel to the central business district can only be effectively performed by mass transportation which today, as thirty years ago, carries 70 per cent of this concentrated load. The share of transit to places of work in the wider central area has declined slightly. However, as more places of employment are located in outlying areas, journeys to work in peripheral direction are increasing rapidly, and most of these require travel by automobile. As a result, today at least 60 per cent of all employed persons travel to work by automobile, compared to only 35 per cent eight years ago.

The people of this area avail themselves of the wide choice of opportunities offered by the metropolis not only for work, but also for shopping, business, social-recreational, and many other purposes, and most of these journeys, made at all hours and in all directions, are made by automobile. On an average weekday about 1.75 million residents of Metropolitan Toronto make almost three million trips, covering over twelve million miles, about one-third by transit and two-thirds by car.

GROWTH SINCE 1945, CHARACTER AND EFFECTS

This growth in trips has been phenomenal, as has the growth in population, employment, housing and developed land.

Since the end of World War II, the population of Metropolitan Toronto has increased by over two-thirds of a million persons, or by 70 per cent. All of this growth has taken place in the suburbs. If the larger metropolitan region is considered, including the fringe area surrounding Metro, the post-war growth has been 800,000 persons or 80 per cent. The 1961 census population of Metro was 1,618,000, and of the fringe 157,000, for a planning area total of 1,775,000.

Employment in the Metropolitan region has grown during the same period by a quarter of a million jobs, or by 53 per cent. Four-fifths of these new jobs are in non-manufacturing, i.e., in the tertiary sector of the economy, comprising the service industries. The 1961 employment total was 700,000.

To house these workers and their families, nearly 200,000 new dwellings have been built in Metropolitan Toronto since the war (160,000 of them in the last decade). 40 per cent of these have been in the form of apartment and other multiple dwellings. (Two-thirds of our current construction is in such multiple dwellings.)

Meanwhile, the urban land occupied within Metropolitan Toronto jumped from less than 60,000 acres to over 100,000 or by two-thirds. For the larger Metro region, including the fringe areas, the nearly 80,000 acres urbanized since the war represent a growth of 120 per cent.

The growth I have been illustrating is not peculiar to Metropolitan Toronto but is found in practically every metropolitan area in the world. It is a secular trend which is an integral part of modern industrial development itself. Just as the earlier development of manufacturing industry was made possible by improved agricultural techniques which allowed the production of surplus food by less labour, so the development of tertiary or non-manufacturing industries, which are characteristic of metropolitan areas, is based upon the dramatic improvements in manufacturing techniques to produce ever increasing floods of goods. Meanwhile, continued reduction in the required agricultural labour force proceeds apace, fortifying the move from country to city. These revolutions in agriculture and manufacturing have been accompanied by a reduction in the portion of the Canadian labour force which owns the productive property or capital with which it works.

The result has been a dramatic increase in the number of workers who can only live by selling their labour, and a corresponding increase in the quality and skills of the labour which they have to sell. This of course is merely the story of modern industrial growth itself, but the vital role of the metropolitan area in this growth can only be understood in terms of industry's increasing dependence upon skilled labour and labour's increasing dependence upon a job market.

The most basic function which a metropolitan area performs is the provision of a very large and concentrated market in which labour and jobs are brought together. The essential role of such a job-labour market in our modern economy need hardly be stressed here. What does require stressing is the fact that only the modern metropolitan area is capable of providing such a market. Those who would propose therefore to control the size of metropolitan areas must realize that they would thereby seriously restrict the economic benefits which only a large labour-job market can provide. For our increases in productivity are in no small part due to the continual rematching of labour skills with job requirements which can only take place if a large and efficient market exists.

As this process continues and the division of labour proceeds, labour itself tends to become more and more highly specialized. But division of labour and specialization mean increasing interdependence as the worker becomes more and more dependent upon his ability to sell his specialized services so that he may buy all the requirements of modern life which he cannot produce directly for himself. This utter dependence upon the market for one's services forces the worker to go where that market is best and it is increasingly in the metropolitan areas that the best choice of jobs it to be found and new jobs are being created.

In many ways the modern metropolitan area is the new frontier, the only place where the rapidly growing non-manufacturing sectors of the economy are concentrated. Metro is therefore the ideal theatre for the entrepreneur, the place where all the components required for a new business venture can be most readily and usually most inexpensively assembled; the nurturing of new enterprises is therefore another vital function of the metropolis.

If the fundamental role of a metropolitan area is a labour-job market, of almost equal importance is its role in supplying the many other inputs of business firms and in consuming their outputs. The extremely wide range of available inputs and the large regional market readily served from a metropolitan location permit firms to specialize in much the same way as labour specializes, concentrating on performing only those functions which each performs best, for only that segment of the market it wishes to serve. But this increasing specialization and interdependence of firms as well as of labour means that markets are required not just for labour and jobs but for everything else which is produced and consumed by our modern society. And the same advantages which a metropolitan area offers in its labour-job market apply also to each of these other markets. In short, in an economic sense, a metropolitan area may be viewed as simply the largest and most varied collection of the broadest markets which man has so far been able to create. It is this collection of markets for all kinds of new and used goods and all types of services which makes the metropolitan area such a vital part of our modern market economy.

Metro is also a place of administrative control, from which these processes may be conveniently directed and in which the vast amounts of information required for rational administrative decisions can be most quickly and readily obtained. The modern metropolitan area is therefore literally the centre for more activities than have ever been collected before in one area.

This vast concentration, along with all the benefits it brings, also brings costs. From the point of view of the individual worker or firm, the keen competition of this vast market place may mean insecurity, which undoubtedly leads to a consistent striving for some secure slice of the market. This is the great push behind the increasing specialization and the ever new attempts to come out with something new which the competition does not have. But from the social point of view—that of the community as a whole—the intense competition among sellers is again one of the attractions of the metropolis, and as a result many goods and services can be bought more cheaply here than elsewhere.

It is in those things of which the supply is limited, where the competition is purely amongst buyers, that the social results are less happy. The most limited thing in a metropolitan area—that which is in some sense absolutely limited—is of course space and it is in the intense competition for space in metro that most of its intractable problems are born. This intense competition for limited space leads directly to the three main problems of a metropolitan area; congestion of living, working and moving about; high land costs and hence high costs for plant space, office space and shelter space and lack of sufficient open space.

In this context the vital role of transportation is apparent. In matching the supply and demand of each of the multitude of markets in a metropolitan area, transportation is absolutely essential. Also, in order to accommodate the multitude of markets which comprise the metropolitan area a much larger area is required than was ever encompassed by former urban areas. In turn the larger area permits the congestion—the high densities of residents, workers and traffic—to thin out.

The point I am making is that this decentralization which is often described by the emotionally loaded word "sprawl", has resulted in some very real and important benefits which we have only begun to understand or measure. What happened was a rather sudden enlargement of the metropolitan commuting area in the early post-war period as car ownership shot dramatically upward. As noted earlier, people suddenly realized that they could commute by car from formerly remote suburban areas with relative ease, and plant managers suddenly realized that they could draw their workers by car without relying upon a location accessible by public transit. This sudden increase in the potential commuting area found land prices relatively low, the only problem being the provision of essential services such as sewer, water and road facilities. The pressure for such services played no small part in the developments which led to the creation of the municipality of Metropolitan Toronto in 1953.

The low suburban land prices, coupled with easy mortgage financing under the National Housing Act, led to rapid residential development, almost all of it in the form of single detached houses at relatively low densities. Similarly, the low land prices attracted the major share of the new factory building, permitting efficiently laid out single-storey factories with adequate parking facilities for employees and ample landscaping opportunities; in addition most of the new factories took additional land to allow for future expansion. Since many of them had been forced to move to the suburbs because of changes in methods of production, and expansion space was not available at their old site in the city, this insurance in the form of land held for future expansion made extremely good sense.

In time, the growth of suburban population led to the development of the suburban shopping centre which began to appear in this area in 1951. Again, the density was low with most stores of one-storey height, and ample car parking provided. More recently, some suburban office buildings have begun to appear.

This then was a new kind of urbanism built at low density with ample space for present and future activities, with a minimum of congestion of either persons or cars, and all of it geared to the new mode of transportation, the private automobile. In the light of the low land-cost structure which meant that suburban homes, factories and stores were often cheaper than in the city, and usually easier to finance, the attractiveness of the new suburban low density in comparison with the old city high density could not be denied. Although much of the architecture in the suburbs was repetitive and the planning poor or non-existent, the combination of low-cost and low-congestion, all of it designed to accommodate the motor car in a way that the central city could not, gave this new form of urbanism undeniable competitive advantages against older high-density forms which had evolved in an era based on a different form of transportation. Here, suddenly, space for low-density living and the efficiencies of low-density factory production, formerly available only to the wealthy individual or corporation, could be had by the average individual and the average manufacturing concern.

In spite of the fact that our metropolitan government was able not only to catch up on the wartime back-log but actually keep up with this suburban growth in the provision of essential services (an achievement matched by few other metropolitan suburbs on this continent), the activities of land speculators and the laws of supply and demand were moving to check the low-density development through a steady increase in the price of suburban land. In addition the growing hordes of suburban automobile commuters were increasing traffic congestion, especially to the downtown area. Although the decentralization of employment along with population was well under way, leading to a stabilization of downtown employment, employment was still not decentralizing as fast as population; and car ownership, especially in the suburbs, was still rising steeply. The increasing commuting difficulties began to set some limit on the distance from downtown at which many downtown workers were willing to live; and the rising suburban land prices began to push the cost of the single detached house beyond the means of many people.

Meanwhile, Toronto, traditionally an area of home-owners rather than renters, had developed an acute shortage of rental dwellings while the increasingly mobile population implied a great increase in the number of those preferring to rent rather than own their shelter.

These trends combined around 1955 to launch a dramatic shift in the area's new residential construction from the low-density single detached dwelling to the high-density apartment and other multiple dwelling types. Since 1955 some 50,000 such dwellings have been completed in Metro, nearly two-fifths of them in the very large outer suburbs of Etobicoke, North York and Scarborough; most of these latter were built on more in-lying suburban sites which had been by-passed by the single-family house subdivisions. The effect on the suburban skyline and on overall suburban densities has been significant. The outward movement of our urban limit has been slowed, and some of the pockets of suburban apartment development are now sufficiently concentrated to support good suburban bus service.

The effects of this shift to apartments on family living have not always been so happy however. Many of the apartments, especially those further from downtown, have been occupied by families with children, and in many cases the environment of a high-rise building with no open play area on the apartment site and no public park nearby is anything but ideal for the needs of growing children or their parents. For such families middle-density accommodation in non-apartment multiple dwellings would undoubtedly be preferable, and it is expected that some of our housing market research, by pointing this out, may lead to increased middle-density residential construction.

The suburban apartments however have permitted greater numbers of those working in suburban jobs to find accommodation they can afford, relatively near their work. Suburban apartment rents (ranging from about $80 a month for a bachelor suite to about $155 for a 3-bedroom unit) are still not low enough however to accommodate most of the suburban factory workers who account for the major share of suburban employment. Except for about three thousand suburban limited-dividend apartments with lower rentals, the suburban wage earner who is unable to buy a suburban house or pay the rent in an ordinary suburban apartment is limited to living in a subletted basement apartment relatively near his work or living in cheaper rent accommodation in an older building in the city or inner suburbs and commuting outward to his job. This situation is a reflection of the tendency of the new suburbs to become almost purely middle or upper class in their income distribution, the poor having in effect been zoned out as a result of the high standards adopted in their building and zoning by-laws.

In spite of the increase in average real incomes (current $6,200 per family) there are still large numbers of low-income persons. This group has become ever more concentrated in the city and a few of the old inner suburbs. Because the city has been the traditional reception area for new immigrants from overseas, being the locus of most of the old housing which lends itself to conversion and overcrowding, the city has become more and more distinct from the new suburbs in the distribution of its people according to income and ethnic origin.

For these reasons the increasing decentralization of employment which would appear to be bringing more jobs into the suburbs near the decentralized population, thereby diminishing the need for commuting, often fails to have this effect because those who work in the suburban jobs often cannot afford suburban accommodation, while those who can afford to live in the suburbs are more apt to work in the downtown area. Nor are the suburbs, under the present limitations of municipal finance, likely to welcome the construction of low-cost accommodation; their concern is rather to ease the burden on their existing taxpayers by encouraging as much non-residential assessment and high-class residential assessment as they can. Nevertheless, the building of publicly subsidized family housing in the suburbs represents the only solution in sight to their problem.

In the light of all this what can be said about the nature of metropolitan man? What kind of a creature is this new metropolitan environment creating? From all that I have said it is already clear that there is no average metropolitan man. There is rather a vast range of metropolitan men, each falling into a certain spot on the age distribution, the income distribution, the family cycle, the ethnic distribution, and countless other spectra. For each of these characteristics the distribution for a metropolitan area tends to be significantly different from that for non-metropolitan areas.

Metropolitan Toronto's age distribution for example reflects the pull its vast job market has had on persons of working age, with over 60 per cent of the Metro population falling in the 20 to 64 years working-age group as compared to only 55 per cent in Ontario and 53 per cent in Canada as a whole. The dip in the under 20 age group reflecting the shortage of Depression babies is of course evident in Metro's, as it is in Canada's age pyramid, but the Metro dip is much more pronounced than is the national one. This relatively lower percentage of the child age groups in Metro is of course merely the obverse of the higher percentage of working age adults.

Similarly the demands of the Metro job market for skills of all kinds coupled with the excellent educational facilities available here has led to a marked difference in the educational background of Metro residents as, compared to those of Ontario or Canada as a whole. Nearly 60 per cent of the Metro population * have more than eight years of schooling, as compared to 49 per cent in Ontario and 44 per cent in Canada as a whole.

In both age distribution and education the metro suburbs again differ markedly from the city. The concentration of families with children in the new suburbs for example has resulted in 38 per cent of their population being under 20 years of age, compared to 28 per cent in the city and old inner suburbs combined. Similarly with education, nearly 65 per cent have more than eight years of schooling as compared to just over 55 per cent in the city; this difference in educational background is of course reflected by the higher average income in the suburbs as compared to the city.

The greater preponderance of working adults in Metro is again reflected in family composition, with a relatively high proportion of single persons not living in families. In Ontario and Canada some 13 per cent of the population falls into this category, compared to over 15 per cent for Metro as a whole and 22 per cent in the City of Toronto; the suburbs on the other hand with their concentration of families, have less than 9 per cent of their population not living in families.

---

* Five years and over not attending school.

In the distribution of persons into dwellings, the less crowded conditions in the suburbs, where only 25 per cent of the dwellings contain over five persons, stand out in contrast to the city with over 45 per cent of its population living in dwellings with over five persons, again reflecting the lower average city incomes.

I don't want to bore you with figures, and I think enough has been said to indicate that for almost any distribution of attributes the population of a metropolitan area is significantly different from that of non-metropolitan areas, and the population of the suburbs is again significantly different from that of the city.

METROPOLITAN MAN DEFINED

Bearing in mind the fact that the differences between city and suburbs may be as great or greater than the differences between metro and non-metro, it may still help to focus much of what I have said by talking briefly about some of the main social attributes of a hypothetical average metropolitan man. For in many ways the ultimate evaluation of this metropolitan environment we are creating must rest upon the effects it has upon its inhabitants. Since the metropolis is at the same time the focus of our modern industrial civilization, the fate of this civilization itself may well be pinned on the kind of metropolitan man we are creating.

At the risk of over-simplification then I am going to try to draw a caricature of metropolitan man stressing what seems to me to be his most significant characteristics.

To begin with he is a worker, well educated with specialized skills which he sells in a highly competitive job market to the highest bidder. His capital investment, as it were, is essentially limited to these skills and in general he does not own productive property. He is therefore utterly dependent on his ability to sell his services in order to obtain the income he requires to live. But having obtained his income, which is considerably higher on the average than that of non-metropolitan man, he then commands an array of riches which the kings of former times could not have imagined. As the economy produces more goods, and to an even greater extent more services of all kinds, he is able to spend his increasing leisure time and his increasing surplus income on a thousand things which only the rich could have afforded a generation or two ago.

He is therefore not only a highly specialized producer, he is also essentially a consumer, consuming a vast array of goods and services at a rate never approached before in history.

He is thus market-oriented to a very high degree, tending to give everything a price; but while much of his consumption is of material things—enough to make him more of a materialist than men of former eras—an increasing proportion of this consumption is non-material, in the form of a multitude of services, many of which have been inappropriately called cultural. He is therefore in a better position to consume culture (if not to create it) than were his predecessors.

The cultural activities of the great metropolis—theatres, concert halls, museums, art galleries and all kinds of entertainment facilities—are among its most important magnets. Metropolitan man is therefore often on a cultural frontier as well as an economic frontier. The opportunities are there for him to be culturally creative and to be a leader not only in his specialized field of production but also in his tastes and consumption.

In short, in many ways man "never had it so good" as he has it now in the metropolis. To take full advantage of its opportunities he has become mobile to a degree never found before; mobile as a commuter between home and work and shopping plaza, etc.; mobile as a job hunter, frequently shifting his employment as he reaches out for better opportunities; mobile as a resident, changing his house on the average of once every five years or less as he seeks a better house or one closer to his better job; mobile as a traveller travelling more often and further on his vacations and business trips; and above all mobile as a social being, striving to move ever upward in the social hierarchy.

The new social hierarchy, however, is increasingly harder to identify as a set of classes with identifiable characteristics as the mark of social position is to a great extent one's spendable income and not one's cultural background, education or tastes. Since one's position in society, as well as one's command over all the goods and services required for the good metropolitan life depend increasingly upon one's job and since there is a widely-held expectation at least among the great metropolitan middle class that one's income should continually increase, and since in fact one's job may be vitally affected by economic developments in another part of town or on the other side of the world, there is a degree of uncertainty and insecurity underlying much of metropolitan life which breeds a troubling anxiety. The rootlessness which is the inevitable corollary of high mobility adds to this anxiety.

And yet, although he is dependent and insecure, metropolitan man is still as independent and secure as it is possible to be in the modern market economy, because he has so many alternatives. He has the insurance of numbers which only a metropolitan area can provide. If he loses one job there are three quarters of a million other jobs from which to choose; if he loses one friend there are countless opportunities to strike up other friendships; if he does not like his neighbours he can easily move to another neighbourhood.

In spite of being rootless he is in some strange way ever more deeply rooted in the metropolitan milieu. He is adapted as it were to metropolitan life, and once adapted can feel at home in any metropolitan area anywhere (though nowhere else).

Thus, while increasing government controls, made necessary by the complexities of our modern urban society, tend to limit many of his freedoms, metropolitan man has open to him new freedoms of choice as to where and how he will live and work.

This may imply an increasing freedom in the economic sphere and a decreasing freedom in the political sphere, although well-informed metropolitan man can have an impact on modern politics which belies any suggestion that he is becoming politically powerless. It may be however that his growing mobility implies a decreasing interest in local government.

At any rate, it appears to me that his political institutions are lagging seriously behind the major developments in modern life. Not only is metropolitan man grossly under-represented in the provincial and federal legislatures (both provincial and federal governments are now belatedly getting around to redistributing the electoral districts) but the very form and structure of our government no longer correspond to the realities of our modern economy.

Bringing our political institutions and governmental structure more into line with the realities of our modern urban economy would therefore have far-reaching effects, among which should be a greatly increased ability to finance the many public improvements which will be essential if we are to see to it that the diverse elements of the metropolitan area and urban regions are brought along in balance.

CONCLUSION

In conclusion the following general observations can be made:

1. The modern metropolitan area is a new form of human settlement quite unlike the forms used in the first 5,000 years of human history.

2. In this country our metropolitan existence has been so short that we are only beginning to understand some of its implications.

3. The nature of the economy of the metropolitan area is a direct result of that phase of history known as the industrial revolution which first produced the nineteenth-century "big city".

4. Toronto's early growth was in its physical form typical of the pyramidal shape of the era. It has now had superimposed on it the characteristic form of the metropolitan area—the rectangle. (Los Angeles is a good example of an urban region which has experienced only the metropolitan form.)

5. In this "seamless web" we still cling to the concept of attaching sovereignty to local units of government which were conceived and developed for a pre-metropolitan society.

6. Traditional community values and organizational mechanisms have become obsolete; the essential qualities of local self-government can only be realized from some form of urban regional government.

7. The concentration of over two-thirds of the total population in metropolitan areas and the consequent high proportion of gross national product created in these areas must eventually lead to a basic shift in the locus of political power from rural to urban areas, and thus have the most profound effect on our political system.

8. Metropolitan man is a relatively new creature. It is hoped that he will learn to adopt an appropriate value system, adjust his political institutions, and participate in the shaping of his new environment to the end that the many economic and social advantages of metropolitan existence will be fully realized.

FORT SASKATCHEWAN : AN INDUSTRIAL SATELLITE OF EDMONTON

P. J. Smith

> Dr. Smith is the Chairman of the Department of Geography, University of Alberta. He attended the planning school at the University of Toronto in 1958-59, and has had planning experience in Calgary, Alberta. From his base in Edmonton, he was able to observe closely the development of the new satellite community, which is the subject of this paper. His account provides an evaluation of the development up to 1962.

Nineteen miles north-east from the centre of Edmonton, downstream from the city on the North Saskatchewan River, is located the small manufacturing town of Fort Saskatchewan. This is one of the oldest settlements in Alberta, but as recently as 1950 it was still no more than a tiny agricultural service centre completely overshadowed by the nearby provincial capital. The past decade, however, has brought radical changes to the community. The establishment of four large-scale industries has changed Fort Saskatchewan's prime function from a service one to manufacturing and at the same time has led to a trebling of the town's population and housing accommodation. This unprecedented growth, in its turn, necessitated rapid expansion of commercial and public facilities and has made comprehensive planning a matter of most urgent necessity. It is fortunate that the Edmonton District Planning Commission, of which the town has been a member since its inception in 1950, has been able to meet the challenge of rapid development in a most commendable manner. Full credit, though, must also be given to the town administration for its desire to follow sound planning principles and to the industrial firms for their willingness to accept the guidance of local officials. In fact, Fort Saskatchewan has become a fine example of the way in which planners, municipal administrators and industrialists can co-operate for their joint benefit.

ORIGIN AND EARLY DEVELOPMENT OF THE TOWN OF FORT SASKATCHEWAN

The initial European settlement in the Fort Saskatchewan area took place as early as 1794 when a North West Company trading post, known as Fort Augustus, was established about half a mile east of the present town. Its function was to intercept the fur-laden canoes of Indians voyaging east to the Hudson's Bay Company posts, and so divert the very valuable trade. The Hudson's Bay Company retaliated by constructing Fort Edmonton close by in 1795 and the two companies conducted a very intense rivalry for about ten years. Rapid depletion of the local beaver and otter populations, however, led to an early abandonment of the posts and the transfer of the trading companies to the present site of the city of Edmonton. The deserted forts were destroyed by Blackfoot Indians in 1807.

Further settlement of the Fort Saskatchewan area was not attempted until 1872 when two French-Canadian brothers named Lamoureux, attracted by the deep sheltered valley and the rich black soils of the uneroded plain, took up land holding along the North Saskatchewan River. They were responsible for the river-lot form of subdivision which still exists for six miles along both banks of the river and which has exerted a prime control on the street pattern and subdivision of the modern town. They also gave their name to the tiny hamlet now sited on the north bank of the river immediately opposite Fort Saskatchewan.

The first settlement on the actual site of the modern town took place in 1874 when a new fort was constructed, on the high bluff overlooking the valley, to accommodate a detachement of the North-West Mounted Police. This detachment was responsible for the supervision of the vast area that is now Central Alberta and was installed at Fort Saskatchewan rather than Edmonton because Inspector Jervis, the detachment commander, believed it to be the more suitable river-crossing point for the projected trans-continental railroad. The protection afforded by the police and the anticipation of the railroad, combined with the agricultural advantages of the area, led to an influx of settlers. The first of these took up irregular river-lot claims, but in 1882 the surrounding region was surveyed for quarter-section homesteads on the regular prairie grid, with special adjustments where the two systems of subdivision intersected. The actual townsite was not surveyed until 1893 but by this time an urban hamlet, with a number of small businesses, had already taken form. There was even an excess of speculative subdivision, beyond the present limits of the town, which reflected the optimistic expectation that Fort Saskatchewan was destined to become the metropolis of Western Canada. This bubble was first pricked as early as 1885 when the C.P.R. constructed its railroad through Calgary and the Kicking Horse Pass in preference to the northern route; it was pricked finally in 1891 when the C.P.R. constructed its north-south railroad from Calgary to Strathcona (South Edmonton). When the Great Northern Railway from Winnipeg reached Fort Saskatchewan in 1905 the railhead at Edmonton was its obvious objective. From that time, Edmonton's growth and Fort Saskatchewan's dormancy were assured. The town, which in 1891 had a population almost the same as Edmonton's, was rapidly outstripped by the city.

The Great Northern Railway, of course, brought some development to the town. A final influx of homesteaders and service businesses helped maintain some of the optimism; population increased from 300 in 1901 to nearly 1,000 in 1915; a thriving brick factory and a municipal thermal-electric plant were using coal mined from exposed seams along the river banks; and a 1911 promotion pamphlet was able to stress "cheap power, cheap fuel and an inexhaustible supply of soft water" as the major industrial advantages of Fort Saskatchewan. [1]

Then came a series of setbacks which ended the optimism. The Mounted Police were transferred to Edmonton between 1909 and 1913; in 1912, a municipal hydro-electric power station and dam were destroyed by floods after only three days of operation, leaving the community with a twenty-year debt; and in 1913, fire devastated a large part of the town's business section. In the face of these blows and the established primacy of Edmonton, "by 1914, the optimism had vanished, and the people settled down to the quiet unchanging life of the center of a farming community". [2]

The Fort Saskatchewan region is eminently suited to agriculture, and particularly to the profitable and stable mixed crop and livestock raising. The chernozem-type soil, with its 12-14 inch black A horizon overlying 18-24 inches of dark brown subsoil, is the most fertile of all the world's major soil groups, largely because of its high concentration of organic matter and nitrogen. The generally level terrain of the till plain and the frequent lacustrine deposits, the boulder-free nature of the soil and the absence of extensive stands of trees greatly simplified the process of cultivation. The only land unsuitable for cultivation is the limited amount taken up by the few steep-sided ravines draining down to the deeply entrenched valley of the North Saskatchewan. The climate is well suited to the growing of commercial grains and to cattle and hog raising, although the moderate average precipitation of 18 inches could support natural woods only along the ravines, around drainage hollows or on the more elevated marginal moraine which rises to the south and east of the town.

This exceptionally favourable combination of physical conditions has produced a density of rural settlement which is comparatively high for the Prairie provinces. The 160 acres of the original homestead units has proved to be satisfactory for permanent occupancy in most of the Fort Saskatchewan area. In contrast to much of the Prairie region, there has been little farm consolidation or abandonment of homesteads so that even today the average farm size is no more than 300 acres. The significance of this for urban development is two-fold. First, a comparatively close pattern of urban service centres and transportation foci will be needed and, second, the towns will be stable and secure. On the other hand, once the agricultural land is fully occupied, and the agricultural system stabilized, there will be little potential for expansion of the urban service functions, and the towns will tend to become static. This was certainly true of Fort Saskatchewan in the period 1911-1951.

The only broadening of the town's functional base occurred at the beginning of the long period of quiescence. When the Mounted Police

---

[1] *Fort Saskatchewan and District Offers Opportunities for All*, Fort Saskatchewan Herald, Fort Saskatchewan, August 1911, p. 18.

[2] Peter Ream, *The Fort on the Saskatchewan*, Douglas Printing Company, Edmonton, 1957, preface. This book is the best single source on the early history of Fort Saskatchewan.

abandoned their barracks, the considerable property was taken over by the provincial government for a penitentiary which has since become a major installation. It has contributed greatly to the town's stability because of the business and service needs of its ninety resident employees.

Figure 1   THE REGION

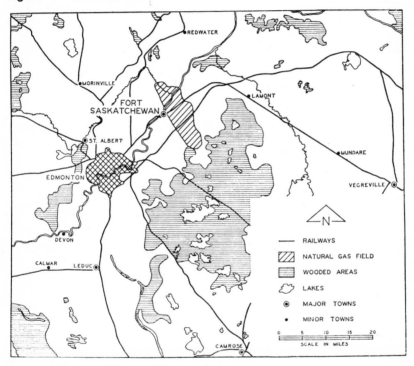

The moderate average precipitation of 18 inches could support natural woods only along the ravines, around drainage hollows or on the more elevated marginal moraine which rises to the south and east of the town.
Large quantities of water are needed in the refining process so proximity to the North Saskatchewan River was a major asset, even though the river water requires very careful treatment, especially at the time of spring run-off.
A satisfactory supply of natural gas very close to the potential site was assured.

By 1951, then, Fort Saskatchewan was a quiet but well-established rural service centre, a function revealed in the almost inevitable grain elevators near the railway station and in the small number of farm supply merchants and implement repair shops. The form of the town was indicative of both its function and its history. A compact and well-defined business core existed on the north side of the railway, and was contained within a single block of it, except for the grain storage area strung along the tracks to the west. To the north and east of the core, between the railway and the physical barriers of the river bluff and Ross Creek, the major residential portion of the town was scattered rather loosely over the grid subdivision which paralleled the lines of the river lots. Minor, and badly scattered residential development was also to be found south of the railway but it did little to lessen the asymmetry of the town's form. This pronounced asymmetrical form could be attributed, first, to the barrier of the railway and, second, to the penitentiary which occupies all the land west of the core. The concentration of business activities close to the penitentiary dates back to the Mounted Police days; the fort, and later the barracks, provided the focus for life in the infant settlement and the town's commercial and professional premises were established as closely to it as possible. The result was a rather unbalanced form which recent growth has not completely eradicated.

RECENT INDUSTRIAL DEVELOPMENT

Fort Saskatchewan's transformation dates from 1952, but the root causes of the transformation go back a little further, to two apparently unrelated mineral discoveries 800 miles and ten years apart. The first was the discovery, in 1941, of a rich and extensive nickel-copper ore body at Lynn Lake in north-western Manitoba; the second, the discovery, in 1951, of the Fort Saskatchewan natural gas field and the successful drilling of the first wells only four miles south-east of the town. The timing of the latter discovery was completely fortuitous but it proved to be crucial for the town's industrial development.

The ore discovery had been made by prospectors of Sherritt Gordon Mines Limited, which for fourteen years had been working the copper-zinc deposits at Sherridon, 150 miles south of Lynn Lake. The new find, however, turned the company's attention to nickel refining, and particularly to the development of a new process which would give "better metal recoveries and lower operating costs than the conventional smelting and refining methods". [3] Between 1947 and 1951, a revolutionary hydrometallurgical process, based on leaching rather than smelting, was developed. The principal reagent in the leaching process is anhydrous ammonia which, in turn, is most readily and cheaply obtained from natural gas. The Fort Saskatchewan gas discovery, then, was most opportune since it came just as Sherritt Gordon was faced with the task of selecting a refinery site.

With the preeminent need for natural gas, as both a fuel and a raw material, the choice of sites in 1951 was obviously restricted to Alberta. It has been said that if the site selection had occurred later a broader choice may have been possible because of the improved distribution of gas through recently constructed pipelines [4], but in 1951 the main concern

---

[3] *Sherritt's Bold Adventure in Nickel,* a publicity brochure of Sherritt Gordon Mines, Limited, p. 11.

[4] Charles A. Hames, "Operations at the Fort Saskatchewan Refinery", paper presented at the Prospectors' and Developers' Convention, Edmonton, February 25, 1957, p. 2.

Figure 2   THE TOWN

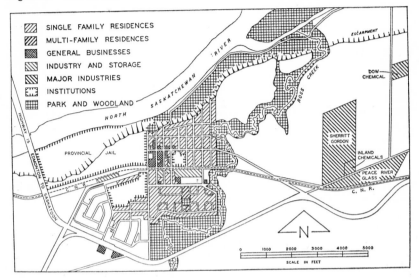

was to be as close as possible to a source of natural gas. The gas alone, however, was not enough to pinpoint the selection of Fort Saskatchewan; several Alberta locations were considered with Fort Saskatchewan favoured for the following reasons :

1. Rail facilities are very important for transporting the bulky ore concentrate from the Lynn Lake plant and as the C.N.R. had constructed a $15,000,000 link track from Sherridon to Lynn Lake it was felt that the refinery should also be on a C.N.R. line. Fort Saskatchewan, on the main trans-continental route, satisfied this requirement.

2. Large quantities of water are needed in the refining process, so proximity to the North Saskatchewan River was a major asset, even though the river water requires very careful treatment, especially at the time of spring run-off.

3. As a result of a private agreement between Sherritt Gordon and a gas distribution firm, a satisfactory supply of natural gas very close to the potential site was assured.

4. The refinery development which Sherritt Gordon was visualizing necessitated an expectionally large land requirement. In fact, the company purchased 800 acres in the Municipal District of Strathcona, immediately adjoining the town. This amount of land could not possibly have been assembled in the Edmonton metropolitan area, and even if it could, it would have cost five to ten times as much as in the rural municipality. On the other hand, Sherritt Gordon wished to be close enough to Edmonton to participate in such organizations as the Chamber of Commerce and the

Alberta and North-West Chamber of Mines and to benefit from other trade and professional contacts.

5. The town site of Fort Saskatchewan provided adequate space for housing for the company's employees. At the same time, all the housing could be less than fifteen minutes' travelling time from the refinery and so qualify for Defence Housing Assistance under The National Housing Act.

6. The stability of the town's administration and finances and its ability to expand utilities and services to meet the needs of an increased population were very favourable considerations. Sherritt Gordon's experience with company town management at Sherridon apparently made the advantages of a soundly established municipal organization seem very attractive. This was reflected later when the Sherritt Gordon industrial area was annexed by the town without opposition.

7. A number of minor factors which influenced the final decision were the availability of electric power and labour and the possibility of developing local markets for by-products.

As a result of the combination of all these factors, Fort Saskatchewan became the approved site without, it is interesting to note, any taxation or other concessions being offered by either the Municipal District of Strathcona or the Town of Fort Saskatchewan. The construction of the refinery began in 1952 and the first nickel was produced in July 1954. Since then, the company has steadily increased its range of products and its plant, expanding the initial capital investment of $24,000,000 to $33,500,000 by the end of 1960. [5] The principal products of the refinery are pure nickel powder, pure cobalt powder, copper sulphide (sold to conventional smelters), nitrogenous fertilizers (ammonium sulphate and surplus anhydrous ammonia) and iron oxide, the residue of the refining process which is sold to local cement plants.

The success of Sherritt Gordon in Fort Saskatchewan and the town's own success in adjusting to its functional change have created abundant interest amongst other industrial companies, and three have constructed plants in the town within the past five years. Two of these, the $1,000,000 plant of Inland Chemicals (Canada) Limited and the $1,250,000 plant of The Peace River Glass Company, were constructed in 1956; the third, a $3,000,000 plant for Dow Chemicals of Canada Limited, has recently begun production.

Inland Chemicals manufactures sulphuric acid from sulphur purchased from Alberta producers. Its principal locational consideration was its market link with Sherritt Gordon which has contracted to purchase 25 per cent of the acid output, with an option on additional purchases. The remainder of the output is distributed to Western Canadian markets.

Peace River Glass, by contrast, has no such direct link with the metallurgical firm. This company produces glass-fibre wrapping used

---

[5] *1960 Annual Report, Sherritt Gordon Mines, Limited,* Toronto, 1961, p. 8.

principally for insulating oil and gas pipelines and its principal requirement was proximity to Alberta oil company markets. The basic raw material, silica sand, has to be imported at present from Ottawa, Ohio, but it is intended to make increasing use of sand from the town of Peace River in Northern Alberta. Proximity to raw materials, then, was not a locational factor but, in compensation, excellent rail connections were essential. A considerable requirement of natural gas was a further factor to be considered. All these conditions, however, could have been satisfied in Edmonton and it has been stated that the critical factor in the selection of Fort Saskatchewan was its much lower land costs and tax charges.

Dow Chemical, the most recent of the manufacturing industries to locate in Fort Saskatchewan, also has no connection with Sherritt Gordon. Its principal products (fungicides, anti-freeze ingredients, and chemicals for removing sulphur from natural gas) are obtained mainly by processing natural gas, though this basic raw material is supplemented by other materials supplied from the parent plant in Sarnia, Ontario, or from other divisions of the company. Proximity to a good supply of natural gas, then, was the major locational factor. A second, more general factor was the need for a plant to serve the expanding Western Canadian market.

These four companies represent a considerable variety of industrial activity and a quite remarkable concentration for a town as small as Fort Saskatchewan. It is all the more significant, then, that there is so much uniformity in the location factors which influenced each of the companies. The three factors which appear to be of major importance are :

1. The convenient supply of cheap natural gas which is used as a fuel in all four industries (though electricity is also important), and as a basic raw material in two of the industries.

2. Direct access to the trans-continental line of a national railway system, which is important for two reasons : first, all of the industries serve Western Canadian and, to a lesser extent, international markets rather than purely local markets and, second, bulky raw materials have to be imported from widely separated areas.

3. The very favourable land costs and industrial tax charges of Fort Saskatchewan and the Municipal District of Strathcona as compared to Edmonton. It should be noted, however, that the provincial government is proposing to standardize industrial tax rates throughout Alberta; it will be interesting to see if this will tend to discourage major industries from locating in small communities.

CHANGES IN THE TOWN AS A RESULT OF INDUSTRIAL DEVELOPMENT

The transformation of Fort Saskatchewan from an agricultural service centre to a manufacturing town has been effected with singular ease. A number of minor problems has arisen but some disruption could be regarded as inevitable since the ramifications of the change have been so far-reaching. That there was not greater disruption was probably due in large part to the efforts of Sherritt Gordon and the Edmonton District Planning Commission : the company took great pains to ensure that it fitted into the town rather than taking the town over, while the Commission provided the machinery and the skills for the comprehensive planning of the development which was a necessary accompaniment of industrialization. In particular, fragmentary subdivision and substandard fringe developments were prevented largely because the adjoining rural municipalities are also members of the Commission and agreed, from the beginning, that all urban development should be restricted to the town.

Care was demonstrated from the first, in the selection of the actual refinery site. Adequate land was available south of the developed area of the town, immediately across the railway tracks, but this was also the obvious and logical area for the residential expansion that would have to follow the establishment of a major industry. Conflict between industrial and residential land demands was avoided when the company selected an 800-acre site one and a quarter miles east of the town centre and separated from it by a thickly wooded valley which is not likely ever to be crossed by housing areas. The distance successfully isolates the town from the undesirable aspects of heavy industry and yet is not at all inconvenient since there is a good access road and all parts of the town are within five to ten minutes driving time. The east side location is also important in view of the prevalence of winds with a westerly component and, though this is not as important as it would have been if Sherritt Gordon had been constructing a traditional smelter, the principle of leeward industrial sites has now been endorsed in the Fort Saskatchewan zoning pattern. All four of the major industries are comparatively nuisance-free but, even so, there are occasional noise, dust and odours which are just as well blown away from the town.

From the point of view of the industries, the principal advantages of the eastern location are abundant space untrammelled by other urban development, proximity of the river and direct river frontage made possible by the long river lots, and access to both the C.N.R. main line and a provincial highway. Of course, only a large company, such as Sherritt Gordon, could have initiated such a definite separation from the town. Small industries would have had to rely on existing water and sewerage systems but Sherritt Gordon's huge demands, which could not have been met by the town systems, made it necessary for independent facilities to be installed. Thus Sherritt Gordon was not confined to the limits of Fort Saskatchewan's utility pattern.

The four industries now provide employement for 650 persons. The totals for each company are : Sherritt Gordon, 530; Peace River Glass, 65; Dow Chemical, 45; and Inland Chemicals, 10. These 650 new jobs obviously have had a tremendous impact on a town which previously offered employment for 250 persons at the most.

In the first place, there was no significant labour reserve in the town which could be called on; the positions could be filled only by attracting new employees to Fort Saskatchewan, either as permanent residents or as commuters. Sherritt Gordon was able to transfer a large number of permanent employees to the Fort Saskatchewan plant, but by no means enough to staff it completely. In total, 125 employees were transferred, 115 of them from Ottawa and ten from Lynn Lake. The remainder were drawn from Edmonton and nearby small towns (330 of the present employees are from Alberta) or were newcomers attracted, through normal advertising procedures, by the employment opportunities. Similarly, the three smaller companies have had no difficulty in recruiting most of their employees from the local region.

Total employment statistics, on their own, do not give a completely reliable picture of the impact of industrialization on Fort Saskatchewan's population. Because of the closeness of Edmonton a certain amount of commuting is almost inevitable, though all the companies encourage their employees to live in Fort Saskatchewan. Sherritt Gordon, for instance, obtained a considerable number of building lots which it sold, at cost, to its employees, and this, combined with the 10 per cent down payment made possible through Defence Housing Assistance, was a major incentive to build in the town. At present 65 per cent of the Sherritt Gordon employees live in Fort Saskatchewan and most of them have become property owners. It has been estimated that 96 per cent of the homes in the town are owner-occupied. [6] Thus, Fort Saskatchewan provides an interesting contrast to the oil towns of Alberta in which the emphasis on temporary trailer accommodation provides a pointed commentary on employee attitudes towards the oil industry. Of the remaining Sherritt Gordon employees, 25 per cent live in Edmonton and 10 per cent in the small towns and rural areas within a twenty-five mile radius of Fort Saskatchewan. A similar distribution can be noted for the other industries; two-thirds of the forty-five Dow Chemical employees and sixty-one of the sixty-five Peace River Glass employees are Fort Saskatchewan residents.

The influx of industrial workers naturally created a sharp increase in demand for urban services. Hence, industrialization indirectly expanded the employment opportunities in retailing, repair and maintenance work, professional services (particularly teaching), local government and similar service fields. All told, as nearly as can be estimated, between 150 and 200 additional jobs were created by the needs of the industrial employees. The net result has been a most inflated rate of population increase, 230 per cent between the censuses of 1951 and 1961, from 1,076 to 3,325 persons. [7]

To accommodate the increased population, some 450 new homes have been built in the past ten years and an additional 225 acres of residential

---

[6] Alberta Department of Industry and Development, *Survey of Fort Saskatchewan*, Industrial Development Branch, Edmonton, 1961, p. 5.

[7] These totals include prisoners at the Fort Saskatchewan jail; if the prisoner population is excluded the 1951-61 increase was 275 per cent.

subdivision have been registered. The earliest new construction was deliberately confined to the area north of the railway, essentially filling in this old sector with its rather scattered and inefficient form of development. Most of the houses are of medium quality, though a number of more expensive ones are to be found along the wooded bluff of the North Saskatchewan Valley and along Ross Creek. There is some incongruity as a result of the juxtaposition of old and new residences, because most of the old structures are in only fair or poor condition, but as yet no tendency to replacement is evident.

The first new subdivision occurred south of the railway but still within the boundaries of the original river lot of the town site. Again, the predominant form of housing is the medium-cost detached bungalow, though a limited number of low-cost, row housing units have also been made available for purchase.[8] The form of the subdivision is rather interesting since it represents a willingness to experiment that is found all too rarely in Alberta. The layout is a modification of the Radburn principle, with houses turned to face an internal system of walkways. The block interior thus provides very pleasant, quiet vistas. The major weakness, as in the Wildwood district of Winnipeg, has arisen from the use of loop streets at the backs of the houses instead of the narrow culs-de-sac of Radburn.

The southern residential area is completely occupied and development is now concentrated in another new subdivision in the south-west sector of the town. Here, the careful control of development is well illustrated. Construction is being allowed to advance into the subdivision only in a compact and orderly manner, following logical but restrained extension to utility lines.

In summary, recent residential development has been characterized by three very worthwhile planning achievements.

1. The unsightly and uneconomical scattered pattern of development of the old town has been replaced by a compact and efficient form. Utilities have been extended with maximum care and economy, public costs have been minimized and replacement of existing major installations has been delayed far longer than would have been possible with continued sporadic development.

2. Careful building supervision has resulted in a generally high standard of construction. Evidences of hasty construction, which would not have been surprising in view of the great need for accommodation, are notably absent.

3. Adequate provision of school grounds and local parks has been ensured and, in addition, the value of the North Saskatchewan valley as a recreational resource has been accepted. The valley is now largely in public ownership and is to be developed for recreational purposes.

---

[8] A Fort Saskatchewan real estate firm is advertising three-bedroom units at $9,995 complete with down payments of $475 and monthly payments of $65.

The old business core of the town has also experienced a certain amount of growth and change. New buildings have been erected, a light industrial and storage zone has appeared immediately south of the railway and the business area has been somewhat expanded, but the total change is by no means as great as would have been expected from the other changes in the town's life. The table provides further evidence of this. In the decade 1950-1960, personal incomes and public income from taxation

Financial Changes in Fort Saskatchewan as a Result of Industrialization

	1950	1960	Ratio 1960 : 1950
Population	1,000	3,200	3.2 : 1
Gross income of population	$1,900,000	9,800,000	5.2 : 1
Assessment for property taxation	$ 810,000	8,240,000	10.2 : 1
Retail and wholesale trade	$1,8000,000	3,900,000	2.2 : 1
Value of manufactured goods	Nil	28,000,000	—
Manufacturing payroll	Nil	4,300,000	—

Source: Office of the Secretary-Treasurer, Town of Fort Saskatchewan.

increased at rates appreciably greater than the rate of population increase; the town's residents therefore became appreciably more prosperous, even when allowance is made for the continuing inflation of the period. The increase in value of wholesale and retail trade, however, lagged far behind population increase, even at face value. If the 30 per cent increase in living costs is taken into account, the trebled population and the 23 per cent increase in average real income have produced an increase of only 66 per cent in trade value. It becomes very apparent, then, that the merchants of Edmonton rather than the merchants of Fort Saskatchewan are benefiting from the increased buying power of the townspeople.

The dominance of Edmonton is very evident in the range of services provided in Fort Saskatchewan. The major retail outlets are groceries, hardware stores and drug-stores serving the most immediate needs of purely local markets; specialty stores are almost entirely absent, and those of good quality are completely so; there are only two banks, and other professional and financial services are minimal. In fact the only outstanding increase has been in the number of building contractors, from one firm to five firms in the past decade.

The retarded development of the business core has been a major disappointment to the town and the District Planning Commission, both of whom expected much greater results from the influx of industrial employees. It has also had two very obvious physical consequences. In the first place, there is still an appreciable number of old and rather inferior residences scattered through the business area; in the second place, in the blocks immediately adjoining the business core, where new residential construction has been prohibited, the land is taken up almost entirely by deteriorating dwellings and vacant building lots. It must be anticipated that the improvement of this blighted fringe will proceed only very slowly.

The major reason for the slowness of Fort Saskatchewan's business development is, quite obviously, the attractiveness of the great variety of competitive facilities readily available in Edmonton. There is, however, another factor which must not be overlooked. This is the fact that the major industries make comparatively little use of the town's business and professional services. In the case of the two national companies, Sherritt Gordon and Dow Chemical, it is only natural that much of such services as banking, insurance and marketing should be handled through Eastern Canadian head offices, but even Peace River Glass, which is a local company, depends heavily on Edmonton services. For example, the company's main sales office is in downtown Edmonton, the general bank account is maintained in Edmonton (though a payroll account is also maintained in Fort Saskatchewan), all insurance is purchased from Edmonton sources and most truck and rail transportation requirements are arranged in Edmonton. Virtually the only goods and services derived from Fort Saskatchewan are drug and hardware sundries, oil and gasoline, lumber, and some printing work. Dow Chemical is much less dependent on either Fort Saskatchewan or Edmonton. It makes use of Fort Saskatchewan's banking facilities but insurance is handled on a national basis; industrial materials are largely imported from other parts of Canada, though Edmonton suppliers are used whenever possible. Sherritt Gordon depends on Edmonton for legal services, industrial supplies, heavy machine work, and engineering and contracting services. In short, then, the industrial companies look to Edmonton far more than to Fort Saskatchewan for the satisfaction of their service needs.

When this fact of close industrial ties between Edmonton and Fort Saskatchewan is combined, first, with the marked dependence of the townspeople on Edmonton's retail, personal and professional services; and second, with the fact that at least 15 per cent of the town's labour force is resident in Edmonton, it becomes obvious why Fort Saskatchewan must be regarded as an industrial satellite of Edmonton rather than a completely self-contained town. The links between the two communities are extremely strong and there is no evidence to suggest that they are likely to be broken in the future.

PROSPECTS FOR THE FUTURE

The interrelationship of Fort Saskatchewan and Edmonton is fully appreciated by the Edmonton District Planning Commission, and the town is increasingly likely to occupy a very special place in the development of

Edmonton's metropolitan region. In particular, the Commission regards Fort Saskatchewan as a major centre for future decentralization of industry and population from the ever-expanding body of Edmonton's metropolitan area. There is, as yet, no formal plan of decentralization within the Edmonton region but there is considerable concern over the form which Edmonton's undoubted continuing growth should take. It can be said that the plan is an evolving rather than an established one. Planning, and particularly the installation of utilities, in the towns of Fort Saskatchewan, St. Albert and Leduc is already based on the assumption that they will grow with Edmonton but it is intended that the processes of regional town growth shall be given long and careful study before a plan is formalized. There is no doubt, however, that decentralization into carefully planned satellite towns, with careful integration of these towns into the total metropolitan pattern, will be a major element in the future evolution of Edmonton's urban structure.

Fort Saskatchewan's special place in the changing pattern of metropolitan growth arises from the fact that, at present, it is the only town which can be regarded as an industrial satellite of Edmonton. Its own growth is not likely to be especially significant in relation to the size of the total metropolitan complex and the District Planning Commission visualizes an ultimate maximum population of only 40,000. Its role as a pilot project in industrial decentralization, however, is of the utmost importance. Small as it is, Fort Saskatchewan has already demonstrated that decentralization can work in Edmonton, even though the city's growth problems have by no means reached the stage at which decentralization could be considered an urgent need. Fort Saskatchewan is providing Edmonton's planners with the invaluable opportunity of gaining satellite town experience well in advance of actual need. It is giving them the opportunity to assess the special requirements and problems of satellite town development in comparative leisure and so should make it possible for the serious short-comings of such forced developments as the British New Towns to be avoided. In brief, Edmonton has an almost unparalleled opportunity to really plan, in a long-term perspective, a model pattern of satellite towns.

Much has already been learned from the Fort Saskatchewan experience. In the first place, it becomes obvious that not all types of industrial enterprise can be located successfully in satellite towns. From Fort Saskatchewan it would seem that decentralization is most useful for those industries with (1) market areas which extend far beyond an individual metropolis; (2) supply and service needs which either can not or will not (because of the national ramifications of a company) be met by the individual metropolis; (3) exceptionally large land requirements; and (4) the financial ability to install their own water and sewerage systems. In addition, such special factors as close dependence on mineral resources may make a metropolitan location impossible, though this is not true decentralization in the sense that a choice was available between city and satellite. Dow Chemical, for example, is not a decentralized industry in the same sense as either Sherritt Gordon or Peace River Glass.

In the second place, a number of basic conditions have to be satisfied by the potential satellite town if it is to be attractive to decentralizing industries. Fort Saskatchewan's experience would indicate that the three most important conditions are : (1) direct access to excellent rail and road communications and preferably to communications which form part of a national pattern; (2) an abundant fresh water supply and river frontage industrial sites downstream from the town; and (3) the physical and financial ability of the town to provide services and utilities, and water most particularly, for a rapidly expanding population. This last factor is likely to prove especially critical for many of the small towns in the Edmonton region which otherwise seem to be in ideal situations for satellite development.

As for the town of Fort Saskatchewan itself, it is impossible to predict the rate at which growth is likely to occur. At present, because of its small size and Edmonton's overwhelming powers of attraction, Fort Saskatchewan can not be expected to grow through its own momentum. There can be none of the "snowballing" effect of continually expanding service businesses or industries oriented to local markets. Instead, future growth must be related directly to the arrival of new decentralized industries, and will therefore be both uneven and unpredictable for many years.

That growth must be expected, however, seems to be certain, and both the town and the Edmonton District Planning Commission intend to be prepared for it. Preliminary consideration is now being given to the ultimate form of the town and to such questions as the public preservation of the North Saskatchewan River valley and the possibility of a link track to the C.P.R. line which passes less than five miles south of the town; the town administration is slowly acquiring land adjacent to the municipal building for the development of a modest civic centre; and a decision on the best method of expanding the domestic water supply, which is now operating almost at capacity, is expected soon. Constant vigilance, though, will be necessary if the still generalized long-term planning aims are ever to be realized. Pressures for piecemeal development have been great and though an intermunicipal pattern of strict subdivision control has completely prevented unco-ordinated development, real estate signs still flank the Edmonton-Saskatoon highway outside the town limits advertising land for sale for "Speculation or Possible Light Industry". Also, the land on the east side of the town is already criss-crossed with a web of pipelines and transmission lines which, if allowed to proliferate haphazardly, could sterilize large areas of potential urban development; fortunately, the only power distribution company is being most co-operative but there is still very little control over pipeline location. Pressures of this kind must be expected to increase in the future, but because of the municipal co-operation and integrated planning ensured by the Planning Commission, they can and will be resisted. The present achievements of Fort Saskatchewan are assured of maximum protection while its potential significance as a planned industrial satellite makes it one of the more interesting and important small towns in Canada today.

ACKNOWLEDGMENTS

Much of the material for this paper has been derived from personal communications from James A. Clark, Secretary-Treasurer, Town of Fort Saskatchewan; Charles A. Hames, Assistant Manager, Chemical Metallurgical Division, Sherritt Gordon Mines Limited; J. M. Pretty, President, Peace River Glass Company Limited; and R. T. Richardson, Works Manager, Fort Saskatchewan plant of Dow Chemical of Canada, Limited. Special acknowledgment must also be made to Frank Marlyn, Executive Director, Edmonton District Planning Commission, for his invaluable advice and information.

5. Perspectives for Regional Planning

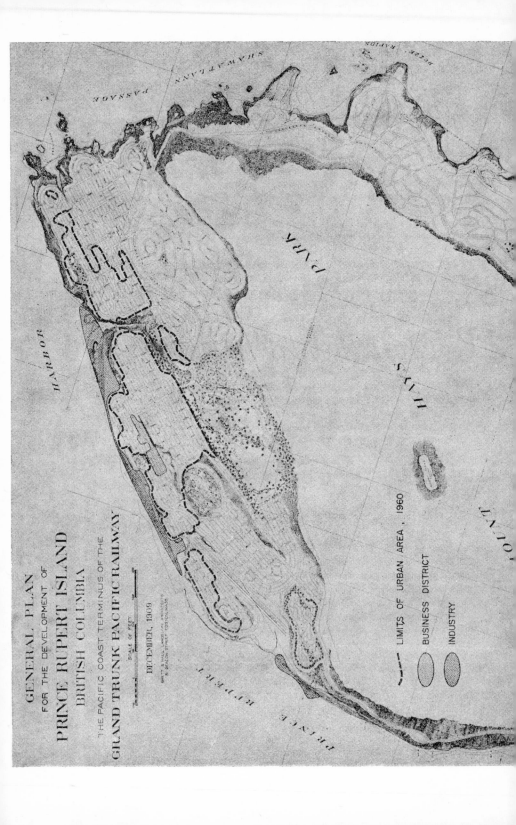

GENERAL PLAN
FOR THE DEVELOPMENT OF
PRINCE RUPERT ISLAND
BRITISH COLUMBIA
THE PACIFIC COAST TERMINUS OF THE
GRAND TRUNK PACIFIC RAILWAY

SCALE OF FEET

DECEMBER, 1909

———— LIMITS OF URBAN AREA, 1960

BUSINESS DISTRICT

INDUSTRY

A TALE OF TWO CITIES

Nigel H. Richardson

The author, a Project Director with Acres Research and Planning Limited, is the former Deputy Director of the Lower Mainland Regional Planning Board, B.C., and Staff Consultant with the City of Toronto Planning Board. He is the current editor of Plan Canada, in association with Professor Benoit Begin of L'Institut d'Urbanisme. The paper is a revised and expanded version of the essay Kitimat, B.C. : An Appraisal, *which was awarded the 1961 President's Prize of the U. K. Town Planning Institute. The T. P. I's permission to make use of the essay is gratefully acknowledged.*

Between the Pacific Ocean and the 4,000-foot crest of British Columbia's Coast mountains, the westernmost mainland range of the Canadian Cordillera, is a rugged, forest-covered land of rivers and fiords. Among the mountains, away from the sea, its summers are cool and its winters bitterly cold; but on the lower levels, along the inlets and the coast, the climate is milder, with mean monthly temperatures between 55° and 65° in July and between 20° and 35° in January. Precipitation is high, reaching 160″ or more annually in some areas, and rain or snow fall throughout the year; except on the seacoast the land is blanketed by thick snow during the winter months.

Until the latter part of the nineteenth century the region was virtually unknown to the white man, though scattered along the fiords and the rivers were the villages of the Tsimshian, Bella Coola and Kwakiutl, dependent on fish for their livelihood as most of their descendants are today. The first systematic exploration was carried out in 1859 and 1860 by Major William Downie, who was impressed by the potentialities of the Skeena Valley as a transportation route. Five years later the "Collins Overland Telegraph", which was to link North America with Europe across the Bering Straits and Siberia, reached the Skeena. But, in 1866, came the news that a cable had been successfully laid across the Atlantic, and the project was abandoned. Many of the workers stayed to look for gold, which in due course was found on the upper Skeena, and by the seventies the rush was on. The riches of the Skeena, however, did not compare with those of the Yukon and the Cariboo, and, as elsewhere, frustrated prospectors turned to less colourful occupations : logging, farming, or fishing, for the most part. By the 1890's fish canneries were being established at several points along the coast and the rivers. European settlement was firmly established by the end of the century.

Surveys for a transcontinental railway were carried out as early as the 1870's and it seems that serious consideration was given to the adoption of a northern route through the Yellowhead Pass and along the Skeena Valley. But the C.P.R. chose the southern route instead, and Vancouver rapidly blossomed from a cluster of shacks along the shore to British Columbia's chief city. However, the possibilities of the northern route were not forgotten. In 1903, with the support of Sir Wilfrid Laurier, the Grand Trunk Pacific Railway Company was incorporated. The Grand Trunk Pacific was the brain-child of C. M. Hays, General Manager of the Grand Trunk Railway, a line beset by chronic financial difficulties. It was Hays' scheme to build a second transcontinental railway to compete with the C.P.R.; and, in fact, by bringing the railway five hundred miles closer to Oriental ports, to outstrip the C.P.R. in the race to carry the rich trade that was expected to develop with the Far East. Construction of the line eastward from the coast was started in 1907; in 1914 the route was completed from North Bay, Ontario, to the Pacific.

PRINCE RUPERT : NEW TOWN, 1904

Meanwhile, even before any track was laid, a site had been chosen on Kaien Island, some ten miles north of the mouth of the Skeena, for the city that was to be the line's western terminus. The company bought 10,000 acres of land from the provincial government at $1 per acre, on condition that a quarter of the townsite and a quarter of the waterfront would be reserved for government use. It then took a step of considerable significance in the history of Canadian town planning by engaging a prominent U.S. firm of landscape architects, Messrs. Brett and Hall of Boston, to design a townsite layout for the new city of Prince Rupert.

The planners were faced with a twofold objective. First, they had to plan for a city of 100,000 people, which might before very long have a population considerably exceeding that figure. If that now seems a trifle ridiculous, one must recall that in 1904 Vancouver, which was barely a village at the time it was reached by the C.P.R., less than twenty years previously, already had a population nearing 50,000 and in fact was destined to reach 100,000 only seven years later. A spectacular rate of population increase was no more than consistent with the rosy prospects that were thought to lie before Vancouver's rival.

Second, Brett and Hall were expected to design a city of beauty and dignity, according to the formal civic aesthetics of the day, on a topographically difficult site consisting largely of rock and muskeg and covered by dense forest. Considering the circumstances, their layout was remarkably successful. A series of monumental thoroughfares, terminating in natural elevations or sites for public buildings, was skilfully adapted to the form of the land. The streets connecting them were laid out broadly on a grid, but where topography demanded it the planners were prepared to modify the grid or even depart from it altogether. In fact, the care and deftness with which a formal street layout is fitted to a rough and broken site commands great respect, particularly when the Prince Rupert plan is compared with the infinities of rectangles which were being imposed elsewhere upon the land of British Columbia with brutal disregard for hill, stream, or coastline. The two main axes which dominate the plan, with their related systems of avenues, circles, crescents and public sites, were in fact intended as the commercial and institutional foci of a great city. The residential areas which were to house a hundred thousand people were to be more freely and informally laid out, their streets curving along the sides of the hills that rise behind the city centre. [1]

In anticipation of the tremendous boom that was to occur when the railway was opened to traffic and the docks of Prince Rupert were crowded with transoceanic shipping, and in an attempt to regain some of the money that it had spent, the Grand Trunk Pacific soon began to sell lots. In the euphoric atmosphere of the time, and with the rosy image of a Canadian San Francisco before their eyes, many people bought them. Streets, sidewalks, and utilities were laid in the forest. Within a couple of years of establishment of the town, Prince Rupert had a population of over four thousand, a council, an apparently firm financial base, electricity, water supply and a telephone system.

PRINCE RUPERT : DEVELOPMENT AFTER 1912

Then the bubble burst. In 1912 Hays went down in the Titanic; the new docks were almost unused; the real-estate boom was over; the city was in serious financial difficulties. In Prince Rupert's hinterland there were riches of minerals and timber indeed, but the time was not yet ripe for them to be tapped. Farming was scattered and marginal. In 1914 Prince Rupert was stagnant, and the coming of war destroyed what hope there might have been that the opening of the railway would revive the golden prospects of a few years before. Eight years later the Grand Trunk Pacific was absorbed into the Canadian National Railways. In 1929 most of the land purchased by speculators twenty years before began to revert to the city for tax delinquency. In 1933 the city itself went bankrupt.

For a quarter of a century Prince Rupert's population remained almost unchanged at about 6,500 people engaged mainly in fishing and fish processing, but also in government and other services, logging and sawmilling. The Second World War brought a temporary boom (during which the population, including servicemen, rose to some 20,000), plus the more lasting benefits of enlarged docks, a seaplane base, and, most important of all, a road which for the first time linked Prince Rupert to the provincial highways system. A pulp mill was established near the city in 1951; a new

---

[1] For a contemporary account of the planning of Prince Rupert, see George D. Wall, "The Future Prince Rupert as conceived by Landscape Architects", *Architectural Record*, 26.2. August 1909.

airport has recently been built, and a ferry service to Alaskan ports will soon be started. The city's population, which dropped to 8,500 after the war, reached 12,000 by 1961.

Physically, the city's growth has taken place almost entirely within the area originally intended for commercial, institutional and governmental use. Ironically, however, the street which was intended as the principal boulevard of the city is now not even the main business street, chiefly because speculation raised lot prices so high that businessmen preferred to establish themselves on a parallel street a block away, which is now in effect Prince Rupert's "Main Street"—a lesson not without contemporary relevance. Prince Rupert is still not a wealthy place; shabby frame houses and weed-grown vacant lots adjoin the wooden sidewalks of streets built over gullies or blasted through rock, streets that were to have been lined with tall and stately buildings. Comparing the vision of 1905 and the plan which grew out of it with the reality of a half-century later, one is reminded of an impoverished family squatting in the ballroom of a palace abandoned long before it was completed.

But from the viewpoint of physical development Prince Rupert has two great assets. Almost all its unused land is in public ownership, amounting in total to over half the city's land area; and, partly as a consequence of this, the built-up area is fairly well-defined and compact, with a minimum of "sprawl". There is, however, a housing shortage, and much existing housing is in poor condition.

Today, the future of Prince Rupert looks brighter, perhaps, than it has since 1912. The old dreams are unlikely ever to be realized, but new transportation links to the south and north, development of timber and other resources, and tourism, hold out hopes of better times to come. At the same time, the silver lining has a cloud in the form of indications of a decline in the city's staple industry, fishing. In the face of these prospects, the City Council recently engaged a Vancouver firm to carry out an economic survey and a study of housing conditions, and a report on planning. [2] These were completed early in 1963, and may provide a sounder basis for future development than the febrile optimism in which Prince Rupert was born. [3]

THE ORIGIN OF KITIMAT

From the beginning of the First World War to the end of the Second, as mining was almost completely abandoned in the face of adverse economic

---

[2] Associated Engineering Services Ltd., *Prince Rupert: Economic Prospects and Future Development,* Vancouver, B.C. January 1963.

[3] For general accounts of the geographical background, early history, and planning of Prince Rupert, see A. D. Crerar, *Prince Rupert, B.C.: The Study of a Port and its Hinterland,* unpublished M.A. thesis, University of British Columbia, 1951; and P. D. McGovern, "Prince Rupert, British Columbia", *Town and Country Planning* XXVIII 4-5, April-May 1960.

conditions, the north coast—Skeena region as a whole depended almost entirely on fish and lumber for its livelihood. By 1951 it had only 20,000 people, about a third of them Indian. 8,500 people lived in Prince Rupert and the remainder mainly in small towns strung along the railway—now part of the Canadian National Railways system—or in isolated logging communities scattered along the coast and in most cases accessible only by sea or air. Sea and air are still the only direct means of communication between the region and the main population centres of the province. But in addition to fish and forest the north coast had an almost untapped reserve of hydro-electric power from the drainage of the Nechako Plateau between the Coast Range and the Rockies, estimated at three million kilowatts. It was this potential supply of cheap power which in 1951 led the Aluminum Company of Canada (Alcan) to decide on the establishment of a major aluminum smelting plant; for while the raw materials of aluminum reduction can be shipped cheaply in bulk by sea, the process requires enormous quantities of power—20,000 kilowatt-hours for every ton of ingots produced. Smelters are thus tied to sites near sources of ample power and with deep-water docking facilities as well as road and rail transportation, requirements which were met at the head of the Kitimat Arm, some fifty miles inland, and connected with the railway and the Prince Rupert-Prince George highway by a convenient valley. [4]

To provide the power, Alcan undertook several major engineering projects, including the reversal of the drainage of an entire lake system. The physical and economic problems were thus overcome; but the human problem remained. The plant, located in almost virgin wilderness forty miles from the nearest town, needed a work-force of thousands, and to get and keep a stable and contented work-force meant providing living conditions that would compare favourably with those obtainable in the cities and towns to the south. Thus Kitimat was born, the region's second planned "new town", only eighty miles as the crow flies from its first, making them next-door neighbours in the terms of that vast country.

THE PLAN FOR KITIMAT

Alcan, like the north coast, had had previous experience with new towns, and in the company's case, like the region's, the experience had not been entirely happy. It is likely that the problems created by Arvida, established under similar circumstances on the Saguenay in Quebec in 1926, had a good deal to do with the care devoted to the physical and administrative forms of the new venture. To shape the general conception

---

[4] For general accounts of the Kemano-Kitimat project, see: Aluminum Company of Canada Ltd., *Kitimat-Kemano: Five Years of Operation, 1954-1959*; Paul Clark, "Kitimat— A Saga of Canada", *Canadian Geographical Journal*, XLIX, 4 October 1954; L. G. Ecroyd, "Start-Up at Kitimat", *Western Business and Industry*, 28.7, July 1954; "The Nechako-Kitimat Development", *The Engineering Journal*, April 1953 and November 1954; "Kitimat: A New City", *Architectural Forum*, July and August 1954; Pixie Meldrum, *Kitimat— The First Five Years*, Corporation of the District of Kitimat, 1958.

Aspects of Kitimat

A natural slope permits two-level shopping on one side of Kitimat's main shopping centre.

An isolated case of a conscious attempt at house grouping, marred by utility poles and excessive asphalt. Note the use of the street as a playground.

The "pedestrianways" through blocks of houses tend to degenerate into littered mud-tracks. There is little evidence that they are much used.

and principles of the town plan for Kitimat, the company engaged Clarence Stein, the author of the Radburn plan, working in collaboration with the New York firm of Mayer and Whittlesey; while a team of experts prepared proposals on the administrative, fiscal and social aspects of the scheme. The result was a remarkably comprehensive series of detailed studies and plans embracing every important consideration which could be expected to apply to the building and operation of a town of ten thousand or more people in a virgin wilderness, forty miles from its nearest neighbour and four hundred from a large city. [5]

Twelve years have now passed since the decision was made, and a decade since Kitimat was formally incorporated as a Municipal District by a special Act of the British Columbia Legislature. The town is today generally recognized as one of the most significant of contemporary North American contributions to planning principles and practice, and one of the few ventures on the continent to compare in scale and character with the British New Towns. A first assessment of the true extent of its achievements can now be attempted.

In doing so, however, one must bear in mind the physical circumstances and the handicaps which were imposed upon the planners thereby. When Alcan came, the country was largely unexplored and unsurveyed. Since it was covered by dense timber, mistakes were made even after aerial photography, mapping, ground surveys and test drillings. Ravines were discovered that had not been suspected, and the site of the City Centre was found, after construction had actually started, to consist in part of muskeg, and the intended arrangement of the centre had to be drastically altered.

These were the circumstances under which Stein had to devise his plan. There were two courses which he could have adopted : to adapt to geography and climate or to adapt to people and culture. The former would have meant probably a tight design, a huddling together of people and buildings about a compact, perhaps multi-levelled centre, a solution such as has been adopted in northern Sweden and has been proposed in other parts of Canada. Instead Stein chose the latter. He assumed that the people of Kitimat would be the same sort of people as those of Vancouver or Winnipeg or Toronto, living as far as possible in the same way; and he adapted to the rugged landscape the "Radburn idea", the principle of the loose-knit community based upon but not subjected to the use of the automobile. He designed a pattern of traffic-ways linking the City Centre to neighbourhood centres, and, connected to the traffic-ways a series of loops and culs-de-sac around which the houses are built. Among the buildings run pedestrian walks and park strips by means of which supermarket, drug-store, movie theatre, church and school can be reached on foot, in complete safety from vehicular traffic.

---

[5] See Clarence S. Stein et al., *Kitimat Townsite Report,* edited and reissued by the Corporation of the District of Kitimat, December 1960.

All this presupposed a car-owning society, and although the car is kept in its place, serving but not dominating the houses and excluded entirely from the inner ways which link homes to community facilities, the mobility which it gives and the demands which it makes have clearly been the chief determinants of the pattern of the town to the almost complete exclusion of any deferring to the exigencies of land and climate. Kitimat has as a result been described derisively as "Radburn revisited" and "A suburb without a city", and indeed it seems at first a little strange to find amid the forests and rugged hills of British Columbia a town which would seem quite at home in the suburban fringe of any North American city. But social values and habits are facts to be faced as much as are snow and muskeg, and less easily overcome. This being so, Stein's application in Kitimat of the principles which he had pioneered in Radburn to permit peaceful co-existence between man and machine was not only sensible but perhaps inevitable.

KITIMAT ASSESSED

In fact, if any criticism can be levelled at Stein's general conception it is that he did not fully appreciate the extent of automobile domination. While he allowed in effect for two separate but equally complete systems of circulation, one for motor traffic and the other for bicycles and pedestrians, it has proved in practice that much of the latter has been neglected and has served little useful purpose. While the internal "green-way" or park belt is well used, the connecting footpaths running between the rows of houses have mainly degenerated into mud tracks littered with garbage cans and junk, and they are likely to be abandoned in the design of new neighbourhoods. It could be argued that for a town set in the midst of a wilderness of tremendous potential for hunting, fishing, skiing and other forms of outdoor recreation, with fifteen feet of snow in the winter and much rain the rest of the year, the whole system of parks and greenways is unrealistically generous; that for its real value the cost of landscaping and maintenance will be too high. The present municipal administration would not agree, but as time passes and the consciousness of and pride in being part of a new venture fades, future municipal councils may well look on all this open space flowing through the town with more jaundiced eyes.

While the quality of the two-dimensional plan of Kitimat can be considered worthy of the tremendous enterprise of which the town is a part, the same unfortunately cannot be said of its physical form. Once the decision was made to go ahead with the project, time was of the essence; production had to be started and houses for the workers had to be built as quickly as possible. For several years shortage of accommodation was a chronic condition, and quality of design and construction was hardly considered. Alcan in any case left the provision of housing to others as far as possible; where necessary it had houses and apartment buildings erected

The Greenway

Through Nechako neighbourhood one can walk from the elementary school along a paved pathway, through the "greenway" . . .

. . . under the road by way of a practical but rather unattractive pedestrian underpass (left background of the top photograph) . . .

. . . to the high school and "Nechako Centre", which, with its movie theatre, library and stores, still rivals "City Centre" as the focus of the town.

to rent to its workers, but for the most part it sold land to private developers, mainly from the Vancouver area, and left them to build as they saw fit. This meant in practice that the standards of construction were those imposed under the National Housing Act as a condition of N.H.A. financing, while the standards of design were aesthetically speaking, nil. In terms of space, Kitimat houses and apartments are quite acceptable; in terms of solidity of construction, they are no better than N.H.A. minimum, which is not high; in terms of appearance, they are at best undistinguished and at worst quite bad. One looks in vain for any evidence or care for civic design. Among other things, the visitor to Kitimat quickly notices that the builder, accustomed to the standard Vancouver suburban grid was clearly puzzled by the Stein concept of the inward-facing house turning its back upon the street, which is quite contrary to the North American convention. It is obvious too that the same applies to many of the residents; the consequence is that some houses are oriented toward the street, in the usual manner, with the orderly, well-trimmed "front yard" located accordingly and the washing hung out at the back; while others are reversed according to the Stein conception to face the pedestrian ways or greenways. [6] As a consequence, the vista whether of the street or of the interior frontage is generally scruffy.

To such criticisms Alcan's reply would be that its business is to produce aluminum, not to build towns; and that its policy, based on its Arvida experience and pursued vigorously by means of second mortgages at N.H.A. rates, home-ownership bonuses and repurchase guarantees, is to encourage its employees to own their own homes, to avoid the "company town" stigma, and generally to encourage Kitimat to become in every possible way a "normal" Canadian community. These principles are sound enough, and have undoubtedly greatly helped the town to become, as it now is, a vigorous community largely free of company paternalism. Nevertheless, it is a matter for regret that Kitimat's physical manifestation is so far removed from the high aspirations of Stein's original conception; and it is particularly regrettable that no attempt has been made in the building of the town to take account of its geographical circumstances. The same buildings might equally well have been erected in Vancouver or Halifax or for that matter in Chicago or Boston; in conception they are as much mass-produced as cars or coffeepots. As a single example, the canopy which surrounds the main block of the City Centre—the commercial heart of the town—is perhaps six feet wide, a token shelter which is of little value in a place with heavy rain or snow during most of the year. This failure to respect, even to consider, the nature of the place is unfortunately completely characteristic of the building of Kitimat; no attempt whatever has been made to try out ideas and methods geared to the circumstances of the site rather than to custom and convention. Even apart from the lack of experimentation the general level of design is low. There is not one building in the town with any claim to architectural distinction,

---

[6] After this was written the author was informed that this was in fact a deliberate attempt to introduce "variety". If so, it succeeded only in introducing visual chaos.

though there are several examples of uninspired but respectable contemporary design. The only obvious examples, in fact, of imaginative design lie in a few such details as the street-name signs, which are colourful, legible and handsome (and made of aluminum).

There has in fact been a general lack of concern with the quality of execution, all the more striking and disappointing when contrasted with the care and skill devoted to the preparation of physical, administrative, fiscal and social plans. There has been a similar lack of concern, the job once having been done, with the success of these plans or with finding out how they have worked, despite the largely experimental nature of the project and the enormous potential value of such an experiment for the planning not only of future ventures of a comparable nature but of new communities generally. In particular, it is impossible to know how successful the conception and execution of the scheme has been for the people most closely concerned, those who live in the town, and it is impossible also to know what relationship exists between physical conditions, planned and unplanned, and their way of life and the degree of satisfaction which it provides.

This failure to consider Kitimat as anything but an expedient designed, however competently, to meet the exigencies of an immediate practical problem has in fact been apparent from its very inception. Consider the circumstances: here was a town established in a region with a great and almost untouched store of natural resources, a town confidently expected to be the largest in hundreds of thousands of square miles, yet next door to another which had been founded only a few decades earlier amid even rosier hopes only to become a shabby fishing community. But almost no thought was given to its prospects as a regional centre, almost none, in fact, to the eventual settlement pattern of the region or to the appropriateness of Kitimat's location from this point of view, or even from the point of view of the eventual development of resources other than hydro-electric power. Here was a site that met the requirements of the company for the production of aluminum; that was sufficient. Its suitability in terms of the future economic development or human settlement of the region was simply not a relevant consideration.

To sum up, Alcan must be given credit for the care which was taken in the planning, physical and otherwise, of Kitimat. The site plan is not beyond criticism but it is unquestionably distinguished. But a townsite had to be planned and from a purely businesslike point of view it made more sense to do the job well than to do it poorly. Good industrial relations and a stable labour force were important to Alcan, and anything necessary to aid in maintaining them made sense. This attitude was hardly novel. Alcan is in the direct line of descent in this respect from the New England millowners of the early nineteenth century, from Salt, Lever, Cadbury, Pullman and other industrialists who, over the last century and more, have provided their workers with better living conditions for the sake not only of social ideals but of hard cash. Alcan probably had its eyes fixed more firmly on the latter rather than the former than had some of its distinguished predecessors. As evidence, one may point to the three main areas of criticism which have been discussed: the lack of interest in the quality of building design, particularly from the aesthetic viewpoint; the failure to make any but the most tentative efforts to learn from so valuable an experiment in town planning, social organization and local administration; and the lack of regard for Kitimat's place in the economic, geographical and social evolution of the region as a whole. Kitimat was, in short, seen in exactly the same light as was the Kenney Dam, the Kemano powerhouse, the plant itself, or any of the other components, as a single tremendous industrial project: as a job to be designed by the best men available, to one end only—the production of aluminum.

THE LESSONS OF PRINCE RUPERT AND KITIMAT

A comparison of the histories of Prince Rupert and Kitimat produces some striking parallels. Both towns were created (almost exactly half a century apart) as integral parts of great commercial enterprises intended to tap the vast resources of the north. Both towns received generous allotments of land from the provincial government but both were developed entirely by private enterprise, with little or no government interference. Both towns were planned by American firms according to the most up-to-date principles of their time.

But the most significant similarity lies in the fact that neither town has achieved what was to be its appointed destiny. In the case of Prince Rupert, the economic base upon which a great city was to grow proved to be an illusion; the second Canadian transcontinental railway was a failure; and the new town, almost stillborn, had to struggle along on a single industry which had hardly, if at all, entered the calculations of its founders. The economic planning which produced Kitimat was more thorough and more realistic. The ingots flow from the Alcan plant and will probably continue to do so—but they are not flowing at the rate that was originally expected. In the face of unexpected adverse conditions in the world markets, production has levelled off and has even been cut back, instead of rising steadily as was anticipated when operations were started. Furthermore, the company and the municipality have so far found little success in their search for new industries to broaden the community's economic base and lessen its dependence on Alcan. Consequently, the town's population seems to have stabilized at a figure between eight thousand and eight thousand five hundred having dropped from a peak of ten or eleven thousand accounted for by construction workers. This may be compared with the estimate of 35,000 to 50,000 used by Stein as the basis of his plan.

Today the attention of Canadians is turning more and more to the north—to the last land frontier, with what we are assured is its vast storehouse of riches. Where there are riches men will certainly go; new communities will come into being; thousands of people—eventually, perhaps, millions—will call the north their home. What lessons do the stories of Prince Rupert and Kitimat hold for us as we contemplate this prospect?

That depends on the answer to another question. When we talk about northern "development" (a word which, as every planner knows, covers a multitude of sins), do we mean resource development or do we mean regional development? Because, in practice, these are very different things involving very different philosophies. Resource "development" is too often mere exploitation of natural riches for financial gain, without regard to the long-run fate of the region which supplies them or of the communities to which the process gives birth. Canada can supply many examples: the fact that no consideration other than the requirements of aluminum production entered into the choice of Kitimat's site is only one illustration. It may well be that in this particular instance no other location would have served, but in view of earlier experience in other parts of Canada—experience in which Alcan has been involved—it seems most regrettable that so little thought was given to future regional development. The case of the Saguenay-Lac St. Jean region may be cited: this part of Quebec offered a variety of natural resources, including, as on British Columbia's north coast, minerals, timber and water-power; but each of these resources was exploited independently without reference to the development of the others or to the future of the region as a whole. The result today is a settlement pattern consisting of a scattering of small or medium-sized one-industry towns (including Alcan's Arvida) within a relatively small area, in some cases only a few miles apart, none of which can aspire to the size or functions of a genuine regional centre. The economic dangers, human deficiencies and general inefficiency of such an arrangement both for the individual community and for the region as a whole are obvious enough, yet the same pattern seems to be emerging around the Skeena Valley.

The best known example of the alternative approach, of course is TVA. Certainly TVA was concerned with making use of resources, but always as part of the process of developing, improving, and helping a region. TVA's achievement lies not in the number of dams it has built or the number of kilowatt-hours of energy it produces, but in the fact that the Tennessee Valley is a better place, its economy stronger and more diversified, its communities more prosperous, the lives of its people fuller, healthier and more secure, than they were thirty years ago. This is regional development in the true sense of the word, and it is to be hoped that the future settlement of Canada's north and the utilization of its resources will be carried out in this spirit. On this assumption, let us return to the question: What lessons can be learned from the experience of Prince Rupert and Kitimat?

First, a single industry is not a satisfactory basis for a permanent community. This is perhaps a truism; certainly after the experience of Elliot Lake, to name only the most famous recent example, the point is unlikely to be disputed. But even if an industry is soundly based, stable and prosperous, it is not a healthy thing for a community to be almost solely dependent upon it for employment, for tax revenue, sometimes even for welfare assistance, entertainment and social facilities. Sometimes it may be unavoidable; but when a new town is to be created, every effort should be made to find a site with the best possible chance of attracting industries other than the one which called it into being; and every effort should be made to encourage such diversification within the community and the concurrent development (in the true sense) and settlement of the area around it. In other words, the enterprise should not be seen as a matter of a single industry and a community serving and subordinate to it, but as the initial phase in a coherent regional development program whose object will be not only the exploitation of the region's natural resources but also the establishment of a sound and broadly based local economy and of a full and secure way of life for the people of the region. Really successful new town planning, in short, is inextricably bound up with regional planning and economic planning; regional planning and economic planning are but two sides of the same coin.

The second lesson to be drawn from the history of the Skeena-Coast region is that regional development planning of this coherent and comprehensive kind cannot be expected from private enterprise. This is no criticism of the Grand Trunk Pacific or of the Aluminum Company of Canada or of any other private firm. Their function is to run a railway or to produce aluminum or whatever the case may be, and to pay dividends to their shareholders, not to design towns or to develop regions. It is to the credit of both the GTPR and Alcan that, in the nature of their commercial activities requiring the creation of new communities, they went to considerable pains and expense to create good ones, at least to the extent that enlightened self-interest dictated. They could not be expected to do more. It follows, therefore, that if future regional development based on the exploitation of the natural resources of the north is not to be the hit-or-miss process that it has been in the past; if the tapping of natural riches is to provide the basis for permanent and stable settlement assuring the best possible way of life for the entire regional community, then public participation will be required in very considerable measure.

NEW APPROACHES TO BUILDING FRONTIER REGIONS

Let us consider briefly where models of such participation might be found.

Several Canadian provinces, notably, perhaps, Alberta and British Columbia, have legislation providing for the establishment of regional planning agencies. But these are clearly envisaged as essentially inter-municipal bodies operating in settled areas. Their function, broadly, is to prepare plans to regulate private development and to guide the works programs of other public agencies. Several provinces also have statutes providing for special forms of administration for new communities. [7] But again, this legislation is in general terms designed to provide a special form of local

---

[7] E.g., Local Improvement Districts in Newfoundland and Manitoba; Mining Towns and Mining Villages in Quebec; Improvement Districts in Ontario; New Towns in Alberta; Local Administrative Districts in the North-West Territories.

government to apply during the life of a temporary settlement or pending the establishment of normal municipal administration. In neither case does it appear to be envisaged that the special agency, either regional or local, will play a very positive role in the development of the area under its jurisdiction. On the other hand, there are a number of agencies established by federal statute—the Prairie Farm Rehabilitation Administration, the Agricultural Rehabilitation and Development Administration and the Atlantic Provinces Development Council, for example—whose purpose is quite explicitly to play an active and constructive part in the development or revitalization of the economy of some part of the country, including making changes in the accustomed manner of land use. None of these, however, is concerned primarily, if at all, with the opening up of largely undeveloped and uninhabited areas, but rather with improving the situation of regions where development has been unsoundly carried out or has not kept up with the more prosperous parts of the country. (One is tempted to suggest an analogy to urban growth, wherein the profitable building of new houses at the edge of the city is left to private firms while government assumes the cost of tearing down the old and decayed areas at the centre and replacing them with something better.)

Thus there exist in this country at least the seeds of three relevant ideas: regional planning, special administrative arrangements for new towns, and government action to aid and stimulate the economies of particular regions. But in pursuing possible avenues of approach to Canadian regional development it is also worthwhile to consider two cases outside Canada, neither of them new: the British New Towns Act of 1956 and the Tennessee Valley Authority itself, born in 1933. Both are too familiar to Canadian planners to warrant detailed description, but it is useful to recall briefly the features of the two schemes which are particularly relevant.

The New Towns Act, based upon the Scott and Barlow Reports and upon Abercrombie's Greater London Plan, had as its chief object the dispersal of population from Greater London. What is of interest here, however, is not the purposes of the New Towns but the manner in which they are established, financed and operated. A New Town, under the Act, is the responsibility of a Development Corporation appointed by the Government with the power to acquire land, to build, to construct utilities, to provide community facilities, and "... generally to do anything necessary or expedient for the purposes of the new town or for purposes incidental thereto" (the words of the Act). Apart from the fact that they are financed by Government loans and grants, the role of the Development Corporations in relation to the New Towns has in fact been very much the same as the role of the Grand Trunk Pacific or Alcan in relation to their respective offspring—with the very important exception that the former are instruments of national policy rather than private investment, and that consequently the first consideration has been the establishment of sound, viable and permanent communities, and each New Town (apart from special cases such as Corby) has been carefully sited and designed with a view to attracting a wide range of industries and not just to serve the needs of one.

The special relevance of TVA lies in the fact that the utilization of a resource was regarded not as an end in itself but as a vehicle for the economic and social enrichment of an entire region, and that this enrichment took many forms and was effected in many ways—direct action by the federal government being the exception rather than the rule. TVA's way was to educate, to demonstrate, to assist, to encourage, not to step in and do the job itself, beyond its immediate statutory task of harnessing the Tennessee River for power production, navigation and flood control; but it did these things to such good effect that a poor and primitive region achieved prosperity and vitality.

From all these—from present Canadian regional planning and special local administration legislation, from PFRA, ARDA and APEC, from the British New Towns and the American TVA there are valuable lessons to be learned, and it is to be hoped that they will be noted and applied. For the experience of Prince Rupert and Kitimat shows unmistakably that good town planning under the aegis of private firms is not enough. Each of the two towns is a fine example of the best town planning thought and skill of its day, and the differences in approach, planning and execution provide a fair measure of the progress that has been made in this field in half a century. But in origin and concept, in the kind of consideration that led to and conditioned the establishment of the two communities, there was no significant change at all. In each case the first consideration was economic exploitation, not the creation of a good environment for living or the future well-being of a region. It is here that progress in thinking is long overdue; it must be understood that the use of the resources of the north means the building of new human communities, urban and regional; that the creation of such communities demands an enlightened and comprehensive economic development and regional planning policy; and that this in turn requires a large measure of public participation, public initiative and public responsibility.

While the manner in which these responsibilities could best be exercised is obviously a matter for careful and expert study, the requirements of the job as well as experience both in Canada and elsewhere indicate the need for some special form of regional planning and development agency, adequately financed and with the authority and capacity to undertake a variety of functions, including resource surveys, provision of roads, harbours, airports and other elements of the economic "substructure", industrial promotion and investment, town planning and building, and perhaps also local administration. There is no exact model to be slavishly followed in meeting the special conditions of the Canadian north, but there are many examples to learn from, not only those already mentioned but others in many parts of the world. By such means, not only could the resources of the north be brought into use more rapidly and more efficiently, but settlement and urban development could take place in a stable and orderly fashion to the lasting benefit of the people. In the final analysis, that is what really matters.

REGIONAL PLANNING

Hans Blumenfeld

The author's concept of regional planning is a distillation of a rich and diversified planning career in the United States, Canada, Russia, Germany and intermittently, Puerto Rico, Israel, and other developing countries. His work has been focused in Canada since 1955 when he became the Assistant Director of the Metropolitan Toronto Planning Board. His present activities include consulting work both in Toronto and Montreal and lecturing in the Department of Town and Regional Planning, University of Toronto. He is the author of the recently published book, The Modern Metropolis, Harvest House, *Montreal. In 1966 Dr. Blumenfeld was elected a Fellow of the Town Planning Institute of Canada. In the spring of 1968 he received an LL.D. from the University of Montreal.*

Regional planning is the extension of planning into a new field. Like all planning it means exploring interaction and attempting to order all actions so that they will help rather than hinder each other.

This new field has been approached simultaneously from two directions, both of which have gradually enlarged their scope; on the one side from local, physical planning; and on the other, from segmental or departmental, functional, planning. It lies in the nature of planning as a discipline concerned with interrelations that it must constantly expand its field of study and of action, as it discovers ever wider and more complex interrelations and attempts to influence them. But in addition to this "subjective" reason for the expansion of planning into new fields there is an even more important "objective" one, deriving from the nature of contemporary society.

It is commonplace that the world is getting smaller. With the development of means of transportation and communication local isolation is being broken and what was once an unrelated event in a distant area now becomes part of the locality's own life. But it is equally true to say that the world is becoming bigger. There are three times as many people living on this globe than there were 200 years ago and they engage in more varied activities and transform the face of the earth more strongly than any previous generation. Ever new skeins are woven into the increasingly complex tapestry of life.

Because the world is getting smaller, town planning, the core of the work of the members of our Institute *, is forced to extend beyond the boundaries of the individual community to encompass its surroundings and its relation to neighbouring communities, leading to comprehensive planning primarily of metropolitan areas but beyond that also of larger and more loosely connected regions.

Because the world is getting bigger, populated by more people making more claims on its resources, functional planning, the planning of the activities of an industry or of a government department, is forced to take into account other activities going on in the same area, on which it is dependent and which may compete with it for land, water or other resources. Out of the attempt to co-ordinate all functions within a given area has been born another type of regional planning, which on this continent is best represented by the planning activities of the Tennessee Valley Authority or of the Commonwealth of Puerto Rico.

Functional planning and physical planning have developed as two different disciplines; but, as far as I know, only one western language, Russian, has developed two different terms; *planirovanye*, regarded as a branch of economics, for the former, and *planirovka*, regarded as a branch of architecture, for the latter. They answer different, though related, questions.

Functional, economic, planning asks: what to produce, how much, at what cost, when? and only in very general terms: where?

Local physical, planning deals, from the economist's point of view, with one scarce resource, land. It asks primarily: where and how? However, it has increasingly turned to a study of the economic and social aspects of planning; by scheduling and "phasing" it attempts to answer the question "when?" and by capital budgeting the question "at what cost?".

On the other hand, functional planning, with increasing competition for land, has to deal very specifically with the question "where?" and with an increasing complex technology, it must be able to answer the question "how?".

Thus the two types of planning converge and merge into a new discipline which we call regional planning. Our French colleagues who use the term *urbanisme* for town planning have coined the term *aménagement du territoire* for this discipline.

I will not attempt to touch that sacred cow, the definition of planning—the poor beast has been milked pretty dry anyhow—but I can not quite avoid talking about the definition of a region for planning.

The term "region" has long been used by geographers to denote homogeneous areas such as the Laurentian Shield or the Wheat Belt. It seems to me that for a planning region homogeneity is not a suitable criterion. Planning is concerned with interaction and interaction occurs between heterogeneous elements which supplement each other rather than between homoge-

---

* Town Planning Institute of Canada.

neous ones. It is often stated—frequently in exaggerated form—that any planning unit should be relatively "self-contained". The more homogenous an area, the more it is dependent on supplementary activities in other areas, and is consequently less self-contained. Therefore, heterogeneity, rather than homogeneity, is characteristic of a planning region. I would define such a region as an area within which interaction is more intense than is its interaction with other areas.

From this concept follow two important considerations. As interaction is impeded or facilitated not only by natural, but also by man-made factors, planning regions are defined not merely or exclusively by natural boundaries, but equally by political or administrative boundaries; most strongly, of course, by national borders, but to some extent by any administrative division. Therefore, the act of defining an area as suitable for planning administration does to some extent determine a region, not merely discover one.

However, the greatest care should be taken to discover where interaction is most developed and where it falls off. Thus the concept of the planning region as an area of intensive interaction leads to the concept of the "watershed". Various methods have been developed to find the boundaries separating neighbouring "watersheds". The German geographer Walter Christaller in his pioneering work on "the central places in Southern Germany" used the number of long-distance telephone calls made from any given location to one or another "central place". Newspaper distribution, wholesale trade in various commodities, and many other activities can be used to find boundary lines. No two lines will ever coincide completely. There is no such thing as an ideal boundary for a planning region. Whichever one is adopted will be a not wholly adequate compromise with conflicting existing conditions; but the fact of its adoption adds a new condition which makes it more adequate.

The problems dealt with by regional planning may vary widely, but at their core will be generally the use of land and of water and the development of transportation facilities; and these in turn very largely determine the distribution of economic activities.

Two different questions arise in this connection: distribution between regions and distribution within a region. Planning for the former is undertaken mainly by large corporations or by national governments; but distribution within a planning region can be guided by provincial and various levels of municipal governments, dependent on the size of the region.

Perhaps more important than difference in size is the difference between "monocentric" and "polycentric" regions. Intensive interaction has in most cases developed from an urban centre which has thereby transformed the surrounding area into its own region. In particular in modern industrial society the metropolitan region is becoming the dominant form of human settlement.

However, there are some areas which are characterized by the existence of several centres in close proximity to each other. Probably the most important of these is the Ruhr region in Germany. But in Canada, the industrial towns of the Grand River Valley form a comparable constellation, though, of course, with a much smaller volume of population and economic activity.

In monocentric regions much of the drive for regional planning is likely to come from the central city; but in polycentric regions it will generally have to be initiated by a larger unit. In any case, regional planning requires active participation by non-governmental agencies, because so many of the crucial decisions are actually made by private enterprise. In this connection the German *Landesplannung-Verbaende* (Regional Planning Associations) are worthy of study. Their membership comprises provincial and municipal governments as well as representatives of the utilities, of industry, agriculture, trade unions, etc.

While active participation of such non-governmental bodies is essential, it appears that under our Canadian conditions the initiative for defining regions and organizing planning bodies within them must rest with the provinces. The time is ripe for regional planning. To assist in its development is a challenging task for the Town Planning Institute of Canada and all its members.

INTERNATIONAL TRENDS IN URBAN AND REGIONAL PLANNING

Ralph M. Rookwood

A native of Edmonton and now in the United Kingdom, Mr. Rookwood is a former Director of Town and Rural Planning for the Province of Alberta. He is at present chief planner of the Covent Garden redevelopment scheme in London, England. Events since the writing of this paper almost ten years ago have not diminished the impact of the central theme—"We are faced inevitably and unavoidably with the greatest era of city-building in the history of man."

Current problems are so pressing and our resources in the planning field are still so limited that we are all ordinarily obliged to focus on a relatively narrow field of interest in order to crystallize decisions and generate effective action. When we have time to think about it, we all acknowledge the dangers of limiting our outlook to this extent, however necessary it may be for the achievement of immediate objectives. We as planners least of all want to be caught winning the last war instead of preparing for the next one. But ordinarily we cannot avoid our daily preoccupations. A major advantage of our annual Town Planning Institute Conference is that we can remove our self-imposed blinkers to have a look at the broader scene and broader issues. With the choice of International Trends in Urban and Regional Planning as a subject, no one can accuse the conference organizers this year of neglecting their opportunities.

The subject is an important one because it may help us to clarify issues and concepts, and because as planners we cannot avoid the consequences of growing world integration and interdependence. There are broad trends in the development of the world as a whole that will ultimately (often in the near future) affect our work at its very foundations, although these trends may be temporarily obscured by impermanent local conditions. Local grain surpluses obscure growing world food shortages. Local wide-open spaces obscure the significance of growing population pressures. Current terms of trade in world markets may obscure a potential shift in favour of food and raw materials with all the implications this would have for Canada as a major world producer of both—implications of fundamental importance for future town design and the planning of the physical environment in general.

It is the purpose of this paper first, to discuss some of the most important of these trends affecting the physical development of the world, second, to describe the present operation of the planning profession in various countries at both urban and regional levels, and finally, to suggest some developments in the profession which may be necessary if planners are to function adequately in meeting the demands likely to be made on them in the future.

THE INTERNATIONAL SCENE

We live and work as planners in a world with a rapidly growing total population and an even more rapidly growing urban population. Moreover, the expert estimates of the rate of growth are still being revised upwards. The report entitled *World Population and Resources* published by P.E.P. (Political and Economic Planning) in London in September, 1955, states ". . . this startling acceleration of growth is of recent origin. After centuries of comparative stability the inhabitants of the globe have doubled in the last hundred years, and at the current rate of growth they will double again in little more than half the time. World population in 1955 almost certainly exceeds 2,600 million; within fifty years humanity will be confronted, if present growth persists, by the staggering problem of feeding, housing, and clothing nearly twice its present numbers." [1]

In April of 1958, only three years after these figures were prepared the United Nations Population Division had increased the total by 100 million, estimating present world population at more than 2,700 million, and predicting that it would rise to more than 6,000 million by the end of this century. Thus, the current United Nations estimate is that world population will considerably more than double in just over forty years, which means a rate of growth of more than 1.5 per cent a year.

In the next few years, then, world population will grow each year by approximately forty-five million, or three times the present population of Canada, and within the working lives of most planners the number added each year will probably be much higher than that.

This increase in total world population would, in itself, require a tremendous amount of new development of all kinds, even just to provide the basic essentials of life—food, clothing, shelter—and the tools to produce them. But there must be added to this essential minimum development, the additional development required to raise standards of living well above the present unsatisfactory levels found in many parts of the world and suffered by the majority of those now living. The authors of the Political and Economic Planning report comment that "it is impossible to foresee a tolerable world situation until ways have been found of feeding adequately the existing population and the expected annual increase in population and of providing the resources needed for a widespread rise in living standards". [2]

---

[1] Political and Economic Planning, *World Population and Resources*. London, 1955, p. 3.
[2] *Ibid*. p. XXXV.

There has beeen a great deal of discussion and unresolved argument as to the implications of this double-headed problem of accommodating a vastly increased population and substantially raising existing standards of living. The argument has centred on the balance between total world population and total world resources and has unfortunately concentrated mainly on the ultimate adequacy of resources in some undefined future, rather than on the comparative rates of increase of population and resource utilization.

We do not know what ultimate limit there is, if any, to our ability to produce new resources to replace those that become exhausted, except that space on the surface of the globe is limited, and eventually we might find we had standing room only. (Professor W. A. Lewis has calculated, for instance, how long it would take at a 1 per cent rate of growth to reach the state where there was only 1 square yard of land per person.) [3] What is of far greater immediate importance is that "for the next twenty-five years the countries of the world will be engaged in a neck and neck race between population and production, and there is no assurance at present as to which will win".

The U.S.A. has already outrun or is in the process of outrunning its resources base and has become a net importer of food and raw materials, as clearly recognized in the Paley Report to the President. This is the traditional situation attained successively by all the highly industrialized countries, which have always assumed the existence of inexhaustible supplies abroad to balance local or national shortages. It is in this kind of world situation that the underdeveloped countries containing most of the world's population have now embarked on a determined program of industrialization, having in fact no alternative if they wish to provide for growing populations and a rising standard of living.

The most obvious planning problem resulting from such a world situation is just the sheer amount of development of all kinds required to provide for the new needs of the new population and the increased needs of those now living. Forty-five million additional people each year to be fed, clothed, housed and employed if one thinks solely of physical necessities for survival. Another forty-five million people each year to be supplied with some additional food, clothing, improved shelter and productive machinery, if the underprivileged are to be provided with the minimum advantages of anything that could reasonably be called civilization, by the end of this century. Development programs throughout the world thus require plans to be made for housing, industry and related development for close to 100 million people a year if the objective is merely to achieve the "tolerable world situation" mentioned earlier, without any provision for the rest of us who all think we should be improving ourselves too.

Most of this development, of course, will occur in urban centres. This is inevitable for a number of reasons, including the improvement of

---

[3] W. A. Lewis, *The Theory of Economic Growth*. London, George Allen & Unwin, Ltd., 1955.

agricultural techniques, the urbanizing effects of industrialization, and the increasing attractiveness of urban centres as the source of all those civilized values for which improved standards of living will create an effective demand. Nearly all studies of the related problems of increased production, reduced population growth and improved living standards, have come to the same conclusion that industrialization and urbanization are the twin indispensable conditions and consequences of success.

These are the circumstances making it inevitable that the rapid city growth of which we are so well aware in this country will persist and accelerate and will probably become typical of all countries before the turn of the century. What is the probable magnitude of this growth in the world's urban centres ?

If all countries experience the shift in the urban/rural ratio which has been experienced in the past by the countries which are now extensively industrialized and have comparatively efficient systems of agriculture, we would expect an increase in world urban populations of 2,200 to 2,400 million on account of the general population growth, plus a further 500 to 1,000 million due to the movement into urban centres of those now living on the land. This would mean a total increase in world urban populations of between 2,700 and 3,400 millions. In other words, the total increase in urban population can be expected to be roughly of the same order as the increase in total world population and might conceivably even be greater. It is this combination of factors, for instance, that accounts for the recent announcement that 92 per cent of Canada's total population increase during the past two years is found in urban centres of more than 1,000 people.

How are these basic trends affecting world development expressed in terms of trends in urban and regional planning ? And what are the implications for planning theory, planning training, and planning practice during the working lives of those present ? These are the questions to which the main body of this paper is devoted, and on which a brief account of present practices and trends may help to throw some light. Let us turn our attention, therefore, to the planning profession as it now exists and operates in various countries within this world context.

CURRENT PRACTICES IN URBAN PLANNING

In reading and talking about current planning problems and objectives in various parts of the world, one is struck first of all by the almost exclusive concentration on urban planning and secondly by the surprising similarity, almost to the point of uniformity, that prevails in this field. It is really only with very rare exceptions that it would be possible to tell what country or what climate, what form of government, what historical background, even what world region was the context for a particular account of current urban planning problems and proposals once the place names have been removed. To illustrate this point, here is an abbreviated account of the planning proposals for a national capital, which I will leave nameless until the end of the description to give you a chance to guess the location.

The Capital City has grown rapidly since the war and provision is made in the plan for a further increase to 460,000 in 30 years, by which time an additional 300,000 people will live in 6 satellite towns situated from four to eleven miles from the centre. By this method of development everyone will live within easy reach of the open countryside and the city will not straggle and become unwieldly.

The road network has a subarterial system of three ring roads and principal radials leading to the hinterland.

The open spaces forming the major park system would limit the overall growth not only of the capital as a whole but also of its component parts. Central area proposals relate mainly to the solution of traffic problems and the replacement of obsolete buildings. The designation of areas of comprehensive redevelopment is regarded as essential in order to create three major shopping centres, each largely pedestrian in character, and to provide appropriate business and residential accommodation in the heart of the city. Adequate off-street parking is planned and through traffic will be discouraged by the completion of the inner ring road.

The city is divided into 7 districts each consisting of several neighbourhood units varying in size from 3,000 to 10,000 persons, with an average of 5,000. Throughout the city, both for central apartments and houses in outer neighbourhoods, the super-block is the basis of residential planning, in order to protect smaller housing units from through traffic and to create some feeling of intimacy.

All 6 satellites are on completely new sites. The two nearest are in the inner green belt and are purely residential in character, with populations of 30,000 each. The other four will provide for local employment and will have populations of approximately 60,000 each. [4]

Well, this description of problems and planning proposals is typical of many different city planning reports throughout the world. With modifications of a few of the details, it could certainly refer for instance, to Edmonton, Alberta. In fact, the capital city in question is Addis Ababa, Ethiopia.

Is this example really typical? There are a number of reasons why it might not be, as for instance the fact that the Addis Ababa master

---

[4] Town and Country Planning Association, London, *Town and Country Planning*, Vol. XXV, No. 10, October, 1957.

plan was prepared by Sir Patrick Abercrombie and a team of British planners, which might account for the nature and form of many of the proposals. After all, it is not unknown for even the most eminent of planners (equally with other professions) to impose preconceived solutions on alien ground, rather than letting them grow out of local conditions.

But the planning proposals for Addis Ababa are in fact typical of much of the planning being done today in all parts of the world, in all sorts of conditions under all sorts of governments, whether prepared by foreign consultants or local planners.

Thus as we read through account after account of current planning problems and their related solutions, there are certain situations and ideas which constantly recur, as the following examples show : [5]

Vienna : Much sporadic development due to lack of adequate planning control. Large areas to the south of the city now reserved for agriculture, the week-end enjoyment of the Viennese and preservation of the city's water supply.

Copenhagen : A growing traffic problem. An outer zone established for agriculture to banish urban sprawl.

Great Britain : Decentralization to relieve the congestion of the old cities, and to end wasteful sprawl on the city outskirts causing the unnecessary loss of agricultural land. The use for urban purposes of about 30,000 acres of agricultural land each year.

U. S. A. : Prodigal use of 1,000,000 acres a year for urban expansion, and expenditure of enormous sums in almost vain attempts to keep urban traffic flowing.

Nigeria : Town Planning Officer introduced to an oil company agent as "The man who refuses to let us put service stations where they are required" to which he replied "On the contrary, I'm the one who has to find the odd residential plot in between your wretched stations." Nigerians prefer residential lots 50 $\times$ 100 feet. The major problems of Lagos are slum clearance, overcrowding, and traffic congestion. Measures are to be introduced to control density, height of building and car parking.

Portugal: A special technical commission after four years' work has advised the government to undertake the building of several new towns south of Lisbon, with heavy industry to the east of them. Portugal has 46 per cent of its people living sparsely on the land, must have heavy industry in the next ten to fifteen years.

Spain : Central area of Cordoba to be closed to cars so that people can work, eat, shop and talk in peace and safety. Four

---

[5] Abbreviated abstracts taken from various planning journals, mainly *Town and Country Planning* and *Town Planning Institute Journal.*

satellite villages of about 10,000 people each now being built outside of Granada. Need for industry to employ a growing population and to serve the surrounding agriculture.

Israel : The housing problem of Israel is one which calls for great urgency. The population has been more than doubled since 1948. New dwellings have had to be located in relationship to the planned agricultural and industrial development of the country.

USSR : The principles emerging out of the Moscow plan were set down and later elaborated into a code of which the following points appear as the most significant.

1. Limited population size and growth of cities.
2. Planned construction and servicing of cities.
3. Eliminating differences between city and village.
4. Super-block to be a basic planning unit for the city.
5. A program for community services.
6. Individual approach to each city.
7. Regard for national approach to each city.
8. The city as a living organism.
9. Other principles including: priority for housing and favourable living accommodation; utilization of standard designs for residential projects; development of the city centre as a political, administrative and social core.

Indonesia : In common with the rest of Asia, there has been a continued movement of population away from the rural areas into the towns, resulting in congestion and squalor. For example, Djakarta, with approximately half a million population prior to 1939, now has a population of over two million. In this instance a Master Plan is in preparation, which will provide for a large degree of industrialization and also improved housing facilities. The main problem here however is to try and prevent any increase in the movement from the rural areas into the city, and if possible to slow it down. The only way that this can be done is to provide housing and employment facilities in the rural areas themselves, and there is a growing realization that, if town planning is to be both realistic and effective, such planning must take place within the context of regional planning. If this is not done the final result may end in conditions far worse than those prior to the preparation of the town plan.

These are extracts taken at random from accounts published within the past few years of current planning problems and proposals, and they can be multiplied almost indefinitely. It is evident that physical planning in the sense of the preparation of development plans for specific urban centres is widespread throughout the world today and that there are surprisingly few countries where some examples of urban planning cannot be found. Moreover, the planning problems being tackled are remarkably similar and the major principles being adopted in their solution are common to most countries.

It would be unwise of course to exaggerate the extent of these similarities between countries and various parts of the world. It may be true that all countries are facing common urban problems and it may also be true that they are reaching quite a degree of disagreement on the basic principles of urban design and layout, but here the similarities end. There are still, of course, enormous differences between countries in the extent and effectiveness of their planning machinery and their ability both to create plans and to put them into effect : differences in legislative framework, in administrative machinery, in the availability of planners, in the quality of planning personnel and in the experience of all concerned with the planning process and its integration with the general machinery of government and development.

However, in spite of these important differences I feel that the lines of advance are clear, and that the great progress already made in the development of common concepts of urban physical planning give clear promise of the eventual practice by all countries of urban planning combining all the best and most effective principles and methods already practised in many countries today. The major defects of city form and function have been identified and are being analyzed; the design principles for the building of future cities have been broadly formulated and are being elaborated and refined. The problems hardly need any further restatement, but four simple basic principles might be usefully noted :

1. The reintroduction of human scale into all units of urban organization.

2. The grouping of development into balanced units which satisfy related groups of needs and have some recognizable identity.

3. The limitation of urban growth both outwards and upwards on the basis that effective planning for unlimited growth is impossible, and unrealistic in any case in terms of the fundamental requirements of a balanced human environment.

4. The grouping of urban centres in a rational regional pattern of related urban and rural uses.

REGIONAL PLANNING TODAY

The foregoing description of urban planning is indicative of the kind of work most commonly done by planners throughout the world today. We have progressed to some extent from the particular to the general, from housing and sanitation and drains and roads to the urban environment as a whole; but we have not generally made the further progression from the urban scene to the larger regional environment within which we all work and live, and within which common problems require joint solutions.

However, there is a growing recognition that many urban problems (particularly the basic ones) demand regional solutions, and there is also a growing demand for regional planning to provide a rational framework for resource development programs, i.e., the twin aspects of world trends discussed earlier. Instances of both approaches are contained in the following examples of attempts which have been made to deal comprehensively with physical development on a regional basis. [6]

France : Planning on a regional basis was introduced under the law of 1935 with special provisions for Paris in a measure of 1936. Some regional planning has been carried out but usually of a metropolitan character concerned mainly with housing and communications and done under the advice of outside consultants whose plans are not necessarily implemented by the communes within the region.

The Rhone Valley scheme is a resource development scheme involving improved navigation, power production, and irrigation. With the development of river transport and cheap electricity the industrial development of the towns will increase apace, and population and overspill problems may become as difficult here as elsewhere among the great agglomerations. There does not appear to be so far a regional plan that envisages these problems and makes adequate provisions for their solutions.

Germany: The need for regional and inter-authority arrangement has been realized for some time and some attempt has been made to plan land use on a regional basis. In 1949 the regional planners of the *Laender* set up their own joint advisory board to act as a means for discussion and sorting out the regional problems, but it has no federal status and is purely an advisory body.

In 1951 the Federal Minister of the Interior created a co-ordinating committee to which belonged any ministers with regional planning responsibilities. However, like the *Laender* regional planners board, it is only an advisory body with no executive powers whatsoever. The Ruhr Basin is an example of a resource development region, but having many of the problems of a metropolitan region. In March 1950, the *Laender* passed the Country Planning Act to enable them to tackle the problems of the Ruhr and its surrounding areas on a regional basis. The implementation of the earlier individual town planning schemes has been found quite impracticable and the town-planning department is gradually bringing together the surveys of all the other departments of states and relating their plans to one another.

---

[6] Extracts taken mainly from *Regional Planning in Europe,* an unpublished paper prepared by Leslie B. Ginsburg for the International Centre for Regional Planning & Development, 1955.

As a result of the preliminary work, various joint committees are at work and the authorities seem to be aware of the necessity to consider the problem as a whole and not merely in its separate parts. Among the problems requiring solution and for which plans are being put in hand are the following : introduction of secondary industry into mining areas; movement of population from overcrowded towns; land reform and agricultural resettlement; rehabilitation of derelict land; prevention of soil erosion by afforestation; conservation and distribution of water supplies; incorporation of transport into the European road and rail system.

Great Britain: Greater London: The idea of regional planning for Greater London was stimulated by the Barlow Report of 1940 which stated that the continued drift of industrial population to London "constitutes a social, economic, and strategical problem which demands immediate attention", and recommended a program of decentralization and dispersal of both industry and industrial population and the redevelopment of congested urban areas.

Three advisory plans were made for the physical development, reconstruction, and reorganization of the whole of Greater London region. However, there is as yet no clear overall direction of planning nor regional co-ordination of development. There is no regional planning authority of the kind recommended. Lacking any strong regional direction the various authorities and public bodies are left to formulate their development proposals according to their own needs, although some decentralization of population and industry has been achieved.

The Clyde Valley: The problems of the area were investigated in 1944 when Sir Patrick Abercrombie produced his plan, and for those interested in this type of region much valuable information on methodology can be gained here. The plan itself was purely advisory. The problem of the Clyde Valley region is linked closely to that of the neglected Highlands of Scotland. The former has attracted half of the population of the country with resulting urban overcrowding and rural depopulation and inadequate development of the country's other resources.

Sweden : It is now appreciated that it has become more necessary than ever to evolve a suitable machinery for inter-municipal planning, and regional plans have been produced dealing with the areas around the larger cities. The Gothenburg Plan demonstrates best the more usual type of regional planning in the country.

The area concerned is Gothenburg itself with three surrounding districts which includes thirty large municipalities, five of which are cities within a twenty-four mile radius. The plan is administered by a committee of seven members from the suburban area and two from Gothenburg who deal in practice with road communications, the repercussions of airfield and port development, and the question of urban and rural open space for recreation purposes of all kinds.

South Africa : Co-ordination of planning by adjoining municipalities in Cape Province. Joint Town Planning Committees formed in several regions to ensure co-ordination by preparation of Joint Schemes which possess legal force. The schemes are sub-regional in character and embrace location of routes for arterial roads as well as siting of industries relative to communications. They also exercise broad control over land use, but do not override detailed town planning proposals of individual local authorities.

Norway : Regional planning was formally established in Norway in 1949 when the government set up a council of regional planning under the chairmanship of the Secretary of Labour. Its twelve members were drawn from other government departments and universities. The impetus for setting up this council for regional planning came from the economic problems of the country, particularly those of the northern provinces which were brought into sharp relief after the war.

The comprehensive nature of the council's task is made clear by the decree of May, 1953, which states "through surveys and analysis regional planning shall serve to elucidate the possibilities of a better exploitation of natural resources, and a serviceable localization of economic activities and population settlement".

Work has been started; but so far preliminary analysis for a few provinces has been completed and the council is very much aware of the fact that no one has as yet any experience in utilizing such material for regional planning. However, regional planning in Norway is becoming more and more important and is gradually being accepted in the field of economics and land use over the country as a whole.

Pakistan : The Thal development project is probably the largest project in the world for the reclamation of desert countries. The project is designed to make possible the cultivation of wheat over an area of some two million acres. River control with the dams and irrigation channels again form the basis for the project. The creation of industry to utilize the power produced in the barrages, the planned development of new towns to service the reclaimed area, as well as the settlement of half a million people in new villages are all facets of the scheme. Two hundred and fifty new villages have already been established.

Israel: The national plan for the development of the new State of Israel is an example of comprehensive regional planning. The country is planned on a regional basis and the development of settlements is integrated with industry, agriculture and water supplies, as well as social welfare designed to integrate an immigrant population coming from many lands. An essential part of the plan deals with desert reclamation, afforestation, and the exploitation of mineral resources.

These examples make it clear that regional planning such as it is today, exists generally in only the most tentative and primitive way in most countries of the world. However, it is equally clear that in spite of the limited progress made so far in the development of effective regional planning machinery, there is a growing demand for planning at a level which can take account adequately of man's relationship with his whole environment instead of attempting to deal with it on the usual piecemeal basis. Probably the most complete attempt to answer this demand is being made in the Netherlands, where regional planning has been granted a truly effective place in a general hierarchy of plans : municipal, regional and national. [7]

All plans regulate the use of land within their purview, but they do so from the respective points of view of the commune, the region, and the nation as a whole. They are arranged in order of rank, in the sense that the principles contained in the higher plans must be accepted and worked out in the lower. As a rule, only the lowest level of planning, that of the local authority, is directly binding upon the public.

The logical sequence of events would be for levels of planning to be built up on the principles laid down at national or regional levels. In reality somewhat the reverse has taken place, due to the chronological precedence of the municipal plan, both in legislation and in practice.

The regional plan was instituted in 1931, with the realization of the need for supra-municipal planning. One regional plan has been approved, several others have been passed and are ready for approval, and many others are in course of preparation.

The National Plan was provided for in 1941, and the Government Physical Planning Service is now undertaking research into fundamental issues of physical planning with an immediate objective the determination of a national planning policy.

In certain respects a clearly defined trend can already be discerned in the national policy—for instance with regard to the decentralization of industry via regional concentration.

The co-ordination of the projects put forward from time to time by the various ministries constitutes an important element in this work.

Beyond the national plan, there are the international aspects.

---

[7] Government Physical Planning Service, *Physical Planning in the Netherlands*. The Hague, 1955.

International economic co-operation will eventually require that its consequences in the field of land use designation should be gone into jointly. A start has already been made. In 1952, the ministers entrusted with physical planning in the three Benelux countries established a joint committee for these problems. This committee will make a comparative study of the legislation, of the planning research methods and of the planning methods themselves, while every effort will be made to ensure that the planning activities in the three countries are more closely attuned to one another.

It is not surprising that the Netherlands should be the first country to reach this advanced stage in planning, since it is one of the countries in which population pressure has become most intense, and in which land really has to be regarded a scarce commodity. However, the same problem can be anticipated in many countries in the next 50 years, and it seems obvious that all countries eventually must recognize the validity of Mumford's remark that "the grasp of the region as a dynamic reality is a first step toward a constructive policy of planning, housing, and urban renewal".

On a deeper level than this, the demand for regional planning can be expressed as the demand not only for the improvement of man's whole environment in order to provide the physical framework for a richer and fuller life, but also for the development of a more stable and sympathetic relationship with the natural environment.

Arthur Glikson in his book, *Regional Planning and Development* [8] puts it in this way :

> What then is the background of the compelling need for regional planning which has become apparent recently in countries of all continents ? What is the emergency that threatens the habitability of various regions and countries in our times ? Does not technology lead us headlong towards even greater comforts, towards more leisure and the other amenities of life? Regional planning is one of the contemporary social expressions which try to expose the error of this official international doctrine, which try to point out the dangers lying in wait for civilization as a result of the treatment of its material and human resources, and which try to replace it with a social aspiration towards integration with nature, mutual help and a more peaceful stability of life. In the words of Benton MacKaye it is 'the most immediate function of the regional planner, ... to take sides in this coming conflict of human values against values of an exotic mechanized civilization'. Regional planning sees a change of outlook as a prerequisite for the continued existence of civilized life.

---

[8] Arthur Glikson, *Regional Planning and Development*, The Hague, Netherlands Universities Foundation for International Co-operation, 1955.

Regional planning works on a program of actual works to be done in order to improve man's relation to his environment. The idea motivating this kind of planning strives at the co-ordination of human needs and the special characteristics of man's material environment, not by blind utilitarian behaviour but organically in a manner by which man finds the place of a co-operating partner in nature's land communities and cycles.

IMPLICATIONS

Assuming that the foregoing description of present trends and future needs in the planning field is correct, and that what is needed most urgently today is a rapid expansion of physical planning techniques, knowledge, and organization at the regional and higher levels, what are the implications for the planning profession during the next forty years? There are many possible answers to such a question, and I would like to mention only three which seem to be among the most fundamental :

(1) the re-examination of planning theory so as to remove any conceptual blinkers which may limit planning to something less than comprehensive action dealing in an integrated way with the whole of the physical environment;

(2) a great expansion of the number of trained planners of all kinds;

(3) the development of international agencies to advance the knowledge and practice of regional planning.

Professor Handler has already given us a notable contribution to the re-examination of planning theory [9], and I do not want to spend any more time on this point except to note that the nature of planning practice throughout the world at both urban and regional levels strongly supports his definition of planning in terms of comprehensiveness, focus on physical improvements, and organizing principle.

Turning then to planning education. A tremendous increase in the number of trained planners will be necessary in the next forty years, if the planning profession is to be equal to meeting the demands that will be made upon it as resource development programs increase in number and scale, and as the growth of urban centres accelerates.

In order to make a very rough assessment of the numbers involved, I have made what I think is probably a generous estimate of the existing number of planners as 10,000. This is of course a real "guestimate", since I certainly did not have available even rough estimates from many countries which are not actively engaged in planning of various kinds.

However, using this figure of 10,000 for lack of a better one, the number of planners available today is about 100,000 short of the number

---

[9] See *supra*, Benjamin Handler, "The Fundamental Aims of Planning".

required to serve the existing world population, if one uses a ratio of one planner per 25,000 total population, which is somewhat lower than the standard adopted by Frederick J. Adams in his recent study of planning education.

Over the next forty years, if we can accept this as the period in which extensive industrialization and urbanization must be achieved in most countries of the world, we must add to this present deficiency of roughly 100,000 planners the additional numbers required by the increase in population and development over that period, which amount to an additional 120,000 planners to be trained, or a total of about a quarter of a million graduates required from planning schools by the end of the century.

Existing training facilities will have to be enlarged, and new planning schools will have to be established in those universities which are presently without them. It is desirable of course that planners should be trained in the country in which they will be employed, (or at least in the same world region where geographic and social conditions are similar) and that the present practice of sending planning trainees from all over the world to be trained in alien conditions in the United States or Britain should be superseded as soon as possible. However, many of the countries most deficient in planners are also short of universities (e.g., Indonesia, with two universities for a population of eighty million); and until more universities are established it may be necessary to set up special planning centres serving whole world regions, within which geographic and social conditions, and problems of planning and development, are roughly similar. A proposal of this nature was made in the last few years, for example, in connection with the Central Statistical Institute in Calcutta, to serve the whole of South-East Asia. Such an international training centre would, in fact, have great advantages in facilitating the international co-operation in physical development that will ultimately be necessary and unavoidable, particularly in such areas.

As to the type of training required, there is obviously a great deal still to be done in providing for the participation of an appropriately wide range of specialist planners at all levels of planning. The need may be more immediately obvious at regional and higher levels, but even at the urban level we recognize that the city is far too complex to be dealt with successfully by one so-called master planner. I do not wish to minimize the importance of any particular specialist in the planning process, nor to overlook the preeminent importance of the architect/planner in designing the final physical form of development as an integrated and artistic whole to delight all our senses. I merely wish to get the priorities straight so that we can create an environment which is economically efficient and socially satisfying as well as being an aesthetic delight—satisfying all three criteria rather than giving undue weight to any one to the ultimate detriment of them all.

There is a real challenge here to the planning profession as a whole to help prepare the way for a great and carefully conceived expansion in training facilities throughout the world in the next decades—an expansion that will undoubtedly be assisted by projects of various international agencies, but will be largely dependent on the help obtainable from the existing planning schools and institutes in those countries that have already reached a fairly advanced stage.

Let us now turn from planning training to the question of an international body for advancing regional planning knowledge and techniques. Such a body was in fact established in 1954 in London, England, under the name Association for Regional Planning and Development; and has now been reconstituted as the International Centre for Regional Planning and Development with a General Secretariat in Brussels.

Those of us who worked for the establishment of the International Centre felt that there was still a great need for an organization that could devote its attention exclusively to the planning of physical development at the regional level, collating existing knowledge from all over the world, acting as a clearing house for information, undertaking research on regional planning techniques, building a library, and eventually establishing a training centre or centres where all persons concerned with regional planning and development (whether physical planners or not) could develop their competence in this particular aspect of planning. Existing information in the field was so limited and so difficult to obtain, experience so limited and difficult to share, the need to develop regional planning organizations so great and the time so short—that only a body international in scope and devoted exclusively to regional planning could operate effectively in the development of this particular aspect of the planning field—this was our assumption. The success of the two international conferences held in London in 1955 and the Hague in 1957, the support given to the Centre by several West European governments, and the improving liaison with the Housing and Town Planning Bureau of the United Nations, all seem to justify the original assumptions on which the Centre was founded.

The Centre as such was formally established in September, 1957, with a General Council representative of many different countries and professions and intended to be even more broadly representative than at present in both the geographic and professional senses. A sub-committee on membership has been set up with members in as many different countries as possible who are responsible for helping to broaden the membership of the General Council in their respective countries. It is the intention that eventually there will be established in most countries a National Group of the Centre, such as has already been formally established in France, Belgium, Holland, and Great Britain. In this way it is intended to build up an organization which can function continuously rather than just at an annual or biennial international conference, and throughout the world rather than just at one localized centre. The National Groups already established have each undertaken the responsibility for research on a particular aspect of the Centre's work, in an attempt to get as much work done as possible even during these early days when there is no full-time paid research staff at the Centre itself, and to steadily build up interest in and knowledge of the

Centre and its work. Of course this is obviously easier to do in compact countries like the Netherlands or Great Britain, than in countries like Canada, but even here we now have large enough concentrations of planners in some parts of the country at least to permit the organization of an effective Canadian National Group of the Centre.

It is hoped that the Centre will quickly develop into an effective agency by which planners in all countries can make a substantial and timely contribution to this branch of planning which has been so neglected for so long, in spite of our lip service to Geddes and other leaders of planning thought to whom planning was something a great deal more than the superficial and one-sided urban design aspect of the field that has predominated for so long and that now leaves us so ill-prepared for the problems now lying ahead.

CONCLUSION

I have tried to indicate in this paper (which is all too brief for such an extensive subject) some of the more significant trends observable in the world today in the whole field of physical planning. I feel that it is only a matter of time before our concepts of the aims and functions of planning, the qualifications of the ideal planner, the proper levels of physical planning, and the relation of physical planning to government generally and to all kinds of environmental development, will be considerably modified and many problems substantially resolved through the general recognition of the true nature of planning as a comprehensive activity co-ordinating all aspects of the shaping of the physical environment, in which stable regional habitability and a humane urban form can both find their proper place in sympathetic relationship to each other.

But the phrase "only a matter of time" is a significant one, and much remains to be done if the rapidity of development is not to leave us hopelessly behind. I feel sure that the success of a body such as the International Centre for Regional Planning and Development could contribute much to the solution of the problems which are manifestly insoluble within particular administrative boundaries, or even within individual urban or metropolitan agglomerations. I feel equally sure that only with this comprehensive kind of planning for our whole physical environment will we ensure that our objectives for the cities of the future will be achieved.

We are faced inevitably and unavoidably with the greatest era of city-building in the history of man : it is now up to us to use every means in our power to ensure that this statement has more than quantitative significance, and that we create the framework for the building of truly great cities, in which human values (both social and individual) take precedence over the mechanistic materialism which now threatens us.

PLANNING OF THE METROPOLITAN REGION

Gordon Stephenson

Professor Stephenson is Consultant Architect at the University of Western Australia in Perth, Australia. He is well known in Canada as the former head of the Town and Regional Planning Division, University of Toronto, and as author of numerous planning studies. He is the former editor of the Town Planning Review, the University of Liverpool Planning Journal, which he re-established when he was the Lever Professor of Civic Design.

METROPOLITAN REGIONS

At the beginning of the Christian era, the city of Rome had a population of over one million. It had become the power centre of the ancient world. The congestion in the city was appalling, and for a long period wheeled traffic moved only at night. The city never slept, there were daily circuses, and the delinquency rate, both adult and juvenile, must have been exceedingly high.

In the middle ages Rome was a small provincial town. It is now a growing, changing modern city-region, with a population somewhat larger than that of the imperial centre which it once was. Modern Rome sprawls over the countryside but the structure of the relatively small inner part of the city-region has been determined by two thousand years of history. Congestion in the centre is greater than ever. Wheeled vehicles fill the streets day and night.

One hundred years ago New York City was confined to the lower end of Manhattan Island, with the newly landscaped Central Park on the northern edge of town. It was about the size of ancient Rome and a growing centre of world trade, competing with Boston and Philadelphia for the role of chief agent to the northern Atlantic seaboard states.

According to a narrow interpretation of our definition, the New York metropolitan region now contains some sixteen million persons; but in truth it has become the major element in a continuous urban area, stretching from Washington to Boston and beyond, with a population of about thirty million. This situation shows clearly on current density maps. Fifty years ago the scientist-planner, Patrick Geddes, was predicting not only this 500-mile long Atlantic coast city-line, but also a "Nearctic Mediterranean" stretching along the Great Lakes, from Montreal to Chicago, over an even greater distance. This is now becoming discernible.

Without wishing to be a Geddes, one may reasonably predict that by the end of the century south-eastern Australia, lying between Newcastle and Geelong, will have an urban population greater than the total population of Australia today. There may be about five million in the Newcastle-Sydney-Wollongong city-region, between four and five million in the Melbourne-Geelong city-region, and Canberra might be a surprise in having upwards of half a million population. Without much doubt urban influence will be felt throughout the 500-mile long city-line, and expressed in terms of ever-increasing land subdivision.

CONCENTRATION OF POPULATION

In the last two centuries there have been profound changes in agricultural techniques and the opening up and development of vast continents. The agricultural revolution of seventeenth-and eighteenth-century England was a prelude to the Industrial Revolution. Both have shattered and reshaped political, social and economic systems throughout the world; both are continuous processes and lead to the concentration of population in ever-growing city-regions.

In Australia, as in many other countries, agriculture is an efficient industry seeking always to reduce labour while increasing productivity. With other primary export industries it has provided the economic foundation for further development. In the nineteenth century the capital cities were firmly established not only as political, commercial and administrative centres but also as the main ports and the hubs of the land transport networks. In turn they have become the centres and chief markets for secondary industry. They are the great magnets attracting population, and it would seem certain they will continue in this role. They grow at a greater rate than the rest of the country, and already the metropolitan regions contain some 60 per cent of the total population.

Looking backwards, it may be seen that the population of Australia has increased by almost five times in the last eighty years. The first census in 1881 recorded a population of 2.25 million; the census of 1921 a population of nearly 5.5 million; and that of 1961 a population of 10.5 million. Consecutive estimates suggest that the country as a whole will have a population of twenty million in another forty years' time.

By the end of this century it is possible that some 70 per cent of the population will live in the metropolitan regions. There are those who consider this to be a frightening prospect. But is it ?

THE SPREADING METROPOLITAN REGIONS

With the increasing tempo of urbanization, the city-regions are changing their form. As they spread far and wide, they are no longer places to be comprehended by ordinary folk. Although they are drawing great numbers of people towards them, they are also scattering many others in various directions over ever-increasing distances.

It is almost impossible to see the end of the process of "scatteration". The more the means of communication improve the more the process is encouraged. An affluent society will allow a person living in Canberra to work in Sydney. Even today he could make the peak hour journey by air in a shorter time than that required by many travelling to work by car from an outer suburb.

The building of great new highways to accommodate heavy peak flows creates new problems. Scatteration is further encouraged and because of this the provision of reasonable community services is made exceedingly difficult. The new arteries fill to capacity as they approach the old and growing work centres, and the congestion in those centres is often appalling.

The ever-increasing use of private cars, congestion in centres of activity, and obsolete roads, cause a steady deterioration in public road transport. The provision of rapid transit by rail becomes increasingly difficult as densities drop and suburbs spread at random. We pay heavily in time and frustration for the shapeless, sprawling city-region. We also learn to accept unlovely urban scenes and unlovable city centres. The main roads are lined by tawdry totems, and the cathedral is hidden behind the financial temple and the treeless car park.

The city-region is full of people, young and old, married and single. They think and dream, enjoy life and despair, love and hate and jostle for position. They nearly all seek the good life as they mould and shape their immediate environment, which is part of a gigantic artifact imprinted by millions of human touches. It is art and non-art telling the story of our time.

SCHOOLS OF THOUGHT

Town and Regional Planning is at the same time an art and a science; an art which is social and aesthetic, and a science which is political and practical. It must therefore, be under continuous debate and at times generate heated controversy.

The modern planning profession is no better and no worse than society as a whole. It includes the educated and uneducated, leaders and disciples, the clear and the woolly-headed. It is moved by many forces and makes judgments ranging from the scientific to the emotive. Because town planning is an art as well as a science, personal views and judgments are sometimes of great importance, and these should take into account a whole range of human needs which are spiritual rather than material.

In a recent issue of the *Architectural Record*, Charles Abrams, a thoughtful observer of the urban scene and eminent authority on housing, made a plea for better understanding of what a city is. In order to make his points on four pages he painted his sketch in black and white. The main arguments were well founded, but he performed the remarkable feat of condemning, on the same page, Ebenezer Howard's "garden city" or "new towns" idea and Le Corbusier's notion of a metropolis as a well-spaced array of huge buildings set in a park. It could, perhaps, be said that he was lambasting the disciples and not the two most important theorists of the twentieth century. Planning certainly has its dogma and clichés, but we should only move backwards if we were to dismiss theory and replace it by sentiment.

Moved by the large-scale replacement of old New York residential neighbourhoods by huge apartment projects, Abrams made a strong plea for sensitive surgery rather than butchery, regenerative pruning rather than wholesale felling. In his inimitable way he was fighting for a city moulded by countless men, rather than a mechanical perfection of great filing cabinets and barracks, with machines flowing in streams between them. He was arguing for a human scale and the richness and variety that come from the human touch.

Within its 400 acres, largely bounded by water and parks, central Sydney has the liveliest concentration of buildings and people in the Commonwealth. There is an overlapping of complementary functions; it is full of human interest and sufficiently small in compass to be at a pedestrian scale. Central Sydney works well largely because, some ninety years ago, a far-sighted railway engineer saw the need for an inner ring railway to serve the centre of the city. It is true that it was completed as an underground electric railway, but this could be regarded as bringing up-to-date a fundamentally sound proposition. As it takes twelve to twenty highway lanes of freeway standard to carry the same number of passengers as a rapid transit line (without taking into account the insoluble parking problem of central areas), it should clearly be understood that the very costly new inner-ring freeway will be far less effective than the inner-ring railway (which causes no parking problem). The freeway is necessary, but if allowed to flood more vehicles into central streets, it may further disrupt and impede pedestrian movement and by so doing destroy the feeling of a city for pedestrians and the intricate balance of central functions.

Central Sydney would not work if access were only by motor vehicle. Once a city-region grows beyond a certain size it is vital that the high-density central area should be served by an up-to-date rapid transit system. This idea was basic in Le Corbusier's *Ville Contemporaine*, of 1922. Disciples please note.

A city-region based primarily on motor transport will work efficiently, have form and character, and evoke deeper human responses and understanding, if it is a whole series of related self-sufficient communities separated by generous open spaces. The regional open-space system might be used for local or national parks, catchment areas, agriculture, or for the considerable range of institutions and facilities requiring park or farm settings. This thesis has been developed by Clarence Stein, co-designer of the important Radburn layout system. He freely acknowledges his debt to

Ebenezer Howard, author of the Garden City idea, who foresaw, at the beginning of the century satellite towns as an alternative to suburban sprawl. Howard envisaged a constellation of railway-age towns, Stein an ever-growing city-region of the motor age.

We are fortunate that basic theories have been developed by several pioneers of the early twentieth century. They allow room for an infinite variety of development and redevelopment solutions within the framework of a regional plan. The main essential in metropolitan regional planning is to have a communications framework and a balanced disposition of residential communities, centres of activity and work places and open land.

The heart of a metropolitan region will obviously be very different in character and function from the newest outer community. But, in both, buildings and civic space should satisfy a range of human needs. Unfortunately, there are all-or-nothing brigades, including one which advocates high buildings for everybody on every occasion, and another which believes that new land subdivision for low-density development is all that matters. Then there are the no-hopers who, having accepted laissez-faire a century too late, are twentieth-century nihilists. Belief in the present and the future is sometimes necessary.

THE SHAPE OF THE EVER-EXPANDING CITY-REGION

Theoretically, a city-region could grow to enormous dimension. Practically, such growth may be seen in the north-eastern United States, and along the London-Birmingham-Manchester and Liverpool axis. The development of lightning speed telecommunications, fast motorways and air travel has made it possible for business associates to live as "neighbours" fifty or 100 miles apart.

Unfortunately, in nearly all countries, city-regions are spilling over the countryside and congesting their "lungs and arteries" at the same time. The more they absorb the fast motor car as a means of getting to and from the centres of greatest activity, the more they slow it down to the speed of the horse. On suburban road layouts, still designed as if for horse-drawn traffic, cars begin to show their capabilities (and their power as lethal weapons). One of the results is that extensive stretches of countryside are peppered by the same kind of building, ranging from dwelling houses for the same income group to factories in large industrial "estates". The richness of the older, more intensive and varied city is lost.

Metropolitan regions will vary in size according to importance, function and topography. Some may reach across thousands of square miles, others mere hundreds. They should grow according to a plan if only to maintain economic efficiency. This is obvious. It is more difficult to make argument for comfort, happiness, health and spiritual enjoyment.

A shapely design for a city-region will have a clear-cut network of routes, embracing freeways, rapid transit and freight lines. Roads will be classifield, with freeways in the highest category and minor residential roads in the lowest. The network of routes will serve, and not dominate : a whole series of communities, each with an active centre; industrial and other special work areas; recreational areas; and, of vital importance, the hub of the whole city-region. The major routes will be on the scale of a late nineteenth-century urban railway system, but as compared with such a system they should pass between rather than through the communities. They should, indeed, be in the open-space system, which will both separate and give identity to the elements in the plan (see the effect of open space in central Sydney and central Adelaide). If any element were to be given priority in building up a sound structure, is should be the open-space system. Colonel Light knew this when he prepared the plan for Adelaide. In the great city-region of tomorrow the open-space system will consist of very large open areas, and an open-space network joining them together and containing the lines of communication.

It is astonishing how often we fail to see what is before our eyes. Yet no responsible planner would try to prepare a plan without first gathering together the maximum number of relevant facts. The past and the present point to the future.

The main elements of an "ideal" city-regional plan are to be seen in Australian cities. There are magnificent regional open spaces in the County of Cumberland. Sydney harbour is of tremendous importance visually, as well as for trade and recreation. There are other open spaces on the grand scale : Ku-ring-gai Chase in the north, the National Park, Military Reserve and Catchment Area in the south. The centre of Sydney works well because it is a little "Manhattan Island" surrounded by water or parkland. The role of the inner-ring rapid transit line has previously been mentioned. Colonel Light's 130-year-old parklands form the most distinctive element in Adelaide. Metropolitan Perth already has six miles of freeway, including an important river bridge, and also many miles of reservations, four to six chains in width, for the planned freeway system. In all the metropolitan regions, there are new industrial areas on a twentieth-century scale.

The evolving Canberra plan is important. In a century Canberra could be the best arranged city-region in the world. The elements, including the monumental national triangle, are distinct and the setting distinguished. The landscape flowing between districts augurs well for an articulate solution. There is the great advantage in Canberra of single land ownership. Without this physical planning is more difficult.

It is agreed everywhere that there is a need for regional government, especially for the planning and execution of large-scale works and to determine policies with a sense of direction. Experiments are taking place in the metropolitan regions of Sydney, Melbourne, and Perth. In the latter the state and local governments are working together in one regional authority. There is the opportunity to succeed. The state must be concerned with comprehensive development, the countless matters of detail should be the concern of the local governments in the many communities forming part of the city region.

If we believe in planning there is cause for optimism.

20

Imprimé au Canada

Printed in Canada